CONFRONTING
RACE

CONFRONTING

WOMEN AND INDIANS ON THE FRONTIER, 1815–1915

RACE

GLENDA RILEY

UNIVERSITY OF NEW MEXICO PRESS
ALBUQUERQUE

10   09   08   07   06   05   04   1   2   3   4   5   6   7

Library of Congress Cataloging-in-Publication Data

Riley, Glenda, 1938–

Confronting race : women and Indians

on the frontier, 1815–1915 / Glenda Riley.

p. cm.

Rev. ed. of: Women and Indians on the frontier, 1825–1915. c1984.

Includes bibliographical references and index.

ISBN 0-8263-3632-9 (cloth : alk. paper)

ISBN 0-8263-3625-6 (pbk. : alk. paper)

1. Women pioneers—West (U.S.)—History—19th century.

2. Women pioneers—West (U.S.)—History—20th century.

3. Women pioneers—West (U.S.)—Attitudes.

4. Indians of North America—West (U.S.)—History.

5. Frontier and pioneer life—West (U.S.)—History.

6. West (U.S.)—Race relations.

I. Riley, Glenda, 1938– Women and Indians

on the frontier, 1825–1915. II. Title.

F596.R56 2004   978'.02—dc22

2004009064

Printed and bound in the USA by Thomson-Shore, Inc.

Typeset in Bembo 11/14

Display type set in Serlio

Design and composition: Robyn Mundy

DEDICATED TO

DEBORAH L. ROGERS AND SAMUEL E. GRIFFET,

FOR THEIR UNWAVERING HELP, SUPPORT, AND LOVE

CONTENTS

ILLUSTRATIONS

Introduction

When this study first appeared in 1984 it was distinctive in that it took into account the role that gender, race, and, to a lesser extent, social class played in white-Indian relations. Before that time, scholars generally assumed that Anglo men and women held similar prejudicial attitudes toward Indians. White men and white women feared, fought with, or fled from Indians at pretty much the same rates and for pretty much the same reasons.[1] By taking a close look at men's and women's documents, however, *Women and Indians* demonstrated that white women traveling west by overland trails and establishing homes there had significantly different reactions to American Indians, and thus very different interactions with them, than did white men. On the trail and in settlements, female gender roles moderated women's racial and social-class beliefs, thus allowing Anglo women to become colleagues of sorts with Indians, trading items of food and apparel or sharing child-care hints with Indian women, and hiring Indian women and men to help inside their homes and out. At the same time, Anglo men, especially those charged with protecting their families, obtaining land, and clearing an area of its original inhabitants, developed an adversarial relationship with Indians, in which white men frequently engaged in assessing the number and potential of warriors, weapons, and horses they would have to overcome.

During the two decades since 1984, scholarship regarding westering women, Native Americans, and the interrelations of racial and social-class groups has exploded. Now, in the early twenty-first century, the University of New Mexico Press has extended to me the opportunity to prepare a second edition of *Women and Indians* that combines the first volume's extensive research and emphasis on gender with recent findings and theory, which gives a slightly different twist to the revised edition.[2] Now titled *Confronting Race: Women and Indians on the Frontier, 1815–1915,* the study demonstrates that in spite of white women's changing attitudes toward Indians, women remained solidly colonialist in outlook toward all other groups. The new version remains accessible to general readers, including teachers, students, and laypeople interested in understanding the legacy of white expansionism in the West and gathering information to aid in present-day problem solving.

The underlying argument also remains the same: that women who migrated westward—after lifetimes of listening to popular and often prejudicial discourse—carried with them certain deeply ingrained images and preconceptions of themselves as nineteenth-century women, as well as racially based expectations of the indigenous groups they would meet. As on other colonial frontiers, Anglo women responded to Indians, at least initially, in the ways expected of properly indoctrinated white women of the literate classes.[3] As Anglo women discovered their own resilience in the face of the harsh demands imposed on them by the western environment, they rethought some of the conventional wisdom that said that women were passive, weak, and silly creatures who would certainly quake at the mere mention of the word "Indian." Moreover, as Anglo women realized their own strength and courage, many were able to view Indians not just as dangerous enemies, but as real human beings.

Because these women were somewhat educated, they gave voice to their thoughts and experiences in diaries and journals, which were seldom written for publication. Rather, they were personal records of daily events of significance to a particular woman or perhaps to her family "back East" or in Europe. She had no reading public to please other than herself or her immediate family and friends. Except for memoirs and reminiscences, a woman's writing mirrored her immediate feelings and reactions. Those used here include diaries kept by trail women, journals and daybooks of women settlers, accounts by army wives, records of female missionaries, and several unpublished statements of women involved in white-Indian conflicts.[4] Additional resources are popular-culture sources, including the novels that women read, and the reflection of women in newspaper accounts.[5] The sources used here represent the trans-Mississippi West, ranging from Iowa and Kansas to California and Oregon, and, as a comparison, the Panama route to California.

One characteristic these documents share is that they were not intended as descriptions and critiques of Indians. Their authors had no vested interest to promote, nor did they hope to influence public opinion. Anglo women's writings reflect the attitudes and beliefs of a cross-section of western women who participated in the casual, intermittent contact with Native Americans that was typical of most frontierswomen, rather than those of women who were missionaries and teachers and thus had more prolonged, intense intercourse with Indian peoples. Trail diaries are especially useful because they often revealed changes in female migrants' reactions to Indians as they moved westward, whereas such sources as missionaries' accounts were less helpful because female missionaries frequently held deep-seated and fairly inflexible perceptions of American Indians peculiar to their own sense of mission and unrepresentative of Anglo frontierswomen in general.[6]

Another salient feature of these women's documents is that they were not accurate sources of information regarding American Indian peoples and their principles and practices. In no way were white women writing Native American history or recording culture and ethnography.[7] These women's writings leave no doubt that their perceptions were skewed by colonialist precepts, including a belief in white superiority. Derived in large part from their own bigotry and cultural values, these women's observations of Indians demonstrate their ethnocentric biases toward Indian societies rather than the realities of Native American culture. From today's perspective, Anglo women's views of Indians were seldom defensible. Although a few freed themselves sufficiently from colonialist teachings so that they even criticized their own menfolk, attacked the American government's Indian policy, or married Indian men, the eyes of the majority remained clouded by colonialist and white-supremacist sentiments.

These women had difficulty reconciling their firsthand observations with their long internalized values. Most recognized that the tales of primitive and savage Indians appearing in dime novels, in "penny dreadfuls" or captivity narratives, and in newspaper reports were more hyperbole than truth. The more seasoned among them disdained the bombastic style of such authors as the one who wrote in 1875: "The very sight of Indians were terrible to many women on the frontier. The savages could not be looked upon without calling to mind the horrid work of the tomahawk and the scalping-knife—the desolated home and the butchered relatives."[8] Yet these women clung to "white" beliefs and teachings that had often begun in early childhood, and caused them to remain always slightly aloof from Indians. Although Anglo women often got closer to American Indian men, women, and children than did Anglo men, the haze of colonialism continued to obscure their view whenever and wherever they ventured on the western frontier—along a plethora of trails, in temporary camps, and in raw settlements.

Unfortunately, resources relating to Native Americans are not abundant. Because they had no written languages, documents are few. Unsurprisingly, Indians have guarded their oral traditions from Anglos, often including scholars. When documents or transcripts existed, they are too often ignored by Anglos who write histories and establish archives. Thus, Indians were frequently absent from a society's memory and identity. Some evidence of the subaltern voice is found, however, in the writings of white women. When a woman described Native Americans as lazy, felonious, or slow to adopt white teachings, she described people who showed their discontent by working slowly, appropriating food and other goods to supplement their inadequate wages, and took from Anglos only what they found to be meaningful.[9] When these or other sources are available, the perspectives of Native Americans are included here.

Of course, other types of people inhabited the West as well. Female migrants included Hispanas, African Americans, Asians, and Mormons, or members of the Church of Jesus Christ of Latter-day Saints, who often found themselves caught between Anglos and Indians.[10] In addition to American Indians, Anglo women observed and criticized these groups, sometimes in a positive way, but more often in a negative one. Anglo women also pushed anyone who was not white or mainstream Christian into internal colonies within the West.[11] Despite the supposed egalitarianism of the West, white women considered themselves free and equal to a greater extent than others, which revealed far more about Anglo frontierswomen than about their targets. Although these peoples' histories are not included here, the presence of Hispanics and Mormons is invoked to demonstrate the encompassing nature of Anglo women's racialist and colonialist thinking during the era of successive frontiers.

For the purposes of this study, the frontier period encompasses the West's greatest decades of white settlement from the mid-1810s until the eruption of World War I in Europe in 1914 captured the nation's attention and, in 1917, its military support. This spectacular era of expansion began after the War of 1812 when the Peace of Ghent with Britain in 1814 convinced Americans that the earlier American Revolution was not a fluke, that the United States had the capability to repulse stronger nations who tried to take advantage of the fledgling country. Although the treaty did little more than end hostilities, some Americans dubbed the War of 1812 the "Second American Revolution," meaning the United States had again pushed the British out of its boundaries. The war also accelerated the Industrial Revolution in the young United States, so that factories multiplied and urban trade centers grew. Women's traditional home work, spinning and weaving, moved into factories, drawing women into paid labor away from their homes. Every year, the rapidly industrializing United States attracted more immigrants from other countries, all anxious for better lives than they had known at home. At the same time, the Transportation Revolution resulted in roads, canals, and eventually railroads that made internal migration feasible. Soon the nation resembled an amoeba, pushing this way and that looking for places in which to expand.

The West seemed to present the ideal solution. The Louisiana Purchase, bought from France by farsighted President Thomas Jefferson in 1803 and explored between 1803 and 1806 by Meriwether Lewis and William Clark, appeared to lie waiting for American settlers, including growing numbers of women. Although Indian peoples with long-established governments and cultures already lived in the area, white Americans viewed purchased land as open for the taking. Soon, would-be settlers coveted lands that lay outside U.S. borders. In 1834, although the United States did not own the expanse along the Northwest coast, Reverend Jason Lee explored the Willamette Valley and founded the first mission and farming colony there. Explorers, missionaries, and settlers soon followed, making their way to the "Oregon Country." Among these were the first female missionaries to cross the Continental Divide in the Rocky Mountains, Narcissa Whitman and Eliza Spalding, who in 1836 helped establish the Walla Walla mission. In 1842 and 1843, the first great wagon trains rolled out of Independence, Missouri, beginning the "great migration" over the Oregon Trail. In 1847, another religiously inspired migration, the first contingent of Mormons, or members of the Church of Latter-day Saints of Jesus Christ, escaped the boundaries of the United States to settle near the Great Salt Lake in present-day Utah where they hoped to be free from discriminatory treatment due to their religious beliefs. A few years later, in 1848, the discovery of gold in California drew thousands to the coast. In that same year, the Oregon Treaty gave the Northwest Territory to the United States. Two years later, the Treaty of Guadalupe Hidalgo with Mexico secured the Southwest for the nation. In 1853, the Gadsden Purchase of land along the U.S.-Mexican border completed the boundaries of the continental United States.[12]

Beginning in 1861, the Civil War interrupted the flow of western migration. When the war ended in 1865, migration swelled. Additional discoveries of gold and silver, the mushrooming of railroads, and the Homestead Act of 1862 encouraged people, including white Europeans from such countries as Norway and Denmark, to settle the Great Plains, which earlier migrants had disdained as the Great American Desert. The emergence of the "long drive" of cattle from Texas during the 1860s and 1870s spurred the development of such railroad towns as Abilene and Dodge City in the Kansas territory, as well as giving the frontier new dimensions: hard-riding cowboys, fast towns with dance halls and saloons, and abundant prostitution. During the early 1880s came a gold rush in northern Idaho. In 1890, the U.S. Congress transformed Indian

Territory into Oklahoma Territory and opened it for white settlement. Also in 1890, the U.S. Bureau of the Census declared the frontier "closed" by virtue of having an average of two residents per square mile.[13] Despite that startling announcement, migration continued, with settlers filling in sparsely developed areas from Minnesota to New Mexico.

These and related events created a volatile situation for western-bound women and the American Indians who lived in the West or had been relocated there from their ancestral homes east of the Mississippi River. Throughout the era, proper nineteenth-century women—along with those who were not so proper—found themselves heading west, many hoping to "do good" among Indian peoples. Meanwhile, American Indians were pushed, hassled, dispossessed of their lands, forced into poverty, and relocated on reservations of questionable merit. Virtually all Indians resisted, some by violence, which led to altercations ranging from the Black Hawk War in the upper Mississippi Valley in 1832 to the widely heralded capture of the feared Apache leader Geronimo in the Southwest in 1886. Other Indians protested more subtly through deceiving whites, ignoring their offers of "help," and rejecting aspects of white culture that did not suit them. Thus, the Anglo women and American Indians who met in frontier zones all over the West sometimes met with tragic results and sometimes with favorable consequences.

In the following pages, western "frontiers" mean geographical zones where two or more types of people met, with the members of one intent on subduing the other and imposing their government, economy, religions, and cultures on those aboriginal to the area. Besides geography, frontiers also involved procedures. Consequently, here frontiers have four phases. The first is philosophy, meaning the ideology that propelled white migrants westward. Called Manifest Destiny in the United States, this belief system might also be characterized as colonization or even colonialism.[14] As in many of the world's other colonized countries, the introduction of Anglo dominance led to such hegemonic stages as war, colonization, decolonization, and a movement for social justice.[15] The next three facets of frontiers are the process by which migrants relocated and imposed their ways on indigenous cultures, the geographical place where cultures met and often clashed, and the product, or aftereffects, of the frontier era.

Based on this four-part scheme, the first two chapters deal with philosophy, namely, the American and European discourse that prepared women to be proper females, encouraged them to go westward, at least in part to help others, and to expect the worst at the hands of Native Americans. Chapters 3 and 4 address issues of process, especially the vilification of Indians, the fear-based contact and conflict that resulted between Anglos and Indians, and the eventual humanizing of Indians by numerous white women. Chapters 5 and 6 look at place: how the geographical frontier brought types of people together, especially during the early years, and how colonialist attitudes endured. Chapter 7 summarizes frontier product, in this case, long-lived enmity between racial groups that reaches into the early twenty-first century.

Several notes on terminology are in order. Manifest Destiny, a term first coined in 1845, means the conviction of white Americans, Canadians, and Europeans that God intended them to migrate to and shape to their own ends the frontier West. Regarding terms for groups of people, white people are also called Anglos. Indians are also termed American Indians or Native Americans. Hispanics are sometimes called peoples of Spanish heritage. Blacks are frequently referred to as African Americans. Those from Asia are Asians.

The examples and case studies of Anglo-Indian contact used here are wide reaching. They derive from all areas of the trans-Mississippi West, ranging from the Old Wild West of the prairie and Great Plains to the far-flung Southwest and Pacific Northwest. Examples also come from the entire period between the 1810s and 1910s. Although western frontiers changed, perhaps through improved technology or the infusion of immigrants of color, these were not sea changes. And, even though some of the situations of Anglo women modified during this period, including taking up paid labor, entering the professions, and, during the early twentieth century, even daring to smoke in public, their interrelations with American Indians on various frontiers had an eerie sameness. This occurred, at least in part, because the more women changed, the more writers of such prescriptive literature as etiquette and guide books for women urged their readers to be "true" or "proper" women by remaining within their domestic sphere and maintaining passive demeanor. Thus, especially middle- and upper-class women of the nineteenth century and those of the early twentieth century stepped out on the trail with very similar injunctions in their heads.

In addition, anti-Indian prejudice increased throughout the era rather than abating. Even though a pro-Indian reform movement emerged after the Civil War, it was based largely in the East and drew many former abolitionists to its ranks, factors that limited its outreach and potency. Moreover, as Indian resistance spiraled in the West, creative authors of dime novels, ambitious journalists, and profit-hungry editors happily brought to eager readers outrageous tales of Indian "atrocities" and "depredations." At the same time, William F. "Buffalo Bill" Cody and a host of imitators took touring Wild West shows to Americans in the East, South, and Midwest, as well as to viewers in such countries as England, France, and Italy. Even though Cody had hoped to present an authentic portrayal of the West and of Native Americans, he soon found himself ruled by the bottom line, which mandated giving viewers what they wanted—fierce, savage, and rapacious Indians. Consequently, an Anglo woman of the early twentieth century was no more sensible and knowledgeable regarding American Indians than those of the early nineteenth century. A third factor leading to the repetitive nature of Anglo frontierswomen's reactions to Indians was the frontier setting in which they interacted with Indians. These venues were usually isolated, in their early stages relatively unpeopled by whites, and very frightening to women who thought of themselves as weaklings devoid of courage. Anglo women, who were accustomed to neighbors, laws, and the absence of Indians, had to cope, often on their own, with people who had reputations as murderers and takers of captives, especially of women and children. Many white women did learn to manage and, in doing so, adopted new ideas about themselves and about Indians. Because damaging constructions of race, gender, and class were widespread and hardy during this era, a similar procedure repeated itself over and over among white women at many times and in many frontier zones.

Therefore, this study concludes that gender, race, and even social class mattered. Although literate Anglo women went west with fathers, brothers, and husbands, and only occasionally left their sides, they had

9

a different experience than did those men. It also indicates that, in the end, women who saw Indians more clearly and related to them more intimately than most men, were still unable to free themselves from colonialist attitudes. Although some gained enough objectivity to criticize the imperialism of Manifest Destiny, they had neither the insight nor the power to bring it down. Thus, in the final analysis, Anglo women helped perpetuate racial problems that otherwise might have lessened.

―――― **Chapter One** ――――

FRONTIER PHILOSOPHY: NINETEENTH-CENTURY AMERICAN DISCOURSE ON WHITE WOMANHOOD AND ON THE AMERICAN INDIAN "OTHER"

Early nineteenth-century women did not have to think for themselves about themselves. Womanhood was defined for them from pulpits, from Chautauqua rostrums, and in a variety of print media. Primarily male voices carried on a brisk discussion regarding the ways in which white American women should feel and behave. In a post-War of 1812 nation in the throes of an industrial revolution, a transportation revolution, growing immigration, women entering the paid labor force, urbanization, and rising crime and divorce rates, male leaders felt compelled to try to keep white womanhood "pure" and women in the domestic realm.

No one specifically stated that these messages were intended for white women, particularly of the middle and upper classes, but their tenets were seldom applicable to women of color, especially black slave women, and even to white women of the lower classes. It was also unclear how useful such ideas would be to women about to join the nation's expansionist phase, known as Manifest Destiny, by transplanting their homes, their families, and themselves to the vast and promising region that lay west of the Mississippi River. It turned out, however, that American women who joined the westward movement were well schooled as incipient colonialists. They were thoroughly indoctrinated into the ideals of domesticity, also known as "true" womanhood or the moral-guardian theory, that assured them they had a moral mission in life, whether it be to family members or to unknown peoples in a region far from their homes.

Yet a number of questions hung in the air. Would westbound women of the early 1800s carry these values with them or would they leave them behind like so much refuse as they crossed over the threshold of the old homestead for the last time? How would such ideas and aspirations serve them as they confronted indigenous groups? Would women discover that their customary ways of looking at female roles and at Indian "others" were inappropriate in the less structured world of the West?

The answers are clearer now than they were in the 1800s and early 1900s. To the first query, the answer is yes; female migrants did indeed carry feminine value systems with them to their new homes in the West. To the second and third questions, women only gradually replaced parts of the ideology of domesticity or the tenets of the moral-guardian theory in favor of a more flexible, liberating set of ideals spawned by a frontier environment.[1] Because these women had been exposed throughout their lives to assertions and pronouncements regarding the qualities of white females and of Native Americans, it is not surprising that they took this dogma westward as an integral part of their cultural baggage. This fact that they did so makes it necessary to explore and understand the climate of opinion from which they came.

—— On Womanhood ——

Assertions that women should stay in the domestic sphere were hardly novel sentiments. Ever since the first women migrated to the shores of British North America, they were regarded as repositories of virtue and piety, as well as guardians of home and family. As early as 1692 the noted minister Cotton Mather had summarized and idealized such thinking in his widely read *Ornaments for the Daughters of Zion*. During following decades, numerous other writers reiterated and enlarged upon Mather's view of American womanhood. In 1814, Abigail Adams, longtime advocate of expanded roles for women in the new United States of America, endorsed the idea of separate spheres for men and women when she wrote: "I believe nature has assigned to each sex its particular duties and sphere of action, and to act well your part, 'there all the honor lies.'"[2]

Throughout the nineteenth and early twentieth centuries, these tenets gained force so that white women grew up with a set of feminine ideals that permeated their very beings. As the century progressed, so did these social constructions of womanhood gain a hold among Anglo women. Such sentiments were widely purveyed through a proliferating prescriptive literature increasingly written by women.[3] The very volume of ladies' periodicals, domestic novels, epistolary guidebooks, annuals, gift books, printed sermons, and speeches that appeared in the middle decades of the nineteenth century—all attempting to imbue women with the precepts of "true womanhood" and to guide them into customary female functions—suggests a pressing societal need to allay a growing dissatisfaction with, and questioning of, traditional gender roles, largely by literate white women.

Even though this literature was heavily didactic, it attracted a widespread and devoted readership among American women. Due to improved literacy rates, decreasing costs of books and magazines, and the introduction of specialized literature for women and children, "domestic" literature, as it was called for its emphasis on home and family, boomed. It attracted larger numbers of readers, representatives of more social classes, and members of more age groups. Although now forgotten and gathering dust on library shelves, many domestic novels were runaway best-sellers in their own eras. At the same time, many ladies' periodicals enjoyed varying degrees of success in the new market created by the increased leisure, money, and education of middle- and upper-class women. While some of these publications vanished within a few years, others, such as *Godey's Lady's Book,* earned fine reputations and extensive circulations that lasted from several decades to over half a century. Indeed, women's magazines had the widest circulation of all types of nineteenth-century periodicals.[4]

By the mid-nineteenth century the concepts of domesticity and separate spheres approached the status of a cult. In 1843, for example, a popular American ladies' magazine exhorted its readers that women's "more delicate sensibility is the unseen power which is ever at work to purify and refine society."[5] Supporters of domesticity and its associated values routinely proclaimed that a woman's influence was "the all-mighty principle in order of social economy." Women, they maintained, were not only to "refine the tastes, ennoble the principles, and soften the asperities of man," but were also to fulfill the "noble charge of train-ing the youthful mind in the paths of virtue and true happiness."[6]

These lofty and somewhat abstract pronouncements were intended, at least in part, to answer the issue of women's inequality in an era that was becoming increasingly committed to a democratic ideology of equal rights. Women could hardly help but notice that as opportunities for white males increased, their own roles became more circumscribed. Even the growing throngs of mill girls who flocked to new textile fac-tories as "operatives" of spinning jennys and power looms knew from their wages that their work was worth less to American society than men's. Women were reassured that equality was a moot issue because men and women operated in different spheres, each gender being equally important within its prescribed domain. These spheres were sup-posedly determined by the unique physiology and intellect of men and women. According to the male novelist T. S. Arthur's 1848 guidebook, *Advice to Young Ladies,* the very shape and size of women's heads indi-cated the development of brains and minds different in approach and function from men's. Because of these obvious differences, Arthur believed that men made decisions according to intellect and women by love. It then followed that men and women were in a strange sense equal because each acted within their own capabilities, limitations, and of course, spheres.[7]

Domesticity, designed also to give meaning to the lives of the newly leisured middle- and upper-class women, further argued than such women had not become superfluous. Instead, it maintained that these women were absolutely crucial as guardians of morality and virtue for a capitalistic society. Advocates of these doctrines preached that women should adopt passive, or "feminine," ideals to balance the capitalistic or "male" standards that were allied with economic growth, industrial and territorial expansion, and urban development. As defenders of home and hearth, women would protect traditional values, yet they were not to interfere in any essential way with the developments that were catapulting America toward prosperity and power.

It may seem odd that women accepted doctrines that had obvious limitations, but there were many reasons for them to do so. It would have been false of women to naysay the importance of wifehood, motherhood, and family care in their lives. After all, they lived in a time when marriage and childbearing were believed to be women's top-ranking goals. Nor could they reject the belief that women were more moral, pure, and virtuous than men, for this not only gave them a modicum of power in their homes, but established their authority over men concerning domestically related matters. Also, interpreted and applied in certain ways, domestic teachings offered women the hope of finding meaning in a world radically altered from that of their grandmothers— or even of their mothers—where a woman's labor often had been critical to family survival. For mill girls who had followed women's work of spinning and weaving from their homes to factories, domesticity assured them that they had not lost significance as wives and mothers. For middle- and upper-class women, seemingly devoid of purpose and trapped in their homes while the menfolk left to labor in another part of the city, domesticity justified their very existence. Consequently, even "intellectual" women such as Margaret Fuller, editor of the Transcendentalist journal *The Dial* and author of *Woman in the Nineteenth Century,* who railed in her 1852 memoirs against the limitations of women's "sphere," could see potential usefulness in the concept of separate spheres for men and women.[8]

Because progressive thinkers concerning women's roles, such as Adams and Fuller, accepted the potential of the separate-spheres concept, it is unsurprising to discover that many other American women also adopted the notion. Women were beginning to see that the philosophy known as domesticity held out certain attractions. Even women who intended to move westward saw merit in domestic ideals. Like their sisters, they were open to the possibility that their otherwise subordinate female roles would earn status, respect, and esteem as women's moral impact upon society was amplified and idealized.

The implications of domesticity for women's roles and status could be enormous. If women developed feminine ideals based upon what one scholar has termed the "four cardinal virtues," meaning piety, purity, submissiveness, and domesticity, at the same time refusing to sully themselves by entering into the male domain of business and politics, their salutary influence could be virtually unlimited.[9] As a result, a number of tropes, or themes, appeared in domestic literature for women. First, male and female writers and commentators, who agreed that women exercised a set of mental characteristics different from men's, stressed that women were particularly capable of religious feelings. As early as 1826, guidebook author Hester Chapone claimed that religion provided the guiding principle for women and their sphere. She advised women that because of their softness and sensibility they would have an easier time meeting religious proscriptions than men.[10] In 1859, writer Harriet Beecher Stowe carried religiosity to a new high. In *The Minister's Wooing,* Stowe's character James admonishes his wife Mary, "You girls and women don't know your own power. . . . You are a living Gospel."[11]

A second trope suggested that, given their incredible spiritual powers, wives and mothers could resolve even the worst of family problems. A spate of domestic novels demonstrated how women were to accomplish such feats. The heroine of an 1854 novel, *The Lamplighter* by Maria Cummins, presented the epitome of the reforming female. Morally flawless, Gerty not only inspired every man who was fortunate enough to come into contact with her, but saved her sinning father by simply letting her tears fall on his sleeping face.[12] The following year, Marion Harland's *Alone* portrayed its protagonist, Ida, as reforming those around her by her own perfect example. Despite the disadvantages of being orphaned, young, and unmarried, she developed such moral strength that when her sickly guardian heaped abuse on her for trying to cheer him, she smiled and "bore up bravely until God gave her strength."[13] Similarly, the heroine of Caroline Lee Hentz's *Ernest Linwood,* published in 1856, reformed a maliciously jealous husband through her constancy and fortitude.[14] Why would women not want to read such heroic tales about themselves?

Moreover, domestic novelists implied in a third trope that women could affect larger communities as well as families. In 1839, a Dr. Blair stated that "the prevailing manners of an age depend, more than we are aware of, or are willing to allow, on the conduct of women: this is one of the principal things on which the great machine of human society turns."[15] A few years later, in 1842, Elizabeth Sandford's epistle titled *Woman, in Her Social and Domestic Character,* stated the matter more strongly. In Sandford's view, American society in general received its "balance and its tone" from women. "She may be here a corrective of what is wrong, a moderator of what is unruly, a restraint on what is indecorous," Sandford asserted. "Her presence will be a pledge against impropriety and excess, a check on vice, and a protection to virtue."[16]

Domesticity was extended a step further in a fourth trope: even the country as a whole could be affected by women's behavior. Women were counseled to take note of the affairs of their nation, but not in a partisan way. Rather, by acting as nurturers, teachers, and moral exemplars to young men, who comprised the future citizens of America, women could be "allies of legislators" and even "have agency in the prevention of crime."[17] By training both female and male children to cherish their country and its government, women could affect the United States as well as its impact on the world. "Mothers of America!" the *Ladies Repository* reminded women in 1848, "the destiny of this mighty republic is under your control, and hence the consequent freedom and the political and moral elevation of humanity throughout the world."[18] Clearly, women had a role to play in emerging nationalism and the country's westward expansion.

Catharine Beecher, an educator and leading theorist of domestic philosophy, was particularly interested in the link between women, the well-being of the country, and the West. As early as 1837, Beecher argued that even though women held a subordinate relation to the "other sex," as men were increasingly known, it was not because Providence destined women's duties or influence to be any less important or pervasive than men's. Rather, God intended that women's mode of gaining influence and of exercising power should be altogether different and special.[19] During following decades, Beecher worked tirelessly to remedy "the fact that the honor and duties of the family state are not duly appreciated" and "that women are not trained for these duties as men are trained for their trades and professions." She believed that if schools were established to train women in their profession, appreciation of "the science and training which its high and sacred duties require" would develop.[20] Beecher envisioned domesticity not just as professionalism in duties, but as social theory. Women were, Beecher argued, not only the protectors of home and family, but the saviors of democracy in America. In her view, women filled a subordinate position in American society in order to promote the general good of society as a whole. Thus, to Beecher, women preserved the virtuous qualities of life that provided the very underpinning of the American democratic system.[21]

These four themes were heady ideas not only for Anglo women in general, but for those migrating westward. They would be moving to the West their households, families, themselves, and their moral influence over lesser folks, including untutored backwoodsmen and pagan Native Americans. Beginning in the late 1820s, Catherine Beecher explicitly stated that it was women's mission to go to the West as teachers of children, immigrants, and the unschooled lower classes. To this end, she conducted fundraising and promotional tours and founded seminaries for the training of women teachers.[22] In her opinion, teaching was the only acceptable paid profession for women, one that provided them with "honourable independence and extensive usefulness." Beecher also believed that inhabitants of western regions needed women's ministrations in the classroom. In promoting her scheme to send women teachers to the West during the 1840s, Beecher explained that she hoped to "engage American women to exert the great power and influence put into their hands" and "to secure a proper education to the vast multitude of neglected American children."[23]

Beecher was not the only one to suggest western missions on the part of Anglo women. In 1844, the *Ladies Repository* asserted that societies only progressed in science and literature during eras in which women exercised their "proper influence."[24] A decade later, in 1854, novelist Lydia Child selected examples from world history to demonstrate that "even under the most barbarous and tyrannical forms of society, the salutary influence of good and sensible women was felt and acknowledged."[25] What more could women ask to assure them that moving to the American West was the right decision for them?

Such arguments appealed to women about to migrate. Applying altruism to needy western societies rationalized any misgivings they may have had about seizing others' land; they would trade their help to Native Americans for land, which whites considered open to development.[26] Even Anglo women who went west to advance themselves in some way came to believe that their presence would help, if just by being living examples of white civilization. Thus, what one scholar has termed "conquest through benevolence"[27] attracted not only Beecher's female educators, but numerous other women who believed that their ability to give to the poor, ill, and non-Christian indicated the high moral tone of American society, especially of its women.

Of course, such inflated rhetoric, and the prominence it extended to women's roles, strongly attracted many Anglo women during the mid-nineteenth century. Blocked from exercising the right of suffrage and holding pubic office, unable to own property or control their wages, and certain to lose their children in a divorce action, these women understandably adopted many aspects of domestic philosophy. Through the arguments of domesticity, women's subordination and imputed inferiority served lofty purposes, including the redemption of all humankind. Moreover, its tenets even implied superiority for women, at least in the realm of morality. If women were the moral guardians of American society, the argument went, then the "other sex" must be lacking in this area.

Some women quickly understood that their moral powers might be the springboard that would considerably widen women's sphere, whereas they acted innocent of entertaining thoughts of enlarging or even leaving their sphere.[28] One of the most articulate of these women was Sarah Josepha Hale, who in 1837 became editor of *Godey's Lady's Book*. A decade earlier, Hale had made it clear in her first novel, *Northwood,* that she believed that "'constitutions' and 'compromises'" were "the appropriate work of men." In Hale's eyes, women were to be "conservators of moral power, which, eventually . . . preserves or destroys the work of the warrior, the statesman, and the patriot."[29] Having said this, Hale spent subsequent years enlarging women's activities. For example, in novels, articles, editorial comments, and personal crusades, Hale demanded that, to fully exercise their morality, women needed "improved" education.[30] Hale expanded women's spheres on other levels as well. She maintained that morally uplifting novels should be written by women who were, after all, the moral shapers of society. Hale often said that impressionable children should be taught only by women rather than by the "other sex." She also thought that the poor and destitute should be aided by women through charity organizations, and that the heathen of the world should be rescued by women serving as missionaries.[31]

Thus, to Hale, women's duties included writing, teaching, community volunteer work, and missionary endeavors far from home. She never suggested, however, that women leave the domestic realm to enter such male affairs as business and politics. Although Hale herself was a successful career woman, she always wore black, an unmistakable sign that she was a widow who had to work for pay. At the same time, she warned women against getting caught in the "the ocean of political life" that heaved "with the storm of partisan passions among the men of America." Instead, Hale wrote in 1850 that women, the "true conservators of peace and goodwill," should spend their time cultivating "every gentle feeling" and avoiding participation in the political "reforms of the day."[32]

Hale believed, however, that women were indispensable to the moral movements of the era, although it would naturally be improper for women to play leadership roles. Hale thus supported a fifth trope, that women should actively engage in reform even if it took them outside their homes. As early as the 1830s and 1840s, women had been called upon to exert their influence against the evils that had crept into American life. Because so many women were economically dependent on fathers and husbands, the growing opposition to the overconsumption of alcohol seemed a natural cause for women to support. A woman who was the daughter or wife of an alcoholic was urged to fight his "perversity" with all the moral power at her command. Unmarried women were advised to shun the "society" and refuse "the addresses" of men who drank. Since men could not do without the society of women, the thinking went, they would "take the jewel [a woman] and throw away that [alcohol] which makes so many miserable outcasts."[33] In one of the most popular novels of the 1850s, *Ten Nights in a Barroom* (1854), the male novelist T. S. Arthur supported the idea of women as temperance reformers. Arthur's protagonist was caught between the moral influence of his wife and daughter and the power of wickedness, symbolized by a rum seller.[34] To combat the problem of alcoholism women formed temperance societies, held temperance conventions, and encouraged wives of alcoholics to desert their husbands.[35] By acting as if overdrinking was exclusively a male disorder, female reformers expanded women's moral powers over men in yet another area.

Other reform movements embraced women as well. For instance, whether there would be peace or strife in the country seemed to depend on women.[36] They not only organized peace groups, but supposedly displayed peaceful behavior in their own lives as examples to the larger American society. Charitable work outside of the home also became part of women's province. As early as 1836, the social observer Elizabeth Sandford explained that such demands were justifiable because women not only had more leisure time than men, but were particularly suited to caring for the destitute and ill. In 1842, the social commentator Margaret Coxe insisted that Americans could reasonably expect women, who were sympathetic and caring, to take charge of such people. Throughout the 1840s and 1850s, Hale mounted a crusade for the holding of Ladies' Fairs to raise money for institutions devoted to training female nurses and to provide funds to female "visitors of the sick and the poor." In 1852, Hale pushed the connection between women and medical care by proposing that female physicians be trained for the care of sick women and children.[37]

Hale received little support for either female nurses or female physicians, but her plea for female missionaries fared better. By mid-century, most mission boards, which were all male, had accepted the proposition that women's mandate to help the "poor and ignorant" included carrying Christianity throughout the world.[38] As early as 1836, the American Board of Commissioners for Foreign Missions sent as missionaries Narcissa Whitman and Eliza Spalding to the far-flung Oregon territory, thus opening the way for other women missionaries—such as Mary Richardson Walker—to go west. According to poet Lydia Sigourney, female missionaries were quite fitting, for they were the "stewards of God."[39] Other writers eulogized women missionaries, lauding them as more courageous than medieval knights. A typical appeal to women during the 1840s explained that teaching others Christianity allowed them to exercise "those peculiar talents and virtues" that were "resplendent" in the female character. In 1848, the *Ladies Repository* encouraged young women to become missionaries, thus realizing in their own lives "all that is lovely in woman's character, or sanctified and ennobling in woman's high ambition."[40]

Closer to home, women exercised their religious virtues by becoming Sunday-school teachers. Because female morality earmarked women as obvious teachers of religious tenets, many a young lady came to include a Sunday-school class among her other good deeds. In 1846, Hale expressed satisfaction with women's progress in religious endeavors, claiming that the United States owed "much of her glory" to women who supported the "cause of Christian mission, Sabbath schools, and charities of every kind."[41] In 1855, the domestic novelist Marion Harland added her stamp of approval in *Alone,* whose heroine found the Sabbath a "season of delight" because of the "band of little girls" who eagerly awaited her teachings.[42]

Of all the reform movements in which women participated during the mid-nineteenth century, abolitionism attracted the greatest number of women. In 1836, reformer Angelina Grimké pointed out that although women could not make laws against slavery, they could read, pray, talk, and even act on the subject. Grimké explained that women could speak to relatives, friends, and acquaintances, at the same time educating or even freeing slaves they owned or controlled as a result of prenuptial agreements. In the same year, Elizabeth Chandler appealed to women to boycott slave-made goods and to form protest groups. In 1860, Lydia Maria Child, author of several abolitionist tracts, declared that even though male legislators had the final decision, women could help create public opinion supporting abolitionism.[43]

Writer Harriet Beecher Stowe, best-known for her antislavery novel, *Uncle Tom's Cabin,* offered specific suggestions to women interested in the abolitionist movement. Stowe urged American women to learn about the subject and to commit themselves to wielding their influence against slavery. Next, women could spread information upon this vital topic through their neighborhoods, financially support lecturers, circulate abolitionist speeches given by members of Congress, and obtain signatures on petitions to Congress.[44] Although these tasks would draw women out of the domestic realm, it was in support of a moral and thus appropriate cause.

Anglo women who engaged in one of the above reform movements learned many lessons. Perhaps the most significant was that when women ventured outside their homes they lacked tangible power. Unable to own property, to vote, to hold office, or even to speak in public without censure, women rapidly became disillusioned by their own ineffectiveness in achieving reform. As a result, many women reformers became advocates of yet another kind of reform, that of women's rights. In 1848, Lucretia Mott and Elizabeth Cady Stanton put a notice in the *Seneca County Courier* of July 14 announcing that "a Convention to discuss the social, civil, and religious condition and rights of woman" would assemble at Seneca Falls, New York. Mott and Stanton had been stewing since 1840, when they walked out of the World Anti-Slavery Convention in London protesting rules that seated them behind a curtain and prohibited them from speaking and voting. Although the Seneca Falls meeting was intended for women, it attracted a number of men as well. This group adopted a "Declaration of Sentiments," based in form and style on the Declaration of Independence, that demanded more personal liberty, control of property, and increased participation in government for women, including the right to vote. Although the declaration stated that "we anticipate no small amount of misconception, misrepresentation, and ridicule," its signers were aghast at the public derision they faced. According to Stanton and Anthony, the proceedings were "unsparingly ridiculed by the press, and denounced by the pulpit, much to the surprise and chagrin of the leaders" who were "wholly unprepared to find themselves the target for the jibes and jeers of the nation."[45]

Caustic responses were to plague the women's rights movement throughout succeeding decades. In 1859, the *New York Times* reported a women's rights meeting held in New York City, during which many in the capacity crowd interrupted with "sneering and scoffing" at such well-known and respected speakers as Lucretia Mott, Antoinette Blackwell, Ernestine Rose, and Wendell Phillips. Pleas from chairperson Susan B. Anthony were of little avail in quieting the crowd, and the confusion that prevailed seemed, to the *Times,* to be an embarrassment to the entire city of New York, which had not even provided police protection.[46]

Women's rights leaders also recoiled in shock at learning that a large number of American women opposed the idea of women's rights. As early as 1844, when reformer and editor of *Yankee,* John Neal, gave a public lecture supporting rights for women, some of his most vehement critics were women. One called Neal's ideas "insane crudities" and his suggestions "characteristic absurdities."[47] A number of female writers also weighed in against women's rights by creating "assertive" heroines who lost their lovers, received rebukes from relatives, hastened parents' deaths, and ended their lives in insane asylums, all because they had worked for women's rights.[48] In 1850, this controversy spurred one female poet to write:

> *It is her right to watch beside*
> *The bed of sickness and pain;*
> *. . . to train her sons*
> *So they may Senate chambers grace*
> *. . . to be admired*
> *By every generous, manly heart,*
> *What would she more, than to perform*
> *On earth, life's holiest, sweetest tasks?*
> *When you a perfect woman find*
> *No other rights than these, she asks.*[49]

Obviously, the argument for women's sphere and their effectiveness as moral guardians of home and family had taken too great a foothold in American thought. Although domesticity had expanded to include areas ranging from teaching to missionary work, significant numbers of Americans were not ready for women's rights. Having given women the domestic realm, they wanted women to remain in it.

For women turning their faces toward the trans-Mississippi West, the divisiveness in thinking regarding women's issues was in some ways unfortunate. They heard as much or more about their moral powers and responsibilities than they did about their prerogatives. Rather than being encouraged to seize rights in the unsettled, flexible milieu of the West, women were reminded that, as carriers of Christian civilization, they had much work to do in the West.[50] In 1854, writer Lydia Sigourney spoke to these women in verse, saying that it was in women's character to take on courageously such challenges:

> *How beautiful is woman's love!*
> *That from the play-place of its birth . . .*
> *To stranger-bands, to stranger-home . . .*
> *Goes forth in perfect trust, to prove*
> *The untried toil, the burdening care*
> *The peril and the pang to dare.*[51]

This sermonizing implanted in the minds of westering women the notion that they were migrating not just as settlers, but as desperately needed moral missionaries. Women looking toward the West had already learned that they were in demand as wives. With so many men migrating to the West the marriage market also moved west. Because men outnumbered women and much work needed to be done, there was an almost constant campaign by westerners to attract women settlers.[52] In 1837, one western newspaper advised women that "every respectable young woman who goes to the West, is almost sure of an advantageous marriage." Anglo women soon discovered that westerners also understood women's potential as "civilizers." In another issue, the same newspaper noted that "whatever may be the customs of a country, the women of it decide the morals."[53] An 1860 poem titled "Idyll of a Western Wife," which appeared in yet another western newspaper, took a slightly different approach, insisting that the rustic "housewife merry" marked the advance of civilization into the West.[54] After hearing so much of this, some women must have wondered how the inhabitants of the West would get along if they did not migrate. Certainly, the belief that female morality would be served by westward migration softened the blow for those women who were not enthusiastic about their impending move. One can almost imagine many of these women heaving a sigh and determining to perform their moral duty in the West, at the same time that other women envisioned the West as a vast moral wasteland that they would redeem.

Unsurprisingly, the Civil War of 1861 to 1865 and the Reconstruction period that followed, lasting until 1877, put a crimp in many people's plans. Women's rights leaders, for example, set aside their campaigns in favor of supporting the war effort. People who hoped to migrate to the West also put their dreams on hold. After the war period, however, women's rights leaders resumed their crusade with a new impetus, whereas westward migration not only increased, but now included newly freed black Americans and a surge of immigrants from eastern Europe.

Thousands of Anglo women believed it was time for changes for themselves as well. For example, war widows and wives of disabled veterans who had to support themselves and their children wanted fair wages and reasonable working conditions. Other women found that in the postwar economy they too had to work for wages to help support their families. Even middle- and upper-class women, especially those who had learned through volunteer work how to speak, conduct meetings, raise money, handle finances, and serve as executive officers, were unwilling to return to old ways. They were in the forefront of women demanding better education, as well as the freedom to write other than didactic literature, enter the professions, and become artists and musicians. Some also wanted the ability to divorce shiftless or abusive husbands.

Women's rights leaders supported all of these causes. With vigor, Elizabeth Cady Stanton took up the last by renewing a campaign she had begun in 1860, then set aside during the war years: ease of divorce. Stanton condemned the "slavery" of a bad marriage, saying that divorce was to enslaved wives what the Underground Railroad had been to slaves of African descent. On more than one occasion, Stanton shocked her readers or listeners with her assertions that every "slave" who fled "a discordant marriage" gave her satisfaction. She hoped that "the education and elevation" of women would lead to "a mighty sundering of the unholy ties that hold men and women together who loathe and despise each other." Few women's rights' advocates endorsed all of Stanton's views, but they did agree that wives of alcoholics should be freed from destructive marriages. As a result, by 1871 thirty-four states, two-thirds of which were in the South and the West, added drunkenness to lists of grounds for divorce.[55]

Anglo women—whether in the East, South, or West—had a

plethora of additional issues. A significant number argued for their right to vote and hold political office.[56] Many wanted to control childbearing; some used abortion to that end. Some wanted separate women's prisons. Others hoped to see more female ministers. Huge numbers of farm women joined the Farmer's Alliance and the Grange, or Patrons of Husbandry. Urban women founded clubs and service organizations. And so many women committed themselves to the cause of temperance that the Women's Christian Temperance Union, founded in 1874, became the largest women's organization in the nineteenth century with, its officials claimed, a branch in every county in the nation.[57]

One might expect all this furor to result in the timely death of domestic ideals and the moral-guardian theory, yet this was not to be. Instead, the furor caused insecure Americans, who had not yet recovered from the Civil War and Reconstruction, to cling to the past. Consequently, domesticity not only lived on, but gained momentum. At the same time that energetic women left their homes for a portion or all of a day, articles and books about domesticity and womanly virtues grew in number and vehemence. Stay home, authors told women, for your own good and that of your family. When Catharine Beecher and her sister Harriet Beecher Stowe formed a partnership in 1870 to write *Principles of Domestic Science,* they repeated the same old shibboleths. In this and subsequent editions, they described women's profession as the care and nursing of the ill, the training of children, and practicing economy in their domestic pursuits. By adding that women's duties included the instruction and training of servants, the sisters revealed their social-class bias; they still wrote for middle- and upper-class white women. Their support was not on behalf of women's rights or woman suffrage, but for better domestic training. If, they wrote, women received preparation for their duties as men did for their trades and professions, domestic labor would no longer be "poorly paid, and regarded as menial and disgraceful."[58] Although proponents of new home-economics programs agreed, most women's rights leaders were determined to push hard until their status changed appreciably.

A similar traditional view of westering women also hung on. In the 1880s, old ideas reached their zenith in a popular work titled *Woman on the Frontier.* Its author, William Fowler, counseled women that it was as "pioneer and colonizer" that their life stories were "potent . . . and interesting." As humanizing, refining, and civilizing agents of the frontier, women were truly the "founders of the Republic." According to Fowler, "the household, the hamlet, the village, the town, the city, the state" rise out of their "homely toils, and destiny obscure." He observed that women must execute their usual moral functions in the West—including inaugurating Sunday schools, introducing religion into the "frontier home," and serving as "unconscious legislators"—since their very presence rendered "more desirable life, property, and the other objects for which laws are made." He added that women as a group must also serve as the "great educator of the frontier" and should work with Indians to soften the "fierce temper of the pagan tribes."[59]

Like women's rights leaders, a significant number of Anglo women decided to modify such traditional advice to serve their own ends. They kept going, finding ways to appear domestic while doing what they wanted to do. For example, women who enjoyed the outdoors hiked and climbed mountains wearing long skirts, corsets, and wide-brimmed hats. Their one concession was to don boys' boots. Others played sports. One case was that of Louise Pound, who during the 1890s and early 1900s, took up lawn tennis and golf. After she earned a Ph.D. at the University of Heidelberg and became a professor at the University of Nebraska, she supported a women's basketball team and founded a female military company, whose members drilled carrying 1880-model Springfield rifles. Other women entered the professions, especially in the West where 14 percent of women were professionals as opposed to 8 percent nationally. In 1889, for example, Ella L. Knowles passed the Montana bar exam with distinction, after which she practiced law in Helena and campaigned for woman suffrage.[60] Yet other women of the era sought autonomy and personal freedom by seeking divorces. The Victorian Age—despite its emphasis on hearts, flowers, and romantic love—produced more divorces than any other era or any other nation: twelve or thirteen out every one hundred marriages ended in divorces, two-thirds of them granted to women.[61] By the turn of the twentieth century, the image of the New Woman struggled with that of the Gibson Girl. The term *New Woman* applied to those who, like President Theodore Roosevelt's daughter Alice, smoked in public, or to "strong-minded women" who demanded their rights. The Gibson Girl, created by Charles Dana Gibson during the 1890s for *Life* magazine and appearing on everything from magazine covers to wall calendars, was a softer rendering of white American women. Gibson Girls wore their hair upswept in bouffant coiffures, favored long skirts and corsets that made them incredibly thin-waisted, and for the beach donned one-piece wool bathing suits with legs that covered their "limbs." Long black stockings, gloves, and parasols completed the outfit in which no one dared swim for fear of drowning.[62] Although Gibson Girls were more liberated than their mothers, they still were "ladies."

The contrast between the New Woman and the more traditional Gibson Girl is best seen in the career of Annie Oakley, the female sharpshooter who, beginning in 1885, appeared with Buffalo Bill Cody's Wild West for sixteen seasons. Cody's Wild West brought a living and breathing West to viewers who, up to that point, had only read about the West or seen artists' renditions. Annie Oakley added a female element, portraying a western woman skilled with guns and horses, yet so feminine and ladylike that she appealed to young and old, conservative and liberal, New Women and Gibson Girls.[63]

During the late 1880s and 1890s, Cody and Oakley created the first public image of the cowgirl. Because popular culture, such as Fowler's book *Women on the Frontier,* characterized women as victims, Cody hired actresses who screamed and fainted in such vignettes as "The Attack on the Settlers' Cabin." But there were also forceful and scrappy women in the West. During the 1890s, for example, women who went west as homesteaders accounted for 11.9 percent of Colorado's homesteaders and in Wyoming were 18.2 percent. The existence of these and other women forced Cody to recognize that in the West, as humorist Josh Billings put it, "wimmin is everywhere."[64]

From Cody's point of view, Annie Oakley made the perfect cowgirl. She was an exceptional shooter rather than a disreputable "show" girl or a New Woman and was intent on preserving her "ladyhood." Cody encouraged Oakley in her interpretation of the cowgirl. In 1889, he stated that women should be able to vote and earn wages, but he opposed rodeo women who wore "bloomer pants" or rode bucking horses. He first billed Annie and other cowgirls he hired as "rancheras,"

"prairie beauties," and "natural flowers" of the American West and vehemently denied that they were New Women. Only a few of them rode
their horses astride; Oakley was not among them. She termed riding
astride a "horrid idea" and did her riding with a sidesaddle.[65]

Annie Oakley herself hoped to embody what she termed the finest
of female qualities. Annie, who was five feet tall and weighed about one
hundred pounds, wore her hair long and loose, avoided makeup and jewelry, and donned calf-length skirts, leggings, and low-heeled shoes. In
1888, a reporter admitted that he expected Oakley to be a "strong, virile,
masculine-like woman, of loud voice, tall of stature and of massive proportions"; instead he found a "pretty little lady" who spoke with him in
a gentle, refined voice.[66]

Oakley, who thought of herself as a Victorian "true woman," demonstrated the five attributes she associated with ladyhood; she was married,
modest, domestic, benevolent, and a civilizing force. Annie was married
for fifty years to shooter Frank Butler, who spared her from immodesty
by handling all business arrangements, including publicity. The domestic Annie adorned her tent with a Brussels carpet, a marble-topped table,
and a rocking chair, in which she sat between acts doing fancy embroi-
dery. The benevolent Annie gave money and gifts to everyone from
family members to orphans, whereas Annie as a civilizer disapproved of
cursing, smoking, or drinking alcohol, especially in her presence.[67]

Throughout her career, Annie Oakley maintained her feminine persona. Although she entered the male realm of what she called "arenic
sports," Annie said she did not want to be a New Woman. Nor was
Oakley a suffragist. She opposed woman suffrage because she feared that
"not enough good women will vote." As the first American cowgirl,
Annie offered the era's women a model of achievement blended with
traditional femininity. Oakley not only rode and shot in Cody's Wild
West, but set records in shooting matches and was an accomplished
hunter. Yet she also was ladylike in conduct and in appearance. For
instance, Annie Oakley was partly responsible for the bicycle craze of the
1890s. She brought one back from England and was soon riding and
shooting from bicycle-back, wearing a modest suit of her own design,
with hidden garters that held down the skirt as she pedaled. Later, when
Oakley, who retired from the Wild West in 1901, made a comeback with

Vernon Seaver's Young Buffalo Show between 1911 and 1913, she still wore her usual clothing. Although some rodeo cowgirls favored trousers, men's boots, and Stetson hats, a fair number of them emulated Oakley, who had maximized her opportunities during the late 1800s and early 1900s without becoming a pseudo-man.[68] Like Sarah Josepha Hale years before, Oakley subtly subverted usual gender roles to fit her own ends, but did it so graciously that she received kudos rather than criticism.

Clearly, then, women who went west between the end of the War of 1812 and the beginning of World War I had rich and varied examples to emulate. Also, because these women had internalized many messages in their lifetimes, they carried considerable mental baggage with them as they headed west. Anglo women had a sense of white superiority enhanced by female superiority, with a strong undercurrent of mission. Once on a frontier, most expected to model white "civilization," including helping establish white agriculture, which was a mode of colonizing the West.[69] They would also act piously and help the destitute, ill, and needy. Although they had a deep awareness of social ills and a need, as women, to correct them, the only curative they knew was to exhibit their own moral rectitude. They also had a vague uneasiness that they had been deprived of certain basic rights due them as human beings and as highly moral women. Yet, whether it was 1850 or 1900, they had very ill-defined ideas about how to claim such rights. They had not been told that change often comes from listening and communicating.

Only the intensity and specifics of Anglo women's mindset varied from the 1810s and 1820s to the 1890s and early 1900s. A female migrant of the 1830s, for example, might interpret her mission as helping uneducated white children and black slaves, of which there were many in the West. She might also hope to have the opportunity of some education and perhaps poorly paid employment. A woman of the 1870s and 1880s was probably aware of the Indian "problem," as defined by journalists and reformers, and looked forward to gaining such women's rights as improved education and possibly professional opportunities. By 1900, a woman might be thinking ahead to aiding reservation Indians and helping subdue such "renegades" as the Comanche and the Sioux. She might also plan to work for woman suffrage in the West. In virtually every case, however, Anglo women were not well-informed citizens who were capable of advancing gender reform, interracial contact, and the nation's best interests in positive and effective ways. In other words, Anglo women went west with an attitude.

—— On the Indian "Other" ——

Because the number-one recipient of Anglo women's imputed morality and charity was to be the American Indian, female migrants were urged at every turn to exert their moral powers on behalf of native peoples. Female "civilizing" gave to women's migration a powerful organizing force, a mythology, a higher meaning in migrating westward.[70] Far from being considered travel, which offered new experiences and novel ideas, the objective of women's westering was to establish the known in a more conducive setting. In 1849, for example, missionary Mary Eastman published a book intended to draw attention to "the moral wants of the Dahcotahs." In a similar vein, the frontier editor Jane Swisshelm admonished her female readers not to let themselves become bored with the oft-discussed cause of the American Indian or to have their attention diverted from Indian problems by more immediate causes, including the Civil War.[71] Novels of the period reinforced this message, especially among middle- and upper-class readers, who drew upon them for entertainment and guidance. In one, the young heroine, Natalie, displayed laudable talent in saving the souls of Indians and blacks. She was duly praised, in dialect that most whites thought appropriate to natives, by an Indian convert to Christianity as he lay near death: "Me love Great Spirit; Great Spirit so good to send his little white-face to tell me how to get home."[72]

This trend of depicting women as the special liberators of American Indians was so accepted that it intensified by the end of the nineteenth century and continued well into the twentieth.[73] No one seemed aware of a basic paradox: white women had reason to leave the old society yet they went west believing the society they had rejected was the best. For most white women, the rejection was more symbolic than real. They took with them every psychical and psychological bit possible of the old, hoping to recreate it in a newer and purer form. Thus, women's aspirations were lofty ones indeed.

Dime novels, written by male and female authors, played an especially important role in defining women and Indians.[74] In a 1911 dime novel, the only apologist for and defender of what the author described as "fanatical and cruel redskins" was a woman who claimed "there are some good Indians that are not yet dead."[75] Such sentiments had a ripple effect—reaching working-class and homebound women through excerpts in newspapers, tracts, pamphlets, sermons, speeches, street plays, their children's school and personal books and periodicals, chapbooks, jokes, folklore, and other manifestations of popular thought. These direct and indirect exhortations to women to provide moral direction and otherwise aid American Indians put Anglo women in opposition to the more natural, freer world of Indians. Moreover, Anglo women put themselves at odds by envisioning themselves as harbingers of civilization and seeing Indians as representative of primitive and inferior culture. Convinced of one basic fact, that the American Indian was a savage, women tended to see Indians as contemptible objects, salvageable only through women's civilizing influence. That many women believed they indeed could overcome the supposedly savage nature of Indians was demonstrated by the avowed eagerness of so many of them to venture into western areas as missionaries to American Indians.[76]

At the same time that women planned to minister to Indians, their number-one fear of migrating to the West was American Indians. Women had been taught to view themselves as weak and helpless, and thus very likely to be victims. As they were reminded of the strength of their morality, they were also lectured on the weakness of their physical being. Because men were physically strong, they were the doers, but because women were physically weak, they had to seek male protectors. Women's dependence upon men was thus seen as a product of their own physical inferiority.[77]

These ideas accosted women from every side. During the mid-1830s, in lectures to Emma Willard's Troy Seminary students, educator Almira Phelps emphasized women's' physical deficiencies. The "delicacy" of women's nervous systems, she warned, "subjects her to agitations to which man, favored by greater physical strength and more firmness of nerve, is exempt." In an 1836 tract titled *Female Improvement,* Elizabeth Sandford added that there was "something unfeminine in independence." Because women had to rely on help from men, she explained, they should encourage men's protective instincts by acting "dependent" and "grateful." In 1848, a male guidebook writer explained that men and women resembled two halves of a circle: the man possessed physical strength, the woman sensibility and patience.[78]

Godey's frequently reiterated such interpretations of women's "natures" to their readers. In the "Editor's Table" in 1851, Sarah Josepha Hale declared that women were not mechanical, inventive, or strong because God had given those characteristics to men. Instead, God had granted women "moral insight or instinct, and the patience that endures physical suffering." Thus, Hale reasoned, women would not advance by "becoming like man, in doing man's work, or striving for the dominion of the world." Rather, women worked best through "obedience, temperance, truth, love, piety."[79]

Novelists also stressed the idea of women's inferiority in matters requiring physical strength. Domestic novelist E. D. E. N. Southworth's 1856 novel *Retribution* presented a heroine who at one point exclaimed, "Talk of woman's rights, woman's rights live in the instincts of her protector—man." It was not only women's, or domestic, literature that advocated these views of women. Popular novelists such as James Fenimore Cooper characterized women as weak, passive, docile, and submissive, rewarded in the end by the prize of a hero, tailor-made to her needs and desires. Although Cooper occasionally created an atypically strong heroine, she always ended up unhappy. In 1848, in *Jack Tier,* for example, Cooper's heroine, deserted by her husband, disguised herself as a man and followed him to sea for several years. She was totally "unsexed" by the experience. Cooper pointed out that Molly Swash desexed herself because she chose to act on her own behalf rather than accept the actions and decisions of the male. In 1856, one of Cooper's characters in *The Sea Lions* added another argument: if women realized how much power their "seeming dependence" gave them with men they would refuse to tolerate those "who are for proclaiming their independence and their right to equality in all things."[80]

In response to these social constructions, women about to go west must have asked themselves many questions: Would they survive in the arduous environment of the West? Would male protection be sufficient to carry them through? And the most crucial question of all: Would male strength prove equal to that of American Indian "barbarians" who reportedly attempted to assault and rape white women? Even though women "knew" that female morality would triumph over evil, the West, a seeming "land of savagery," appeared less than an ideal arena in which to test that belief.

Fortunately for westward-bound women, an opposing portrayal of women appeared during the mid-nineteenth century. Even as the "fact" of female physical inferiority was heralded across the land, the capable woman made her literary debut. The capable woman could not only care for herself in certain situations, but could occasionally aid a man. A close reading of Catharine Sedgwick's popular 1836 novel, *A Poor Rich Man and a Rich Poor Man,* provides a case in point. Its heroine supported a large family on an impossibly small income and, in her spare time, engaged in charitable endeavors. Only a year later, Hannah Lee's heroine in *Elinor Fulton* sustained her entire family after bankruptcy, as well as provided unwavering inspiration until her father worked his way back to solvency.[81]

This is not to suggest that these early capable heroines won over American readers completely. According to book sales, the public still preferred Hannah Lee's flighty, squandering Jane of *Three Experiments of Living* (1837). Meanwhile, however, certain events opened readers' minds, including the women's rights conventions of the late 1840s and 1850s, and the liberating effects of the Civil War on women during the early 1860s. Near the war's end, the height of the capable woman appeared in E. D. E. N. Southworth's *Capitola* (1865). Young and daring, Capitola entered the story disguised as a boy. After flouting her guardian, fighting a duel, outwitting her kidnappers, and romping through a number of people's lives, she received the supreme compliment from her guardian, who declared that she deserved to be a man. That many readers loved and possibly imitated Capitola was proven by the book's sales, for it joined the works of Charles Dickens, William Thackeray, and George Eliot on the best-seller list and was republished several times in subsequent years.[82]

Perhaps inspired by these novels, *Godey's* began to include the capable woman among its other features. In the mid-1840s, *Godey's* published on a regular basis sketches of heroic women of the American Revolution. "The women of that era were equal to the crisis," one author wrote; they contributed "active assistance, by the labor of their hands; by the sacrifice of their luxuries; by the surrender of what had been deemed necessaries." About the same time, accounts of female heroism in other eras appeared. In 1845, one tale recounted how an explorer's life had been saved several times by women. Another story celebrated the wife who realized that a robber was hiding under the bed and bravely detained him by staying in the room for two hours until help arrived.[83]

The emergence of capable women also manifested itself in *Godey's* through an increased emphasis on exercise, diet, health, beauty, and fashion. The argument was that women could perform their moral duties only if they were healthy and strong. Women therefore needed to learn how to take proper care of themselves. As early as 1841, *Godey's* dared to suggest that the "delicate" young lady was becoming passé; that a woman should "go forth into the fields and woods, if you live in the country—take long walks in the cool morning and evening hour, if you are in 'populous cities pent'—let the minimum of these daily excursions average at least two miles." When indoors, dancing provided excellent exercise, as did the practice of modest calisthenics. Even a revision of *Godey's* fashion plates was justified by the appearance of capable women. During the 1840s, *Godey's* launched a campaign to do away with stiff and pudgy figures, replacing them with healthy, graceful ones.[84]

The contradiction between woman's weakness and her capability were especially apparent in the dime novels of the late nineteenth century and early twentieth century. On the one hand, women were characterized as "gentle maidens" who required protection from men. When one heroine of the 1890s was accosted by a bully demanding a kiss from her, she cried out, "Are there no men among you who will help me?" She was saved by a stalwart hero who proclaimed that he "never hesitated to face death in defense of a woman." In another tale, "white maidens" were placed in a grotto by their male protectors, who fought off "savages" on their behalf.[85]

On the other hand, capable women also existed in dime novels. During the 1890s, a woman threatened Deadwood Dick at gunpoint, insisting that he marry her. In the nick of time, Dick's wife, whom he thought dead, appeared to challenge his tormentor to a duel. Dick observed the resulting fight, a "strange, exciting combat between two infuriated women." At the struggle's end, Dick's wife lunged at her opponent who "fell back, with a blade run through her heart—dead." In a later story, *White Boy Chief* (1908), a madwoman and a young girl rescued the hero from a band of "red devils" and "cussed redskins." After the hero commented, "what a head piece yer have got, old gal," the author explained that "notwithstanding her demented condition, she was a woman of iron constitution and will." By 1917, the capable woman seemed to have triumphed, at least in dime novels. In that year, a heroine threw sandbags out of a hot-air balloon on the heads of Sioux Indians, used the revolver she always carried to further discourage her pursuers, and capped her unladylike performance by returning to camp where "with several of the females of the settlement," she "engaged in making coffee for the men."[86]

Women who found themselves caught between messages that they were physically weak yet physically capable hoped they would be fortunate enough to encounter "good" Indians. Although the good male Indian was rare in nineteenth-century white discourse, he did exist. This was the Noble Savage who was pure, virtuous, and gentle. It was to this streak of natural nobility in American Indians that women could turn for protection from elements of the western environment that included ruthless and rapacious American Indians they might meet. During the closing decades of the century, writer and Indian reformer Helen Hunt Jackson portrayed their ilk in her popular writings, as well as in her reform treatises.[87] The good Indian survived well into the twentieth century. In 1907, Gray Feather appeared in *Kid Curry's Last Stand*. Gray Feather "had a reputation among the cow-punchers of being a good Indian, for they had always found him truthful and reliable." Gray Feather spoke beautiful and correct English, referring deferentially to himself in the second person. "Gray Feather is pleased to see you, White Chief," he greeted one of his acquaintances.[88] Gray Feather was obviously one of the "good" Indians to whom an Anglo woman could turn for aid.

At the same time, Anglo women heard far more about the under-side of the Indian—the "bad" Indian, who was brutal and very fright-ening. The creation of negative stereotypes and splitting native peoples' personas into good and bad was not uncommon in colonial discourse, but from these negative social constructions women were predisposed to view the Indians they encountered in the worst possible light.[89] As moral missionaries embarking on a crusade to the West in general and to American Indians in particular, women had prejudice toward Indians firmly in mind before they even set foot upon the westward trail. If women had any doubts regarding the brutal natures of most American Indians, they were dispelled by the climate of prejudicial opinion that marked the nineteenth and early twentieth centuries. Anti-Indian sen-timent was longstanding, emerging first during the American colonial period as white settlers attempted to enslave, civilize, assimilate, or reshape into settled farmers the original inhabitants of the New World. When their attempts to "elevate" Native Americans met with resistance, some early Americans concluded that the only alternative for American Indians was eventual extermination.[90]

Later generations of Americans elaborated upon earlier themes. They helped create the stereotype of the Indian, lumping together more than two thousand native cultures—and called "The Indian"—all of them savage, heathen, and barbaric. Because most Indians were "bad," meaning naked, dirty, mean, and hostile, they deserved removal or destruction by a progressive and civilized white society.[91] Throughout the nineteenth century, accounts depicting American Indians as savage barbarians became a well-developed art, especially in the literary genres of captivity narratives, or "penny dreadfuls" as they were known in Europe. These chronicles of brutal treatment inflicted upon white cap-tives by Indians appealed to, and reinforced, the anti-native prejudices of readers. Appearing first during the American colonial period, 1607 to 1776, captivity narratives clearly manifested the fear and hatred of colonists toward the native peoples of North America. In one of the most well-known captivity narratives, *The Narrative and Restoration of Mrs. Mary Rowlandson* (1682), the author described her captors as "mur-derous wretches" and a "barbarous enemy." As the nation continued its westward expansion into the Ohio Valley during the post-Revolution years after 1783, the popularity of captivity narratives continued. The story of Mary Jemison, taken prisoner by Indians in 1758, was released in 1824 and subsequently republished some thirty times.[92]

By the mid-nineteenth century, captivity narratives originated all over the West, including Mormon trails and the borderlands of New Mexico.[93] The most usual setting for these horrifying dramas, however, was the prairie region of the trans-Mississippi West. In Iowa, the story of the Spirit Lake Massacre of 1857 was written by survivor Abbie Gardner-Sharp, who sold the book in a souvenir shop in the cabin where the "depredations" reportedly occurred. In Minnesota, the New Ulm Massacre of 1862 also received its share of attention, especially from Mary Renville in her *Thrilling Narrative of Indian Captivity* (1863). In 1892, Emeline Fuller, attacked by American Indians in 1860, published her story under the title *Left by the Indians* (1892). Fuller recalled that she had seen unburied bodies bearing "marks of torture too devilish for any human beings to inflict except Indians." Still, Fuller concluded her story on a charitable note: "Let those who have never suffered as I have pity the fate of the noble red man of the forest."[94]

Journalists also reported grim tales of captivity, lacing their accounts with invective. In relating the return of two female captives to their family in 1866, the *Leavenworth Daily Times* noted that "they were in captivity about ten weeks, and in that time suffered all the cruelties that the fiend-like malignity and heartlessness of their cowardly captors could invent." A few years later a correspondent for the *Kansas Daily Tribune* reported that a Mrs. White had lost a daughter to the "hands of merciless savages."[95] Eastern newspapers eagerly picked up news of captivities and their attendant "outrages" on whites, especially women and children. In 1859, the *New York Times* noted that the commissioner of Indian affairs had identified seventeen children harmed as a result of the Utah "massacres" of 1857. In 1868, the *Times* offered its readers a detailed report of the execution of thirty-nine Indians in Minnesota for various crimes: "capture of women and children," "took a white woman and ravished her," "murder of a white woman and of design to ravish her daughter," and "shooting and cutting open a woman who was with child." In addition, the *Times* routinely informed its readers of Indian "uprisings," "atrocities," drunkenness, and continued captivities of whites.[96]

In whatever media they appeared, captivity narratives fulfilled different functions throughout the nearly three centuries of their existence. During the American colonial period they were largely religious tracts concerned with the salvation of those who escaped captivity. By the end of the eighteenth century and well into the nineteenth century, they expressed anti-Indian sentiment. These narratives rationalized the extermination of American Indians and the taking of their lands. During the mid- and late nineteenth century, captivity narratives demonstrated the courage and fortitude of frontiersmen and women, thus becoming tall tales that exaggerated the exploits of captives to indicate the bravery of American settlers. They were highly fictionalized and even used as school texts in moral values.[97]

Meanwhile, a similar stereotype pervaded other nineteenth-century forms of popular culture.[98] Like all groups of human beings, whites sought truths about "others," often constructing them without much evidence.[99] Because literature, including periodicals, was the primary form of media during the early nineteenth century, it played a key role in white colonization of Native Americans. Authors who misrepresented Indians conditioned white Americans to accept almost any travesty against Indians.[100] For instance, in 1835, William Gilmore Simms's novel *The Yemassee* presented Americans with one type of ignoble savage, and in 1837, Robert Montgomery Bird's *Nick of the Woods* created another. James Fenimore Cooper also contributed to Indian stereotypes; for example, his Indians were quintessential Americans who were not Americans at all, in that they fell outside of white American society.[101]

Meanwhile, the Romantic historians George Bancroft and Francis Parkman produced widely read histories filled with barbaric American Indians. In historical narratives more like fiction, these historians made no pretense at objectivity. Convinced of Indians' inherent savagery, Parkman wrote that although white settlers must take into account the "good qualities" of Indians they must also be aware of the "impassable gulf" between the two groups.[102] Indians were also depicted in negative ways in many popular Currier and Ives prints, such as the 1813 *Death of Tecumseh at the Battle of the Thames,* whereas the renowned artist Frederic Remington often had Indians skulking through his engravings, paintings, and sculptures. According to Remington's portrayals, such as those in *Sign Language* (1889) and *The Luckless Hunter* (1910), the Indian was an inferior being destined for eventual extinction.[103]

Bad Indians also turned up in immensely popular dime novels and other pulp literature, all of which reflected and exploited anti-native sentiment. Dime novelists described American Indians as "pesky red-skins," "red skunks," "bloodthirsty wretches," and, of course, "savages." In 1907, one author even put these words into the mouth of an Indian character: "You may not know it, but the wild blood that flows in an Indian's veins craves for the excitement of the torture stake if that Indian be a bad one."[104]

Stereotypes of Indians included Indian women as well. Like male Indians, females were lumped into a few categories, whose members shared the same characteristics.[105] There were good female Indians who were sensitive, human, and warm hearted. One type of good Indian woman was the peacemaker. A specific case from the 1890s was not only "fully cultured, and of fair education," but, because of the peaceful influence she exerted, received many valuable lands and money gifts from settlers and Indian agents.[106] There were also good Indian women who were sympathetic to whites, sometimes helping them escape Indian captors, even their own husbands.[107] And there was the Indian Princess, who, like Pocahontas, was willing to aid whites in their campaign to overcome her people and seize their lands. She appeared in many guises, as Magawisca in Catharine Maria Sedgwick's *Hope Leslie* (1827), as Little Deer in Robert Strange's *Eoneguski; or The Cherokee Chief* (1839), as Moinoona in Osgood Bradbury's *Peripold the Avenger* (1848), and as the Indian princess Winona in an Isabel Moore Kimball statue (1902). Always the paragon of beauty, usually the daughter of a chieftain, and favorable to white expansion, the Indian princess seemed to embody American national pride in things and people uniquely American.[108]

Typically, these characters derived from the prototypical Indian princess, Pocahontas, who was saved from savagery by her relationship with an Englishman. Elevated to the status of a princess because of her marriage to the English gentleman John Rolfe, Pocahontas adopted the white name Rebecca, wore such white-style clothing as corsets and ruff collars, and allowed herself to be presented to the English court. As a result, writers and artists depicted Pocahontas as more white than

Indian.[109] A seventeenth-century portrait of her, titled simply *Pocahontas,* depicted a fair-skinned woman with a ruff around her neck and a fan in her gloved hand. An eighteenth-century painting by Mary Woodbury, also titled *Pocahontas,* showed a woman with her dark hair pulled back, her fair skin set off by a ribbon around her neck, her sloping shoulders and narrow waist accented by a lace-trimmed dress with voluminous skirts, and her delicate hand holding a single flower. In the nineteenth-century portrait by Robert Matthew Sully, also called *Pocahontas,* there was slightly more suggestion of naturalness in the subject's flowing hair and in the outdoor background. Yet here too was the face of a white woman with Cupid's bow lips, soulful eyes, and bejeweled ears, displayed above an elaborate gown.[110]

White eyes saw the Pocahontas they wanted to see. She was to reappear in many other forms throughout the nineteenth century. Introduced on the stage first in 1808, through James Nelson Barker's play "The Indian Princess; or, La Belle Sauvage," she was to flit over many platforms, rescuing white heroes in the process. She was also the subject of countless poems, such as Lydia Sigourney's 1841 *Pocahontas.* To Sigourney, Pocahontas was "a forest-child" whose "spirit-glance bespoke the daughter of a king." After many stanzas recounting Pocahontas's story, Sigourney concluded that although her people were gone, her memory should be preserved. "It is not meet," Sigourney wrote, that Pocahontas's "name should moulder in the grave."[111]

Pocahontas's legacies were not all positive, however. Because her marriage to John Rolfe proved that "savages" could be Christianized, it provided something of a rationale for Indian women–white men relationships.[112] Still, whites generally opposed such marriages, which would undermine notions of white superiority, social class formed by breeding, and white nationalism based on white superiority and class. Whites who hoped to ensure racial purity had to control sexual desire, making intermarriage as far out of bounds as possible.[113] As a result, many writers opposed interracial unions. As early as 1827, Cooper's *The Prairie* made it clear that intermarriage, or miscegenation as Americans later termed it, was unacceptable. The white hero refused the offer of an Indian wife because he opposed "the admixture of the species, which only tends to tarnish the beauty and to interrupt the harmony of nature."

Later in the same story, a female character excoriated her husband for even listening to an offer of an Indian wife. "Would ye disgrace color, and family, and nation," she cried out, "by mixing white blood with red?"[114]

A similar point was made in later years by many others. In an 1841 love story in *The Ladies Companion,* "Malaeska; the Indian Wife of the White Hunter," author Ann Sophia Winterbotham Stephens presented the tale of an unfortunate Indian princess married to a white man. Although she had promised at her husband's deathbed to raise their son like a white person, the boy was torn from her by whites who wanted to ensure his "proper" upbringing. Bereft of husband and child, she returned to her tribe.[115] Judging from dime novels, this debate continued into the twentieth century. In a 1908 story, a young white woman who was appalled and insulted by a marriage proposal from an Indian chief graciously accepted her brother's impending marriage to a young Indian "belle" living among whites in St. Louis.[116]

Little wonder that advertising seized upon such images, which were popular with white consumers. Especially between 1870 and 1910, when big business flourished in the United States, American advertisers appropriated the image of American Indians and turned it to their advantage. Advertisers were able to steal Indian likenesses because they possessed power—as whites, they were a cultural force, and as entrepreneurs they had economic clout. Numerous companies distributed trade cards in shops and with products. It soon became a fad to collect these postcard-sized pictures, which used Native Americans to advertise such products as corn starch and coffee, and to promote such businesses as a clothing establishment in downtown Indianapolis. A little closer to the actual product were trade cards portraying attractive Indian women on behalf of "Indian Queen Perfume" and "Oswego Bitters." The point was not that the pictured Indian used the product, but that his or her image grabbed the attention of white consumers.[117]

Despite the existence of a female Noble Savage, however, the dominant prototype of the Indian woman in various types of media was the "squaw," an unfortunate and exploited female who did all the camp work. This image was an inaccurate objectification of American Indian women that has continued into the twenty-first century.[118] The "squaw" has a long history. In 1830, a white male observer declared that Indian men saw their women as "a kind of slave, or beast of burthen." In 1841, in *A New Home,* white commentator Caroline Kirkland depicted a French trader's Indian wife as a withdrawn woman who refused to talk with white visitors, conversed only with "some wretched looking Indians who were hanging about the house," and seemed pleased when her white guests departed. Kirkland, like most nineteenth-century commentators, saw native women as pathetic, depressed figures who had little control over their own marital and sexual destinies.[119] Decades later, in 1868, a correspondent for the *New York Times,* who had traveled among the Navajos of New Mexico, demeaned women moving a camp on horseback and on foot as presenting little more than a "funny and interesting scene." The correspondent also included an account of an Indian woman "who gave birth while walking, picked up her child, and traveled on."[120]

Artists, too, represented Indian women falsely. White observers often thought that Indian women were exploited by the practice of plural wives and the seeming willingness of Indian men to trade a woman for a pony or for trinkets. Because whites misinterpreted such practices they thought that American Indian women were chattel to be bought and sold at the whim of their men.[121] In *The Trapper's Bride* (1850), the romantic artist Alfred Jacob Miller, who traveled through parts of the West noting Indian practices, depicted a lovely young Native American woman being sold to a white trapper by Indian men for six hundred dollars' worth of guns, tobacco, alcohol, and beads.[122] Apparently, white onlookers often trivialized Indian women, at the same time overlooking the existence of matrilineal Indian groups, the status accorded Indian women for economic activities, and Indian women who served as warriors, shamans, healers, and religious leaders.

For a significant number of whites, then, the Indian woman was an inferior and abused creature who earned little esteem among even her own people. Sadly, such views achieved the status of truth in the minds of many nineteenth-century Americans, who also came to believe that such women were brutal to captives. As withered hags, as hideous crones, and in a variety of similar characterizations, fictional American Indian women perpetrated outrages consonant with their own "barbarous" state. In *The Prairie,* Cooper's "crones" heaped verbal abuse on their unfortunate victim. In Cooper's words, "they lavished upon their unmoved captive a torrent of that vindictive abuse, in which the women of the savages are so well known to excel." In other fictional accounts, women physically attacked their captives. In an 1830 story titled "The Bois Brule," Indian women "unsheathed their knives and would have immolated the prisoner on the spot had they not been restrained by their men." In 1835, William Gilmore Simms, in *The Yemassee,* described Indian women as directing blows toward a captive. He explained that these women had "lost the gentle nature of the woman without acquiring the magnanimity of the man, which is the result of his consciousness of strength."[123] Although some of these scenes touched on reality, such actions by Indian women were highly ritualized and usually in retribution for one of their own dead.

If white women who became westward migrants managed to escape all these types of social constructions of Indians, they probably had seen the fierce warrior and his obedient squaw, both caricatures bordering on buffoonery, in the many circuses that crisscrossed the United States. By the latter part of the nineteenth century and the early years of the twentieth, Indians also appeared in Buffalo Bill Cody's and other Wild West shows, as well as in numerous "congresses" and "expositions."[124] Cody was one of the few who tried to present authentic Indians, whom he recruited largely from Sioux reservations in the Dakota territory. Cody soon learned, however, that his audiences cared little about real Indians and their cultures. They wanted excitement, action, and blood, all of which Cody grudgingly gave them. Prior to a performance, Cody put on display in a store window the scalp and feather headdress he claimed to have taken from Yellow Hair, also known as Yellow Hand. Cody elevated the "Battle of Summit Springs" from a minor skirmish into a major battle, replaying it with gusto during every performance. In the "Attack on the Settlers' Cabin," Cody raised the possibility of rape and the abduction of women and children by Indians, a fate from which white men mounted on powerful horses saved them.[125] After Sitting Bull's tragic death, Cody retrieved the horse he had given the chief. Cody had trained the horse to raise its front leg and shake hands. Now he added it to his program, billing it as Sitting Bull's horse. Cody also made a point of setting up a separate camp for Indian performers and, at the end of shows, inviting audience members to stroll around, talk with Indians, and view "Indian life."[126]

Indian reformers opposed Cody mightily. Although they stopped him from displaying the scalp and headdress, they never won their campaign against the use of "show" Indians. They maintained that Cody and other Wild West entrepreneurs represented Indian men as savage warriors and women as passive yet cruel squaws, destroying the Indian Bureau's work in turning Indian men and women into productive and "civilized" people. Reformers especially feared that viewers would believe Cody's claims that his Wild West presented Indians as realistic rather than recognizing them as actors who not only never died, but sold souvenirs and programs after shows. Reformers even criticized the establishment of an Indian village on every show lot, saying that these villages gave white visitors inaccurate impressions of Indian life.[127]

Cody recognized, however, that people wanted Indian attacks on wagon trains, burning cabins, and scalping, and Cody the businessperson had to keep his eye on the bottom line. Thus were Anglo girls and women treated to vivid but inaccurate characterizations of the native peoples they would meet in the West. Many an impressionable little girl carried into adulthood her memories of tomahawks and scalp locks, expecting on her trip west to see them at any moment.

In other words, white people created the simplistic category of "Indian." In a monumental act of cultural appropriation, whites took such images as the warrior, the Indian pony, and the buffalo and shaped them to fit whites' ideas of the Indian "other." During the late nineteenth and early twentieth centuries, white women who wanted to "help" Indian women gain self-sufficiency through their crafts also commercialized in the white marketplace such Indian symbols as baskets and pots. Indians who were not allowed to be politically sovereign were stripped of their cultural sovereignty.[128] Representing Indians and their world had been subsumed by whites. As the Ojibway Lenore Keeshig-Tobias said in 1990: "'Indian' is a term used to sell things—souvenirs, cigars, cigarettes, gasoline, cars. . . . 'Indian' is a figment of the white man's imagination."[129]

For westward migrants, the image of bad American Indian men and women did little to reassure timorous white women already intimidated by tales about the areas in which they intended to make their new homes. If white women looked to Indian women for deliverance from Indian men, the squaw stereotype hardly encouraged such hopes. Because pejorative interpretations of both American Indian men and women have persisted through twentieth-century "western" films, we can understand from our own experience just how pernicious and damaging such media treatments can be. Could we expect nineteenth-century women to have been any less gullible than ourselves?

As women's attentions swiveled from Pocahontas and other good Indians to representatives of bad Indians, and back again, many recognized the incongruities between the two. This contradictory manner of thinking about Indians created in the minds of women migrants a good deal of confusion and perhaps even misgivings about their western venture. By the time they struck out for the West, they had to choose between enigmatic visions of themselves as moral but weak, or perhaps capable in certain situations. They also had visions of Indians as superior native beings who were friendly, kind, and courageous, or apparitions of inferior native peoples who were bad, hostile, and vicious. Combined with the uncertainty in their thinking from mixed messages they received about their own natures, roles, and responsibilities, the equally mixed messages concerning American Indians created a tremendous potential for misunderstanding and misinterpretation.

How might one expect these women to act when they met their first Indian "other"? Most would rely on racial profiling rather than on their own observations. They would draw on long-held stereotypes and frame their reactions accordingly. Of course, their actions only helped polarize racial animosities. On the other side, virtually no one offered American Indians any information concerning the hordes of white settlers invading their lands. Because whites judged Indians as inferior and stupid, there were no ambassadors or outreach programs to make cultural confrontations go smoothly. Rather, Indians, who were in reality bright and curious, would annoy and irritate Anglo women to no end by staring at them, touching their belongings, and asking "stupid" questions.

On an even more tragic level, nothing prepared Anglo women for the widespread despair and death among the people they displaced. Stunned by their inability to help, women would soon learn that their morality and piousness meant little on Indian-white frontiers. The many social constructions that women had absorbed back home were as useless as greenback dollar bills after the introduction of the silver standard. As complex as things were for Anglo women, however, they were complicated even further by an influx of European ideas that poured into the United States during the nineteenth and early twentieth centuries regarding white women and American Indians in the frontier stage of the great American West.

Figure 1. Anglo women, who frequently went west with minds filled with misinformation and eyes dark with trepidation, clung to a belief in the divine and superior nature of white womanhood that would protect them from violent enemies. "Madonna of the Prairie," 1984, by the western illustrator W. H. D. Koerner. Courtesy of the Buffalo Bill Historical Center in Cody, Wyoming.

Figure 2. The author Sarah Josepha Hale, who in 1837 began a long editorship of the widespread and influential *Godey's Lady's Book*, touted women's separate spheres, yet encouraged women to expand their realms. Frontispiece, undated, *Godey's Lady's Book*. Courtesy of the author.

Ætatis suæ 21. Aº.1616.

Matoaks als Rebecka daughter to the mighty Prince
Powhatan Emperour of Attanoughkomouck als Virginia
converted and baptized in the Christian faith, and
Wife to the wor.ll Mr Tho: Rolff.

Figure 3. In a quest to make American Indians more appealing to Anglos, early writers and artists turned the image of Pocahontas into that of a properly dressed, white-style "princess." "Pocahontas," 1661, by an unknown artist. Courtesy of the National Portrait Gallery, Smithsonian Institution, Washington, D.C.

Figure 4. Late nineteenth-century Americans continued the trend of visualizing Indian women in highly romanticized ways. Drawing of a Nez Perce woman, 1898, by the American illustrator Frederick S. Church. Courtesy of the Museum of New Mexico, Santa Fe, negative number 107725.

FRANCES TROLLOPE

Figure 5. An English woman who also visited the United States and wrote about the West and its peoples was Frances Trollope, perhaps best known for her *Domestic Manners of the Americans* (1832). Undated. Courtesy of the author.

Figure 6. Settlers who lived in wagons on trails and in basic dwellings in settlements had little defense against weather, animals, and human assailants; thus they felt especially vulnerable to Native American assailants. A homestead in the area of Terry and Fallon, Montana, undated, photograph by Evelyn Cameron. Courtesy of the Montana Historical Society, Helena.

Figure 7. The remains of a temporary agency on the homeland of the Warm Springs or Mimbres Indians, led by Chief Victorio, who wanted only to be left alone in this still unproductive area of western New Mexico. Most Anglos dubbed Victorio a "bad" Indian due to his resistance to white settlement. Ruins of the Warm Springs or Mimbres Indian Agency, west of Truth or Consequences in the Black Mountain Range, 2003. Courtesy of the author.

Figure 8. White women migrants and settlers who favored elaborate clothing, jewelry, and bonnets, and who liberally doused their bodies with toilet water, nonetheless criticized Indians for their choices in clothing and jewelry and for their "peculiar odor." Fashion plate, 1840, *Godey's Lady's Book*. Courtesy of the author.

—— **Chapter Two** ——

FRONTIER PHILOSOPY:
NINETEENTH-CENTURY EUROPEAN
DISCOURSE ON WESTERN WOMEN AND
ON THE AMERICAN INDIAN "OTHER"

The philosophies and ideologies of westward-bound migrants originated not only with American thinkers, writers, and artists, but with
Europeans as well. At the same time that Americans engaged in a spir-
ited discourse regarding the nature of white women in general and in
the West, as well as of American Indians, so did Europeans speculate on
the makeup of those white women who migrated to western frontiers
and on the character of the peoples they encountered there. Some
European observers traveled in parts of the American West, whereas
others became western settlers; both frequently made their reactions
public. Thus, the "philosophy" stage of American migration drew heavily on European perceptions and misconceptions.

The most significant European prejudices and vanities to influence
emerging images of the American West and its people were colonialism
and supposed white superiority. Because a number of European
countries—notably England, France, and Germany—were expanding
to frontiers in India and Africa during the nineteenth and early
twentieth centuries, they argued that white Europeans had the right
to divest native Indians and Africans from their land and resources,
replacing them with European-style farms, businesses, and
governments. European colonialists, who spent a great number of
written and spoken words justifying their behavior to themselves and

their critics, were understandably intent on how the United States, so recently colonies itself, would pursue its own white colonialist phase in the American West.

As a result, when Europeans confronted the topics of white western women and Native Americans, they filtered everything through the distorted lenses of imperial and racialist thinking. White frontierspeople, as seen through European eyes, frequently loomed larger than life. As inhabitants of a strange new region characterized by danger and opportunity, they often seemed to Europeans to be highly unusual specimens of humanity. A magnified portrait of Indians also developed, but, predictably, Native Americans had far more vices than virtues.

Moreover, wish fulfillment on the part of Europeans complicated the process of trying to fathom the American West. Europeans tended to see what they hoped to find in this promising "new" world. Increasingly during the nineteenth century, they viewed the American frontier as the child who would bring to reality their own thwarted wishes and dreams. The literary scholar Jerzy Jedlicki has suggested that the Polish fascination with America began as compensation for things missing at home, such as conceptions and realities of space, freedom, human rights, land, abundant food, and progress. The result, according to Jedlicki, was that the heroes of authors such as Henryk Sienkiewicz "vied with those of James Fennimore Cooper and his successors in rousing the imagination and dreams of derring-do among Polish adolescents."[1]

Jedlicki also correctly implied that Americans themselves contributed to European perceptions of the West. From Cooper's *Leatherstocking Tales* to the sagas of domestic novelists, American interpretations reached a huge number of European readers. During the 1850s, for example, Elizabeth Wetherell's *Wide, Wide World* sold more copies in England than any other American novel to that date, and was also translated into French, German, Swedish, and Italian.[2] Later in the nineteenth and well into the twentieth century, dime novels supplied Europeans with stock images of western women and of Indians.[3] Women ranged from damsels being rescued from peril by heroes named Flying Floyd and Deadwood Dick to heroines waging sword duels, shooting Indians, rescuing in a hot air balloon a lover appropriately named Young Wild West, and thrashing an amorous young man for impertinence.[4] These formula novels also regaled European audiences with Indians who were called "savages," "pesky redskins," "red devils," "cussed redskins," and "blood-thirsty wretches," and spoke hackneyed English.[5]

Undaunted by their lack of hard data regarding frontierswomen and American Indians, European writers did not hesitate to inform their readers about the nature of these inhabitants of the western United States. These European attempts toward interpretation contributed significantly to the body of information about American westerners that engulfed both European and American female migrants prior to their departure for the frontier. Thus did European attitudes toward the West circulate among Americans and would-be settlers, making their expectations more complex, and also more unrealistic, than ever.[6]

—— On Womanhood ——

European observers and commentators who enthralled European and Americans alike with portrayals of the American frontier were legion in number; a complete collection of their works would consume incalculable library shelf space. Yet, despite the torrent of words that these spectators expended upon describing, analyzing, and criticizing the westerners who so fascinated them, they seemed to understand little about the West and its female settlers. Just as white Americans appropriated Indian cultural symbols and shaped them to suit themselves, Europeans seized American images and put them in the form they preferred. They created an American frontierswoman that few real frontierswomen would recognize or own.

This happened for many reasons. For one, European visitors had limited conceptions of the location of the West. Rather than maps, European visitors carried romantic expectations with them as they embarked upon their expeditions to the American West. The popular French writer François René de Chateaubriand, who derived most of his ideas about the West from other authors, traveled briefly once in 1791 to upstate New York, yet proceeded to write a spate of novels and commentaries regarding the western frontier.[7] Similarly, in 1818 the "West" of William Cobbett was Indiana; in the 1830s Alexis de Tocqueville's West was New York and Michigan; in the 1840s Albert Koch's West was the Keokuk-Burlington region of the Iowa territory; and in the early 1850s Moritz Busch's West was Ohio and Kentucky.[8] During the same period, Isabella Bird approached Rock Island on the Mississippi River, rhapsodizing, "On we flew to the West, the land of Wild Indians and Buffaloes."[9] Also during the 1850s, Swedish observer Fredrika Bremer waxed eloquent: "the West is the garden where the rivers carry along with them gold . . . this enigmatic, promised land of the future, I shall now behold!"[10]

For another, how could European interpreters of the American frontier possibly write with objectivity and impartiality while pressure toward misrepresentation swirled around them? Largely middle and upper class, well educated, and usually male, they were unprepared by virtue of their background or experience to serve as accurate reporters of the western American scene. Whether they analyzed the New England frontier of the 1600s, the Midwestern frontier of the early nineteenth century, the Far West of the late nineteenth century, or vestiges of the frontier that continued to exist into the twentieth century, European observations were permeated with image and myth. Factual reporting was elusive at best and impossible at worst.

Moreover, Europeans whose nations had joined the world race for colonies were awash in colonialist sentiment. Although Americans stood largely united behind Manifest Destiny, Europeans, beginning around 1870, experienced a tremendous discussion of whether imperialism was "right."[11] In England, for example, Britons who wanted to be proper at all times found the question of entering other peoples' lands momentous and often distressing. Some had specific reasons to criticize colonization. Those opposed to high taxes needed to fund colonial developments spoke against expansion. Advocates of "free trade" claimed that economic gains would be minimal. Others argued that imperialism and its "racial theory" were destructive to indigenous peoples and their cultures.[12]

At the same time, various versions of what Americans called domesticity inundated white European women. Especially in England, the idea spread that English-speaking societies were innately superior, and that it was women's duty to spread white "civilization" and "truth" around the world. Women's culture demanded that women serve others, especially "savages" and "inferior" peoples. Dating from the sixteenth century was the growing belief that white Christians must save from the depths of depravity nonwhite peoples, who were basically noble. Women, also noble at heart, had a special mission to save those who were "primitive" and "barbarous." Because whites believed they were distinct and exceptional, they developed a will to power that underwrote colonialism.[13]

Like middle- and upper-class white American women during the nineteenth and early twentieth centuries, English women of the same classes came to view benevolence as linked with white dominance. Gendered maxims assured women that they were to "civilize" wherever they went, do good as they understood it to others, and provide a model of womanhood and of the "civilized" world for all peoples they encountered. According to female ideology, white women would bring improved health, religion, and lifestyles to indigenous peoples on world frontiers.[14] For women, Christian morality blotted out the reality that England stood to gain economically from colonization.[15] By the mid-1800s, women's literature immersed its readers in the idea that white Victorians could change the world.[16] Thus did growing numbers of English women join the ranks of teachers, missionaries, and settlers heading toward India, Kenya, and the American West.

Reformist sentiment drove white women all over Europe to join one migration or another. They fully expected to take over the invaded area, even if original inhabitants resisted. As in the United States, the opportunity to help others was compelling because it affirmed a woman's strength of character and willingness to forego a life of comfort to relocate in a "primitive" place for the good of others. Even women who succumbed more to the parts of migration philosophy that urged people to "make good" or to "succeed" in capitalistic terms believed they would still be helpful. Because women would carry white "civilization" with them, even those who were not missionaries and teachers would model and spread the "superior" ways of white peoples. As late in the world colonial era as 1895, the British prime minister,

Lord Salisbury, told English women that they were capable of helping supply the "energy, initiative, the force" that colonization demanded.[17] Consequently, women who thought about migrating to the American West, where "barbarous" peoples needed their ministrations, as well as women who planned to stay firmly planted in their homes, developed immense interest in America's westering women. They helped swell the nineteenth- and early twentieth-century reading audience, already expanded by improved education, increased leisure time, and decreased costs of books and periodicals. As early as the 1840s, European women of almost all social classes were avid readers of novels and periodicals.[18] Due to the increasing availability of print media entering employers' homes, even domestic servants became part of the rapidly growing reading public. Laborers, too, were urged to read by evangelists, Mechanic's Institutes, and purveyors of sensationalistic literature. Those who withstood such blandishments were exposed to the American West in other ways, including street theater, sermons, speeches, folklore, jokes, and other forms of popular culture.[19]

At the same time, European images and interpretations of the West and its women circled back to American women, primarily through the print media. European novels and excerpts from them, newspaper articles, tracts, pamphlets, humorous pieces, plays, and the commentaries of travelers in the West inundated American readers. Anxious to know what other nations thought of their fledgling country, many Americans consumed anything that provided images of themselves through European eyes. Although they were not always pleased with what they read or heard, as was the case with the writings of Charles Dickens and Harriet Martineau, their attitudes and prejudices about themselves were determined to some extent by European thinking.[20]

Naturally, European writers responded to the growing demand. Especially prolific were European travelers to the American West. Despite the difficulty of finding any authentic information, visitors seemed to have little hesitation in projecting their own values on the land and cultures around them. They frequently lavished extravagant numbers of pages of imaginative prose upon the question of how the white women who inhabited the American frontier looked, acted, and thought. In so doing, they usually saw what they hoped to see. The continuous frontiers emerging in the American West encouraged the European tendency toward wish fulfillment. Each successive frontier appeared to be one more promise, one more opportunity for the eventual redemption of the European world through colonization into less "civilized" parts of the world.

Thus, many commentators reached new heights of exaggeration and inaccuracy in their analysis of frontier America. This willingness on the part of Europeans to perceive the American frontier in terms of their own needs and wishes still exists in the twenty-first century. Wild West novels, poems, and movies are best-sellers throughout Europe, where western wear and country music are popular consumer items. Cowboys and Indians is a game widely played by European children. And adult western cultists and buffs throughout Europe continue to breathe life into a colorful but inaccurate image of the American West.[21]

Despite their inaccuracies, European views of western Americans are well worth exploring for the effect they had on generations of settlers, politicians, and policymakers. It is clear, for example, that when their traditional values clashed with the new, liberal, and innovative ideas demonstrated by generations of western women, confusion filled the minds of European observers. Given their customary and conservative notions about women's "place," what could Europeans possibly think when they confronted relatively independent, free, and sometimes even gun-toting western white women? The resulting ambivalence on the part of Europeans resulted in contradictory judgments regarding western women that ranged from outrage to praise.

Yet, in light of their belief that the God-given superiority of white people was destined to triumph over the West and its native populations, Europeans were committed to perceiving western women as intrepid conquerors. The single view upon which European observers generally agreed was that frontierswomen, shaped by the crucible of the western environment, were exceptional among women. Seemingly liberated and freed by the frontier setting, these women were considered by many Europeans as a distinct and even superior breed of female. Much as they looked upon their own white women as "mothers of empire," they thought of western women as tools of Manifest Destiny, as veritable saints of western expansion.

Of course, many Europeans completely neglected to mention white frontierswomen as a separate category in their commentaries. In the fashion of the era, many onlookers, both male and female, either sub-sumed women under the category of "men" or ignored them entirely. Thus, when observer Francis Grund stated in 1837 that nine-tenths of western emigrants were farmers or planters, one might reasonably assume that he meant that women also engaged in agrarian pursuits. But when W. Faux announced in the 1820s that 90 percent of the adult pop-ulation in the West owned land and Charles Dickens noted during the 1850s that westerners of any grade could climb the social ladder, it is likely that these writers literally meant "men."[22] They tended to disre-gard women because they did not visualize females as being personally or legally qualified to own land or having social status of their own.[23] Such assumptions perpetuated a myth that the experiences of many women in the West contradicted. Some western women occasionally owned or controlled land and had social status of their own.

The small size of the female population in relation to men also affected European opinion. Some Europeans ignored white frontiers-women simply because they were relatively few in number, at least in certain areas or during the early years of settlement. Others, however, emphasized the dearth of women.[24] One British traveler who visited Texas in 1841 collected the following statements from Texas men: "a maid is hardly to be met with in a day's march"; any woman "has only to go to Texas to charm and fascinate at least one-half of a town's bach-elor population"; and "Wimmen was powerful scarce in these diggins, and almost any sort of one was looked on as a reglar find."[25]

Apparently, the shortage of women enhanced their importance in many people's eyes, especially in men looking for wives. As late as the 1870s, an Italian traveler in Colorado estimated the ratio of men to women as fifteen to one, whereas a British traveler placed it as high as twenty to one. "The cry is everywhere for girls; girls; and more girls," the latter wrote.[26] Another Briton claimed that a Denver man was will-ing to pay "a ten-dollar piece to have seen the skirt of a servant-girl a mile off." In 1881, a British publication, the *American Settler,* repeated a Durango newspaper's claim that the greatest want in Colorado was women, especially those "who can wait at table" and "above all . . . for sweethearts."[27] Late in the 1880s, the newspaper reported that only one unmarried woman lived in the town of Delta in Washington Territory and that in Modoc County, California, "ladies are rare birds."[28]

Despite this reported scarcity of white frontierswomen, some Europeans included them in their commentaries. In the manner of their time, but in a way that would now be termed sexist, they usually focused first on women as sexual and ornamental beings, concentrating their remarks on physical appearance, beauty, and dress. It seems that not only gender, but ethnicity, could affect how a nonwesterner looked at western women. For example, the Frenchman Edouard de Montule declared, as one might stereotypically expect of a French male, that although western women were "on the whole very pretty and shapely" he had only encountered one woman who in his opinion had "truly lovely breasts (which American women rarely have)." In 1821, he again complimented some and damned others. In his view, frontierswomen were "generally pleasing; and, with due respect to the amiable ladies of Philadelphia, they are much more attractive in the West than in the regions bordering the coast."[29]

In other cases, neither gender nor nationality carried any weight. Some Europeans concurred with Montule in his assessment of western women. In 1828, the Englishman Charles Sealsfield asserted that they were "considered very handsome" and the German woman Fredrika Bremer said that in the American West "one seems to meet nothing but handsome faces, scarcely a countenance . . . may be called ugly."[30] But many thought that western women grew old prematurely, with their beauty fading and their health disintegrating. They attributed this to a variety of factors, including climate, heavy labor, and poor diet.[31] One British traveler, William Shepard, added that scores of western women displayed dull, expressionless faces due to hard work, poverty, and cheerless lives.[32]

The French traveler Alexis de Tocqueville carried the debate to a higher level, that of inner beauty. He agreed that even though most women endured "fever, solitude, and a tedious life" in a "comfortless home" in the "Western wilds," they had not lost "the springs of their courage." To him, their features might be impaired and faded, but their looks were firm: they appeared to be at once sad and resolute. "I do not doubt that these young American women had amassed," he continued, "in the education of their early years, that inward strength which they displayed under these circumstances."[33] Thus did de Tocqueville pronounce, if not the last word, a sensible one on this rather superficial concern.

Just as perfunctory was the question of western women's dress, in which European observers also exhibited great interest. They were generally pleased with what they saw. De Tocqueville considered the women walking along the streets of Albany to be "well turned out"; Busch thought that Kentucky horsewomen dressed "in modish costume"; and Hungarian traveler Theresa Pulszky judged women standing at the doors of longhouses in the Alleghenies of the 1850s to be "elegantly" dressed.[34] During the 1840s, the German observer Friedrich Gerstäcker pronounced that women "even of the lowest classes . . . were simply but tastefully dressed." During a Fourth of July celebration, he was startled to learn that the women changed their dresses four or five times between noon and the following morning. He sensibly concluded that since women had little chance to display their wardrobes they had to seize any opportunity to do.[35] Other commentators mentioned Sunday church services as the occasion on which most frontierswomen flaunted their apparel. According to the English traveler Frances Trollope in 1832, women attended church in "full costume." Edward Montule agreed that Sunday was indeed an important day, sartorially speaking, on most frontiers. He explained that "confined within the small, cleared spaces in the midst of this wilderness, they impatiently await Sunday, the only day when they can see each other, and be seen; therefore, they make the most of the occasion."[36]

After commentators finished with attractiveness and dress, they turned their attention to more substantial questions. One of these concerned how western women fared at the hands of reputedly rough and unpolished western men and what their treatment might indicate about the position of women in western society. Gender apparently influenced commentary to a considerable extent. European men were generally impressed that western women received a great deal of courtesy and respect from western men, but claimed that this was due to the character of women themselves. For instance, Charles Sealsfield believed that graceful western women were "well entitled" to chivalrous attention. Gerstäcker added that women inspired respect by their energy and grace.[37] Many others agreed that women's moral standards were high and that they exhibited a certain delicacy in their manners, both of which elicited male esteem.[38]

Furthermore, European men made excuses for seemingly cool and indifferent frontiersmen. One stated that such behavior did not indicate a lack of affection, merely an attempt to maintain privacy and dignity.[39] Others argued that undemonstrative men showed their true feelings by allowing women to appear anywhere without fear of insult or injury.[40] In 1849, the Englishman Alexander Mackay was astounded to discover that men would perform "gallant self-denial" by stopping spitting and hewing in the presence of women.[41] One wrapped up the debate by saying that western men had self-reliance, common sense, and "the manliness that under all circumstances does honor to itself by the uniform respect paid to woman."[42]

On other issues, European men disagreed among themselves. For instance, Gerstäcker disliked the frontier custom decreeing that women could eat only after the men had finished. During the 1820s, a German traveler claimed that women were always served before the men. In 1842, English author Charles Dickens noted that "no man sat down until the ladies were seated." In 1845, the naturalist Charles Lyell stated that women always seated themselves at the table before men.[43]

When female travelers, who were far fewer in number than men, offered their opinions on the respect extended to western women they revealed a very different situation. They felt that chivalry on the part of frontiersmen was little more than a sham, phony in intent and limited in nature. In 1838, Harriet Martineau, an English author and traveler, derided chivalry as a poor substitute for justice. In her eyes, western "ungentle, tyrannical" men fell far below their own democratic principles in the treatment of their women.[44] Another Englishwoman, Frances Trollope, also doubted the value that western men placed upon their women. As she watched women "amusing" themselves by engaging in strange religious exercises at a frontier revival, she raised the question that if western men valued their women as men ought, "would such scenes be permitted among them?"[45]

Unarguably, most onlookers failed to address the basic issue raised by Martineau and Trollope, of whether men's chivalry toward women stemmed from a deep, lasting esteem. Instead, most observers assumed that polite treatment connoted respect. Consequently, many travelers, men and women alike, were impressed by the safety with which a woman could travel over all parts of the West.[46] In 1845, for example, Prussian traveler Friedrich von Raumer emphasized that women could travel alone through the "whole country" because even those men who were rough with other men extended courtesy to women. Gerstäcker similarly maintained that "often one will see young girls and women undertake long journeys alone. . . . We know here in the forest of nothing more cowardly and mean than the mistreatment of a woman."[47]

These observations were problematic in that European travelers toured America for a short time and derived their opinions regarding women from limited contact on steamboats and stagecoaches. Thus, they drew conclusions from superficial evidence rather than delving deeper into women's situations. Consequently, steamboat and stagecoach stories regarding the preferential treatment of women became legendary. A Norwegian traveler of the 1840s described one captain's table as having empty chairs that separated the ladies and the captain from the male passengers.[48] A French traveler recalled a steamboat captain who brandished a kitchen knife at a passenger who had directed a mild curse toward a lady.[49] That "ladies" did not always live up to their genteel reputation, however, was demonstrated by an incident in which two steamboat gamblers, having decided to fight with only gun butts in deference to the ladies present, were cheered on by these "ladies" who climbed on chairs and tables to get a closer view.[50]

On stagecoaches, gentlemanly behavior also repeatedly assumed extreme proportions. In 1857, Hungarian traveler John Xantus was amazed to learn that a filled stagecoach stopped for a woman; the last man to board got off and waited for the next coach, which could take a week to arrive, or proceeded by foot. Xantus had difficulty believing that the man involved did not grumble, but acted as though giving up his seat was the most natural thing in the world.[51] Another male traveler told of a stage journey through a heavy rain, during which a Houston merchant held an umbrella over a woman, protecting her but drenching the other passengers. "The water fell like a cascade over unfortunate me," he wryly noted.[52] Regarding stagecoaches, female travelers agreed. The Englishwoman Lady Duffus Hardy stated that to a woman "the manly heart yields his interest in car or stage, gives her the best seat, that she might be screened and curtained, while he broils in the sun; for her he fights a way to the front ranks of refreshment rooms, skirmishes with the coffee pot, and bears triumphant ices aloft."[53]

Some European male spectators of the western scene were astute enough to look deeper than behavior on public conveyances. They probed the educational opportunities offered to women in the West, agreeing that "female" education was widely available and of high quality. Pulszky pointed out that schools for young women were more common in the West than in the East, whereas Busch, upon viewing a Cincinnati ladies' school, remarked that "an offspring of fashionable refinement does exist and is flourishing."[54]

Were these male observers impressed by the mere existence of schools for western women or were they struck by their quality? Because they were accustomed to girls being taught such female "accomplishments" as doing fancy needlework, playing the pianoforte, and cultivating an interest in literature, they viewed such education as being of high quality. Although female students received little education in English, history, and science, they appeared to observers to be reaching what one called "a high taste for literary and mental accomplishments."[55] Too, women living in boardinghouses in western towns filled their hours with a great deal of reading and with their attendance at public lectures.[56] And western white women in general were given more time to cultivate accomplishments, so that they were more "civilized" than western men.[57]

Male visitors were similarly overwhelmed by widespread coeducation. In 1869, after studying coeducation in Kansas, the Englishman William Bell stated that it was little wonder that political contests in Kansas were marked by "petticoats . . . well to the front," and that "woman's suffrage and equal rights form part of each platform in every election." He added that it would take a particularly bold Kansas man to oppose "openly the phalanx of political Amazons" that the Kansas educational system produced.[58] This less than salutary reaction was heard again and again. As late as the 1890s, French author Charles Varigny wrote that it was "strange instruction that, and strange schools, those, in which girls and boys sat together." Like Bell, he concluded that women emerged "sure of themselves, able to compete with men, and capable of eliciting respect from men."[59]

Again, gender mattered. Even though such female visitors as Fredrika Bremer noted that "an important reformation in female school is taking place in these Western states" largely due to the efforts of reformer Catharine Beecher, they also noted many deficiencies. For instance, female critics of frontier schools for women believed that the existence of young ladies' schools, a skill in "accomplishments," and even coeducation did not indicate the existence of meaningful education for women. After visiting upstate New York in 1818, Frances Wright, a Scottish reformer, decided that although there had been strides in women's education, it was still puerile. Until it became "the concern of the state," she argued, women's education would offer little of real use to women.[60] Harriet Martineau added that women's education was based on rote method rather than intellectual activity.[61] She was especially incensed by a young ladies' school that she visited in New Madrid, Missouri, during the late 1830s. "There are public exhibitions of their [the pupils'] proficiency, and the poor ignorant little girls take degrees," she wrote scathingly. "Their heads must be so stuffed with vainglory that there can be little room for anything else."[62] Fredrika Bremer was even more vitriolic than Wright and Martineau on the subject of western women's education. Visiting St. Louis in 1850, she was disgusted to find girls weakened by an "effeminate education." She charged that they lived little more than a "harem life." She declared, "The harems of the West, no less than those of the East, degrade the life and the consciousness of women."[63] Martineau complained that the only possible life course open to women educated in this manner was marriage.[64]

Of course, this direction was not totally inappropriate because in the West women were in demand as wives. For generations, men had emphasized the need for wives. Assuming, as did most people of the era, that all women desired matrimony as soon as possible, western men were far from subtle in their statements. One Norwegian man declared the West an "El Dorado" for women, whereas another advised his hometown newspaper in Norway to publish the advice, "Go west, young woman."[65] Another explained that even women who "crossed the line"—a Norwegian folk expression for those who strayed from the straight and narrow—would be marriageable on the frontier.[66] This opinion was widely held. Some men even listed locales where women would have "mountains of gold dust" laid at their feet "in exchange for their hands."[67]

Conservative voices were in a minority. When an 1884 issue of the *American Settler* warned that ardent swains might already have "a surplus wife or two in the East," it confirmed the fears of such critics as Wright, Martineau, and Bremer.[68] Weak, gendered education and a demand for wives would prematurely lead American women into marriage. These women had a point. As early as 1698, an English farmer had stated that the American woman usually married before twenty, and soon she "hath a child in her Belly, or one upon her Lap." The following year, another Englishman claimed that American women were "very Fruitful, which shows that Men are Industrious in Bed, tho' Idle up."[69] This proclivity toward early marriage and childbearing moved westward with the frontier, where brides of age thirteen to fifteen frequently received mention in traveler's journals, immigrant's accounts, and western novels. Because Wright, Martineau, and Bremer wanted more for western women they urged western women to want more for themselves.

Even though early marriage and immediate remarriage were more apparent than real in the West, a number of frontierswomen did marry young and immediately remarry after the death of a spouse.[70] For one thing, it was an economic necessity in an era and a region where a married couple constituted a business partnership. For another, marriage and childbearing were considered the ultimate goal of every woman's life. "I have seen," stated one observer, "young girls of thirteen and hideous old girls of fifty snapped up eagerly as soon as they arrived in the country."[71] At the same time, well-bred European travelers of the upper classes, and thus accustomed to formality in such matters, found it highly unusual that young men and women chose their own mates, agreed to marry without consulting their parents, and ignored the tradition of a dowry.[72] One traveler was particularly horrified when he saw a young couple meet on a riverboat and, within fifteen days, commit themselves to wed. When ice floes prevented the minister they asked to meet their boat from reaching them, the couple kneeled on the deck so the shore-bound minister could marry them.[73]

Europeans were similarly aghast that frontier courtships in general proceeded rapidly. According to Pulszky, a pioneer man simply paid a few taciturn calls to a neighbor's eligible daughter, during which he "places himself in a chair before the chimney, chews, spits in the fire." Within weeks, the suitor offered an equally taciturn proposal of marriage.[74] A German traveler of the 1850s also described suitors as "abrupt"; having "no time to beat around the bush." Pulszky added that a swain met a girl in a shop, the theater, at a ball, or in her parents' home. "He needs a wife, thinks this one will do. He asks the question, she answers. The next day they are married and then proceed to inform the parents."[75]

Europeans objected not just to the lack of formality, but insightfully pointed to a number of negative results that would ensue. Among these were the breakdown of the family as a result of the early departure of the children to form their own family units and a rising divorce rate.[76] Many believed that the greatest underlying ill was the increased power that accrued to wives, who expected their husbands to be extremely affable. As one young western woman quipped in 1876, "if he don't there's plenty will."[77] Worse yet, a husband could go nowhere without his wife, the *American Settler* reported in 1892.[78] Furthermore, such wives purportedly refused to do barn work, legally protected their property before marriage, and even ordered servants to flog errant husbands.[79] If women were displeased with the course of their marriage, they reportedly sought divorce with little hesitation. As early as 1830, English traveler Simon O'Ferrall noted that three divorces were granted during his brief stay in Marion, Ohio. All three were initiated by women: one for desertion, one for physical abuse, and one for general neglect. O'Ferrall added that a woman was seldom refused a divorce in the West because her dislike of a husband constituted a sufficient reason for granting her freedom.[80]

Stories of outrageous wifely misbehavior caused many immigrants to conclude that western women were so spoiled that a proper wife could be found only by importing one.[81] This reputation for brattiness was perhaps undeserved; when critics turned their attention to frontierswomen's domestic labors they were usually complimentary in tone. Although an occasional visitor depicted "wives of settlers" as living in "sloth and inactivity," others were delighted to learn that all women were not as lazy as rumored.[82] Still others represented western women as very diligent indeed. According to Sealsfield, a farm wife was "in motion from morning till evening."[83] The Englishman William Blane was even more laudatory. In his view, women in the backwoods of the 1820s were "the most industrious females" he had ever seen in any country.[84]

Even though frontierswomen labored assiduously within their homes, they reportedly never worked in the fields. Travelers consistently characterized frontierswomen as hard workers in the home but protected from "unwomanly employment" in the fields.[85] In 1841, an Englishman emphasized that "every man here, rich or poor, seems on all occasions sedulously to give place and precedence to females, and the meanest of them are exempt, or I might rather say debarred, from those masculine or laborious tasks which are commonly enough assigned the sex, or assumed by them, in our country."[86] And in 1860, a Swede wrote home that "women never work in the fields—not even milking cows."[87]

Europeans identified a variety of reasons for this practice, which was very strange to Europeans who were used to women working in the fields. Many speculated that the generally high regard paid western women explained the situation. At least one writer suggested, however, that the inordinate cost of imported British goods caused women to be "chiefly employed in making articles of domestic clothing."[88] Generally, observers assumed that the restriction of frontierswomen to domestic labor meant a relatively easy life for them. They often characterized settlers' wives and daughters as "ladies" who refused to draw their own water from a well.[89] In 1848, a Swedish farmer in Illinois wrote home that "women do not have to do any other work here but wash clothes and cups and keep the house tidied up and at some places also cook food."[90] A Frenchman traveling in Kansas during the 1870s claimed that "an American woman's only job is to make a home and to make little Americans; we were never able to make the women there understand that country women in France work on the land and know how to do it almost as well as their husbands."[91]

Again, gender was a determining factor in how one viewed women's work. Some nineteenth-century European women, who had themselves chosen to become frontierswomen, presented another perspective. A Norwegian woman, Elisabeth Koren, felt that frontierswomen did nothing but cook, thus leaving them little time for other chores, much less for leisure.[92] Another Norwegian settler, Gro Svendsen, pointed out that although frontierswomen were supposed to have much free time, she had not met any who actually thought so.[93] And the English settler Rebecca Burlend said that she worked in the fields because her husband was unable to find a hired hand.[94]

These comments by women are probably more reliable than those of male travelers. The experience of these European female settlers demonstrated that frontierswomen worked long and hard hours within their homes and labored in the fields whenever necessary. Other accounts indicate that women also willingly helped with men's traditional tasks and responsibilities. For example, even male visitors remarked on women's ability to take up arms. Busch remarked that in the early years of settlement "everyone was a soldier, and even the women knew how to handle a rifle."[95] Other reporters mentioned female entrepreneurs, judges, journalists, publishers, and university professors.[96]

Obviously, western women, who were not as constricted as European women, achieved some latitude in their roles.[97] This was not good news to male European visitors, who responded to liberated western women with shock, puzzlement, and dismay. Unsurprisingly, most appeared more comfortable with western women who used their talents in accepted female ways, particularly as civilizing forces in the American West. These men had heard so much about female morality and civilizing power that they applauded women who exercised their gendered talents. British visitors were especially delighted that many frontierswomen seemingly exerted a stabilizing force in the West.[98] According to one, women were second only to churches in helping to refine the new society.[99] Another was enthusiastic in his description of women's salutary influence on the frontier: "A lady is a power in this country. From the day when a silk dress and lace shawl were seen on Main Street, that thoroughfare became passably clean and quiet; oaths were less frequently heard; knives were less frequently drawn; pistols were less frequently fired."[100]

Others went on to say that women were the judges of decency, the guardians of humanity, and the very glue of a society that, "without woman, is like an edifice built on sand."[101] Sienkiewicz insisted that women so softened the brutal habits of one frontier town of the 1870s that although men still argued, "Bowie knives remained in their sheaths and revolvers in the pocket." He added that "cards were not played so fiercely and only cocktails were drunk, instead of the usual enormous draughts of whiskey."[102]

Because Europeans believed that female colonists were unusual women, their descriptions of western women portrayed a superior type of being. They also had faith in the redemptive power of frontiers. By helping others—in this case Native Americans—white women rose to the very heights of womanhood. As a result, despite the contradictions and disagreements regarding specific aspects of frontierswomen's lives, roles, and actions in the writings of Europeans, the overall assessment was that frontierswomen had the best situation of any women in the world. To demonstrate this point, Europeans favorably compared American women's lives with those of women in other countries.[103] Europeans stressed repeatedly that western American women received more respect from men than did women anywhere else in the world. They also emphasized that frontierswomen wielded more power in their homes and in society than did women in other parts of the world.[104] One Dutch traveler, Tutein Nolthenius, even claimed that western women "are different from our womenfolk, who are kept inferior female animals from force of habit and superstition."[105] Moreover, Europeans pointed out that western women faced more opportunities within the institution of marriage, in the schools and colleges, and in employment.

Once they recovered from their initial surprise regarding the behavior of western women, European male visitors lauded them for seizing their opportunities. In 1885, the *American Settler* emphasized that Anglo women made "good use" of the "free field" they found in the West.[106] Most seemed to come around to admiration for western women. Some went so far as to say that western women's strengths and skills proved women equals of men in almost every way.[107] As Varigny put it, a frontierswoman was relieved of her "chains" by the environment, but she won equality with men through her own talents. One even suggested that western women who voted be left alone because they were not, at least in his view, creating social upheaval.[108]

Meanwhile, European women visitors found little substance to women's legal and political rights in the West. Again, Harriet Martineau and Fredrika Bremer were in the forefront of critics. They felt that women's rights were more fantasy than fact. Vociferously, they contradicted men who claimed that western women exercised actual rights, and, in fact, were pushing to become more than equals of their husbands. They also shushed men who brought up domesticity, saying that women had a "providential mission in this world" and should adhere to it.[109]

Given Europeans' conservative ideas regarding women's rights, it is understandable that most would react with concern regarding women's changing political situation in much of the West. Male European visitors found it difficult—yet not impossible—to grapple with the realities of women's equality and rights. Female visitors like Martineau and Bremer, however, came with what today would be called a feminist mindset. Because these women were educated and of the upper classes, they had done more reading and thinking than most Europeans about women's position. The fact that they traveled abroad and published their thoughts also marks them as liberal thinkers for their time. Thus, it is understandable that men took one view whereas women took another.

The ultimate question is, given this glut of information and disparity of opinions, what was the average person to think and believe about white women in the American West? The answer is simple. An individual could believe whatever he or she wanted. Accuracy of interpretation was not the goal. Forming an interpretation of white women in the American West, and criticizing them or lauding them, were the points at issue.

—— On the Indian "Other" ——

The image of Native Americans fared even worse than that of western women. For one thing, a wealth of traditions influenced the ways in which Europeans interpreted American Indians. From the time of Columbus, literary and other conventions of the Middle Ages and the Renaissance shaped European thinking regarding Indians. From Greek gods to Judaic heroes to Christian saints, Europeans applied them all. On the other side were folktales of savage hordes, barbarians, and cannibals. The result was a split persona—the Noble Savage and the Ignoble Savage.[110]

For another thing, because Europeans viewed Indians as different and even outrageous in their dress, customs, and culture, they consumed any form of media concerning Indians. From the 1570s to the early nineteenth century, artists depicted American Indians largely as fantasy figures whose primitive nudity was only partially disguised by feathered ornaments. Presented as simple and pure people, these stylized American Indians reflected Renaissance traditions by taking on, in most drawings and paintings, the proportions and classical lines of Greek and Roman figures.[111] By the late eighteenth century, artists such as Benjamin West refined the use of these neoclassical, didactic Indian figures in paintings commemorating historical events.[112]

By the early nineteenth century, European artists began to reflect the Romantic view of the world, and the image of the American frontier changed accordingly. Soon, Romanticism ran amuck in the work of European artists who found it impossible to divorce themselves from European dreams and fears in their representations of western Indians. Such painters as Goya, Girodet, Delacroix, and Doré frequently represented Indians as personifications of the American West, as well as romantic heroes.[113] Although these artists had never seen the western frontier, they believed themselves qualified to purvey its image to Europeans who were anxious for a confirmation of their own preconceptions. Swiss artist Karl Bodmer, a member of German explorer Prince Maximilian's 1833 expedition to the West, was one of the few European artists who attempted to bring ethnic accuracy and anthropological clarity to his drawings of Native Americans. Other artist-explorers, such as Charles Bird King, produced highly idealized portraits of Indians that were more hyperbole than truth.[114]

At the same time, writers and travelers frequently lavished extravagant and imaginative prose on how American Indians who inhabited the American frontier looked, acted, and thought. These European interpretations contributed significantly to the information about American westerners that engulfed both European and American female migrants prior to their departure for the frontier. Once again, writers' own conceptions of colonialism and wish fulfillment underlay their work. The popular French writer François René de Chateaubriand provided an example of such blurred vision. Although he derived most of his ideas about the American West from other authors, he proceeded nonetheless to write a series of highly stereotyped "Indian" novels as well as a detailed commentary on his American experiences.[115] Like so many of his contemporaries, Chateaubriand responded more to his own needs and to those of his audience than to the realities of western American life.[116]

Similarly, discontented Germans looked toward potential colonies and across the Atlantic Ocean for relief and hope. Especially after 1817, when a large number of Germans migrated to the American West, German literature began to focus upon frontier people, who were now the symbols of the land of the future.[117] As in Poland, many popular German novelists developed such frontier motifs as wilderness, violence, and anything having to do with American Indians. Authors such as Charles Sealsfield, Friedrich Gerstäcker, Friedrich Armand Strubberg, and Balduin Möllhausen presented adventure novels, featuring German-born heroes, as authentic accounts of life on the American frontier.[118] German enthusiasm for the American West reached its height with the writings of Karl May, often called Germany's Cooper, who did not visit the United States until after he wrote nearly all of his western American adventures. He was expert at combining his own imagined "facts" with bits and pieces of information to produce tales that well served his readers' wishes and needs. May also inspired Germans to organize "cowboy and Indian societies," much like the fraternal organizations in the United States whose members wore Indian-style clothing and recreated Indian rituals.[119]

Agreed, it was problematic for most Europeans to approach Native Americans with any degree of objectivity. Caught between opposing interpretations of the "good" Indian, who was simple, pure, and virtuous, and the "bad" Indian, who was cruel, rapacious, and predatory, Europeans tended to reflect one view or the other. Seldom did they attempt to blend the two images into a realistic portrait of Indians combining both "good" or "bad." Novelists made up stories based on their own beliefs, whereas visitors with preconceptions tended to see what they expected to see, even when the scene before them contradicted their notions.[120] These were mostly men, although a few women dared to travel to the areas less settled by whites and still containing Indians.

One proponent of the "good" Indian was Chateaubriand. He believed that it was unfair to show only the unattractive characteristics of Indians because in reality their "manners were often charming."[121] Another who staunchly defended Indians was a German physician, Johann Schopf, who traveled through frontier America in the early 1870s. From his observations, he maintained that the moral character of American Indians was not nearly as black as it had been represented. Schopf also maintained that many Indians were innovative and that their medical competence was especially admirable.[122]

A number of novelists took similar positions. The Norwegian novelist Jens Tvedt created a Dakota woman who, as a child of a trapper, grew up among Indians and married a native man. Tvedt put these words into her mouth:

> There are Indians who possess just as many good qualities as any white person. Although you may find some of the worst scum among them, I think that you will find quite as many bad specimens among our own people. You will seldom find such a degree of vile coarseness among the Indians as exists among the whites—at least as long as they have not been corrupted by contact with the whites.[123]

Other novelists championed Indians as well. During the 1830s, the author Charles Sealsfield decried the injustices perpetrated on Indians who were the legitimate owners of the lands that the whites were so ruthlessly seizing.[124] But the greatest supporter of the American

Indian was Karl May, widely known for his 1892 novel *Winnetou*. May deplored the fact that Indians had not been given adequate time to evolve from hunter to farmer to city dweller. Instead, May argued, Indians were expected to make a great leap. When unable to do so, they were killed off by whites. "What could the race have achieved given a chance?" he asked.[125]

Meanwhile, sympathetic observers challenged the widespread use of the term *savage* to describe Native Americans. This objection was not new. As early as the 1790s, Louis Philippe of France said that he preferred to call natives "Indians" rather than "savages." He did not believe "that these people merit that epithet in any way."[126] Subsequently, others suggested that white settlers deserved the term *savage* more than Indians. Half-civilized and brutal in their actions toward American Indians, they were often considered less desirable acquaintances than "the genuine uncontaminated Indian."[127]

To their credit, some Europeans were so outraged by the degradation and destruction of America's native peoples that they felt compelled to lay the blame for it on someone. Arguing that Indians were basically good, Chateaubriand put the responsibility on white Europeans and Americans for debasing and destroying Indian cultures and societies. According to him, "the right of force took independence" from America's original inhabitants.[128] Pulszky also condemned Anglo-Saxons for being great colonizers but ineffective civilizers, who swept native races away in their settlement process.[129] Others indicted arrogant American frontier people for decimating "unhappy savages" and driving the remnants across the land.[130] Still others blamed the U.S. government for the harm done to American Indians by its unenlightened policies.[131]

These apologists were in the minority, however, and the feeling that whites were accountable for the plight of the American Indian was far from unanimous. Von Raumer charged that the Indians themselves were at fault. Their own idleness, he said, had made their assimilation into an industrious white society impossible. He added that their claim to land simply because they hunted on it was invalid.[132] In 1837, English observer Francis Grund supported von Raumer on both counts. Since they possessed little in the way of tradition or moral character, Indians could never be civilized. Because they had not cultivated the land, they had no "distinct title to it arising from actual labor." Grund was slightly different. Although he regretted "the fate of the doomed people," he believed that the "rest of Mankind" would "use the land much more efficiently."[133] Other travelers agreed that rescuing the land from "savages" in order to turn it to industry was a progressive change, and they found it difficult to contemplate America's "growing wealth and strength without rejoicing."[134]

Given such viewpoints, it is little wonder that portrayals of "bad" Indians far outnumbered those of "good" Indians. Most white Europeans, schooled in world colonialism, looked down on peoples of color. As early as 1628, a Dutch minister had described Native Americans as "entirely savage and wild . . . uncivil and stupid as garden poles."[135] This theme was repeated many times throughout the following decades. A French pianist called Indians in his audience "a delegation of savages." A Hungarian naturalist declared Indians to be "completely savage and far, far removed from civilization." And a Prussian traveler insisted that they were "corporeally and mentally so very different" from whites.[136] As late as 1913, English writer and social critic Rupert Brooke proclaimed his judgment of American Indians in the *Westminster Gazette*. "The Indians have passed; they left no arts, no tradition, no buildings or roads or laws; only a story or two, and a few names, strange and beautiful."[137] Evidently, such critics not only adhered to the doctrine of white superiority, but had colossal egos as well.

Unfortunately, some Europeans reacted so negatively to the Indians they met because they had been led by Chateaubriand, Cooper, and others to expect romantic, colorful figures. They were disappointed and disillusioned to find small, wiry folk who could have come "from the lowest mob of our great European cities."[138] Comparisons of Native Americans with peasants, Arabian Bedouins, and gypsies were common.[139] One disenchanted Englishman concluded that "they are a dirty vagabond lot, not unlike our gipsies," whereas another stated that they "appeared like the lowest and worst of our gipsies."[140] Given the popularity of such unflattering assessments, it is unsurprising that other whites described Indians as having "snakes" in the "bosom of their race" and as violent people who attacked white colonies and harbored white murderers, robbers, and rapists.[141]

Even more than their dirty and ragged appearance, the drunkenness of some American Indians disgusted Europeans. Seldom, if ever, did these commentators reflect on why Indians drank or who supplied the liquor. De Tocqueville, for example, recounted several instances of drunken native men and women. To him they were brutalized wild beasts, to be feared when in a drunken state.[142] Other writers ranged from extending sympathy to "poor corrupted frontier Indians" to concluding that Indians would go to any lengths, including selling a wife or child, to obtain liquor.[143] With insight and human understanding, a number of Europeans pointed out that drunken Indians were not typical. Rather, they argued that the most visible Indians were often those whose culture had been destroyed, and who were transformed into lazy, dirty beggars hanging around towns and railroad depots in hopes of a handout.[144] During the 1820s, Paul Wilhelm, Duke of Wurttemberg, pointed out that it was highly unfair and inaccurate to extrapolate from a few drunken Indians to construct an image of all Indians, whereas de Tocqueville searched in vain for the unspoiled Native Americans who had surely retreated into the wilds.[145]

With so many countervailing and often less-than-enlightened conceptions of Indians swirling through their minds, some Europeans reacted by simply giving the topic short shrift. Still others allowed their own shock and disillusionment to interfere with objective and fair reporting. Whatever the cause, the result was often a superficial and biased description of Indian society, customs, and culture. When turning to the subject of Indian women, Europeans assigned Indian females a place on the other end of the continuum from white frontierswomen; that is, Indian women, like Indian men, were considered savages. Europeans believed that white saints would triumph and Indian savages would disappear, for saints deserved to survive, and savages deserved to disappear, a solid tenet of nineteenth- and early twentieth-century colonialism. Given this predilection, the observations of European writers and travelers were shaded, colored, and limned until the portrait of white women became slightly larger than life and that of American Indian women less.

As was the case with white women, writers often subsumed native women under the generic label of "Indian." When they did refer specifically to Indian women, Europeans tended to call them "squaws" rather than use more dignified terms comparable to "Indian," "brave," or "chief," which referred to Indian men. Given the harsh connotation of the term *squaw*, this European usage suggests not only ignorance about the word's meaning but the existence of a negative prejudgment of Indian women.[146] When they encountered female Indians, Europeans again were determined to see what they expected to see.

Even though Europeans categorized Indian women as Indians and as squaws, they also recognized them as women. Thus, although these observers viewed Indian women as inferior females, they were still interested in some of the issues that had concerned them regarding white women. As a result, many of the Europeans who mentioned Indian women were sexist, paying inordinate attention to physical appearance, beauty, and dress. Some characterized Indian women as "seldom ugly," but others described native women as "quite lovely."[147] Still others noted beautiful women in certain tribes. A French naval officer thought that Louisiana Indians had "beautiful wives"; a German novelist said that Choctaw women had "beautiful figures"; and a French traveler declared that Lake Erie Indian women were "the most comely savages I had yet seen."[148] During the 1840s, the English author Frederick Marryat described Comanche women as "exquisitely clean, good-looking, and but slightly bronzed." Marryat also compared favorably Shoshone women to graceful Arabian women.[149]

Such comments do not fit well with the accepted image of the squaw and were indeed an expression of a minority viewpoint. Most Europeans seemed quite convinced that American Indian women were dirty, ugly, and unattractive creatures. They shared de Tocqueville's view that there were no "passable" Indian women, and they offered a variety of explanations for the situation.[150] The hard work performed by Indian women was frequently given as the cause of early aging and ugliness.[151] Uncleanliness was also suggested as a reason for what seemed to some viewers the disgusting appearance of Indian women.[152] Whatever the reason, European men reached similar conclusions. During the 1830s, a German scientist, Prince Maximilian of Wied, consistently characterized women of various tribes in the upper Missouri River region as ugly, plain in appearance, and unappealing in dress and personal hygiene.[153] Another early nineteenth-century traveler summarized his reaction to Native American women more succinctly. "As to personal appearance, with very few exceptions, I can only specify three degrees—horrible, more horrible, most horrible."[154]

Yet when they turned their attention to the matter of women's dress, most Europeans did not seem to be describing ugly, filthy women. After a negative statement about Indian women, Isaac Weld went on to recount the ribbons, jewelry, and profusion of ornaments with which they adorned themselves.[155] Others also spoke of the ribbons, shells, feathers, beautiful dresses, delicate moccasins, and ornaments favored by Indian women.[156] In addition, there were frequent comments regarding carefully arranged hairdos.[157] "Their hair is very beautiful," Xantus wrote of native women in Missouri, "always dressed with great care and falling softly on the shoulders."[158] Even those who encountered poor Indians complimented women's dress. Harriet Martineau was impressed by native women in Oneida, New York, who were neatly dressed and wrapped in clean blankets. Fredrika Bremer complimented Indian women in St. Paul for being "less painted, and with better taste than the men."[159] And in 1898, the English observer Trevelyan stated that Indian women dressed "like shabby Americans."[160]

Oddly enough, this was not the way American Indian women appeared in most European novels, where they were often presented as lovely young maidens or as princesses in exotic garb. During the early 1840s, Marryat characterized them as adorned in doeskin shirts, embroidered moccasins, ankle and wrist bracelets, and with jewels in their luxuriant hair.[161] In 1845, another writer visualized his heroine in an elegant sheepskin cloak, porcupine-quill work, and elks' teeth ornaments.[162] Beads, tinkling silver bells, scarlet leggings, partially nude bosoms, hair that reached almost to the ground, and wampum belts were also mentioned by many authors.[163] In 1878, Gustave Aimard created a prototype of these maidens when he introduced Ova, a chief's daughter, who wore "a tunic of water-green colour, fastened around her waist by a wampum-belt, with a large golden buckle." According to Aimard, she was much loved by all; when she danced for her father, "the old man's forehead became unwrinkled" and her lover brought her "perfumes of grizzly bears' grease, necklaces of alligator's teeth, and wampum girdles."[164]

Clearly the contradiction between the "good" Indian and the "bad" Indian affected Europeans' interpretations of Native American women. Were they pure, simple, lovely princesses clothed in exotic attire, or were they ugly, filthy, ragged squaws who deserved extermination? It seemed easier for Europeans to adopt the first view while reading a romanticized novel, sitting by a warm fire somewhere on the continent, than when they were traveling through the American West observing real women. Arriving as they did with specific ideas about how women, even those of a supposedly inferior race, should act and be treated, Europeans were troubled by what they saw. Superficial topics, such as physical appearance and dress, created problems for them; but when they considered deeper issues, such as sexual behavior and marriage customs among Indian groups, their responses ranged from rationalization to acrimony.

Sexual relations between American Indian women and white men particularly evoked a complex spectrum of reactions from Europeans. One quandary concerned whether white men should cohabit with or marry native women. From the time of John Rolfe and Pocahontas, Europeans believed that Providence sent white men to guide and fulfill American Indian women in a way that Indian men were incapable of doing.[165] Because Pocahontas was considered an Indian "princess" who was presented to the royal court in London, having an Indian woman in a family could bring it honor. In 1837, Marryat noted in his diary that a chief's daughter had brought heraldry into a white family and that the Randolphs of Virginia still boasted of their association with Pocahontas. Further, Marryat noted that there were practical reasons for an alliance between a white man and a native woman. "They labour hard, never complain," he claimed, "are always faithful and devoted, and very sparing of their talk."[166] Indian women could also ease a white man's way among Indians.[167] Some women even brought with them land rights or other kinds of income. According to von Raumer, "many improvident or dissolute whites marry Indian girls in order to share their income."[168]

It was also said that a white man could obtain a mistress or a wife by purchasing her with ponies, liquor, or baubles.[169] This assertion, however, was largely a misunderstanding of the Indian custom of compensating a woman's parents for her loss. One male writer who understood the concept behind the bride price was the novelist Percy B. St. John in

The Trapper's Bride, who noted that bride price existed in all societies. "Is it alone amid the wild Indians of the American prairies that this custom prevails?" he asked. "If we look around, we shall find the fair daughters of Europe brought to market not so universally, neither so openly and avowedly, but still bought and sold as nakedly and as foully as any poor Comanche or Eutaw maiden ever was."[170]

Nor did Europeans analyze why native women became involved with white men. They failed to consider either political or economic motivations on the part of American Indians. They also ignored the possible legitimacy of Indian customs that proscribed sexual and marital behaviors for women. Instead, Europeans were quick to justify their own actions and dismiss those of Indians. Few voices challenged the assumption that Indian behavior was immoral. Despite good reasons for establishing liaisons with American Indian women, many European men rejected the practice. Not every one believed that white men helped advance Indian women or that a chief's daughter was a princess. Rather, some felt that the practice of marrying Indian women was detrimental to Indians. During the 1820s, the Englishman Adam Hodgson expressed concern that intermarriage between Indians and whites undermined Native American customs.[171]

Most Europeans who opposed Indian–white relationships did so on the basis of traditional white attitudes of what was acceptable and what was not. A Hungarian traveler rejected what Americans would later term *miscegenation* because he thought Indian women were unattractive.[172] The protagonist of a Hungarian novel refused the offer of an Indian bride because he believed that these women became dirty and untidy wives.[173] And the hero of a Polish story fled an impending marriage with a native woman because he found her customs repulsive. As he watched his bride-to-be presiding at a prenuptial banquet, he was repulsed. He said that his betrothed "sat there disemboweling the ox" and "would plunge her round arms into the interior of the beast and then pull them out, dripping with gore and warm fat that she would offer to the whole company." The sight of his beloved eating raw meat "as if she were eating caramels" moved him to plead to his commanding officer for a distant mission.[174]

Other Europeans were similarly repelled by what they deemed

primitivism among Indians.[175] Rather than spending time and energy trying to understand Indian customs they were quick to judge and condemn. During the 1850s, one German traveler maintained that Indians knew "little of the pure feelings of shame and love."[176] Others explained that they avoided insult when rejecting the offer of an Indian bride by pointing to their wedding rings or giving presents to her family and friends.[177] Even Karl May, who was favorable to American Indians, had trouble dealing with the issue in his novels. In one, May's Indian character declared: "The great Spirit has cursed every red woman who loves a white man; therefore, the children of such a woman are like the worm." In another, May went to the extreme of killing Winnetou's sister to halt any further affection between her and his hero, Shatterhand.[178]

The seeming liberality of premarital sexual practices among American Indian groups also upset many Europeans. "When an unmarried brave passes through a village, he hires a girl for a night or two, as he pleases, and her parents find nothing wrong with this," the French naval officer Jean Bernard Bossu puzzled during the 1860s. He could more easily understand why chiefs would urge young girls to give their bodies to white men, an action which offered status and other advantages.[179] Paul Wilhelm had a less kind explanation of why native women got involved with white men and bore children out of wedlock. To him, these women were outgoing, kind, and overly fond of ornaments.[180] To European eyes such practices not only appeared immoral and dangerous, but led to European-style prostitution, which Indians had not known before the coming of white men. Apparently without scientific evidence, Weld claimed that prostitution among native women caused sterility and therefore a decline in the Indian population, which not all white men would have considered bad.[181]

Europeans also reacted harshly to the fact that Indian fathers chose mates for their offspring. Coming from nineteenth-century Europe where the concepts of romantic love and companion marriage were on the rise, they considered parental mate selection a travesty. Observers were often as shocked by the rigidity of this system as they were by the lack of forethought that seemed to characterize white marriages on the frontier. Fredrika Bremer thought one of the worst features of Indian women's lives was that they were seldom able to choose their own mates.[182] The practice of arranged marriages also provided the raw material for hundreds of nineteenth-century fictionalized stories of love that was sometimes fulfilled but more often thwarted. The Indian maiden who committed suicide rather than marry a man she did not love became a standard in European literature.[183] Although such deaths shocked and thrilled European readers, it failed to reflect the reality of Indian custom, which was marked by considerable deliberation and usually the consent of the young people involved. During the 1879s, a Polish analyst who looked into the situation explained that women's lack of choice was not as absolute as it first appeared. According to him, Indian women had recourse against forced matches. A man who took a wife against her will, he said, was "brewing a whole pot of trouble," for "the maiden will sulk, bite, throw herself on you with a knife, hide away, malinger, and after a few days will flee back to her father, or at worst, with some other lover."[184]

Europeans also found it very curious that women who appeared to them to be sexually free before marriage were expected to be chaste afterward.[185] One eighteenth-century author explained in a dismissive way that "liberal to profusion of their charms before marriage, "they are chastity itself after."[186] If wives violated standards of matrimonial fidelity, they were often harshly punished, even by physical disfigurement such as having an ear or nose cut off.[187] Some travelers were wise enough to see that a woman's sexual liaisons were not judged immoral when approved beforehand by a husband, father, or brother, but it still remained incomprehensible to them how this could be so.[188] Had Indians known about European society, where sexual affairs were kept secret and infidelity could lead to death, they might have been equally puzzled.

Europeans also found it strange that women of many Indian tribes left their homes during menstrual periods, bore babies alone, or could discipline female children but never male.[189] They agreed, however, that motherhood conferred a certain amount of respect and status on women[190] and that native mothers were caring and affectionate toward their children.[191] In return, children, even males, listened to their mothers. "A crime considered frightful and unheard of among the Indians is that of a son rebellious to his mother," Chateaubriand wrote in 1827: "When she grows old, he feeds her."[192]

The practice of polygyny, or plural wives, among some Indian groups especially shocked European visitors. Because the practice was not part of their own cultural background, they were unprepared to find any validity in such an institution. Travelers frequently commented upon it at length, and many novelists incorporated it into their works as a commonplace of American Indian life.[193] The usual interpretation was that polygyny implied disdain for Indian women by their men. Louis Philippe claimed that plural wives had to be "contemptible" in men's eyes. Von Raumer took the position that polygyny contradicted the mild and happy relationships that Europeans assumed to exist among Native Americans.[194] Other travelers recounted dramatic tales of women's responses to what Europeans viewed as reprehensible treatment. These included stories of wives who fought violently the admittance of another wife into their home or who took their own lives and those of their children rather than tolerate such an indignity.[195]

The feature that most struck European spectators about Native American families was the women's total accountability for all domestic and agricultural labor, whereas the men were expected "only" to hunt, fish, care for animals and weapons, and conduct warfare. The list of men's duties might appear to some to be demanding, dangerous, and exhausting, yet to most Europeans, who came from settled agrarian or industrial backgrounds, such tasks seemed incidental and even amusing. Montule depicted Indian males as "by nature very lazy in cultivating the land or in working as do civilized people." To him, they seemed to have energy only for amusing activities, that is, hunting, fishing, and preparing for fighting by playing war games.[196] Very rare indeed was the traveler such as Friedrich Gerstäcker, who argued that "in a state of society where the lives of the family, depend upon the success of the hunter, he must have his arms free and unencumbered for action at every minute, and dare not toil under a heavy load, for it would make his aim unsteady."[197] Rather, visitors endlessly lamented the plight of the poor woman who did all the domestic chores, labored in the fields, and took complete care of family and housing matters, whereas her mate did little or nothing.[198] Such statements were repeated so often that they became truisms. Some observers even claimed that American Indian men did no work at all and "sometimes had to be carried on their wives' backs when they grew too lazy to walk home from hunting."[199]

These inaccurate portrayals of the roles and duties of Indian men and women occurred because commentators usually observed only the village life of traditional hunting and military societies. They had many opportunities to watch native women carry out the domestic chores that were their responsibilities, yet seldom had the same chance to witness native men conducting a dangerous and demanding buffalo hunt, fighting in deadly warfare, or performing such rites as a sweat lodge ceremony. Coming from an industrialized society where hunting and fishing were considered little more than leisure-time sports and where warfare was a matter for a trained few, Europeans had no notion of the skill and peril involved in such pursuits. Thus, in their eyes, native women got the very worst of the bargain, whereas men seemed to get the very best.[200]

Complicating the matter still further was the absence of meaningful contact between observers and Indian women, so that visitors could hear women's opinions. Nor were women's words available in written form among tribes who depended on oral traditions and history. Even the trappers and missionaries who got to know American Indian women allowed their self-interests or perceptions to bias their reports. In addition, white commentators virtually ignored women operating outside the domestic realm. Although American Indian women among many tribes became equestrians, warriors, medical practitioners, and religious leaders, it has been left to modern anthropologists, historians, and native women who serve as tribal, family, and personal historians to reveal the stories of Indian women such as Elk Hollering, Running Eagle, and Old Lady Drives the Enemy.[201]

As a result of the blinders they wore, European commentators emphasized what appeared to them to be a cruel and unfair division of labor between American Indian men and women. "The man smokes peacefully while the woman grinds corn in a mortar," Louis Philippe wrote. "The men in domestic life are exceedingly slothful," traveler John Davis added. Another claimed that "women perform all the household drudgery....The active employment of the men is war and hunting."[202] "The squaw has to toil," Pulszky claimed, "the man but to fight, to hunt, to play, and to speak in council."[203] According to Hodgson, "the women were hard at work, digging the ground, pounding Indian corn, and carrying heavy loads of water from the river, while the men were either setting out to the woods with their guns, or lying idle before doors."[204]

European onlookers concluded that the domestic toil performed by Indian women placed them in the category of an animal or a slave. In 1817, English botanist John Bradbury thought that the plight of native women was so dire that he concluded that mothers who performed infanticide on deformed or ill babies actually destroyed their female children, "alleging as a reason, that it is better they should die than lead a life so miserable as that to which they are doomed . . . also it is said that suicide is not infrequent." The negative interpretation of Indian women continued in later decades. "The women are forced to do the hardest work, and are treated like slaves," one author stated in 1845.[205] "The wife of an Indian is his marketable animal; traveling, or in a campaign, she carries the burden of his baggage on her back," another added in 1849.[206] During the 1850s, John Xantus was shocked to discover that women "do everything, even the most degrading tasks we would be embarrassed to ask our servants to do in Europe."[207]

European novelists reinforced these unhappy images of American Indian women by representing them as drudges and their men as "haughty" husbands who "amuse themselves with hunting, shooting, fishing."[208] Authors frequently characterized Indian men as indolent, lazy tyrants who smoked and chatted while their women labored their lives away.[209] Only Karl May rejected this interpretation in favor of an enlightened Indian hero who vowed to make his wife "a lady of the hut and the tent, as the women of the palefaces!"[210] Perhaps May could not bear to present his friends, the American Indians, as complete tyrants. Or perhaps he suspected that such a depiction of the roles of Indian men and women was too extreme in its dimensions to be totally accurate. At any rate, he elevated an Indian man to the "civilized" level of white men by having him swear to make his wife a white-style lady.

There were, of course, reasons for these European perceptions of Indian women. Because of their attitudes regarding the limited roles and inferior position of women in European society, it was difficult for them to grasp many native groups' concept of men and women as separate but equal.[211] Yet, to Indians, it was a matter of pride that men and women had their appropriate duties, which they performed faithfully and well. An Indian woman could insult another most severely by saying, "You let your husband carry burthens." To European ears, however, this sounded like a complaint rather than an expression of pride in one's duties.[212] Europeans could not understand that an American Indian male walking in front of a female did not signify the woman's inferiority, but indicated that since the male was expendable he was placing himself in the way of an attack and thereby protecting the more valuable female, who would propagate and care for the race.[213] Nor did they see that separate dances and amusements did not automatically indicate male disdain for women.[214]

In addition, European critics apparently failed to see the contradictions in their descriptions of native women, who were portrayed as beribboned and bedecked with ornaments, beads, and finely worked clothing, which hardly signified contemptible and degraded slaves. They also did not seem to see any problem in their accounts of love-struck Indian swains, who went to great lengths to court their loved ones, or their descriptions of elaborate marriage ceremonies, both of which indicated esteem for women. Another paradox occurred in Europeans' comments when they praised the exquisite basketry, ingenious quill work, and fine weaving of the women.[215] Europeans were apparently unaware that such skills could not be achieved nor such crafts produced by slave-like beasts of burden who had neither leisure time nor the necessary status to develop the marks of a cultured and productive society.[216]

Evidently, the view of Native American women as unfortunate workhorses, who became brutalized and cruel as a result of their husbands' treatment, was more amenable to most Europeans than the depiction of Indian women as skillful, respected, and well treated. Consequently, travelers frequently rendered accounts of "savage women" who were "as insolent as the men were cruel."[217] Novelists too—even May—often portrayed native women as outrageous figures capable of inflicting the worst kinds of tortures upon their victims.[218] Occasionally a dissonant note challenged this account of American Indian women. In 1859, a Norwegian traveler described a huge, respectful assemblage gathered around the pyre of an Indian woman.[219] A female British novelist stressed the existence among the Huron Indians of an elected governing council of matrons who ruled coequally with the council of elders.[220]

Opposition also came from female traveler Fredrika Bremer, who pointed out that a native woman could achieve power "from her mystical, witch-like attributes, when she is possessed of a powerful character."[221] In her 1850 travel letters, Bremer critiqued the usual European view of American Indian women as degraded savages. After watching Native American women in St. Paul, visiting them in their homes, and commenting upon their heavy workloads, she was moved to write, "With inward wonder I regarded these beings, women like myself, with the spirit and feelings of women, yet so unlike myself in their purpose of life." She added that as she "thought of hard, gray, domestic life in the civilized world . . . hedged in by conventional opinion, with social duties . . . with every prospect of independence, liberty, activity, and joy closed, more rigidly closed by invisible barriers than these wigwams by their buffalo hides," she concluded that the Indian woman's life was happier. She also thought it more healthy: "There they sat at their ease, without stays or the anxiety to charm, without constraint or effort, those daughters of the forest."[222] Bremer's remarks also suggest that the position of the white frontierswoman was not really very liberated, despite the tendency of many Europeans to paint it in rosy hues. Hemmed in by social convention, treated unequally in almost every area of life, and committed to a lifetime of low-status domestic labor, white frontierswomen did in fact face a great number of restrictions and problems. Yet most Europeans did not see the situation that way. Compared to the tradition-bound circumstances and limited status of European women, Anglo frontierswomen at least appeared to be free and equal. And as inhabitants of the wonderfully progressive New World of the American frontier, white women were often assumed to be recipients of humanitarianism and equalitarianism.

Conversely, Indian women, who symbolized opposition and challenge to white expansion across the West, had to be viewed as primitive and savage. While they could occasionally be credited with a spark of beauty, warmth, or creativity, in the last analysis they had to be grouped with their men as poor, degraded folks meant for extinction.

The willingness of Europeans to see white women as near saints and Indian women as total savages was the logical outcome of the belief that white people were destined to inherit the earth and, most immediately, the American West. This message was surely not lost on generations of European and American women who, when migrating westward, found themselves cast as "natural" opponents of American Indians.

These European perceptions greatly influenced European and American philosophies regarding female migrants and American Indians. European writers encouraged the idea that the mettle and moral powers of white women were to be tested on western frontiers. Although men were physically stronger, women possessed exceptional virtue. Women's moral fortitude would not only carry them through, it would enable them to help the throngs of native peoples they encountered. But would Native Americans want what these women had to offer, namely white morality and virtue? The stories white women heard regarding debased and rapacious Indians suggested that Indians might reject women's gifts, yet this circumstance made "helping" the Indians more challenging. Even those white women who had little interest in aiding the Indians believed that their very existence in the West would be a civilizing force.

Thus, the philosophy phase of frontier migration was strong, rationalizing whites' entry into someone else's domain. Women especially believed they were doing the right thing, especially if Indians were as "bad" as depicted. Naturally, danger was involved, but women's genteel nature could overcome almost anything. The next step was to set frontier process in motion by venturing out onto a trail, whether by land or sea, thus testing the validity of frontiering ideology. Confused by inaccurate beliefs about themselves and American Indians, westering women were soon thrust into a climate of rumor and alarmism. Primed to believe the worst, many frontierswomen would need time before they could replace the attitudes they had learned with more accurate perceptions derived from their own day-to-day experiences in the West.

⸺ Chapter Three ⸺

FRONTIER PROCESS: VILIFYING
AMERICAN INDIANS

For migrating women, the switch from absorbing frontier philosophy to putting into effect frontier process occurred as they and their group moved toward a trailhead. For New Englanders, this might be St. Louis, Missouri, or Kanesville (today Council Bluffs), Iowa. For those who crossed the Isthmus of Panama, New York City was the takeoff point. For Canadians, it might be Toronto in the East or Vancouver in the West, and for Europeans a wide variety of port cities.[1] Whether they traveled during the nineteenth century or the early twentieth, these women were well versed in frontier ideology, notably regarding American Indians. As a consequence of their long exposure to American and European thinking about the contradictory nature of American Indians, most westering women struck out for the trans-Mississippi West with their minds conjuring apparitions of inferior native peoples who were hostile, vicious, and evil, interspersed with enigmatic visions of superior native beings who were friendly, kind, and courageous.

Because the likeness of the "bad" Indian was usually dominant, most female migrants' expectations tended to be negative rather than positive. When they set foot on the trail, their nerves were taut with fearful anticipation; they were ready for the worst of fates at the hands of American Indians. When they reached the end of their journey, most were considerably more savvy, but not entirely cleansed of their prejudice. Teachings about women's moral authority, white superiority, Manifest Destiny, and European-style colonialism were so deeply entrenched, they remained always at the back of women's minds. Even though a significant number of white female migrants adjusted their thinking toward Indians, they retained a great deal—which they passed on to their children and grandchildren.

—— On the Trails ——

After 1840, so many people went west that an industry sprouted, supplying everything from wagons to guidebooks. Preparations might take a few months or an entire year. By the time migrants reached their particular trail, they were already anxious and overwrought, only to find themselves thrust into a climate of thought rife with rumors and alarms. Pioneering was as much human adaptation to a new physical environment as anything else. In these new environments, where there were not many people or the customary social institutions, white peoples reacted in ways they would not have at home.[2] Those who came from lesser situations adjusted better, but this was not the case for most white migrants who were of the middle classes and had the financial wherewithal to migrate.

Women, as well as men, were convinced that they were about to come face to face with the fiendish visages of creatures who were little more than consorts of the devil. The specter of savages hung heavy around them as they stepped gingerly upon the trail. Indian "sign" was everywhere they looked—lurking beside the trail, hidden in every bush and tree, or outlined along the horizon by the rays of the rising or setting sun. If women's nerves were not already thoroughly frazzled by the time they turned westward, the gossip that enveloped them as they began their trek was enough to bring them to the edge of terror in a very short time. Aggravating the situation was the pettiness and meanness with which whites and natives often treated each other; thus injecting an element of truth into the awful tale-telling.

By translating their fears into ubiquitous rumors, migrants created a climate marked by nervousness and tension. While a state of anxiety kept them alert to possible danger, it also made them so apprehensive that they were incapable of dealing effectively with the native populations they encountered. That many violent outbreaks and tragic confrontations occurred between American Indians and the migrants intent upon settling the West is a widely known fact. It is also true that many "uprisings" and "massacres" were little more than the work of people's overactive imaginations. Problems with Indians were frequently derived far more from the migrants' worries about what could happen to them than from what actually happened.

The process of distilling anti-Indian bias had begun for migrants when they were children listening to family folklore. Quite often the focus of these yarns was the custom of scalping attributed to American Indians. Scalping was the very stuff of Indian tales. Dramatic, colorful, and capable of inducing little prickles of dread in an audience, stories of scalping could be depended upon for titillation. Moreover, late in the nineteenth century and into the early twentieth, William F. (Buffalo Bill) Cody's Wild West, as well as his many imitators, reinforced the existence of scalping on the frontier. Every evening and twice on matinee days, Cody and his troupe enacted historical vignettes that included a scalping or two. Even as late as 1915, viewers could pay their money and see how scalping supposedly was done in the old West.[3]

Therefore, many women had already served childhood apprenticeships as potential victims before they took their places in the wagons. Rather than realizing that Indians fought to protect their families and lands, white women thought them to be belligerent and renegade.[4] Harriet Smith, migrating as a young girl in the 1840s, vividly recalled her grandfather's chilling tales of the Indians he had encountered while serving in the War of 1812. "Naturally we were somewhat afraid," she commented when the members of her party spied their first natives. During the same decade, Virginia Reed Murphy also carried with her the terror that her grandmother had instilled in her with frequent recitals about the "fearful deeds of the savages" and the trials of an aunt held captive for five years.[5] As late as 1900, Lucy Jennings admitted that she had heard so many horror stories about Indians that she was terrified to step out of the family wagon.[6]

Because the possibility of scalping dominated the minds of many women, such thoughts led to a variety of protective measures. Going west as a child in 1861, Lucy Fosdick not only heard much about scalping, but had her hair cropped short by her mother before departure.[7] In 1874, another young woman, Emily Andrews, was so certain that two Tonqua Indian guides had a peculiar "desire for light haired scalps" that she "kept a good distance from them" throughout the journey.[8] Even near the turn of the twentieth century the situation had not noticeably improved. Although Native Americans were largely vanquished, the rumor mills continued to churn. One woman of the 1890s said she had heard so much about the Indians she was convinced she would be scalped. One of her contemporaries related her consternation in more detail. As a girl of sixteen in 1895, Mary Ellen Williams joined her father's family, consisting of a Choctaw wife and offspring; she confessed she "was absolutely scared to death." She continued, "I didn't expect anything else but to be scalped if Dad got out of my sight."[9] As late as 1899, Martha Lowrence remembered her neighbors in Missouri warning her family that Indians "would kill us and scalp us and burn us up and that they were bad people."[10]

It is little wonder that many women expected to be scalped when they actually met American Indians for the first time. With so many traumatic stories fresh in their minds, more than one woman's thoughts focused immediately upon her hair as natives approached. When shadows against the sky materialized into Indians, Annie Baker reacted in a typical fashion by "expecting momentarily to be scalped by the Redskins."[11] In 1870, some ten years after the Baker episode, Mabel Beavers displayed a similar response when she was met at the train by "a couple of full blood Indians." Despite the fact that she had come to teach school in the Oklahoma Indian Territory, Beavers was consumed by fright. "I just knew," she said later, "that if one of those Indians had touched my hair, my scalp would have come off without any pulling." Although Indians treated Beavers with respect and consideration, she remained a prisoner of her uneasiness. Her explanation was a simple yet telling one: "They were Indians. Horrors!"[12]

Because the inflammatory family legends of American Indian atrocities that spurred such reactions pervaded the nineteenth century and continued into the twentieth century, neither the degree of settlement of western regions nor increasing white control and decimation of native populations seemed to affect the nature or proportions of these accounts. Rather, the legends were based on what whites living in Europe or in non-frontier regions of America believed to be the situation in the West. Those folks who decided to move westward, in spite of Indian horror stories, found little escape from the tales once they had embarked on their trek.

Migrants' concerns with more immediate issues, such as food and water supplies, failed to deflect their worries about Indians. Not only were guidebooks filled with dire warnings about Native Americans, but the jumping-off places were hotbeds of rumor and gossip. One young traveler of 1852 wrote: "As we drew near Council Bluffs on the Missouri River, the cry of 'Indians, Indians,' turned me into stone. . . . The air was thick at Council Bluffs with tales of Indian massacres, starvation and pestilence. . . . The one refrain was that the plains were alive with Indians on the war path."[13]

Once on the trail, travelers were thrust into an even more intense climate of dramatic reports regarding American Indian activities. They soon learned that there was little relief from terrible and often ill-founded portrayals of native peoples. Even during eras characterized by reasonably good relations between whites and Indians, travelers related concerns about Indians. During difficult periods, migrants related only slightly more trouble. Perceptions of Indian problems depended more on the traveler's jumpiness than on his or her actual circumstance. Consequently, accounts of trail experiences almost always included mention of rumor-mongering regarding American Indians and what were termed their "depredations."

Male and female migrants recorded the alarms they encountered as they progressed along one of the many westward trails. On the Oregon Trail of the 1840s and 1850s, scarcely a traveler escaped receiving secondhand intelligence of a horrifying nature.[14] Those heading toward California were also recipients of frequent rumors along their route.[15] As a case in point, in 1849 Dr. Jonathan Clark, journeying from Iowa to California, mentioned notes relating Indian activities "stuck up in a conspicuous place near the road" by advance parties.[16]

Other migrants were exposed to more startling conveyors of news. On her way from Wisconsin to California in 1850, Lucene Parsons noted that bones were used as bulletin boards to report the exploits of Native Americans. "We see writing on bones every day stating the deeds of the Indians," she wrote. A few days later she added, "Here we saw a bone stating that Indians had run off 17 mewls & horses."[17] Later in the decade, Helen Carpenter remarked that, in spite of the many rumors, her party had not been overly concerned about Indians until they too "found little messages by the roadside, written in pencil, on the bleached bones of animals such as 'look out for the Indians; Indians ran off all the stock of train ahead'; etc. etc."[18]

Apparently, when it came to reporting "Indian troubles," whether real or fabricated, ingenuity and imagination were unlimited. In 1850, Margaret Frink was disturbed by a rather sophisticated alarm system in the form of printed circulars distributed to emigrants. She was further distressed when the natives and "their doings" became the focus of camp conversation. Soon she began "to think that three men, one woman, and one eleven-year old boy, only armed with one gun and one Colt's revolver, are but a small force to defend themselves against many hostile Indian tribes, along a journey of two thousand miles."[19]

Other migrants were also intimidated by conjecture and storytelling.[20] The after-dinner fireside especially encouraged such activity. In Cyrus Hurd's view, "It will do in the States to tell those stories for fun, but when you come to the spot it ain't so pleasant."[21] More than a decade later, in 1864, Mallie Stafford lamented the effectiveness of a fireside gathering she attended in what she called "the middle of Colorado Indian country." She declared that "the conversation naturally, under the circumstances, centered on Indian stories, Indian attacks, crossing the plains, etc., and as the night wore on they grew more and more eloquent—it seemed to me they were gifted with an awful eloquence on that particular subject."[22]

For most migrants, the word-of-mouth reports that constantly buffeted the wagon trains served as the main source of their consternation.[23] Helen Love said she had listened to so many stories that by the time she reached Fort Kearney in 1853, she could no longer sleep. She thought she "heard wolves howling and Indians screaming and all sorts of noises."[24] While moving from Iowa to California in 1862, another woman remarked that "there is great tails about the Indians." During years that followed, yet another woman had difficulty in sleeping because of constant reports of "depredations of the Indians."[25]

Such stories came from a bewildering variety of sources. The license to purvey Indian intelligence was to be had simply by asserting that one "knew" something, that one held a key piece of information that could avert a disaster or save a life. All kinds of people became reporters, and often their news was more alarming than helpful to those who received it. In 1861, Lucy Fosdick pointed to the drivers of teams as the source of her unease. "The teamsters, to be sure, generally ended their advice by telling us that if we were well armed we should probably get through all right," she explained. "But we naturally felt very uneasy," she added, "and from that time dated my fear and hatred of 'Lo, the poor Indian.'"[26] Helen Carpenter mentioned trader's reports; Charles Robins cited the tales carried by a priest; and James Miller, on his way to Virginia City, identified a dragoon as the person who regaled him with stories of Indian attacks.[27] Other migrants were less specific. In 1862, heading toward California, one writer noted simply that "we hear many stories of Indian depredations." In Texas in 1868, another traveler mentioned that "we hear of Indians being seen at every foot." In 1875, in Wyoming Territory, still another wrote that "the air is full of Indian rumors."[28]

Because emigrants' nerves were honed to such a fine edge by reports like these, they mistook an incredible variety of occurrences for Indian raids.[29] Expecting to see a native at every turn, to lose one's scalp or to receive the fatal blow at any time, a traveler's eyes and ears interpreted things in the context of Indian. They literally transformed the landscape, their stock, and their own companions into threatening menaces. Images of Indians were evoked by a passing deer, a wandering dog returning to camp, four little pigs that had escaped, and some jittery cattle.[30] Wolves were quite often the cause of terror in a camp. Maria Schrode related that one man's wife thought "some wolves was Indians and she screamed louder than the wolves howled and frightened some of us considerably." Sometimes flocks of birds started the trouble, as in the case of Mary Powers, who wrote that "the Indians that had so frightened us were nothing but a flock of filthy bussards."[31]

Not infrequently it was train members who generated the scare. When two young women rushed through the dark toward a young man on the fringe of camp in revenge for some of his practical jokes, they were appalled to see him dash into camp raising an Indian alarm.[32] Similarly, a man in another train jokingly fired a shot to awake a sleeping guard, thereby raising the entire camp, stampeding the stock, and causing the guard to be run over and seriously injured. In recounting the episode, Mary Saunders commented that "it taught Mr. Baker and all the guards that they could not break the rules with safety."[33] Harriet Ward also disparaged the tendency of some travelers to use scares for their own purposes. When her son was hit by an arrow, the entire camp readied itself for a full-scale assault, only to find that "the much dreaded arrow was but a harmless little stick" thrown into the midst of the children "to frighten them, by one of the boys whose slumbers were disturbed by their merriment."[34]

Moreover, a variety of people along the trail were sometimes taken for Native Americans. Mary Warner remarked that a member of her train was fired at by an Indian as he passed through a canyon, or rather, she explained, "he supposed it was them."[35] Lucy Cooke related a similar incident about one of her fellow travelers.

> He had not gone far when, looking back, he saw someone in pursuit, and fearing it to be an Indian, jumped off his horse and took to his heels and hid in the tall grass, leaving his horse for Mr. Indian. The pursuer proved to be one of his own men, so he got well laughed at for his fright, and would have lost his horse had not an Indian caught it and brought it to camp.

The captain of the train justly rewarded the Indian with a dollar for his honesty.[36]

The soldiers sent to protect the migrants also elicited their share of cases of mistaken identity. Ada Millington described the men of her party loading their guns and regrouping the train when they thought they had sighted wigwams in the distance and Indians firing guns. When the Indian camp turned out to be tents and United States soldiers, she said that "we had a good laugh over our scare."[37] Emily Andrews mentioned that her party grew very excited about a small body of riders on a distant hill, only to learn on approaching them that they were Texas Rangers.[38]

In this state of constant agitation, male and female migrants blamed American Indians for any misfortune or irregularity that occurred. Indians automatically became the villain of virtually any mishap. Because prejudice and near hysteria achieved dimensions that defied rationality and reason, natives did not even need to be in the area, nor was it necessary for any shred of evidence to exist to suggest that they had perpetrated an incident; they were immediately and irrevocably indicted. When cattle stampeded, Mary Warner indicated that the guards assumed that Indians had been the cause.[39] Katherine Dunlap explained that when stock wandered it was "natural" to think that it had been stolen by Indians, who were assumed to be always "skulking around the camps."[40] When observing Native Americans for her first time, Lucy Sexton noted that "they were mounted, and one of them on a fine American horse, undoubtedly stolen."[41] And Emily Horton offered a particularly harsh judgment when some of the men of her train brought a bleached skull into camp. According to her, it was "all there was to show that one of our race had perished far from home. No doubt death was caused by savages."[42]

When real Indians were spotted, ensuing accounts led to great precautions. Despite their demeanor or intentions, natives were blamed for all kinds of deeds. One man rushed into camp hollering that Indians were chasing him. He raised fifteen to twenty armed men, only to discover on tracking down the natives that they wanted "to smoke peace" and beg for food. These same men remained convinced that a full-scale attack would hit their camp that very night. Despite their fears, it failed to materialize.[43] In another instance, the mere presence of American Indians in the vicinity caused train members to dress and prepare for night combat. On the next day an oxen, "full of arrows, but still alive," was found on the trail. After shooting the animal to end its misery, these people concluded that some other train moving ahead of them had been struck.[44]

This is not to argue that there were no violent and tragic interactions between frontier people and Native Americans, for there were many such unfortunate instances. Rather, the suggestion here is that myth and media overemphasized such calamities to the point of distortion. Moreover, some migrants were not above inventing incendiary tales. In turn, newspapers, in the East and West, always searching for ways to expand their subscription lists, published these fabrications with additional embellishments so that by the mid-nineteenth century mythical massacres were sensational and commonplace.[45]

It is meant to demonstrate that the willingness of overlanders to permit rumors and gossip to rule their lives imposed great rigidity on their activities. On the trail they joined with so many other travelers that parties became unwieldy and often created difficulties in locating campsites, water, and grass. However, it was generally thought to be better to experience the problems of a train that was too large than to take the chance of being overpowered by unfriendly American Indians.[46] As Lavinia Porter pointed out, the warmongering attitudes and actions of train members could actually create more danger than they deterred. After remonstrating in vain with hostile train members, she and her family, fearing retaliation from the Indians whom the migrants had abused, left the train to attempt the journey on their own. Their experience was instructive: not only were they never bothered by Native Americans, but one traveled with them for three days as a guide. When she learned that he had been sent to protect them, she remarked, "If that were true, it went to prove that there was honor among these savage tribes of the wilderness."[47] Other migrants who were less trusting stuck close to their train, refraining from enjoying the countryside or even from killing game "for fear that the Indians might be near."[48]

Even though many of the alarms lacked credence, they did serve a purpose for the migrants in reminding them to be cautious.[49] As trail discipline gradually relaxed, people did things like taking what one woman called "fool-hardy" walks. Scares encouraged them to exercise more precaution.[50] In response to the rumors, many trains regularly circled their wagons, posted guards, and kept night fires burning in an effort to protect their animals from theft. In 1840, for instance, Abigail Smith wrote to her brothers and sisters that while crossing Missouri her party routinely circled their wagons and posted night guards.[51]

Apparently, for many migrants rumor was far worse than reality. Their fears were seldom realized, and their trepidations proved to be largely unfounded. Although they tortured themselves and one another with apprehensions that kept everyone on tenterhooks, most travelers were actually more harassed and plagued by their own angst than by Native Americans. A surprisingly small number of chronicles by emigrants and settlers recorded any violent interchanges with Indians,[52] yet the majority did contain some mention of tension, agitation, and dread concerning the possibility of altercations with natives. Such malaise often evaporated by the end of the westward trek, leaving a traveler feeling a bit sheepish. It is perhaps best expressed in a statement by a member of the Donner Party, Virginia Reed Murphy. Although terrorized by Indian tales before leaving home, Murphy later wrote, "let me say that we suffered vastly more from fear of the Indians before starting than we did on the plains."[53]

As time passed, women even became skeptical. Although some white-Indian altercations occurred, the more usual narratives were punctuated by impending crises and predictions of doom, ending on rather anticlimactic and peaceful notes. Oregon migrant Margaret Chambers's remark in 1851 that "we had no trouble with the Indians— only some scares" was typical of trail accounts.[54] When Charlotte Pengra heard a "frightful tale" about four hundred revengeful natives blocking her party's path she was at first concerned. She soon added: "Have seen no Indians so conclude the tale we heard was false." Some days later, the appearance of a "hostile" Indian village again caused distress; "we anticipated some trouble," she wrote, "but realized none." By the end of her 1853 chronicle of her move from Illinois to Oregon, she declared that "I have heard lots of bugbear stories about the Indians. . . . I conclude the stories are about as true as they ever will be."[55] On the way to California in 1859, Lavinia Porter exchanged what turned out to be her "groundless" fears for an almost favorable attitude toward Indians. "From their general demeanor they rather inspired us with a confidence which seemed to sanction our presence in their midst," she wrote at one point. On another occasion, when an Indian returned her train's wandering cattle to them, she remarked, "It truly seemed to us in our long journey traveling alone that the Indians watched over us."[56]

It is also instructive to pursue the writings of some individuals who were the most terrified when beginning their westward journey. Their accounts disclosed a reversal in their attitudes toward American Indians. Terror was routinely replaced by equanimity, aversion by acceptance, and hatred by affection. For instance, Lucy Jennings, the young woman who had been afraid to leave the family wagon, met some Oklahoma Indians who were "very nice" to her and her family.[57] And Mary Williams, the young trail girl who had so dreaded living with her father's native wife and children, not only learned to love her new brothers and sisters but eventually married a Choctaw herself.[58]

—— In New Settlements ——

Despite some softening of attitudes, especially among women, travelers who reached new settlements seemed to need to repeat the cycle of terror, alarms, sheepishness, and diminishing fear. As a result, trails were far from the only breeding grounds for anxiety about Indians; an omnipresent dread of Native Americans accompanied the migrants into their new settlements. Like trail folk, the specter of savage beings haunted settlers' minds as they slashed at the trees or cut the sod to build their first cabins or soddies. Consequently, settlers typically continued to restrict their actions and lives. Some men wore guns at all times, including working in the fields, which made them vulnerable to attack.[59] Women refused to go on rides or picnics, to attend war dances and other ceremonies, or to observe the splendid sight of a government-endorsed hunting party.[60]

Others made more substantial efforts to protect themselves. They engaged in subterfuge, such as lacing their own liquor supply with morphine in case troublesome Indians appeared or placing in their yards hollow logs in which they intended to hide.[61] Band after band of informal "frontier guards," "rangers," and "brigades" drilled zealously, only to disband without having seen action.[62] In many regions, forts, stockades, and blockhouses were built to shelter settlers when the dreaded horde descended upon them.[63] Sometimes the local rangers staffed these garrisons; on other occasions, formal troops were ordered out, often by the thousands.[64]

Once again, the number of American Indians living in a region, the degree of settlement that the area had achieved, the number of problems encountered, or the point in time did not seem to have any discernible correlation with the quantity of stories in circulation. Rather, people's interpretation of the dangers inherent in their situations influenced the number and scope of the tales. One Oregon woman of the 1840s remembered that "often the news would come that the Indians would murder us," rumors that resulted in her parents keeping all-night vigils.[65] Another Oregon woman maintained that although her family experienced several scares they were never molested and were probably "never in actual danger."[66] A Texas woman of the 1860s recalled that an attack became so imminent that men "wore guns in the field and at all times." In explaining people's fright, she exclaimed, "And Indians, Oh horrors, we expected to be massacreed at any time."[67] Significantly, these women not only survived to make these statements but retained both their wits and their scalps in the process.

As with trail events, newspaper editors were quick to print, and often enlarge on, stories concerning Indian "atrocities." Hungry for news to fill their pages and anxious to enlarge their readership, editors often printed Indian atrocity tales that were unmarked by any degree of taste or discrimination. As one woman noted in 1856, she was sure that a friend had received all the Indian news available from Oregon Territory and "perhaps more" since news accounts "do not generally lose anything."[68] The same journalists who used rumors and scares to justify the practice of excessive literary license, gave authentic armed conflicts, such as one near Fort Phil Kearney in 1866, the grand treatment. Army wife Margaret Carrington commented that "as there was no one to contradict, and no one who knew the truth, a large margin was left for the play of the fancy, and the imagination was drawn upon with great freedom and success."[69]

Such unfounded tattle reinforced in eastern minds images of marauding Native Americans. One female visitor to Wyoming, whose travel account appeared in *Lippincott's Magazine* in 1875, said she refrained from discussing the "Indian question" because "everybody all over the East has an opinion ready formed upon the subject."[70] Other writers were not so reticent. They offered to their readers accounts of "uprisings," embellished beyond belief. In 1876, the Nebraska settler Caroline Winne denigrated such overstatements. "Oh what a farce it is," she wrote her family back East. "Come to get down to the facts of Crook's expedition, the one hundred Indians killed amounted to just 4 killed." She added that "as there were four soldiers killed and light wounded . . . we failed to see the success—but twas a famous victory."[71] Still, easterners who wanted to believe such bilge did so. The parents of traveler Ellen Biddle became so alarmed that they entreated her to return home. Biddle explained that the reports of an Indian alarm had reached her family through "newspapers in the East, and had lost nothing in transit."[72]

Yet it was settlers themselves who caused the most chaos. Anything that moved was suspect by these anxiety-ridden frontier people. Tumbleweeds driven by the passing wind were imaginary Native Americans for some Nebraska homesteaders. A colt alarmed some Kansans, a screeching hoot owl frightened some Oklahomans, and a lone mouse trying unsuccessfully to climb out of a tin dish of water became an Indian intruder in an Iowa farmhouse.[73] Shadowy Sioux dressed in their white blankets and stalking through a dark and foggy barnyard were discovered by other Iowa farmers to be no more than a flock of geese, while a hired man carrying a featherbed through the fog alarmed still others.[74] The era seemed to make little difference in peoples' fear. Near Denver in the early 1800s, for example, some Mexican cattle drovers were discovered to be the source of similar trouble.[75] In Oklahoma, nearly one hundred years later, a noisy charivari party following a wedding was enough to convince people that Native Americans were killing and scalping their neighbors. Although the citizens of the nearby town rallied to the call by organizing an army of defense and emptying the hardware stores of arms and ammunition, no Indians appeared and one more uprising failed to occur.[76]

In addition, as on the trail, settlers often mistook a dismaying array of people and things for American Indians. With their consternation at an untenably high level, they determined that an attack was imminent from the flimsiest evidence. During the 1870s in Texas, May Tansill concluded that a man approaching her was an Indian because he wore something red. "I had always fancied that Indians wore some thing red about them," she later explained, "so I jumped to the conclusion that an Indian was approaching me."[77] Another young woman was embarrassed when, armed with a shotgun and "thinking only of wild Indians come to scalp us," she opened the door to encounter a startled young farmer from Kansas standing on her doorstep.[78] Later, yet another woman precipitated a massive Indian scare when she "started running and screaming to a neighbor's house" after mistaking her son—approaching home and wearing a jaunty feather in a newly purchased hat—for an American Indian.[79]

Moreover, some frontier people perpetrated hoaxes simply to scare their companions or to make an attempt at humor.[80] Settlers reported perverse attempts at humor on the part of their neighbors. After a night of terror, one woman sarcastically remarked that had they been able to identify the prankster who raised the alarm "there would have been some hair lost, but not by scalping."[81] Another woman described her own participation in an attempt to reduce the bumptious male attitudes of a local judge and attorney by surrounding their wagon with whites masquerading as natives. When the "Indians" struck with appropriate shouting, yelling, and shooting, the driver of the wagon fell backward with the exclamation, "I am shot; everyone for themselves"; the judge fled the scene, and the attorney ran to a nearby fort to return with two groups of soldiers.[82]

Such scares frequently caused people to flock into a town's center. Convinced that strength as well as ultimate survival lay in joining forces, settlers willingly left their homes, fields, and businesses to devote excessive, and usually needless, amounts of time and energy to preparing their defense. Men drilled, and women sewed all day to make tents, but often it came to nothing and the distraught populace soon dispersed.[83] One Oklahoma woman of the 1880s recollected many such gatherings, admitting that she could not "remember of there ever being a fight." On one occasion, her mother "cooked up a whole sack of flour into bread and baked several hens, boiled hams, etc.," to last them through a coming siege. Rumor had it that the Indians were holding a war dance preparatory to killing all the "pale faces," yet, given a little time, it too blew over.[84]

Men and women spent inordinate amounts of time, energy, and resources in "fortin up."[85] Often this meant that they gathered in someone's well-built house, barn, or other outbuilding. Others resorted to utilizing mine shafts, specially dug caves, hotels, and town squares as their forts. Time after time they spent sleepless, terror-filled nights during which no siege transpired.[86] In some places, notably Texas, these precautions were necessary. One early Texas woman, Jonaphrene Faulkner, claimed that the worst times came during the full moon because Indians preferred nights of "Commanche moons" to attack. In her community, she added, people "began to look forward with dread to those beautiful seasons that had heretofore been our greatest joy; and many families accustomed themselves, upon such nights, to 'fort up,' in the largest and strongest house in their settlement."[87] In another area of Texas, the women and children forted up and the men lay out in the fence corners under the full moon to protect their stock.[88] Unfortunately, unscrupulous whites took advantage of these occasions. One group of Texans entrusted their stock to a concerned army captain while they forted up, never to see their animals or the man again.[89]

In many locales, such structures as forts, stockades, and blockhouses were built.[90] In places that rapidly "settled up," forts never logged a battle. At Fort Dodge in Iowa, which became a state as early as 1846, soldiers spent three years without incident. In 1853, the fort was dismantled and sold at public auction. The following year, the local man who purchased it founded the city of Fort Dodge on the fort's original site. In nearby Sioux City, the fort was never finished, and its timbers were sold for firewood and building material.[91]

Understandably, frontier people living in viable forts stretching across the West were especially prone to such scares.[92] Because they were in the center of native populations and because it was their primary function to control these peoples, conflict with American Indians was always an imminent possibility. Even given their belief in white superiority, fort dwellers were afraid and suspicious of the people of color who surrounded and outnumbered them. They were unwilling to test whether white goodness could stand in the face of attacking "savages." Hence their nerves were frequently rubbed raw with foreboding. As a case in point, Frances Carrington warmly described the friendly Cheyenne living around Fort Laramie, the "feeling of perfect security" at the fort itself, and the large number of American Indian children who frequented the fort. Yet she noted that a serious alarm had been created by nothing more than a herd of buffalo.[93] Another army wife, Ada Vogdes, who considered herself a "nervous excitable person," stated that she was unsuited for life in places such as Fort Laramie and Fort Fetterman during the 1860s. As a result, she spent most of her time being "frightened to death." This state of mind caused her to mistake coyotes, dogs, two drunken cooks, and a soldier returning stealthily from the quarters of a laundress, for Indians. She refused to leave the fort for outings with her husband because she was "frightened nearly to death for fear we might encounter some Indians." And when an unfounded alarm swept the fort she professed herself, once again, to be "frightened to death."[94]

Given the existence of such tension and worry on the part of so many settlers, it is little wonder that when actual Native Americans appeared they were blamed for all manner of misdoing. Expecting Indians to be disreputable and troublesome, settlers eagerly laid a wide spectrum of offenses at the feet of available natives. An Iowa woman of the early 1830s described the alacrity with which some whites assigned a missing hat and ax to Indian theft. When they discovered the articles, they simply dismissed their mistake with a "hearty laugh."[95] Some years later, during the Civil War, another Iowa woman quickly jumped to the conclusion that a begging Indian was undoubtedly a Sioux spy.[96]

Such reactions were usually irrational. Several Oklahoma women admitted that they had feared American Indians because they did not know how to handle difference, in this case, clothing, dirtiness, singing, and "jabbering and grunting" speech. In reality, Indians had never harmed them.[97] Another Oklahoma woman remembered that her distrust of Indians was instilled in her by her mother, who would spend Sunday mornings distractedly watching natives file by the house on their way to church at a nearby mission.[98] On one particular Sunday morning in 1884, in Cañon City, Colorado, ragged and begging Indians disrupted church service and caused a general chaos during which many people screamed and others fainted. Yet once they had been given bread and other foodstuffs, the Indians quietly departed.[99]

Many settlers responded to an Indian's approach by fleeing, either to hide for days or weeks in a barn or in the nearby woods or to desert the area entirely.[100] According to the Iowa settler Ambrose A. Call, after the Spirit Lake disaster in 1857, "every stranger was viewed with suspicion, and if seen on the prairie was run down and captured as an Indian spy." He added that as panic grew, "cranes were magnified into Indians, prairie fires were mistaken for Indian camp fires and the very howling of the April winds sent a chill of horror to the hearts of mothers as they clung closer to their babes." Of those families who fled, Call remarked, only a few ever returned. Predictably, no Indians were ever found in the area so affected by their supposed presence.[101]

Other settlers stood their ground, but with weapons they were often ill prepared to use. As a result, whites destroyed their own goods, stock, and companions. After mistaking his mule for an Indian intruder, one fellow shot his mule twice. Another shot an oxen through the head. An Arizona woman who fired at an "Indian" through her cabin door wounded a neighbor's burro, for which her husband had to pay two dollars in damages.[102] Settlers also frequently took aim at each other. Ella Bird-Dumont drew a bead on an approaching Indian, only to learn that she had almost shot her own husband, who was searching for her.[103] During an Oklahoma scare of the 1890s, a local judge obligingly took command of the "troops" of local men. As he drilled them with supposedly empty rifles, he ordered them into formation and then gave the command to fire. One recruit discharged a cartridge that he had accidentally left in the chamber, hitting the dust in front of the judge's feet. The judge, angry and disgusted with his recruits, threatened to resign and shouted at his men, "Let the confounded redskins butcher you all."[104] In another area of Oklahoma during the same decade, a native dance occasioned a scare that resulted in a young boy fatally shooting his own brother.[105]

As if all this were not enough, settlers developed a "frontier psychology," that is, a near obsession with recounting the dangers of the West and their own heroic victories over all challenges. Within a decade or two of settlement, whites formed Old Settlers Associations, which met regularly and sometimes distributed printed proceedings. The members' purpose was to recall and recount their hardships and their triumphs. Sadly, these retellings of hardships not only exaggerated Indian behavior, but caused whites to swell on the possibility of additional danger. Such hyperbole led to rumors and scares and to hundreds, or perhaps thousands, of invented massacres, in which the brave U.S. Cavalry emerged victorious.[106]

As on the trail, however, many women eventually settled down. Mabel Beavers, the young teacher who had been so afraid of her American Indian charges, discovered that "those people were lovely to me, and were and are yet, some of the warmest friends I have ever had."[107] The young woman who had answered her door with shotgun in hand, and who on other occasions had run for the house and barred the doors and windows in the face of approaching Indians, recollected that the anticipated war whoop never reached her ears. "Finally we were not so afraid of them," she observed, "becoming well acquainted with dozens of bucks and squaws in later years and counting them as some of our best friends."[108] The little girl who timorously watched American Indians pass by her house on Sunday mornings grew up to marry "a full blood Comanche Indian," and upon his death she wed "a full blood Cherokee."[109]

Evidently, many settlers came to realize that Indian rumors were usually nothing more than figments of someone's overactive imagination. As they became seasoned frontier people, they realized that they and their neighbors seldom experienced serious altercations and confrontations with American Indians. The relaxation of their defensive postures toward Indians allowed them to interact more freely with individual Indians, which often gave them more confidence in the rationality of Indians. As one might expect, however, all settlers did not surrender their biases against native peoples they encountered. Many held tightly to their own preconceptions despite a barrage of challenging evidence. Not only did the scares and speculation confirm what they already believed to be true, but it impeded any meaningful communication with Native Americans that might have reshaped their attitudes. Even though Native Americans rarely played out their parts in the dramas concocted by overwrought frontier people, the more timorous settlers never surrendered their ideas concerning Indians. For instance, as a child Anne Ellis of Nebraska was frightened of starvation, ghosts, and Indians. Long after she outgrew her qualms about food and ghosts, she still dreamed of fleeing from native pursuers, "of running from them till my feet rose from the ground and I ran in the air."[110]

—— The Role of Gender ——

Even though the climate of fear that whites created on the trail and in settlements affected men and women, women were generally more hysterical in their reactions to alarms than were men. Because of nineteenth-century dictums concerning woman's weak and nervous nature as opposed to man's strong and calm disposition, frontier people believed that the threat of Indian troubles was more debilitating to women than to men. On a wagon train en route from Illinois to the Willamette Valley in 1845, the cry of Indians caused the "frightened men," as one person described them, to arm themselves and to form a corral, whereas the women, all in a state of panic, reacted by crying, wringing their hands, and praying.[111] During her 1853 trip from Texas to California, Maggie Hall similarly described male and female behavior in the face of alarms. The "groundless scares in the night," she said, were "very exasperating" to her father, but "they made the women nervous and sick."[112] Some years later, in 1873, on a train moving from Kansas to Texas, Olivia Holmes tersely noted that "we got up a little excitement about the Indians but it did not amount to anything" except to "frighten us women folks."[113]

In numerous cases, women raised the alarms, often to the scorn or amusement of their menfolk. In 1853, on her way from Iowa to Oregon, Catherine Washburn jotted in her diary that "some of the women were very much allarmed to night they thought they herd the Indians coming to attack us which turned out to be the ferry rope splashing in the water."[114] In another incident of "Indian excitement" at Fort Dawes in 1865, Samuel Newcomb disdainfully described distraught women gathering their children and running "from place to place like they had lost all reason."[115] As late as 1900, Lois Brown awakened her husband to inform him that natives were whispering and conniving among some nearby trees, but he took it calmly; he laughed and told her that her Indians were only screech owls.[116]

Yet, in several instances when American Indians were believed to be attacking, some women maintained their composure. They neither cringed in terror nor fell into an incoherent state of hysteria. Instead, they not only conducted themselves admirably in the face of real danger but aided other women whose nerves were not quite so steady. It was remarkable that at least a few women retained their sanity when confronted with an authentic siege. By being constantly reminded that they were by nature weak and nervous, women were told that they were expected to behave in a panic-prone fashion when danger appeared and that it was acceptable for them to do so. That such cowardly behavior was expected and allowed created a situation in which even the most self-possessed woman could easily succumb to the pandemonium created by her sisters. To maintain one's composure as Native Americans were about to invade was difficult enough; to remain calm as one's companions were creating bedlam was nearly impossible. After an 1853 fray, Harriet Ward explained that "I hardly think we ever suffer quite as much when anything of this kind really happens as we do in the anticipation."[117]

In all fairness to frontierswomen, it should be noted that they had two gender-related reasons to be concerned about native assaults. One of these was the dread that almost every woman harbored of being raped, or, to use the nineteenth-century euphemism, of being "passed over the prairie" by Indian molesters.[118] Terrifying accounts of such occurrences intimidated generations of frontierswomen, keeping them close to wagon, home, or fort. As Susan Newcomb phrased it in 1865, she was leery of going very far from Fort Davis, Texas, in this "Indian world."[119] The other danger that alarmed women was the possible seizure of their children by American Indian captors. Charged with child care and lectured on maternal sensibilities, women reacted with horror to stories of Indians who not only stole children but supposedly perpetrated all manner of atrocities upon them. In an 1876 attack on Fort Lapwai that never materialized, Emily Fitzgerald stated that "for a few moments, I think, we women with our helpless little children suffered as much as if the Indians had really come."[120]

Because men were cognizant of these menaces to women, some avoided leaving women and children alone for long periods or alone at all if they could avoid it.[121] If necessity dictated their absence, men frequently left their women with a last resort should Indians appear. One woman's husband, who was about to defend her from approaching

Indians, tossed her his rifle and shouted at her to get in the back of the wagon. "Should they attack us and capture me and you see that you can not escape," he yelled, "you will have the gun and can decide what you wish to do about your life."[122] Another woman with small children wore a locket on a thin gold chain; while beautiful, the locket contained a meticulously folded paper and inside were small pellets of cyanide for her and her children to consume rather than face capture by Native Americans.[123] In these cases and probably many others, the threat came to naught and neither the pills nor the gun were ever employed.[124]

To other men, such precautions were impractical or unattractive. They left their homes and families to conduct business in nearby towns or county seats, to work fields, to hunt, to fight Indians, and for a variety of other reasons. Yet the terror experienced by the women left behind them was crushingly painful, even though it might be inspired by imagination rather than by reality. Given the intensity of their terror, numerous women maintained equanimity and even rejected alarmist thinking regarding natives. Furthermore, despite nineteenth-century stereotypes of hysterical women and stoic men, not all men were as imperturbable as they were reputed to have been. Despite supposedly steady hands and stout hearts, men's courage occasionally displayed cracks.

Men were also scared. Some imagined a few American Indians turning into hordes. In one case, "hundreds" of Indians turned out to be closer to fifteen, and in another instance, "thousands were actually forty Indians."[125] This tendency toward exaggeration was viewed with scorn by more implacable men. Byron McKinstry, a member of a train headed toward the California gold fields in 1850, jeeringly wrote in his journal about a fellow traveler. He wished "the Indians had Potts and half a dozen more of our co. that I could name, then our Indian trouble would be at an end, at least the imaginary part of them." A few days later McKinstry added: "We had a hard rain last night—and an alarm of Indians!!! Blood and murder what shall we do? We shall surely all be slain!! Why did we not make our wills and have our lives insured before we adventured among these horrible savages!" He wrote that later, as he was sleeping in his tent,

> Bang! Bang! from the guns of the sentinels . . . the cry of Indians! Indians! from voices in every direction. . . . I commenced dressing

quite cooly. . . . But soon the voice of our captain and the valiant
Potts made us take to the rain to defend ourselves against those
grim savages. . . . After walking round an hour or so, and listening to many valiant speeches . . . I was permitted to go to bed,
and I got a fine nap before day.[126]

McKinstry thought that some white civilians were as silly as
Captain Potts. During one false alarm, the women of the camp screamed
and swung their bonnets, convincing the men that Indians were killing
them. McKinstry wryly noted: "I don't expect that the poor souls will
get over their fright in a month, and I am not sure that all the men will.
If there had been Indians within hearing they certainly would have
fled!"[127] McKinstry's record also reveals that it was not just women who
were inclined to allow their anxieties to overwhelm them. In fact, one
male migrant on his way to Montana in the 1860s frankly admitted that
he imagined that "every weed and bunch of grass" that stirred was an
American Indian.[128] Like the women, many men imagined all kinds of
people and things to be Indians.[129] In one case, three approaching Indian
warriors turned out, upon closer inspection, to appear more like Indian
women. In the final analysis, they were three emigrant women from that
very train.[130] In another case, some distant objects thought to be war-
ring Indians caused the men to grab their weapons and to fall upon the
ground, concealing themselves from the advancing opponents. "Every
gun was charged & every eye gazed eagerly at the Indians," one partic-
ipant wrote, "when, lo, & behold, the Indians proved to be six large elk
crossing the river."[131]

Men who behaved hysterically were the objects of derision, yet virtually no woman criticized herself or other women for "cowardly" conduct. Women were expected and allowed to display emotions that were
not considered suitable for men. Charged with protecting train members, wagons, and stock, and possessing a supposedly strong nature, men
were expected to demonstrate bravery and equanimity. They were to
stand unmoving in the face of danger. When threatened by an Indian
offensive, they were not allowed to surrender to the luxury of panic that
the women were permitted.

Accordingly, most men tried to live up to dictates for their gender.
Although masculinist tenets were popular throughout the nineteenth

century, they intensified around the turn of the twentieth century. Between Wild Bill Cody's parade of Rough Riders, which he introduced in 1893, and Theodore Roosevelt's military Rough Riders in the War of 1898, expectations of men to be brave and even invincible intensified notably.[132] Whether early or late in the era, however, westering men often showed themselves to be human beings. Predictably, there were instances of outright cowardice, as in the case of the Englishman who took refuge under a wagon during a threatened siege and loudly proclaimed himself an alien while invoking the protection of King George.[133] But most men maintained that they did not fear Native Americans and would route them through strength of arms. Such assertions led to the organization of protective associations, in the appointment of military "captains" to lead trains, in arming and drilling by men, and in the posting of many guards.[134] Often such precautions were found to be what migrant Fancher Stimson described as "cumbersome and undesirable," especially as the fear of Indians was quickly dispelled. Typically, they not only disbanded but became a "subject of merriment."[135] In other instances, such measures remained very much in force so that white people were always prepared for an Indian attack.[136]

These military efforts by frontiersmen etched in sharp relief the differences between the men and women of an expedition. While Samuel Newcomb described the ineffective actions of women, his wife Susan noted in her 1867 diary that "the men over hauled the Indians yesterday." At another point she recorded that some men hunting Indians to locate their camps had returned with three native scalps. Stuck at home, unable to take any action herself, and fearful for her husband's safety, Susan retaliated with invective, the only way available to her to cope with the frustrating situation. She railed against the U.S. government, which she felt did not supply whites with adequate protection, and against American Indians. In her view, President Ulysses S. Grant should personally battle Indians until he was willing to order out enough military power "to scalp every red skin in the universe." When soldiers were finally sent after the "red imps of the earth" she hoped that the army would "scalp the last one of them, for they are too bad to be endured."[137] Her husband Samuel, while also vitriolic in his complaints against the government and the natives, was much more capable of taking such action as negotiating treaties, redeeming captives, chasing Indians, and protecting the stock.[138]

Seemingly, such an aggressive stance on the part of frontiersmen should have allayed much of the women's distress. Yet women were not always impressed with either the good sense or the physical abilities of their men. Instead, they were often doubtful, even caustic, in their statements regarding the protection from American Indians afforded them by their menfolk. There seemed to be too much braggadocio in the air to indicate the possibility of reasoned and effective response by men. As Lydia Waters phrased it: "I should say we had some mighty men of valor with us. The Indians would die of fright as soon as they saw them! These mighty men could fire forty shots out of their wagons without reloading!"[139] Other women joked about their men's military might. Surveying her well-armed husband with his bowie knife and pistols, Lucy Cooke remarked, "Hope he won't hurt himself."[140] And after watching the men of her family fire fifty shots to kill one cow, Maria Schrode wryly observed, "We think the Indians would be in great danger if they should attack us."[141]

White women also suspected white men of causing alarms to gain something for themselves. After enduring several traumatic scares with other terrified women and children, the Texan settler Julia Sinks concluded that they were largely the work of "ladies' men," who had created the threat of siege to excite "a host of fears for the pleasure of allaying them." According to Sinks, there were several men in Austin "who fought windmills diligently, bringing in their somber visages as if laden with the news of terrible calamity." Once the women were sufficiently alarmed, these men would pass among them, "assiduously" offering their protection."[142] Even more than ladies' men, Sinks distrusted the influential white leader Samuel Houston, especially when he took the part of American Indians. Julia Sinks emphasized that although Houston was a charismatic figure with a widespread following, his eloquence on behalf of Indians was wasted. According to her, most Texans "hardly classed" Indians "with the people in its usual sense," and Houston's "sympathies were outside the common pale of thought."[143]

As evil as Sinks's men appear, there were other frontiersmen whose motives were more devious than the solicitation of attention and gratitude from the womenfolk. These were the various traders who used scares to further their own economic ventures and who were considered by some to be "as roguish and treacherous as the Indians themselves."[144] In some cases, they initiated alarms to draw cavalry to the area in order to sell them their corn and other goods. In other instances, they stirred up the natives themselves, intending to plunder their goods during the ensuing confusion.[145] Government agents, renegade Frenchmen, Union and Confederate soldiers, Catholic priests, and Mormons were also often accused of inciting Indian scares to enhance their own economic and religious ends.[146]

Women's remarks reveal a gender-based tension regarding men's and women's abilities to handle themselves in the face of danger. The men clearly expected the women to be nervous and silly. Surprisingly, given nineteenth-century injunctions about male strength, many women anticipated ineptness and even irrationality on the part of men. Evidently, women did not meekly accept the role of helpless protectee to courageous male protectors. Barred by social norms from taking matters into their own hands, they could express their dissatisfaction with the lack of security through jibes directed toward the men. One might even argue that if women had felt relatively safe and protected by their men they would not have acted in the panic-stricken manner that they so often displayed. In turn, the inability of both males and females to grapple effectively with the threat of native violence contributed to rumors and scares.

—— The Indian Perspective ——

In the face of invading whites, Indians initially went about their own business. Because Indians had not been briefed regarding white migrants and their sensibilities, they continued hunting buffalo and other game animals, as well as pursuing petty infighting and more substantial wars among tribes. On the Great Plains and in the Southwest, Indians were effective hunters and fighters. Thanks to the Spanish reintroduction of the horse to North America, these groups were mounted and highly mobile. In addition to customary weapons, they had obtained white weapons and ammunitions from white traders at such places as Bent's Fort in New Mexico. Moreover, Indians were puzzled. Although early white mountain men had mixed with them, observed certain rituals, and had no interest in taking their land, the hordes of whites entering their lands avoided them, were rude, and seemed to want nothing but land. Especially after the whites' war among themselves during the early 1860s, more white troops accompanied white settlers. The Indians had no way of knowing that they were caught not only in a massive white migration, but in the economic transformation of the West to a capitalistic system.[147]

At first, Indians had difficulty in understanding why their everyday activities so alarmed white people. They did not realize that settlers like Agnes Cleaveland believed that American Indians, who had lived by "the natural bounty of the land or the garnered resources of their neighbors," would eventually direct their greed or ire against whites. Seeing no problem, Indians took no precautions to keep their hunts or battles from white eyes.[148] As a result, overanxious whites misinterpreted hunting parties as war parties, ceremonial makeup as war paint, religious dances as war dances, and a lone sentinel as an advance guard.[149] Indians must have thought that whites were superficial observers, a point on which they were absolutely correct.

Internecine warfare among Indians also frightened whites. Peaceful Indians who asked whites for refuge and protection discovered that white reactions varied widely and were seldom satisfactory. For example, one group of migrants sheltered frightened natives, supplying them with food and other small gifts. Another train, however, simply allowed some scared Indians to follow it, as one migrant explained it, to have the advantage of numbers against "the much dreaded Sioux."[150] Other whites extended little sympathy to Indians, especially if they were Pawnee who, due to their constant discord with Sioux and Cheyenne neighbors, were forlorn and starving. One female traveler expressed dismay when what she called "the gallant men" of her train drove the Pawnee "forth without mercy," but another voiced the majority view that because intertribal warfare was a great source of unrest for migrants, the Indians were best dispatched.[151]

Eventually, Indians concluded that it was dangerous to approach whites, the new "other" in their land, who usually flew into a rage and became exceedingly hostile when Indians came near.[152] Indians could see that white people, especially men, were belligerent and ready to shoot before talking. Consequently, thousands of Indians impoverished by white destruction of their animals, grass, and water, or simply curious about the new breed of white people, learned to draw near whites very carefully. Again and again, bright and inquisitive Indians scared white women beyond belief. In turn, anxiety-ridden whites insulted Indians who, as one sympathetic migrant said, "wanted no more than to ask questions, to beg, or to simply visit." In 1846, a typical botched confrontation occurred when a large group of mounted and well-outfitted Native American men approached an Oregon-bound party. The Indians watched as white men hastily distributed weapons and pushed women and children behind wagons. What did these people expect from Indians? they wondered. They surprised the white men by asking only for information. As one white man later remembered, despite the Indians' warlike appearance, they "failed to molest" him and his party in any way, but "told them that they were going to war with another tribe." Although outright disaster was averted, the Indians seized the opportunity to make apparent their ruffled feelings regarding white suspicions. As a result, white men distributed a "generous supply of tobacco" before the Indians departed, convinced that whites were high-strung indeed.[153]

Indians also failed to understand white settlers. Such Indians as Comanches and Apaches, who were running out of their traditional sustenance of buffalo and small game, raided settlers' stock. In return, white settlers accused Indians of theft, a position difficult for Indians to accept since whites had destroyed the wild game. Indians, who had to feed their families, raided settlers' herds with some regularity and often caused outbreaks of violence in the process.[154] To Indians' dismay, when they harmed or killed a white, rumors flew with incredible speed for many miles in every direction. Word-of-mouth reports, letters, and newspapers magnified the Indian threat to unrecognizable dimensions. As early as 1857, for example, two white women settlers in Algona, Iowa, who were buffeted by one story after another about the Spirit Lake Massacre for many months, finally wrote their family in Connecticut that the stories were "large" and so numerous that they did not know what to believe. One added, "If they all increase in proportion, I don't know what they would be when they get to you." The other woman assured her cousin that she hoped not to "see an Indian for ten years" because "it is not very pleasant to be in fear of them all the time." The upshot of the affair was that "for a week we had six persons beside our own family here nights, and six guns well loaded, but we did not use them."[155]

Native American leaders, who were neither stupid or uninformed as many whites thought, were privy to white reactions. In the case of the Mimbres Apaches in New Mexico, for example, Chief Victorio received information during the 1860s and 1870s from his own scouts, as well as from white traders and travelers. He knew when the whites' civil war ended in 1864 and watched with apprehension as grizzled war veterans, Confederate and Union, took their place in the West's Indian-fighting army. Victorio also knew that the citizens of nearby Pinos Altos had raised a cry heard in the territorial capital, Santa Fe. In 1866, outraged citizens implored officials to establish a reservation for the Mimbreños, but instead the legislature gave to whites the right to form volunteer companies to hunt Indians, and take for their pay any plunder they found, including keeping Indian captives as slaves. More than one train halted its journey or disappeared entirely, whereas entire families left New Mexico Territory because of Victorio and his fighting force.[156] All this Victorio knew.

Victorio could have put down his arms and surrendered, but every peace treaty he had ever signed became a travesty. From intelligence, he understood that whites intended to make Indians dependent, unable to feed or protect themselves, and doing as the U.S. government decreed. But he was no longer willing to watch his inadequately supplied people waste away on white reservations.[157] After hiding the young, old, and infirm in havens in the San Mateo Mountains, Victorio's men raided settlers' stock and even seized animals meant to feed the white military. As the number of Mimbreños declined, Victorio could not depend on a white-style draft to replenish his forces. Apache women, who had influence and certain rights, increasingly accompanied men on hunting and military expeditions, as did Victorio's warrior sister Lozen. Apache women performed such domestic work as setting up camps, preparing meals, and giving medical care. They also undertook heavier work, including digging rifle pits, building stone breastworks, standing guard, and carrying knives and pistols that they were trained to use.[158] For all this, Victorio learned that the white leader, the territorial governor Robert B. Mitchell, called Victorio and his people outlaws and asked for their extermination. Although Victorio saw the folly of raiding, especially in lives lost, white policies and promises came to nothing.

When Victorio and other Indian leaders continued their resistance, infuriated whites demanded that the U.S. government "do something." At the same time, a few whites spoke on behalf of Native Americans. In the West, women especially expressed sympathy. In 1868, for example, army wife Margaret Carrington declared that colonialism—popularly called Manifest Destiny in the United States—gave American Indians horrendous choices: "abandon his home, fight himself to death, or yield to the white man's mercy."[159] Meanwhile, back east, an Indian reform movement was taking shape, but its primary weapon was rhetoric. Even at the end of the nineteenth century, many easterners continued to believe negative depictions of Native Americans. For instance, during the 1890s an Oklahoma woman tried to persuade some eastern visitors that some of her best friends and favorite house guests were Indians. She took the easterners to a camp where her native acquaintances would "all gather around" and pat her on the back. Yet the easterners drew back from the crowd, looking like "they were ready to run." Sadly enough, she never convinced her visitors that American Indians were more than malicious and contemptible beings, nor did she ever allay the hurt feelings of her Indian friends.[160]

This lack of empathy between Indians and whites led to some pathetic situations. Indians who begged scraps of food from white migrants discovered that whites frequently refused to speak to the natives who approached them. What the Indians could not know was that whites believed that Indians would perceive them as cowardly or as easy marks for begging and thievery.[161] Following the advice of guidebooks and other migrants, most white travelers treated natives with disrespect, suspicion, and distrust. In 1857, a group of Pawnees came to a camp where migrants were "nooning," and immediately the order went out to not give them a thing. "It was thought," a member of the group,

Helen Carpenter, explained, "that they would follow and be a nuisance if shown any kindness." When the Pawnee continued to hang around, they saw that Carpenter was having trouble eating her lunch. She later explained that she could not eat "with those poor wretches watching every mouthful like hungry dogs." The Pawnee were thankful when Carpenter's mother slipped some food to them. They did not follow the train or give the travelers any trouble, which left Carpenter and her mother free from suspicion. "We do not coincide with all of Uncle Sam's views," Carpenter remarked, "but he is the 'boss' of the train and as such his views must be respected."[162]

Other Indians were disgusted by white attitudes, which usually combined a pettiness of spirit with an utter disregard for the American Indian as a human being. Indians were disheartened by white migrants who, convinced of their inherent right to invade native lands, refused to pay tolls to cross bridges that natives had built. Indians found themselves captured and forced to serve as guides for white parties.[163] Other Indians experienced white needling and attempts to make them appear foolish. They encountered white men who not only swaggered and bragged that they could whip any band of natives, but treated them contemptuously on a personal basis. "It was their usual custom whenever the Indians approached our camp or sat by our camp fires," Lavinia Porter complained, "to tease and play various tricks upon them."[164]

The consequences of white "tricks" ranged from disrespect to physical harm. For instance, American Indians were frequently fleeced in trade, an occurrence that delighted many whites, supposed Christians. Disregard for the basic humanity of American Indians motivated a variety of other schemes that resulted in white profit at native expense. In one of the more macabre tricks, a young doctor allegedly severed Black Hawk's head from his recently deceased corpse and boiled the flesh from it with the intention of publicly exhibiting the skull for a fee. Intimidated by the near uprising he provoked among Black Hawk's people, the doctor was reported to have deposited the skull with a friend, who sold it to a museum that subsequently burned down, destroying the skull.[165] To some Indians, such treatment of an Indian's corpse condemned his spirit to similar disfigurement in the afterworld. To virtually all, it constituted the greatest of insults.

Frequently, a white prank involved potential physical danger to a native. One such incident was related by a Colorado settler who explained that a "future divinity student—although at that time he was harboring no such holy intentions—loaded up some sticks of stove-wood with healthy charges of powder and left them on the woodpile in the hope that some of the roving Indians . . . would carry them off, put them on a camp fire and receive the benefits." Subsequently, the young man forgot which logs were doctored, carried some of them into the house, put one in the kitchen stove, and when the smoke of the explosion had cleared away he realized something was wrong.[166] Although that prankster received a just reward, most of the others did not. Indians usually ended up suffering. For instance, a group of Indians contracted smallpox after trading with white men for infested bedding. When the Indians realized what had happened, they retaliated by steal-ing stock and keeping local settlers in a general state of upheaval.[167]

Indians also received physical abuse at the hands of whites. Indians found it difficult to believe that whites, who deplored such practices among Indians, took scalps, hostages, and captives.[168] Indians thought such whites to be vicious, savage, and barbarous. An early episode demonstrated to Indians just how bestial white men could act. Shortly after the 1847 Whitman massacre in Oregon, whites killed a chief named Pe Pe Mox-Mox. A white man tied one end of a rope around the chief's neck and the other to his saddle horn. He rode through camp shouting at Indian prisoners that the same would happen to them if they killed any more white settlers. White men then scalped the chief, which humil-iated the Indians.[169] During subsequent years, Indians received all kinds of injuries from whites. For instance, Indian women and men were the targets of white men's potshots.[170] As such events tend to do, they often escalated to a pitch that caused not only bitterness and hostility but fre-quently the deaths of natives. As might be expected, Indians usually sought revenge for the pointless murder of their companions.[171]

Understandably, Native Americans felt misunderstood and misused. For revenge, the more unscrupulous among them took advantage of white superstitions and prejudices. For example, aware of white fears regarding scalping, some Indian tormentors were not above deriving amusement from threatening to take scalps. When a number of Indian men entertained themselves by seizing Mollie Stanford's two long braids and brandishing their hunting knives, they ridiculed her for being scared.[172] On another occasion, three Indians cut off two young boys' hair with their hunting knives. They were appalled at their harsh punishment. The terror they inspired in local settlers gained them not only a stern lecture from the Indian agent, but a drastic cut in their rations for that month.[173] Other Indians appeared to delight in scaring whites by wearing scalp locks dangling from their belts, which only intensified whites' concerns.[174]

Yet other Native Americans developed a perverse sense of humor that frequently revealed itself in their teasing and torment of frontier people. An aged Indian couple startled an Oklahoma woman who discovered them standing quietly in her kitchen; they laughed at her discomfiture and departed.[175] Begging Indians accosted a male migrant, thrusting their hands into his pockets, taking a kerchief from around his neck, and mocking him with raised arrows. The man's companion later recalled that the victim gave his tormentors "leg bail for security." The natives laughed uproariously as he scampered back to his camp.[176]

Some Indians even liked to upset white women by threatening to take their children. On one occasion, an Indian chieftain teased an Oklahoma woman by asking through gestures for her two-year-old boy. She recoiled from him. When she recovered enough to shout no in the Indian's face, the man threw back his head, laughed heartily, and departed. According to the woman's white neighbors, "the Indians meant no harm and were merely trying to be friendly," a fact lost on her.[177] In a later case, intoxicated local Indian men entered the house of another Oklahoma woman, where they carried her daughter around and shot bullets into the fireplace. She stood her ground, which elicited respect from the pranksters.[178] One Texas woman was not as stalwart when an intoxicated Indian seized a young boy, telling him that the "sweetest morsel ever known was a white man's heart."[179]

Indian women also engaged in making migrants appear ridiculous before their companions. They especially preyed on inexperienced men who, responding to the women's blandishments, handed over money and headed toward the bushes with one of them. The woman led the way and then suddenly ran off to a group of her own people, leaving the greenhorn to face the giggling and applause of the native women, the guffaws of the Indian men, and the taunts of his own comrades.[180]

Even though some Indians seemed to go out of their way to frighten whites, others hoped to gain something for themselves by creating scares.[181] For example, Indians would warn white travelers of impending attack, sometimes to ingratiate themselves with the migrants, other times to chase a train away from their territory.[182] In other instances, one tribe would revenge itself on Indians who had been friendly to settlers. By raising the cry of depredation, they hoped to turn the settlers against the traitors.[183] Once in a while, an individual American Indian even attempted to aggrandize personal power through implementing the fear of an uprising. In 1889, for example, a Crow medicine man used an alleged vision of white extermination to gain what a white woman settler described as "a dangerous following of restless spirits among his own people."[184]

Perhaps worst of all, even the most well-intentioned Indians found whites impossible to fathom. One Indian stood in the kitchen of the Texan settler, Ellen Bird-Dumont, making his needs known through gestures and actions. Bird-Dumont, however, was so jumpy that she could not comprehend the Indian's intentions.[185] When seven more Indian men pushed their way into her house, they saw that Ella Bird-Dumont was terrified. Their leader increased his efforts to appear friendly and to "talk" to her through motions. The object of their visit was to trade their government-issue clothing for groceries, but Bird-Dumont's stock of food was short and she vehemently shook her head no. When the men discovered her rifle, however, their leader became determined to trade for it. Although she continued to shake her head fearfully, he began showing her the items of clothing that he wore. To the Indians, the woman appeared stupid so their leader took off his clothes, item by item. He was quite satisfied with his trade, clothes for a rifle, but when Bird-Dumont's friend suddenly realized that he thought he had a satisfactory trade going, the two women signed him that there was no trade and he should re-dress himself immediately. Fortunately, he was not embarrassed and, laughing, proceeded to put his clothes back on.[186]

These and thousands of similar episodes demonstrated a lack of sympathy, understanding, and communication between Indians and whites. Indians were as often puzzled by white behavior as whites were by theirs. Had more positive feelings existed, they might have made white entry into Indian lands safer for everyone involved. Instead, miscommunication after miscommunication occurred. During the Civil War, for example, a Choctaw man who tried to help several Arkansas women find their way could only stand and watch as the women screamed and fled. Later, an amused white soldier told the women they had no cause for alarm because the Choctaws "to the last man were Southern." Far from intending to return with "a band of tomahawkers," as they had assumed, the man hoped to assist them.[187] During the 1880s, another pointless incident involved an Indian man wearing a top hat. A white man hired to protect the women of a white family bragged to a companion that he could put a bullet hole through the Indian's hat without touching his head. In fact, he grazed the old man's scalp. Indians retaliated by burning the women's home, destroying the silver and other items of value, and shooting the beloved dog. One of the women later explained that white settlement "was all very kindly up to a point, but beyond the kindness was a blank wall." In her view, the cruelties exchanged between Indians and whites had destroyed "warmth" and made Indians "cynical" toward whites. She added that the hardest lesson she learned in Montana was not to expect any "affection" between members of racial groups.[188]

More recently, a number of Native American women supported the latter viewpoint. One, a Yavapai, born and reared on the San Carlos reservation in Arizona, argued that Anglo-Indian relationships would never work because white people disliked Indians, and Indians disliked whites. According to her, such enmity was inevitable because the two groups were "different tribes." She believed Native Americans were "better off" living away from whites and following their own ways. Other Indian women said they had so often witnessed whites' brutality to their people that the chasm between the two groups would always exist.[189]

During the frontier period, the inability or unwillingness of Indians and whites to communicate led to the victimization of untold numbers of Indians. The ingenuous, the curious, and even the most well-intended

American Indians took the blame for a variety of ills. Whether they had any part in the creation of these problems was often not really germane to the consequences that they suffered. Indians experienced a range of effects from embarrassment to persecution for trouble they had not caused. Also, they often experienced starvation, poverty, and the loss of their land due to misinformed government policies generated by prejudiced and harried bureaucrats.[190]

Of course, Indians also lost their lives. Not only were they exterminated without quarter in many instances, but individual natives also fell at the hands of distrustful frontier people. Byron McKinstry told of one such case, in which a white male traveler swapped horses with an Indian who was overtaken the next day by a rear portion of the same party. When they recognized their companion's horse they accused the Indian of stealing it. Fearing their ire, he fled. His flight was perceived as evidence of his guilt; thus, they fired immediately, killing the innocent man.[191]

From their contact with whites, then, Indian were amused, confused, poverty stricken, or dead. Seemingly, Native Americans had much more to complain about than whites. In reality, white people killed more Indians than were killed by Indians between 1840 and 1860. In addition, some 90 percent of emigrant killings occurred west of the South Pass rather than on the Great Plains, as legend would have us believe. And even when such killings did take place they often resulted from individual incidents rather than from the large-scale murders so often described by the overworked term *massacre*.[192]

On the one hand, it might be argued that white actions were not extreme but were necessary measures against an unstable and threatened native population that did indeed assail and kill whites. On the other, it might be suggested that white behavior created as much trouble with Native Americans as it averted. Aggressive conduct and the harsh sentiments that accompanied it did nothing to encourage peaceful coexistence or harmonious relations between groups. Certainly, the widespread existence of anti-Indian passions and the incidents that they spawned leave little doubt concerning the reasons why so many frontierswomen were apprehensive, at best, and filled with terror, at worst, at the possibility of encountering real American Indians. Between the stories they had heard before leaving home and the rumors, scares, and alarmism they had been subjected to since leaving home, they were primed for a series of traumatic experiences.

Interestingly enough, women's mental states often had little or nothing to do with real American Indians. Whites made no attempt to learn about Indians and their cultures, nor did they send advance parties to inform and ready Indians. All that Indians had in the way of preparation was exposure to white traders, trappers, and missionaries. Because these people were few in number and usually civil, they gave Indians inaccurate expectations about the hordes of pushy whites that would follow. Nor did the U.S. government make an attempt to designate certain lands for settlement and enforce those boundaries. Partly because whites dismissed Indians and thought they had a right to Indians' land and partly because no one envisioned the enormous number of migrants who would go west, American Indians were left to deal with the situation on their own. Consequently, a self-fulfilling prophecy was activated. Anti-Indian sentiment in the "states," in Canada, and in Europe prepared migrants to meet scurrilous natives and the migrants, taut with fear, acted in ways that too often confirmed their fears.

How then would white women react when they met an Indian or Indians personally? Would they see only the Indians whom they expected to encounter, or would they prove to be flexible and open enough to revise their views once they confronted real people? While living with rumors and alarmism, would white women think and act in a rational and independent fashion? These questions have surprising and significant answers.

—— **Chapter Four** ——

FRONTIER PROCESS: HUMANIZING
AMERICAN INDIANS

Since the majority of Americans and Europeans were more receptive to the idea of the "bad" Indian than to that of the "good" Indian, migrants headed west with a view of American Indians that was more negative than positive. Because the existence of bad Indians confirmed the rightness of white migration and white superiority, migrants who turned westward during the early decades of the nineteenth century or started their treks later expected to meet barbarous savages. At the same time, most of these people hoped that American Indians might turn out to be the noble savages described by Jean Jacques Rousseau and James Fenimore Cooper: "nice" Indians who would prove helpful rather than troublesome.

These contradictory expectations resulted from the long, complex conditioning process that migrants experienced in regard to native peoples. Female emigrants had additional reasons for searching out despicable Indians, to whom they would minister, and ennobling Indians, who would help them survive. These women presented portraits of Indians that overstated their undesirable traits and exaggerated their favorable qualities, thus giving a picture of Indians that was paradoxical and fraught with ambivalence.

Further complicating the inconsistency in women's views of western natives was female migrants' tendency to shift toward generous interpretations of American Indians. For some women this change occurred rather quickly, often during the westward trek itself. For others, especially those who were abruptly deposited in a raw frontier settlement by a ship or a railroad, the metamorphosis came more slowly. Whatever the timing, numerous women replaced their conception of American Indians as a combination of saint and savage with a view of natives as human beings to be empathized with, perhaps even liked. Although white women and men were exposed to similar influences, such as the ferocity or the gentleness of the natives they encountered, as well as whether or not their party had violent interchanges with Indians, white men seldom exhibited a like degree of contradiction or change in their interpretations of Indians.

Women's perceptions frequently altered because their perceptions of American Indians were linked to changing ideas about themselves as females. As women's beliefs about themselves modified, women thought of themselves less as civilizers and more as physically adept people. Consequently, they were able to see native peoples in a more humane way. A woman who headed westward with trepidation regarding Native Americans could, and often did, become sympathetic to those very Indians.

—— Finding "Bad" Indians ——

Like Indians, white women were considered by nineteenth-century society to have two sides to their natures, one superior and the other inferior. The superior side of women's character derived from their exceptional moral abilities, the quality that made them moral guardians of home and family. In addition, women's superiority included other admirable traits; they were kind, gentle, passive, religious, domestic, pure, and refined. At the same time, the inferior aspect of women's nature resulted from their weakness. Although morally superior, women were believed to be physically and intellectually inferior. They had small brains and weak muscles. They were helpless, childlike, nonassertive, indecisive, and unable to protect themselves.[1]

Having heard all their lives these assertions regarding female character, most women accepted them and carried them west. As they assessed the various American Indian groups they met, their concepts of themselves helped shape their interpretations of Indians. While viewing themselves as harbingers of civilization, women saw Indians as potential subjects for female reform efforts. Because women were taught to see themselves as moral guardians and the protectors of civilization, they perceived Indians as uncivilized, morally deficient, and brutalized by their primitive existence.[2] Sara Smith, a recently wed minister's wife, remarked:" I long to be telling the dying heathen the story of the cross. O, how happy I shall be in my laboring for the good of those dear Indians. May God prepare me to do them good."[3]

Women's assumed superiority led women to emphasize the American Indian's supposed inferiority. As reformers, white women had to see their subjects as savage and rapacious, in need of women's influence. Women undertook the journey filled with hopeful anticipation at the changes they might bring, yet trembled at the prospect of their first confrontation with a real Indian. Because white women came from a society that emphasized the construction of Native Americans as evil, they spent their days on the trail fearfully scouring the countryside for any sign of Indians.[4] When one California-bound traveler of the 1860s heard shots fired in a nearby camp, she concluded that Indians were nearby. Another female emigrant recalled that an Indian dog who followed her party kept them "in a continual state of excitement."[5] In 1850, one woman even scanned the horizon with a telescope in order to detect Native Americans. Although no one in her party was alarmed when she spotted several Indians and all were able to sleep that night, she not only remained awake but did not change her clothing, "neither shoe nor bonnet." She was prepared for an attack that never came.[6]

Like trail women, female settlers frequently demonstrated a willingness to see things in a dramatic way. During the 1880s, for example, Agnes Morley Cleaveland viewed the long-deserted site of a massacre near her new home in New Mexico. Although it was marked by only two grave-shaped mounds of loose rock and the faintest suggestion of a covering of ash, she insisted that her mind's eye saw the "dash of howling savages" from the timber beside the fading wagon tracks that were the road. In her imagination, Cleaveland witnessed what she called "the swift, terrible slaughter of the surprised and helpless men; the oxen driven away to their own slaughter, leaving behind them the remnants of what had been human bodies and a fire that blazed fearsomely."[7]

What a surprise it must have been for these women to discover that the "first" Indians they met were often friendly. This was the case, at least, during the 1840s, 1850s, and 1860s, when Native Americans had limited exposure to whites. Indians had not yet formed their own social construction of whites. As Indians met mean-spirited, acquisitive whites, their folklore adapted to include the rude invaders.[8] The first meeting between Indians and whites usually occurred just beyond the Missouri River, since St. Joseph and Council Bluffs were the primary departure points for migrants. Even as the American Indians in this region became accustomed to a steady stream of travelers through their domain, they were more curious than predatory. Consequently, women frequently remarked that the first Indians they met were not nearly as troublesome as they had expected. In 1846, for example, while Polly Purcell's family crossed the Missouri River on their way to Oregon they were surrounded by what Polly described as "500 warriors." Although Purcell's group prepared to defend themselves, they were astonished and relieved that no battle ensued.[9] Three years later, Martha Morgan noted that the Sioux her party met in the same area were "ostensibly very friendly."[10]

During the next several decades, women continued to report that the American Indians in the Missouri River region were peaceable, friendly, and annoying only in their habit of begging.[11] Women's fears frequently dissolved into curiosity or even amusement. When Pauline Wonderly crossed the Missouri River at Kanesville (today Council Bluffs, Iowa) in 1852, she felt that she was entering "the domain of the dreaded Indian." Instead of being attacked, however, she was treated to an "exhibition of Indian markmanship in which native men shot their bows and arrows at nickels which the gullible whites gladly threw into the air." As they collected and counted their coins, Indians surely had the final laugh after these encounters.[12] In 1853, while crossing the Kansas River, Elizabeth Goltra was amazed to learn that her first Indians accepted gifts of bread, meat, and a dime, thanked her, and went on their way.[13] In 1862, Ada Millington discovered that the first native Americans she met near Fort Kearney asked not for coins, but simply wanted to shake hands with the migrants and say, "how, how."[14]

Ada Vogdes was another woman whose terror of American Indians was not borne out by her first meeting with them. On her way toward Fort Laramie in 1868, she noted that "it was a fearful feeling to me, in the midst of an Indian country, & far from home." By the time her party reached Chimney Rock, she added that it had seen no Indians but believed it was in the midst of them. "This kind of life," she lamented, "does not suit the female portion of creation. A woman was never intended to cross these Plains." When she finally met some Native Americans near the fort, the incident passed without drama, for they encountered only a small party of friendly Indians on a hunting expedition. Vogdes's pleasant experience did little, however, to change her ideas. Because she clung to her terror of Indians, she made herself miserable for some time. She was unable to enjoy the social life of the fort, spent sleepless nights while her husband was away, and refused to leave the garrison's protective walls for outings.[15]

Clearly, years of being steeped in anti-Indian prejudice were not suddenly erased by a meeting with friendly tribespeople. This was especially the case for women who viewed themselves as moral missionaries to "barbarians." Teachings concerning the moral nature of women and the "savage" natures of American Indians held sway, regardless of evidence to the contrary. Therefore, first meetings with Indians, even if cordial, were tense. "I was very much scared," one female traveler wrote during the early 1850s. Others stayed closer to camp or were caught up in "scares" as a result of Indians' proximity.[16] During the early 1860s, one trail woman viewing her first Indian beggars commented that, although Indians may have looked pleasant to train members who had seen them before, they looked "very savage" to her. She added that "they are monstrous looking creatures to inhabit such beautiful soil as we are now traveling through."[17] In 1864, Mary Warner jotted, "There were two Indians came to camp begging—they were the first we had seen and we were afraid of them."[18]

Such revulsion was not uncommon. Women reacted to the first Native Americans they met in light of their expectations rather than the reality standing before them. As early as 1848, a young woman encountering her first Indians outside St. Joseph explained that to her "frightened vision, dressed in their long macinaw blankets, with eagle feathers in their hair, they looked ten feet high."[19] As late as 1886, Allie Busby, visiting the quiet Mesquakis at the Tama agency in Iowa, responded in a similar manner: "Wild visions of tomahawk or scalping knife arose, while the Indian of romance disappeared altogether from our imagination."[20]

Not all women were intimidated by the presence of Native Americans along their routes. Rather, women displayed a spectrum of reactions. Some, like Lavinia Porter, were annoyed by the Indians, even though her party was not troubled by them to any extent.[21] Others were disillusioned not to find the color and dash that they anticipated. "We had expected to see feathered head-gear and painted faces," one explained. Another, headed for Montana in 1864, complained that the first Indian she spotted was a ragged, ugly creature who "was very disappointing as the 'Noble Red Man' we read about."[22]

The characteristic of American Indians that first attracted women's attention was their style of dress—or the lack of it. Coming from a Victorian culture that advocated covering the body with layers and complex types of apparel, women were shocked that these "barbaric" people wore little or no clothing.[23] Mary Sandford recalled that "the Indians were nude save for a throw over one shoulder, and a strap around the loins."[24] Mary Staples declared that their "clothing was very scant." Sallie Maddock added that they were "mostly naked." Margaret Hecox said that they frequently came "to our camp in a perfectly nude state." And Harriet Smith reported that, in encountering an Indian man, she was "a little streaked for he had nothing on but a blanket and great earrings and bracelet, all brass."[25] Apparently, Indians' state of undress did not stop these good Victorian women from looking, however.

White women were further appalled to discover that Indian children were seldom clothed.[26] Mary Fish wryly commented that the "papooses were perfectly naked and some of the seniors did not come very far from the same predicament."[27] This was a typical observation. Helen Carpenter was distraught that Pawnee Indians she met had "no clothing" and were wrapped only in "very unsanitary looking blankets." Standards of Victorian modesty stayed intact, at least in this situation. Carpenter was pleased to see that Indians were so "adept in the management" of their blankets that there was "no undue exposure of the person."[28]

It also seemed curious to frontierswomen that the very Indians who covered their bodies with little more than loin cloths, blankets, and moccasins wore a "profusion of ornaments" much like what one woman called a "Broadway belle."[29] Moreover, a variety of brass, silver, feather, and shell jewelry and other decoration accompanied bright hues applied to the face and torso. Failing to understand that jewelry and face paint frequently indicated a person's status, women judged some combinations as flashy or even outrageous.[30] To Eveline Alexander, for instance, Indian regalia was overwhelming because of its fullness and complexity. When she first encountered Utah Indians, she noted that their "costume exceeded anything" she had yet seen in its elaborateness and profuseness.[31]

Rather than extending a modicum of approval to the intricate outfits of American Indians, white women, who themselves favored complicated styles of clothing and ornamentation in their costumes, were less than complimentary. They were willing to judge the Indian "other" in dismissive terms. One woman observed that though "some are nearly naked, some dressed most fantastically." Still another noted that they were "decorated in the extreme of Indian dandyism."[32] In 1853, Celinda Hines Shipley remarked that she could not really make up her mind about the first group of Native Americans that she saw fully dressed. Although they seemed rather well clad, she explained in a caustic way that she could not assess them fairly since she had not seen many clothed Indians.[33] In 1856, on seeing her first Indians near Fort Kearney in 1856, Caroline Richardson wrote that they were "drest in their peculiar costome."[34]

White women gave their approval only when American Indian attire resembled white styles.[35] Wearing white-style clothing made Indians look less like the "other." Too, such imitation flattered white women who felt that their "civilizing" influence was already taking hold. Esther Hanna, for example, was pleased that some Sioux near Fort Laramie "prized any article of clothing from a white man very much."[36] Another group of Sioux, who were neatly attired like pseudo-whites, struck Margaret Hecox as "clean and wholesome in appearance."[37] And when Maria Norton came across American Indians dressed "with pants and caps," she pronounced them to be "the most respectable that we have seen."[38]

Obviously, white women imposed the standards of white society on people from a very different way of life.[39] Instead of being attracted by the color, spirit, and verve of native apparel, women's reactions tended toward discomfiture because American Indians dressed so differently from whites. Rather than admiring the craftwork involved in native jewelry, quill work, and beading, many women—at least initially—disregarded such decorations as pagan, ostentatious, or excessive. Given white women's fashions, these judgments were humorous. Characterized through the nineteenth century by such sartorial splendor as bustles, hoopskirts, and leg-o'-mutton sleeves, white women's styles now seem rather peculiar themselves. Women who aspired to a fifteen-inch waist through severe corseting, beginning in childhood, or by the extreme method of surgical removal of the lower ribs, might have shown some tolerance for Indian fashions. Yet these women, who saw themselves as the carriers of white civilization to aborigines, thought their own styles not at all eccentric, whereas they condemned those of the Indians as absurd.

In a similar shortsighted manner, women passed harsh judgments on what they perceived as low standards of cleanliness among Indian groups. White women, who bathed infrequently and doused themselves with "toilet water" and perfumes, disparaged various Native Americans as dirty and even filthy.[40] Although many Indians bathed frequently and cleansed themselves in sweat baths, they were perceived as unclean. Garbed in jewelry, paint, and colorful blankets, they were, according to Annie M. Zeigler, "picturesque" but "often dirty."[41] To Sallie Maddock, they were "disgusting and dirty looking." To Mary Staples, they formed "a filthy set," and to Mary Jane Guill, "a filthy and dirty set of Indians."[42] One woman was firmly convinced that "the romance of Indian life will not bear a closer inspection—they are neither more or less than filthy savages."[43]

As vitriolic as these opinions were, other women were even more vicious. One charged that "filth" and Indian were "inseparable." Another dismissed an entire village of natives with the statement that "the creatures looked too filthy to live."[44] Sarah Herndon maintained that Native Americans were "the most wretched looking human creatures" that she had ever seen. To her there was "nothing majestic, dignified, or noble-looking" about any of the Indians. Clearly disappointed that she had not found a Cooperesque Indian, Herndon caustically wrote, "I fail as yet to recognize 'The noble red man.'" She concluded that Indians were "lazy, dirty, obnoxious-looking creatures."[45]

One indication of white conceit was women's habit of calling Indians "creatures." The repeated use of "creature," which implies something less than a human being, suggests that to many white women American Indians were not really people.[46] One Indian practice that reinforced this view was the habit of some groups eating insects, including crickets and locusts. Women who sanctioned or even advocated drinking alcohol, devouring foods dripping with butter or pork grease, eating highly spiced or sugared dishes, and the use of tobacco and snuff, found the consumption of insects disconcerting, at best, and repulsive, at worst.

Women's appraisals of such practices were quick and acrimonious. When Algeline Ashley observed Utah Indians pulling wings off locusts and harvesting them in sacks, she declared that they were "very low Indians and very ugly looking."[47] The reaction was even more vituperative when the insects were lice. One California settler of the early 1850s watched an Indian woman eating lice from her husband's head, while, according to her, she was feeding him a few of the choice ones. The settler stated unequivocally that Indians were contemptible objects because of the "extreme indolence of their nature, the squalid conditions in which they live ... and the general imbecility of their intellects."[48] Helen Stewart indicated that she preferred Indians to avoid her camp because they were not only "the durtyist creatures I ever saw" but "they will pick the lice out of there head and eat them."[49] Unfortunately, these women seldom analyzed economic realities or customs of Indians. They were equally slow to understand the eating of fare that they found unacceptable. Instead, while white men encouraged Native Americans to entertain them by shooting at targets with bows and arrows, white women seemed compelled to watch Indians eat grasshoppers.[50]

In a similar distortion, white women associated "peculiar" odors with American Indians. They held the notion that the presence of Indians could be detected through their smells.[51] Whites often claimed they could smell a nearby Indian camp or that their horses and dogs responded with fear to the aroma of a Native American.[52] Whites thought that the Indian scent, which was indeed different from their own, was odd, unpleasant, and "strongly Indian."[53] Lydia Waters explained that the smell derived, at least in part, from the Indians' habit of rubbing themselves with "the entrails of some small fat animal, a skunk or raccoon, which looked as if it were dried in smoke." Instead of bathing with water, she said, they "took the greatest comfort lying in the sun rubbing themselves with these greasy insides."[54] Mary Fish claimed that the Sioux smeared their bodies with "oil which they procure from polecats." She phrased her opinion delicately, saying that the "effluvia arising from their persons is none of the sweetest." Frances Roe was more direct in stating that the Indians she met struck her as "simply, and only, painted, dirty and nauseous-smelling savages."[55] Again, white women failed to consider need or custom in judging Indian ways. They simply brushed aside American Indians as deficient in certain areas, a lack that white women intended to remedy.

Many frontierswomen were in for yet another shock. When they got close enough to an Indian to hold a conversation, they discovered that the average Indian spoke little or no English. With dismay, Ellen Adams remarked, "Some of the Indians could not understand a single word of English."[56] Other women noted that the native peoples they tried to converse with could not speak or understand English.[57] And Helen Carpenter called them "stupid" because they could not "understand French any better than they did English."[58] These women denigrated the validity of native tongues and assumed that English was the dominant means of communication for all western peoples. This ethnocentrism grew even more apparent when women found an American Indian who could manage a few words of the white's language, often a discovery to be recorded and sometimes disdained.[59] "They do not understand any of our language," one woman declared with a sneer, "and when they can speak a word of it they seem to think that they have done something very smart."[60] Whether Indians spoke no English at all, some English, or "good" English, they were often the targets of disdain on the part of white women.

As frontierswomen came into contact with various Indian customs, they continued to demonstrate puzzlement, derision, and outright racism. Some were amused by entire Indian villages moving to new campsites with equipment and other belongings mounted on pole carts pulled by dogs or, in other cases, with wigwams' poles strapped to ponies.[61] It would, of course, be revealing to know what Indians thought of white people with their overstuffed wagons and teams of cumbersome oxen. They may have been as amazed and as belittling as Harriet Ward. On her way to California in 1853, Ward said that when Indians moved they constituted "a strange and altogether interesting sight." To her, they were "poor half naked creatures with their all packed upon their horses." In 1854, Mary Burrell concurred. After counting 402 Sioux in a procession, Burrell asserted in a patronizing way that this "astonishing" sight was "equal to 50 caravans or circuses."[62] Evidently, neither Ward nor Burrell could view themselves and their companions objectively enough to see them as "strange," perhaps a veritable circus parade.

Such disrespect turned into outright irreverence when women encountered American Indian burial grounds, where corpses were placed on open racks. Women who thought underground burial was the "right" way to dispose of a corpse were shocked to see bodies in the open air. To Marie Nash, migrating to California in 1861, the bodies presented a "sad sight." Other women minimized Indian burial customs by seeing them as simple practicality in raising the bodies far enough off the ground to prevent pillaging and mutilation by wolves.[63] Some women had so little respect for Indian burial customs that they entered burial grounds to "visit" and to collect beads to wear as ornaments.[64]

White women also found strange the mating practices of American Indians. Given the white social construction of marriage as involving one white man and one white woman and of family as two white parents and their offspring, white women were stunned to find cases of intermarriage and the existence of métis, or what white women called "half-breeds." Moreover, white women feared the disappearance of white superiority if whites and Indians cohabited and produced mixed-race children. Some women reacted by chronicling every French trader who had an Indian wife and "half-breed" children.[65] Mary Fish acted amused by it all. When she encountered a French trader with two native wives, she quipped that "the Frenchmen go for amalgamation." When she saw another with a dozen wives she joked that he was simply "fond of a plural number."[66] Of course, white women's "jokes" denied the validity of Indian beliefs.

An even more condescending reaction to intermarriage was surprise that the parties involved got along well. White women could not believe that one of their own could actually love one of the "other." In 1852, Frances Sawyer was astounded that the children of one marriage seemed "playful and happy." Margaret Frink marveled that one trader's native wife was not only "quite good-looking" but "dressed in true American [meaning white] style."[67] One found it "perfectly astonishing" that "a man who has ever seen civilized people can intermarry with the natives and be contented to settle down and live as they do." She was amazed that Indian wives and daughters were spoken to "pleasantly, even fondly" by their white husbands and fathers, attained a certain amount of status among Indians and sometimes whites, and became respected cultural brokers, that is, go-betweens for white and Indian peoples. Books such as that by Mourning Dove, a southern Okanogan woman, which tried to give an inside picture of mixed-heritage Indians and of their relations with whites, came too late to relieve these women's ignorance.[68]

White women who found intermarriage so counter to their own notions of racial purity in marriage branded frontier intermarriages a "shame and disgrace to our country." Given such attitudes, white women rejected the very idea of marriage between a white man and an Indian woman.[69] Mollie Dorsey was astonished when she observed such a family living "like civilized people." She could not believe that a white man could "live such a way." The most acrid remark of all came from Maria Norton, who viewed intermarriage as an abomination. To her, it was "the greatest absurdity . . . for a white man to live with black dirty squaws."[70] In other words, Norton tried to control white men's behavior, partially through disdain and partly through disregarding Indian women as potential mates.

White women also derided native wedding rituals. From hasty, superficial, and misguided observations, they concluded that men nonchalantly traded ponies and other goods for as many wives as they desired. Although bride gifts were meant to honor the girl and compensate her parents for their loss, Mary Bailey declared that she "was somewhat shocked to think of such a loose state of morals."[71] Despite women's outrage over what they perceived as crass arrangements for procuring wives, they thought it a joke if an Indian male attempted to trade ponies for them.[72] Sometimes, they even risked their safety by insulting and angering Indian men when they agreed to a trade as a prank. When an Indian male returned with the ponies and was rejected, the "joke" discomfited Indians and whites.[73] In other instances, reactions to the offer of ponies ranged from sarcasm to levity. When an Ottawa Indian proposed to Emily Horton, who was on her way to California in 1852, she stated caustically, "I was too unsophisticated to appreciate the honor."[74] In a similar situation in 1862, Harriet Smith jested, "I thought I would wait untill some one would give Unc a lot of ponies for me and I would go and stay awhile with them then run away, and then we would have some ponies."[75] Mary Warner joked that her "Uncle Chester traded Aunt Lizzie off for two ponies but she would not go."[76] And Catherine Bell wrote home that "there was an Indian chief offered Charlie two of his best ponys for me, don't you think he ought to have traded?"[77] Here again, white women made marriage between Indians and whites sound impossible; the fantasy of irrational minds.

Many white women were also outraged by what they perceived as degrading treatment of native wives by husbands. When they witnessed men taking money from women who had earned it by selling their handiwork, men riding horses while women walked, or men expecting women to carry the load while they went unburdened, white women labeled Indian men as detestable and contemptible. Women who had no conception of the variations of domestic power condemned that of Indian women.[78] These misinterpretations of the treatment of native women by Indian males increased white women's forebodings regarding their possible captivity.[79] "I have no desire to go among the Indians in that way," one emigrant asserted. A Kansas settler of the 1850s admitted that she asked her son to watch her while she fetched water so that Indians would not carry her off.[80] When another woman sighted some Indians garbed in blankets and feathers, she too worried that captivity was imminent.[81] None wanted to fill what they saw as the degraded position of an Indian "squaw." Rather, they preferred to stick with forms of gender domination and exploitation to which they were accustomed.

Because white women disapproved of so many features of American Indian life, they decided that Indian character was of the lowest order. What they saw with their own eyes convinced them that the native population of the West was indeed debased, ruthless, and savage. Interpreting native cultures in light of their own white values, white women were quick to judge Indians as poor specimens of human-ity (that is, if they saw them as people at all). White women left no doubt as to their intentions to "civilize" Indians and their support of the estab-lishment of white nationalism. As a result, women employed such epi-thets as "hard-hearted and cruel people," "too devilish for any human beings," "most treacherous mortals on earth," and "ever treacherous."[82] According to other women, Native Americans were "untrustworthy, thieving, and treacherous," of a "sly intriguing nature," "very cowardly," and "ignorant and simple."[83]

One of the most notable personality defects attributed to all American Indians was their reputed laziness. In 1853, Kate Furness, who did not question why Indians near Fort Laramie were idle, proclaimed that "doing absolutely nothing" but standing around and gazing "vacantly into space" made them contented.[84] When, during the mid-1870s, Ellen Biddle attempted to train a Colorado Indian youth as a house servant, she was not surprised when he ran away with some other "indolent" and "worthless" Indians. After that, Biddle wrote, "I have never thought the plan of sending Indian boys to the schools in the East to educate them, and then allow them to go back to their reservations, a good one." To her way of thinking, "there are too many generations of Indians back of them, and the few years of civilization are soon for-gotten." Thus, to Biddle, no amount of civilizing or educating would ever make Indians assimilable into white culture.[85]

White women also attributed to Indians a crazed desire for liquor. This signifier marked Indians as not only inferior "others," but as unsta-ble and dangerous. White women's discourse gives no evidence that they attempted to find out why some Indians sought whiskey. Also, white women generally ignored their own men's propensity to drink, as well as to cause accidents while inebriated. Summarily, white women damned Indians who drank.[86] During the 1830s, settler Mary Rice wrote to her sister that Creek Indians near Fort Gibson patronized a local white liquor peddler. The result, in her words, was that "a com-pany of them git together and drink and git to quarilling and then they will stab one another. . . . they dance and hollow and scream all night and most always on a Satterday night they dont never truble us any by coming near the house onely by going by in the road and screaming."[87]

When in 1846, Catherine Haun explained that her party lightened their load by burying "the barrels of alcohol lest the Indians should drink it and, frenzied thereby, might follow and attack us."[88] In 1852, a white woman who watched an Indian man attempt to trade a buffalo robe for whiskey lamented "Why do we try to thrust our civilization on a people like this?"[89]

White women believed their assertions. They failed to recognize that they condemned a huge number of people on the basis of a few and highly visible cases. Nor could they see that, at least during the early stages of frontiering, they operated on white American and European values. In addition, they seldom asked how white migration had affected Indian standards of living, morality, and aggressiveness.[90] They assumed that whatever Indians were resulted from themselves rather than from white actions. Thus, women's images of Indians do not provide useful or accurate information regarding American Indians, but they do reveal a tremendous amount about the thinking of the women themselves. White women's reactions to a once proud and self-sufficient people now appear intolerant and heartless.

As noted, white women's thinking came from anti-Indian prejudices, as well as from beliefs about themselves as the moral reformers. But frontierswomen's intolerance was also intensified by their need to survive. They guarded their safety and that of their children closely. As the primary providers of food and clothing for their families, they resented incursions upon their limited supplies. Most western women had to work very hard to maintain even an adequate level of provisions for themselves and their dependents. While on the Oregon Trail in 1853, Charlotte Pengra wrote plaintively, "I always have to improve every moment of time when not traveling to provide enough to eat."[91] Because women saw American Indians as potential threats to their safety and their resources, they automatically thought of Indians as dangerous and deadly foes.[92]

White women were also ignorant of American Indian customs. When they came to the frontier, women knew little about Indian standards of hospitality that called for strangers traveling through an area to offer token gifts to the inhabitants.[93] White women were thus amazed to find that Indians were, in Sarah Royce's words of 1849, "desirous of getting something out of us if they could."[94] Women complained mightily, using such phrases as "thieving people," "somewhat troublesome," and "troubled by begging Indians."[95] Even though Indians asked for basics, including sugar, meat, flour, coffee, other foodstuffs, and tobacco, white women seldom questioned why once self-sufficient groups were in such dire economic straits. Instead, they referred to Indians as sly, disgusting, or pesky.[96] One woman wrote, "They are the greatest beggars I ever saw. I do wonder if they are hungry."[97] Others called Indians "born beggars" and "awful thieves."[98] Some were even more stinging in their remarks. "The better Indians come to camp to pay us a visit," Mary Jane Guill wrote in 1860. "Always stay till after supper I suppose it is fashionable for them to stay."[99] In 1864, Mallie Stafford scoffed: "Two large powerfully built warriors, in all the glory of red paint, buckskin, beads, feathers, dignity and general magnificence, condescended to honor our humble camp with a call—a call long enough to eat up and devour everything we had cooked, that being an immense pot of beans and bacon."[100]

Without a second thought, women condemned such behavior.[101] From the Pawnees to the Sioux to the "Diggers," Indians were reputed to take anything they could lay their hands on.[102] Women were especially annoyed that Indians ran off the stock that was so vital to whites' lives and livelihoods. In truth, there were minor and major conflicts all over the western frontier, from Minnesota and Iowa to Montana, Wyoming, Colorado, and into the Far West, that erupted over horses and other animals.[103] A closer examination of these interchanges indicates that American Indians were typically far more interested in taking livestock than taking human lives.[104] Time after time, Indians wanted horses and cattle, not captives or scalps.[105] In 1863, for example, while moving to California, Mattie Walker mentioned that the "men were kept on the alert on account of Indians who made several attempts to drive the stock off."[106] Referring to West Texas of the 1870s, Mary Jane Bell insisted that "the Indians didn't molest anybody, as all they seemed to want was to steal the horses."[107] Other women who worried about horses, mules, cattle, and sheep often suspected Indians of "eyeing" their animals.[108]

Even though native forays on white people's livestock could escalate into violence, such raids were often more annoying than life threatening.

Because of the belief that Indians would steal animals if given "half a chance,"[109] train members circled their wagons at night to form a corral for animals and posted guards. Even at the trail's end, vigilance could not be relaxed. Men and women stood guard over barns, outbuildings, and fields to thwart stock-hunting American Indians.[110] As a result, the vast majority of white settlers completed their trips and established settlements in relative safety.

Women also remained oblivious to Indian rituals involving horses.[111] The same women who congratulated themselves for making "sharp deals" or "good buys" in trading with Indians resented the effort of Indians to strike a favorable horse trade. Women accused such Indians of being out to bedevil emigrants and settlers, drunk, or thieves at heart.[112] Moreover, when Indians returned wandering stock to whites, women were skeptical. "That they were honest enough to be bringing the lost horses to us we could hardly believe," remarked one young trail woman.[113] In other words, white women kept Indians in a no-win position.

Clearly, women's anti-Indian prejudices hung on. Convinced of their moral mission to help "depraved" Indians, women were hesitant to give up their preconceptions regarding America's native population. Whether curious, amused, or decidedly negative, women were not easily dissuaded. Adding women's belief in white superiority to the mix makes even more understandable women's stubbornness and difficulty in seeing Native Americans as legitimate human beings. As one woman tellingly remarked in 1853, she and her party never tired of watching the Indians, for "they were equal to a circus in interest to us."[114] This woman was not the first to condescendingly compare Indians to performers in a carnival or other entertaining show. Although Indians were not consulted about their feelings, their actions made it clear that they found white invaders a source of wonder. Certainly, Indians spent hours gazing through the doors and windows of white homes, churches, wagons, and other structures. To white women, however, this habit was one more disconcerting and vexing characteristic of natives who already seemed to be largely worthless as people.[115]

—— Finding "Good" Indians ——

Even though white women's anti-Indian biases were deep-seated, women had a softer side as well. At the same time that women condemned Native Americans, they often pointed out—frequently, in lavish and extravagantly generous terms—attractive qualities of Indian peoples. Paradoxically, women who appeared so intent on casting Indians as evil, criminal, and primitive simultaneously recognized a number of positive qualities in natives. Although whites in general detected favorable and unfavorable qualities, or "bad" and "good" sides in Native Americans, women had additional motives for viewing Indians as good. White women hoped to see a glimmer of honor in Indians that would respond to women's moral blandishments. Even more importantly, women's view of themselves as inferior in certain respects to men caused them to search for superior qualities in the Indians they met. Because they had been taught to think of themselves as weak, helpless, and vulnerable to harm, they relied on the nobility and fine character of the "primitive savage" for survival. Although white men could defend them to some degree, it was the Indians, in the last analysis, who would—if "good"—make the trail reasonably pleasant for Anglo women, but—if "bad"—could destroy women through thievery, sexual assault, or outright warfare. Therefore, many frontierswomen were inclined to seek out a bit of nobility, a hint of kindness, or an indication of intelligence in the native peoples they confronted. Despite their negative judgments, women also cited positive aspects of the physical appearance, customs, and character of Indian peoples.

Even those women who were malevolent in describing the ugliness, filth, and odor of some Indians characterized other natives with such phrases as "an imposing sight in the wilderness," "good-looking," "fine-looking," and "noble-looking."[116] Contradicting their unfavorable judgments, women depicted some Indians as "grave" and "stately," and "fine looking," with "the appearance of wealth and independence," or as "tall, strongly made," with "firm features, light copper color, cleanly in appearance, quite well dressed in red blankets."[117] A few women punctuated their derogatory remarks with words such as "industrious" and "intelligent." One woman spoke of "mannerly conduct" and "a degree of refinement" that she had not expected to find among "just Indians."[118] Still other women stated that in spite of some unattractive qualities the Indians were also honest, proud, and responsible people, who would not lie, steal, or cheat as many whites would do.[119]

Some women were quick to praise individual instances of ability on the part of Native Americans. Since the home was their bailiwick, white women were interested in Indians' household arrangements. They frequently commented upon the interiors and exteriors of wigwams, wickiups, and teepees, offering observations surprisingly positive in tone. Lucene Parsons thought that an Indian town with "underground" wigwams showed ingenuity. In 1867, the Denver settler Emma Hill said that a nearby Ute village constituted a "pretty picture."[120] Others emphasized the cleanliness of Indian dwellings. Esther Hanna, for example, said she found a wigwam she visited "more comfortable" than she had anticipated. Hanna was also impressed with Indian handiwork, which she maintained was of a surprisingly high quality.[121] Lodisa Frizzell regarded the needlework produced by the native women whom she visited as the finest and most beautiful that she had ever seen. "I must say that nicer work with a needle I never saw," she declared, "or any this more beautiful, it looked like sattin, & was finely ornamented with various colored beeds." Like Frizzell, other women were so taken with the fine Indian beaded bags, moccasins, and shawls that they became popular items of exchange between white and native women.[122]

Unfortunately, women seldom recorded their reactions to childbirth and child-care practices among Native Americans. Whether they lacked opportunity to observe them or whether they felt it was improper for Victorian women to discuss is unclear. Occasional mention was made of the love Indian parents gave their children and the high standards of behavior that parents expected.[123] Susan Magoffin complimented American Indian women for bathing themselves and their infants immediately after giving birth. "No doubt many ladies in civilized life are ruined by too careful treatments during child-birth," she remarked.[124] For the most part, however, white women neglected the topic of childbirth.

Numerous women commented that Indians often expressed warmheartedness. White women who denigrated Indians also thought that they were capable of responding to fair treatment by whites. For instance, some said that respect, courtesy, friendliness, and willingness to share food with the Indians were factors guaranteeing the safe passage of their party.[125] Apparently, these women viewed Indians as human beings with qualities similar to whites. Lavinia Porter argued for such an approach: "Evidently our hospitality and courteous treatment won their hearts, for they showed no signs of hostility to us." Porter added that the Indians' "general demeanor . . . inspired us with a confidence which seemed to sanction our presence in their midst."[126]

Moreover, some women blamed white men, rather than Indians, for "troubles." In their view, whites frequently treated Indians in an unfair or exploitive manner. Showing her obvious sympathy for Indians, Mary Hopping bitterly called two men, who had paid an Indian counterfeit money for moccasins, "smarties."[127] Similarly, Lavinia Porter claimed that she remonstrated in vain with the men in her party who teased and played tricks on Indians.[128] In another instance, Pauline Wonderly empathized with displaced natives by criticizing male emigrants who refused to pay a "reasonable" toll to those who had constructed a bridge across the Elk Horn River. In the ensuing fight, eleven Indians were killed. Later parties, Wonderly prophesied, would pay for the "meanness of the men of that train." White women believed that selling guns and ammunition to Indians was another offense for which later parties of emigrants and settlers would suffer.[129]

Evidently, women were willing and able to express positive feelings toward American Indians. They recognized that many Indians were indeed impressive in stature and presence. Prevailing beliefs about women's physical weakness seemed to encourage them to look for Indians' benign rather than savage qualities. Although women's supposed moral powers encouraged them to see Indians as depraved beings in need of reform and rehabilitation, women's physical weakness led them to seek out qualities of goodness and nobility. The ambivalence of many women toward Indians, which resulted from such dualistic thinking, was illustrated by Ada Vogdes, an army wife at Fort Laramie during the late 1860s. She filled her journal with the expression "frightened to death." She was awakened by imaginary Indian whoops during the night, mistook two drunken cooks for an uprising, and repeatedly declined her husband's invitations to explore the area surrounding the fort. Yet, when a alarm led to a council that brought Indian leaders into camp, she noticed that Red Cloud had a "pleasant smile" and that Big Bear had "the most splendid chest, and shoulders, I ever laid my eyes upon." She thought that Red Leaf had "a fatherly looking countenance, & one to whom you would go in trouble, were we in different circumstances." Although Vogdes remained in "constant fear" whenever she left the fort, she came to enjoy her position as what she termed "a belle amongst the red men of the Plains."[130]

When Vogdes relocated to Fort Fetterman, she went through a similar process. What she had learned at Fort Laramie turned out to be specific to that situation. At Fetterman, Vogdes complained that "this frontier life is terrible for a nervous excitable person as I am, and it seems as if I could not endure it much longer. For nearly two years the Indians have been the bane of my existence." At Fetterman, she thought a soldier returning from a laundress's quarters was an attacking Indian and she shuddered with fear at the sight of Cheyenne Indians passing outside her windows. Again, however, when American Indian leaders came into the fort, she was impressed by them. Although Vogdes considered herself a proper Victorian woman, she enjoyed commenting on the near-naked male form. Of Red Dog, she said that he "had nothing on but the skin in which he was born. . . . I never saw such shoulders, arms, & legs, & hands . . . his legs were equally fine looking." After sitting with him at a table, she maintained that although an easterner would think it strange to see her with Red Dog, whom Vogdes called "this naked man," it did not seem strange to her at all. "I am not shocked if I see them with no clothes on," she added.[131]

Such contradictory assessments by white women of American Indians were not simply a result of what they had been taught about the two-sided natures of women and Indians. They were also a product of the gradual erosion of those attitudes. Women were experiencing a change in their views of themselves. They discovered that their supposed ability to civilize was only one of a myriad of skills demanded of them by the land they now inhabited. Moreover, they discovered that nothing disastrous would happen to them or white society if they could not fully exercise the role of cultural conservator. Although they washed clothes on the Sabbath, listened to oaths, came into contact with gambling, drinking, and polygamy, life went on. White women in the trans-Mississippi West also developed the ability to drive teams, perform trail work, walk for miles over rough terrain, handle weapons, participate in decisions, and make economic contributions.[132] Under such circumstances, frontierswomen realized that their value to society was not eroding, but was taking a new direction.

Given the emergence of women's new strengths and abilities, many suspected that the inferior side of their nature was no more rockbound than the superior side was proving to be. Numerous cases of western women who grew strong, assertive, and confident in their own talents and skills disproved the existence of female inferiority. Such women believed that they could play a role in shaping their own lives, in protecting themselves and their children, and in determining their survival in the West. Logically, then, if women were not of value primarily as moral forces there was no need for them to emphasize the inferior aspects of Indian character. And if women were not weak or incompetent there was little need for them to depend for protection on the superior aspects of Indian character. Women who drove two-thousand-pound wagons, wielded rifles, and survived the rigors of westering no longer needed to find reassurance in an idealized vision of "noble" natives.

Moreover, such changes opened white women's eyes and minds to a more humane exchange with the American Indians they encountered. The result was a growing awareness that Indians were neither "bad" nor "good." As women saw Indians as people like themselves, they gradually rejected their interpretation of natives as a combination of the terribly savage and the wonderfully noble. White women developed a more balanced interpretation of white and native peoples caught in a complex, tense, and potentially explosive situation. Lavinia Porter, for example, recounted the usual tales of begging Indians infested with vermin, lazy native men who expected women to do the work, and degraded American Indians who possessed low moral standards. Like Vogdes, she was frequently "speechless with fright," suffering extreme anxiety about "dangers of savage life." Increasingly interspersed with these statements were Porter's remarks about helpful and kindly natives. At another point, Porter said that an Indian had traveled with them for three days as a scout and guide, which "went to prove that there was honor among these savage tribes of the wilderness after all."[133]

Similarly, Harriet Ward not only overcame her dread of Indians, but maintained that many other women did as well. "I have conversed with many ladies," she declared, "and they all appear happy and in good health." At one point, Ward admitted that she felt uneasy knowing that "hostile" Indians "infested" nearby mountains and, at another, she remarked that a few Indian groups she met seemed "wild," "miserable," and "not to be trusted." Yet she felt confident enough to not lose any sleep over the matter. "We encamped beside the mountain, with not a living being near us except the Indians, who, they say, are watching all our movements," she declared. "We staked our horses near the tent," she went on, "and all laid ourselves down to sleep, which we enjoyed nicely."[134]

Anglo army wives serve as a good illustration of how white women came to understand American Indians better as their contacts with them increased and improved. Army women lived every moment under the threat of attack and the possibility of losing their husbands. They often survived mind-numbing Indian wars, and they were by affinity and marital relationship committed to subduing native populations. Yet they surprisingly had a great deal of goodwill for Native Americans. For instance, despite the death of her first husband in the Fetterman "massacre," Frances Carrington expressed sympathy for Indians who had been forced to relinquish hunting grounds on which their lives depended. Margaret Carrington, whose husband commanded Fort Phil Kearney during the conflict, supported Frances in her interpretation of events.[135] Even Elizabeth Custer, wife of the famous boy-general, grew unsure of her position regarding Indians. When Custer related the story of the Battle of the Washita to a friend she was so sympathetic with Indians that the friend commented that Custer's memories "confused my sense of justice." She added that "doubtless the white men were right, but were the Indians entirely wrong? After all these broad prairies had belonged to them."[136] Obviously, Custer had caused her companion to rethink the usual beliefs regarding Native Americans.

The wife of Orsemus Bronson Boyd also changed her mind about Indians. Stationed at Camp Halleck, Nevada, in the mid 1860s, she was so regularly exposed to Paiute and Shoshone Indians that she wrote, "I soon regarded red men as fearlessly as if I had been accustomed to them all my life." They, too, were interested in her and paid long visits. Indian observers would spend an entire day watching Boyd and her family. When she attended a native dance, however, she noticed that the dancers returned to "their original savage natures." Because the dance was a regulated social function, she could accept the Indians' ferocity. Moreover, she balanced their warlike behavior with their friendly demeanor, so that she could not think of them as "savages." She did not see that friendly Indians fulfilled the peaceful roles that whites prescribed for them. Boyd was simply relieved that her positive attitude helped her avoid the terror "which has made life so hard for many army ladies."[137]

As frontierswomen recognized their humanity and fallibility along with those of Indians, their remarks about Native Americans became more gentle and kind in tone. Also, as Indian tribes were controlled or vanquished, the frontier became safer for white women. As a result, women's contradictions and ambivalence gave way to warmth and even expressions of affection. As women became more balanced and realistic in their attitudes, they recognized that the white social construction of "Indian" did not exist. Individually and gradually, women learned to perceive the divergence between types of Indians, to realize that different groups possessed different qualities, and to reject the image of "Indian" as one amorphous collection of people. Although women recorded the sighting of their first "Indians," they eventually specified, for example, that "we are now in the Pawnee nation" or that "we are now in the Sioux nation."[138]

As women learned to discriminate between Indians, they grew to dislike some groups and to react favorably to others. White women thought the Pawnees of the Platte River country the most troublesome of Indian tribes. Reputed to be beggars and thieves, the Pawnees were considered by some women to be "one of the most dangerous of hostile tribes." The Sioux, on the other hand, encountered farther along the northern trails to California and Oregon, were characterized as the most handsome and the cleanest of all American Indians. To white women, the Sioux were "a fine intelligent looking race"; tall and athletic people who were "friendly to the whites." When traveling from Iowa to California in 1852, Lucy Cooke noted that the Sioux were "a noble-looking tribe . . . so well dressed; such gay trappings on them and their ponies, and beautiful beaded work they wear." During the same year, Lodisa Frizzell judged them to be the "best looking" Indians she had seen, explaining that they were "tall, strongly made, firm features, light copper color, cleanly in appearance."[139] The Cheyennes also elicited women's admiration for their intelligence, wealth, and stalwart appearance.[140]

When women saw the so-called Digger Indians of the Plains region, the tone of their remarks became acrid. They agreed that the Diggers, given this name because of their custom of digging roots for food, were the most loathsome of all Native American tribes.[141] Elizabeth Lord described them as "repulsive creatures, squatty, dark and greasy."[142] When Lydia Waters spied her first Digger Indians she exclaimed that "greater brutes nature never made." She went on to say: "They had never cut their hair which was full of sticks, dried grass and dirt, and their heads looked as large as bushel baskets for their hair stuck out straight." She added that "they were very saucy and would have taken the guns out of the wagons in spite of all the women could do."[143]

Evaluations of other Indian groups along the many trails and their "cut-offs" varied. The Bannock Indians were said to possess countenances that were "fine and some of them even intelligent." The "Piute" Indians "were fine looking" but not to be trusted, according to Harriet Ward.[144] The "Kioose," in Esther Hanna's view, were "intelligent, finely formed, well clad and very cleanly."[145] To Mary Pelham, the "Pima, Papgo, Maricopa," and Yuma Indians were the most interesting.[146] Helen Carpenter saw the "Puitahs" as friendly, but the Shoshone as aggressive and combative.[147] Harriet Bunyard found the "Lemore" Indians "detestable" and the "Maricopis" an "ignorant, silly looking people."[148] An early Texas settler, Mary Maverick, thought the Tonkawa Indians treacherous and cruel. And a woman traveling along the Platte River felt honored to give the chief of the Otoe tribe, "a very fine looking man," a loaf of bread.[149]

Clearly, white women came to realize that Indians were not all alike. They recognized that natives not only varied from tribe to tribe, but also from one area to another and from one era to the next. For instance, a group of once peaceful American Indians might have experienced the ravages of white migration so thoroughly by the 1860s that they became belligerent.[150] Lucy Sexton maintained that when her family moved to California in the mid-1850s "the Indians were peaceable all along the route, and we had no such contentions as later travelers over the same route did."[151] Mary Pelham claimed that there was a difference in time periods and trails. She believed that the northern route was safer than the southern one that her party took on its way from Texas to California in 1853. Pelham voiced a common complaint about alterations in Indians:"How these Indians have changed. Not simple and childlike any more. Until that year very few had ever seen a white man and seldom a white woman or child. They never tired of watching us and our ways of living."[152]

In some cases, time improved Indian–white relations. During the late 1850s and the early 1860s, whites so dominated the San Francisco area that they found Indians peaceable, seldom causing settlers the trouble that was reported from the interior portion of the country.[153] White women seemed pleased that—in their view—Indians had responded to their civilizing influence. Clearly, a significant number of Indians had learned how to act in ways that whites found acceptable. Although Indians may have demeaned whites in private, perhaps by joking or making fun of them, they appeared "civilized" in the presence of whites. In 1867, Cynthia Capron, an army wife, said that most Indians had settled on a reservation where they were "very industrious for Indians," cultivating "a large farm of several thousand acres, and very well too." Evidently, Capron assumed that reservation Indians were happy in their dependent, confined state.[154] In the Mount Hood region of Oregon, white women described Indians, especially the Flatheads and Nez Percés, as friendly, good looking, well clad, and clean.[155] During the late 1860s, the Montana settler Mary Hopping maintained that when the Flathead and Nez Percé Indians passed by on their way to hunt buffalo "everyone was glad to see them."[156]

Modifications in American Indian behavior did not always promote smooth Indian-white relations, however. Some Indians continued to resist violently rather than passively. Some women saw that exploding numbers of whites on the frontier pushed Indians to the edge, marginalizing Indians in terms of land and patience. White pressure compelled

Native American groups to fight whites and to wage war with each other over dwindling resources.[157] Kate Furness explained that when she encountered her first Indians just across the Missouri River they were engaged in war with the Sioux, who had "encroached on their hunting-grounds and killed the buffalo."[158] Other women added yet another factor, "renegade whites," who not only "incited" the Indians, but stole white stock and then blamed the Indians.[159]

Clearly, a significant portion of white women modified or radically altered the conceptions of American Indians that they had brought with them on the westward trail. Many women replaced hate and fear with warmth and sympathy. Neither did women fulfill the widely accepted image of inept and cowering creatures intimidated by vicious, marauding, and sexually abusive natives. As interchanges grew between white women and Indians, few were the dramatic, conflict-filled confrontations portrayed by nineteenth- and early twentieth-century media. How women acted in their dealings with American Indians is vastly different from the story usually told.

—— Changing Attitudes ——

To explore the contention that white women's relations with American Indians were less negative than usually thought, a sample of 150 diaries, journals, memoirs, and letters was assembled. Unfortunately, Indian, or subaltern, accounts do not exist in a written form, only in oral tradition, or storytelling.[160] Thus, documents regarding white female–Indian female contacts were generated by a dominant group—white women. These sources represent most trans-Mississippi areas, the primary eras, and the thoughts and experiences of Anglo women from a range of social classes, ethnic backgrounds, and national origins. When the women's reactions to Indians were studied and counted, it was discovered that 113 writers recorded no trouble with native peoples, 22 noted minor problems, and only 15 reported major difficulties. Although it is not very scientific or sophisticated, this data provides enough evidence to challenge the image of white women victimized by predatory

Indians. Woman after woman employed the phrase "no trouble with Indians" in their diaries, letters, or memoirs.[161] In a specific case in point, Ada Millington concluded her travel diary by writing, "Our journey has been as prosperous, with as little trouble as we expected. No Indian difficulties to speak of, and our stock was not stolen or lost."[162]

Could media accounts have been wrong or perhaps sensationalized? The answer is yes. In spite of white women's assertions, myth and the media promoted the belief that white women and American Indians were at loggerheads more often than not. Violent confrontations that harmed women have held center place, whereas Indians have generally been portrayed as barbarians who pillaged, burned, and raped. A survey of nineteenth-century novels, poetry, drama, tracts, textbooks, newspapers, magazines, sermons, and lectures supports the customary idea of the weak and ill-used white woman and the fierce and rapacious American Indian. The widespread popularity of the captivity narrative is a good illustration of negative views of Indians finding wide audiences among whites.[163] Unfortunately, twentieth- and twenty-first-century myth and media have perpetuated this view rather than questioning and reassessing it. With a few notable exceptions, such as *Dances with Wolves* and *The Last of the Dog Men,* film and television westerns, as well as much print media, remain largely unsympathetic to frontier Indians, preferring to deal in dramatic events.

Of course, what watcher or reader hopes to get a line on the boring truth? Most would rather relish an exciting story. And, in fact, excitement, disaster, and tragedy did occur in the trans-Mississippi frontier West. For instance, Texas in the mid-nineteenth century was the setting for numerous horror stories, no doubt embellished by white storytellers. Beginning with one of the earliest women to settle in Texas, Mary Maverick, the drama that unfolds is one of misunderstanding and confrontation. Maverick not only related troubles between Tonkawa Indians and white settlers, but described in detail eruptions between the Comanches and the whites during the 1830s and the 1840s, including the taking of white captives. Maverick proclaimed that Texas Indians were "cruel and relentless savages" who "daily committed atrocities about us." In a similar vein, Mary Rabb, an Indian Hill settler, maintained that during many years, especially 1835,

Texas Indians were so troublesome that whites went to nearby La Grange to "fort up."[164]

Other Texas women came to hate Comanches, a determined and well-mounted hunting people who needed a vast area to support themselves. Whites who took land and killed buffalo and other game seemed to expect Comanches to disappear rather than to resist. Martha Simmons never forgot an 1839 conflict with Comanches, which resulted in her father's death and the captivity of her and her mother. Simmons claimed that the "devils" tortured her and her mother until they escaped in 1840.[165] Similarly, Elizabeth Owens indicted Comanches' actions of the 1840s. And Mary Locklin referred to Texas Indians as "red fiends" who interfered with what she, being a white woman, naturally called the emigrants' "work of improvement." To her, Indians hatched "deviltry" and attacked "without warning, burning houses, killing stock, destroying property, and murdering defenseless women and children."[166] Another woman, Rosalie Priour, stated that attacks and "atrocities" perpetrated by Texas Indians against settlers in the Corpus Christi area continued well into the 1850s.[167]

Nor did white-Indian conflict diminish. Throughout the 1850s, additional Texas women—Julia Sinks, Martha Gray, Eugenie Lavender, and Mary Baylor—reported that raids by Tonkawa, Caddo, and Comanche Indians kept them in an "upset state."[168] During the 1860s, difficulties continued. Susan Newcomb declared that Indians were "thick and plenty and trying to brake our country." Newcomb had no conception that, in reality, whites tried to "brake" Indian country.[169] Jonaphrene Faulkner, who wanted all Indians exterminated, also offered a stock white interpretation: that troubles occurred because Native Americans "resisted all advances of the white man looking to their subjugation or control and roamed free and vindictive still, and blood thirsty, upon the far western plains."[170] To Indians, of course, the explanation would have been that whites kept coming into Texas, interfering with Indian lives and lands.

Such struggles in Texas continued well into the 1870s. One woman explained that "Indians would often come down on raids during moonlight nights." In 1872, another said that her family moved into town to escape altercations with Jack County natives. And May Tansill reacted with utter disillusionment: "I know the Indians have been unjustly treated and I have a great deal of sympathy for them, but I haven't quite so much sentiment concerning them as I did before I came here and learned so much about their cruelty and depredations."[171]

During the 1880s and 1890s, relations between Texas's white settlers and native groups were erratic. One woman who migrated to Montague County in 1889 lived without incident near her Creek and Comanche neighbors. "We had no truck with them to speak of," she explained, "they let us alone and we let them alone."[172] Another woman, who moved in 1890 to Indian Territory in Texas, became disgusted with Choctaw Indians. According to her, Choctaws were impossible because "Choctaw Beer" made "them both drunk and crazy." In 1891, her family left Texas to relocate in the more stable Oklahoma area.[173] Furthermore, another woman recalled that other Texas families, tired of living in fear of "mean and treacherous" Indians such as the Cheyennes and the Potawatomis, also caught "Oklahoma fever" and left Texas.[174]

The experience of Texas women settlers demonstrates that violence did occur between white women and American Indians.[175] The turmoil in Texas gave white women little opportunity to alter their views of themselves or of Indians. Kept in a state of upheaval, they seldom developed sympathy for Indians.[176] But Oklahoma during the latter half of the nineteenth century gives a different picture of white-Indian interaction. In Oklahoma, women encountered the so-called Five Civilized Tribes, notably the Cherokee, Chickasaw, and Choctaw, who had migrated to Indian Territory (later Oklahoma) beginning with the "removal" policy of the 1830s. Despite the tragic Trail of Tears experienced by these early Indians, a relatively peaceable manner of dealing with Indian-white issues developed in Oklahoma, allowing white women to adjust their perceptions of themselves and their Indian neighbors. Some Oklahoma women who were initially "scared to death" even became "intermarried citizens" by wedding native men.[177]

Oklahoma women went through the process described earlier concerning trail women. Gradually, they felt confident enough to attend native dances, including mourning cries, ceremonial dances, and even mock war dances, where Indian participants acted in ways that would have scared whites outside the ritual sphere. Within the context of social ceremonies, however, Indians could air political and racial antagonisms and express subtle forms of resistance, whereas white women who sensed tension could dismiss it as make-believe. Although both sides claimed to have had a good time, the hegemonic structure had been tweaked, yet stayed firmly in place.[178]

Moreover, whites and Indians also exchanged bits of culture. Even the most stubborn whites and Indians had to recognize that the other group could offer them something. For instance, even as white-Indian conflict continued in Texas during the 1880s, Oklahoma white women learned medical care from Indians and, in turn, taught them to speak English and to use white farming methods. As one Oklahoma settler said, the Indians "acted friendly and we found that they were as good as we were and couldn't help liking them."[179] Only occasionally were such attitudes offset by a female settler who continued to think that Indian were "nasty" people.[180]

As a result of the land rushes in Oklahoma during the early 1890s, scores of white settlers placed additional pressure on the landholdings of the native population. Yet white women were soon visiting with Indians, admiring their honesty, and denying fear of them.[181] Anglo women, who were protected from harm by their membership in the dominant culture, spoke of sharing schools, towns, and reservation lands with Indians in peace and friendship.[182] For the most part, Indians conformed to white expectations. As a result, only a few women judged American Indians as wild, fearsome, or possessing peculiar habits.[183] Rarer yet were the women who remembered "uprisings" and "massacres."[184] One such woman described the establishment of white hegemony; she claimed that Indians, who may have scalped people "at one time," quickly became "civilized." From her perspective, "Indians were sure mean those days but later became our friends."[185] Another Oklahoma woman who migrated to the area in 1901 recalled only one "bad" Indian, or nonconformist who continued his resistance by terrorizing settlers when inebriated.[186]

The positive outlook of Oklahoma frontierswomen does not stand alone. Some declared, as did Lucene Parsons, that "we have some fine times with all our troubles."[187] In 1853, a single woman traveling with an Oregon-bound party insisted her trip had a "refining and ennobling influence."[188] And Harriet Ward maintained: "Indeed I think what is often termed suffering is merely a little inconvenience, for I had so often read and heard of the difficulties and dangers of the overland route to California, and I find from experience that the pleasure thus far quite overbalances it all."[189]

In spite of the ever-present threat of Indian attack, such women slept very soundly.[190] In 1853, Oregon-bound emigrant Helen Love said, "I was not so afraid as to keep me from sleeping."[191] In 1859, Catherine Bell stated that although the Indians were "very bad" she slept as though she were at home.[192] Even the sight of a scalped Pawnee with four or five arrows implanted in his corpse failed to keep Frances Sawyer awake. She wrote, "Morpheus cozily wrapped us all in his arms last night, and the pleasant dreams of our faraway Kentucky home were not disturbed by the Indians, dead or alive."[193] Yet another woman added that she slept with an ax by her side, but never had to use it on an Indian.[194]

These women do not sound terror stricken. Many went from "very much scared" to casual.[195] For instance, Allene Dunham, who crossed the plains to California in 1864, began the trip curled up in her bed because she feared that Indians would cut off her feet if they protruded from the wagon. Dunham concluded the journey by emphasizing how much she had enjoyed her visits to Indian camps.[196] Yet others came to see the humorous side of the situation. After traveling safely throughout the West with her journalist husband during the 1870s, Carrie Strahorn derided the anti-Indian ideas she had picked up in the East. To Strahorn, it was ridiculous that easterners saw life "on the other side" as one of hardship, dagger, bandits, and "rubbing elbows with the slayers of Custer."[197] For Dunham and Strahorn, their experiences were enough to change their minds regarding Indians.

Still other women admired and respected specific Indians. Caroline Phelps, whose husband traded with Indians on the border of Illinois and Iowa between 1830 and 1860, began her life in the West complaining about Indians: they drank, fought among themselves, and would surely rob her. After several disasters that she survived through her fortitude and help from Indians, Phelps began to see herself and American Indians through different eyes. Eventually, she attended native dances and other ceremonies. When her sister from Dubuque arrived for a visit, Phelps persuaded her that there was no danger in attending an Indian dance. Phelps and her sister seemed to have used these occasions to learn something about another culture. Phelps also called an Indian doctor to treat her children and hired an Indian male nurse for them. When John, her children's native nurse, died, she said that they mourned him as though he had been a member of the family. After an 1838 upheaval among Native Americans in the area, Phelps stated that she was glad to "have peace & quietness again after so much howling in the wilderness, if we always had to live as I have for three weeks past I could not stay in the indian country, but I never was very much afraid of them."[198]

Many years later, another woman, Hilda Faunce, also the wife of an Indian trader, had a similar experience. She moved with great trepidation to a Navajo reservation in the Arizona desert. Feeling superior yet scared, she initially branded the residents as primitive, heathen, and immoral. Gradually, however, she came to admire Navajo people and feel comfortable living near them. "As the months passed," she wrote, "I learned to respect the way the Navajos made the most of an arid, rocky land; I admired their architecture; the design of the blankets and the skill and sincerity in carrying it out were real art." She added that "the lazy and the indigent were less common than among whites." As to native religion, Faunce found it "wholesome and clean and their respect for their belief compared favorably with the white man's attitude toward his God." From her new perspective, Faunce blamed Navajo problems on white men who supplied the Indians with alcohol.[199]

Like these traders' wives, military wives went from misgivings to warmth. Although white women arrived at their husbands' frontier posts filled with misconceptions about American Indians, they eventually became more open and receptive. Martha Summerhayes regarded her Indian servants as quick learners and conscientious workers.[200] With time, Alice Baldwin became friendly with several Indian women and praised the "sincerity" of Indian culture and values. She also insisted on describing the disgruntled Chief Joseph as a "wonderful Indian."[201]

The timid and fearful Ada Vogdes is an outstanding example of a white woman's ability to adjust her attitude. In "constant fear" whenever she ventured from Fort Laramie and "frightened to death" at any irregularity while inside its sheltering walls, she was not a likely candidate as friend and supporter of people she thought of as dreaded enemies. Yet she became friendly with the hated and feared warrior, Red Cloud. When Red Cloud brought his men into the fort for peace negotiations, she judged them to be "young bold & dashing." She concluded that, "A more exciting day . . . I never experienced. . . . It was a grand sight." She also entertained and traded with American Indians. She even left the fort for outings and horseback rides that she "enjoyed very much."[202]

Naturally, not all women changed their minds about themselves or American Indians. Some women hardly mentioned Indians. In other cases, such sources as a letter or half-kept diary are too truncated to indicate any change in attitudes.[203] Moreover, some white women did not like Native Americans. For example, during the 1840s, the Iowan Susan Willeford declared that although her Indian neighbors were "peaceful," they "were seldom if ever very welcome neighbors." During the following decade, the Californian Mary Staples and the Oregonian Caroline Budlong had ample opportunity to revise their views of themselves and to get acquainted with the many native peoples who lived around them. Yet these women continued to think that Indians were nothing more than cruel, lazy, and unreliable beggars.[204]

Moreover, factors besides gender affected women's thinking about Indians. Place of origin, previous contact with Indians, age, marital status, ethnicity, race, religion, and personality also affected women's views. The point is, however, that numerous white women demonstrated that social constructs were not absolute. These women developed an ability to replace prejudice with warmth, sympathy, and understanding. As these women grew more realistic and confident about their roles, contributions, and strengths, they were more secure and sympathetic in their relations with American Indians. They were not beleaguered frontierswomen living in terror of marauding and savage Indians. Nor were they routinely at odds with natives or attacked and debauched by them.

If "rape, pillage, and burn" is not a key phrase in understanding relations between white women and American Indians in the early trans-Mississippi West, then what is it? If women did not always play the white female victim, what were their dealings like with American Indians? Did white men undergo a similar adaptation? Or did gender matter?

Figure 9. Understandably, Anglo women were very interested in Indians' domestic arrangements, especially cooking and childcare. Unidentified woman and children, undated, probably California. Courtesy of the Museum of New Mexico, Santa Fe, negative number 91528.

Figure 10. White men showed interest in Native Americans' weapons, horses, and buildings; the latter often constructed of locally available material, even if it consisted of cast-offs. Miwok camp, California, undated. Courtesy of the Museum of New Mexico, Santa Fe, negative number 89917.

Figure 11. Unlike women, white men were seldom invited inside Native American homes, but had to view them for a distance, often from a council fire in front of a chief's dwelling. Pawnee Indian Wind Lodge, ca. 1868–1870. Courtesy of the Museum of New Mexico, Santa Fe, negative number 58632.

Figure 12. Often, Anglo women judged Anglo men, especially soldiers, as too harsh in their approach to Native Americans. Sitting Bull and family, 1882, Fort Randall, Dakota Territory. Courtesy of the Montana Historical Society, Helena.

Figure 13. One of the few ways that American Indians could get white sympathy was by dressing up as whites expected and going on the stage giving lectures and sometimes craft demonstrations to white audiences. The Piute chief and reformer Sarah Winnemucca who lectured during the early 1880s and wrote *Life Among the Piutes: Their Wrongs and Claims* (1883). Photograph undated, first appeared in O. O. Howard, *Famous Indian Chiefs I have Known* (1908). Courtesy of the author.

Figure 14. Another type of Indian that Anglos found acceptable was the beautifully attired Native woman who made and sold exquisite craftwork. Na-tu-ende, Apache woman, ca. 1883. Courtesy of the Museum of New Mexico, Santa Fe, negative number 15910.

85. Maricopa and Pima Indian Squaws,
Southern Arizona.

Figure 15. Even during the early twentieth century, many Anglo travelers viewed Indian women as "squaws" and curiosities, whose photographs they sent to friends back home on postcards. A Maricopa and a Pima woman in Arizona, undated. Courtesy of the author.

—— **Chapter Five** ——

Frontier Place: Gender Matters

Because interchanges between whites and American Indians go unexamined in terms of gender, the assumption stands that white women and men played similar, if not identical, parts in dealings with American Indians. Once gender is introduced into the study of migration and settlement, it is apparent that women and men acted differently in virtually every facet of the western colonialist venture, including behavior toward Indians. White women developed a collegial relationship with Indians, whereas white men played an adversarial role.

Division of labor on the basis of gender caused this split. On the trail and in frontier settlements, women primarily supervised the domestic realm, children, gardens, and chickens, whereas men were charged with care of equipment and livestock, as well as providing protection. During migration and early stages of settlement, women and men frequently shared jobs or overlapped functions. Still, even among European women who performed outside labor, the division of tasks along gender lines was widely accepted, causing a gender differentiation between workers within families.[1]

In this system, female migrants had numerous responsibilities. They fed and clothed family members, provided a home of sorts, and perhaps bore additional children. As they had at home, female migrants also gave continuity to their families and friends, meaning that women kept up people's spirits, continued ethnic and racial traditions, traded for foodstuffs and other goods, and sang hymns and read scripture.[2] Women also were on the alert to protect themselves and others from harm, but at the same time they were concerned with extracting vital resources from the environment and its inhabitants. Women were dedicated to the success of the western undertaking because of their involvement—whether willing or not—and their dedication to the safety of their families, as well as their visions of frontier opportunity. To survive, white women had to develop collegiality with small-town shopkeepers and farmers along the way, and, as they progressed farther west, with Native Americans.

At the same time, white men were adversarial. Following the dictates of Manifest Destiny, they cut paths into the Indians' domain. They pushed wagons, people, and stock over the trails; seized native hunting grounds; and fended off Indians who were intent on protecting their lands and families. Male migrants and settlers, who were on the lookout for any indication that their enemies were in the vicinity, took turns standing guard. Men were committed to the success of these efforts because of their desire to find livelihoods in the West and a belief in their superiority to Indians, who were inferior foes. Consequently, there was little in the contact between white males and Native Americans that fostered sympathy, affinity, or friendship. Rather, most white men approached the frontier and its native population as a piece, to be subdued, controlled, and made to serve through militancy and, if necessary, through violence. Frontier mythology, anti-Indian prejudice, and the male mystique all advocated this approach toward overcoming the challenges in white settlement of the frontier.

―― **White Women's and Men's Perspectives** ――

The contrasting roles played by men and women shaped their interests, values, perceptions, and observations. They asked different questions of the landscape and the people they encountered. They applied disparate standards to their experiences and to their contacts with indigenous peoples.[3] And they frequently noticed and remarked upon divergent aspects of the same scene. Even during the nineteenth and early twentieth centuries, men were from Mars and women were from Venus.

A sample of 150 men's documents and an equal number of women's sources analyzed here demonstrate gender dissimilarities. Although the diaries, letters, and reminiscences were alike regarding trails covered, location of settlement, and eras, the accounts of white men differed in that men's journeys included a significant number of all-male expeditions, parties, and communities. All-male groups included scientists, military, miners, and potential settlers. They consisted of single men and married men, with the latter serving as advance agents for their families. Women lacked a parallel experience. Although single women migrated and settled on their own, a significant portion of women were married and had children.[4] Even though there were a few all-female parties of Sooners in Oklahoma, some predominantly female settlements, and a number of female communes, as in Belton, Texas, these were relatively unusual.

This difference between male and female sources raises an interesting point. One might expect that the all-male groups would demonstrate a high proportion of trouble with Indians. This assumes that men took fewer precautions when women and children were not present. The male documents, however, showed a slightly lower rate of such reports than did the female data. Out of 130 male documents, 124 reported no trouble with American Indians, 17 recorded minor problems, and 9 noted serious confrontations. There were 113 women reporting no discord, 22 mentioning minor difficulties, and 13 recording major conflicts. Although these differences are statistically insignificant, they suggest that men exhibited the same degree of caution in male groups as in mixed parties.

Overall, men's and women's sources were compared in the following categories: propensity to quantify; domestic affairs; childbirth and child care; general observations, such as scenery and weather; and social affairs. Concerning Native Americans, men and women were contrasted in how they described native people, villages, and artifacts; assessed military preparedness; judged customs and morality; handled contacts with Native Americans; developed awareness of tribal differences; and changed (or did not change) their personal views of American Indians.

The divergences between male and female perspectives appeared not so much in their tendency to enumerate, but in the issues that were important to them. One male migrant of 1841 began his trip by reckoning the number of people in his party and the number of oxen, mules, and horses.[5] Men were also very aware of distances covered. Crossing the western plains in 1850, Iowan William Edmundson included mileage figures in each day's notations. The Ohioan Hiram Shutes was so concerned with distances traversed that he concocted a device for a wagon wheel that counted the number of revolutions. From that figure, Shutes calculated mileage.[6]

Even though women shared the same adventure, most were by role and function concerned with other aspects of arrangements. When women remarked on such topics as wagons and provisions they did so from their own point of view. On the Oregon Trail, Kitturah Belknap devoted paragraphs to the way in which she had sewn inner and outer wagon covers by hand, what dishes she packed, what medical supplies she included, what her workbasket contained, and the nature of the tablecloths she tucked into the wagon.[7] Moreover, at the same time that men counted miles, women counted graves. Walking by the wagons a good part of each day, women were in close proximity to newly dug graves.[8] They also demonstrated an almost macabre desire to know the toll that the journey took on individuals.

Men and women also differed regarding daily concerns. Men's accounts focused on wagons, terrain, directions and maps, stock, finances, land purchase and clearing, crops, equipment, and innumerable other technical and mechanical matters. Men typically gave meticulous descriptions of a watering place or campground, a ford or ferry, a land investment, a crop failure, a harvest, or a house-raising. Since the care and safety of stock was of great importance, men also wrote of spending time in herding and resting animals, searching for grass and water, and hunting for lost, strayed, or stolen animals.[9]

Men who had to purchase goods, including wagon wheels or ammunition, or hire such services as help in fording a swollen stream, usually paid cash, especially to white storekeepers and farmers. With Indians, however, white men frequently used threats or sheer pugnacity.

In a typical action, the men of the Burrell party brandished their pistols to seize an Indian-built bridge and scare away the Indian men attempting to collect a modest toll.[10] If white men, taught to be aggressive and profit-oriented, had swapped places with the Indians they would have judged themselves enterprising and ambitious rather than troublesome. For white men, however, an enterprising Indian was an impossibility. White women, long taught to be soft and nurturing, often derided men for violent behavior, whether it be against each other or directed toward Indians.[11] Women made clear their disapproval of the means men used. Steeped in female virtues of the era, women did not believe that the thud of a heavy fist on a native's head guaranteed survival or success. Furthermore, women's lack of physical strength did not encourage them to think in terms of belligerent action. Instead, women pursued a softer course in their dealings with Native Americans.[12]

Besides trade, another state of affairs that called for might from men was flooded streams and rivers. These constituted a challenge to male strength and ingenuity. "Went 6 miles to Dry Creek," wrote A. W. Harlan, while crossing the plains in 1850. He added that Dry Creek had nine feet of water, with a swift current. "We set stakes & stretched ropes & chains across & built a bridge of willow brush," he wrote, "rolled our waggons over by hand, swam our teams across." Before going on their way, he and his companions showed a cooperative spirit with other white trains in lending to drivers their chains and ropes.[13]

Unsurprisingly, men said little about domestic arrangements.[14] Although they mentioned cooking and washing in passing, if at all, they occasionally helped with these tasks. Helen Carpenter remarked on a father and sons who joined "mother" at the fire and cooked their own food.[15] One young man noted that, after the party's cook "suffered an accident along the trail," he did the cooking for "seven adults and a boy about 3 years old."[16]

Even though men in all-male parties did their own cooking and domestic chores, they also made light of them.[17] The forty-niner Edwin Hillyer, for example, was bemused by the sight of men cooking. "Who'd a thunk it, three months ago," he wrote, "that they would see John and Ed away out on the plains ... cooking over a bush fire?" Later, he noted: "I baked bread. Yes I made and baked bread."[18] Another male migrant on the road to Virginia City in 1865 stated, "Baked my first loaf of bread, very good."[19] A migrant on the Oregon Trail wrote his wife that he was "much pleased" with camp life. He reported that "Hank & self have done most of the cooking, and have succeeded thus far, admirably." The men's only problem was cooking sufficient amounts. "The great difficulty we find, is to cook enough—All of us have most voracious appetites. . . . But truly we get along finely."[20] A captain in the Army Corps of Topographical Engineers, surveying the Salt Lake Valley in 1849, sounded as if he too got along "finely." On one occasion he expressed satisfaction with his dinner of buffalo meat, two bottles of claret, coffee, and a "segar."[21]

Besides cooking for themselves, the other major domestic hurdle that confronted these men was cleaning soiled clothing. One man devised a simple solution; after tying his dirty clothes in a blanket, he submerged the bundle in a swift stream.[22] Another bragged that he "suceeded admirabley" at "the art of washing dirty clothes," but that his fingers "suffered some from the effects of very good soap."[23] A man who hurt his back and knuckles on his first washday said that he and his companions wondered why they had ever been "dissatisfied" when their wives were impatient on washing day.[24]

Men traveling alone missed women for more than their domestic services, however. When one forty-niner and his comrades heard "the sound of a female voice" in a nearby emigrant camp, they were quite "cheered."[25] Once men reached the California diggings, they felt lonely for women and regretted leaving home.[26] An unmarried emigrant of 1870 stated that "what goes hardest with me is the loss of the company of young ladies."[27] Others confided their feelings to diaries, wrote long letters, and sometimes turned to available women. One unattached miner wrote plaintively, "Came across a camp of Indians. We had a bottle of Brandy along & treated them. Tried to honey up to some of the squaws, but couldn't come it."[28]

Because women did not migrate in all-female groups, they did not voice parallel complaints about a lack of men. Nor did they squabble about who would cook and wash. It was a given that these were female duties.[29] Thus, on the trail and in new settlements, white women collected and exchanged information, including recipes, instructions for

producing soap and butter, and directions for constructing basic yet
fashionable clothing.[30] Catherine Haun described women walking
along in dust and heat, sharing gossip and recipes.[31] Unlike men who
recorded in a few words their bread baking, women went on at great
length. For instance, Kitturah Belknap offered a complete sketch of her
"salt rising" bread.[32]

A comparison of men's and women's documents from the same
family dramatically illustrates gender differences. Although childbirth
and child care were of crucial importance to women, men apparently
accepted pregnancy, childbirth, and even infant mortality as natural
functions to which they accorded little notice. If men mentioned such
matters, they did so with brevity. The terseness of the following diary
entry was typical:

> Feb. 25, 1868—Tacy, my wife, had a new daughter this A.M. at
> 6 1/2 o'clock.
> Sat. March 7th—I went to Salem and paid Dr. Siveter $10.00.
> I had expected him to charge only $5.00.
> Sun. May 3—Baby died![33]

A stark contrast emerges when this is set beside the statement that
Kitturah Belknap made after her baby died from lung fever. It was, she
wrote, the "first real trial" of her life. When another of her children died,
she noted in her diary: "I have to pass thru another season of sorrow.
Death has again entered our home." Within four days, Kitturah lost her
"dear little John" to "dropsy on the brain." She concluded, "We are left
again with one baby and I feel that my health is giving way."[34]

This is not meant to suggest that men cared nothing about the
birth, care, and death of their children. Men were, after all, expected to
project an image of strong males and family providers. The first prevented them from expressing emotions, whereas the second riveted
their attention on matters important to providers. Thus, men were likely
to mention family matters in offhand remarks. When Dr. Thomas White
delivered a baby on the trail from Indiana to Oregon in 1852, he simply
stated that "the rule of multiplication, will go on, on the plains, as well
as in other relations of life."[35] Years later, in 1865, a prospector commented, "The Indians are still camped near us. There are a good many

pappooses with them, and their squalling reminds me of my own parental home and village."[36]

Like men, women avoided going into detail about pregnancies or births, but for different reasons than men. Because of Victorian reticence regarding personal matters, women seldom spoke of anything related to sex. They did, however, express concern about protecting and caring for children in a frontier setting. Women worried about children's health and safety, especially preventing rattlesnake bites or the jolting of a child off a wagon seat. Men also took precautions to protect their children, and went to great lengths to retrieve them when lost. Being male, however, men acted "masculine" and said little about their reactions.

Even though men's and women's writings differ in the above areas, they converge in general observations and social life. Both genders commented on scenery, weather, meetings with old neighbors, the beginnings of friendships, loneliness and homesickness, illness, death, disaster, entertainments, schools and churches, and similar matters of joint concern. Both were taken with the grandeur of the plains and mountains, the profuseness of prairie flowers, the clarity of water, and the vastness of the sky. Both relieved the boredom of the trail by describing such sights as Scotts Bluff, Independence Rock, and Salt Lake City. Both lavished detail on prairie fires, hordes of locusts, blizzards, and spring floods.

In addition, men occasionally expressed delight and enthusiasm, although not in the same way as women. A man pleased to meet an old friend along the trail might clap him on the shoulder, whereas women would hug and cry. More often than not, men kept their sentiments to themselves. When leaving for the West, Hiram Shutes slipped off to bid his mother goodbye in private.[37] After settlement, a woman who wrote home that letters were like "bread and 'lasses' to a hungry child" suspected that her husband "wept over them" in private.[38]

Furthermore, men were scientific and women literary in the style of their observations, another reflection of societal gender prescriptions. Women emphasized color and light, openness and vastness, and nature's flair for the dramatic, whereas men focused on soil types, dimensions, and nature's ability to enrich or deplete the earth's resources. Women typically envisioned Chimney Rock as a castle or some other fanciful form, whereas men speculated on dimensions and types of rock. The male forty-niner Byron McKinstry's portrayal of the area deserves quoting in full:

> I can see several very high rocks . . . one of them looks like a large building, also more Bluff Ruins on this side 2 or 3 m. farther up.
>
> I should suppose the highest of the "Bluff Ruins" were from 300 to 400' ft. high, and are composed of somewhat differently colored strata. The top of one was of a hard brown rock for 10 feet, then chocolate or clay color for 10 or 15, then white for 3 or 4, then 15 or 20 of the chocolate or clay again . . . the strata nearly horizontal, and any of it except the hard cap rock could be cut easily, and the water had worn some frightful chasms among these hills.[39]

In 1851, the gold-seeker J. Goldsborough Bruff offered another description from a male perspective. Although he acknowledged that "this basin, among the singular and romantic bluffs, is a beautiful spot," he went on to say that "it appears to extend E. & W about 5 ms. and about 3 ms. wide" and that "in a deep gulch lies a cool clear spring and brook." Through male eyes, he also saw "a group of Indian lodges & tents, surrounding a log cabin, where you can buy whisky for 35 per gallon; and look at the beautiful squaws, of the traders."[40] Yet these gruff men, so aware of whiskey and women, once in a while gathered flowers for themselves or compared Court House Rock to a European castle.[41]

Regarding Native Americans, men and women revealed additional differences and similarities according to gender and responsibilities. In the first category—aspects of native people, villages, and artifacts—men noticed the physical appearance and dress of American Indians, but were not as detailed or as judgmental as women. Unlike women (see chapter 4), men were impressed by native dress when intricacy and display were involved, and they did not find it ostentatious. One man described several Potawatomis as "splendidly dressed in white deerskins ornamented with black cloth, small sleigh bells, ribbons, feathers, and so forth." Yet another described some Indians near Fort Hall as "fine looking fellows with there caps and feathers on and there Beed shoes and Bo and arrows."[42] Although men enjoyed Indians' ornaments, beadwork, feathers, and paint, they concurred with women regarding native dress or lack of it. In 1859, Joseph Camp judged some Pawnee Indians to be "very degraded" because "some of them are almost naked and most of the men wear nothing but a tattered blanket and a breechclout. . . . women wear short petticoats and leggins."[43]

When American Indians emulated white clothing styles, women, who saw themselves as civilizers, applauded their attempts to look like whites, but men found it amusing. During the 1840s, a military officer who encountered an "old savage" who had tried to make himself look "as respectable as possible" by dressing in a green frock coat "not of the latest cut," an old pair of epaulets, leggings, and a cap of grizzly bear skin topped by a red feather," declared that "it did afford us a little amusement."[44] Another on his way to California observed that emigrant trains had so influenced Pima Indians that most wore "a shirt, coat or a pair of Pants—though never an entire suit." He added that he was "much diverted" at the sight of a tall, good-looking Indian with a stovepipe hat on his head, a heavy blue blanket coat covering the upper portion of his torso, and absolutely nothing on his "lower extremities."[45] A Utah-bound traveler of 1859 was similarly entertained by the sight of Cheyenne and Sioux Indians dressed in white-style clothing. "I was quite amused," he remarked, "to see some of the Indian women dressed so neatly in calico and crinoline, and some of the boys had on pants, suspenders, calico shirts, and straw hats, but these were rare cases."[46] And a male emigrant of the 1860s, on meeting some Dacotah Indians, stated that "our indians are evidently somewhat civilized as they have trowsers" and "soldiers blouses" and "one gay chap had on a caloco shirt."[47]

When men turned their attention to Indian homes and villages, they seldom saw them as picturesque, concentrating instead upon the manner of construction involved.[48] Men's writings were filled with detailed accounts of building techniques, materials, styles, and dimensions of native dwellings. A typical journal entry read: "This morning I examined the lodge referred to yesterday. It was of a conical form made of dressed buffalo hides nicely stretched over sixteen cottonwood poles."[49] Another male migrant commented on wigwams that were made of "dressed bufaloe skins sewed together" and "are round in shape with a pole passing through the top."[50] A Texas settler of the 1830s offered more details: "They sew together a number of hides, making a long roll of it. When they wish to pitch a tent, they form a circular frame work of forks & hickory with[e]s around which they wrap this roll of skins beginning at the ground and winding round until they reach the top leaving a small hole for the escape of the smoke." According to him, the finished structure resembled a "hornet's nest, and having inwardly very much also of the hornet temperament & severity."[51]

Other frontiersmen took similar pains in reporting huts, teepees, houses, and even ruined native villages.[52] Men only occasionally included descriptions of interiors of Indian homes, presumably because they had little interest in such matters. Even when they were curious, it was difficult for them to gain access to a dwelling's interior. When Isaac Wistar insisted upon visiting an Indian town that intimidated his friends, he, unlike most men, wanted to observe the Sioux's "domestic arrangements at home." When he approached a lodge, so many young men jostled him and tried to examine his weapon that he remained mounted. He shook hands all around, working his way through the male population, who, according to him, "were loudly discussing me or some other interesting object." The conclusions that he drew from his visit were superficial: the Sioux were curious and friendly, and their well laid-out lodges were "characterized by lances and shields in front of each one."[53]

Wistar's emphasis on Indian weapons was common among frontiersmen. Charged with defending themselves, their families, and stock, they were almost obsessed with the weaponry and martial skills of American Indians. Although men sometimes mentioned baskets, beadwork, or other crafts, they mostly discussed such items as bows and arrows, lances, and other weapons.[54] White men's descriptions of Indian men virtually always included weaponry: "The braves were armed with small tomahawks or iron hatchets which they carried with the powder horn, in the belt . . . over their shoulders were leather targets, bows and arrows, and some few had rifles."[55] Other men noted, "their bows & arrows are formidable weapons," "the arrows about 3 feet long with a steel point sharp as a knife," and "chief had his bow & arrows—one had a spear—no fire arms."[56]

Men also concentrated on quantity and quality of techniques, motives, and strength of Indian groups, comparing them to their own tactics, rationales, and military organization.[57] "The Comanchas," explained an early Texan, "are warlike and fight on horseback; they drill themselves & horses on the prairie, their mode of fight is to form a circle round their enemy, & keep riding round & round like circus riders . . . they then draw their arrows and commence attack; still keeping their circular gallop."[58] To some men, Indians were at their worst when after white women. To them, women who fell into Indians "merciless clutches" faced "an ordeal worse than death."[59]

The majority of white men spent even more energy worrying about their stock.[60] Like white women, men realized that most American Indians wanted to take animals rather than captives. Given the crucial role that stock played in westering, men were neither generous nor understanding where animals were concerned. As Isaac Wistar explained after Digger Indians had run off his party's mules, "most of the men have gone after the mules in a desperate hope of recovering them, for life itself here depends on the all-important help of that indispensable but hated animal." He added that men felt terrorized when Indians took their stock, becoming "savage" themselves.[61]

Certainly, women recognized the need for defense measures, but they mentioned it less often than men. Some women even joked about precautions at the men's expense. As might be expected, women were inquisitive about domestic matters, especially customs and morality, marital etiquette, child-raising practices, and crafts of American Indians.[62] As civilizers, white women had vested interests in these topics. Because white women failed to understand Indian ways they most often expressed shock, disapproval, and indignation.[63] Men, who were less concerned than women with the domestic side of life and keeping white morality in force, were nonchalant. They observed that Native Americans practiced plural marriage and intermarried with French settlers. Some men noted that Indians ate insects, were fond of liquor, were lazy, and were inveterate beggars. They were, however, terse in their moral judgments of such practices.[64]

Because many men were curious about the ways that American Indians treated their dead, they wrote in detail about above-ground burials.[65] One emigrant of the 1860s commented that he found these burying grounds "quite interesting," but he, like most other men, extended them the greatest respect.[66] Only one man from the group surveyed here violated the sanctity of Indian cemeteries by taking from one a bead as a souvenir.[67] Unlike women, men treated the dead of any group with esteem. Their attitude is best summed up by the army officer who declared that "in no instance will one nation disturb the dead of another or anything that may be about them, not even when at war." He added that "the Indians deserve great credit for the respect they show their dead" and that no one in his command would dare enter burial grounds or lodges.[68]

Most men also respected or ignored Indian marriage customs, including intermarriage and plural wives. White men seldom disparaged these practices the way white women did. Men recognized that although plural marriage was vastly different from their own ideas, Indians did not engage in what one emigrant termed "indiscriminate cohabitation."[69] On intermarriage, men made such notations as the following: "there is quite a village with stores owned by white men, the most of whom are married to Indian women." Another man said that "there are some ten or a dozen Frenchmen living here in lodges or wigwams, withe Squaws for their wives." Still another man remarked, "I saw a white man with a squaw and several children."[70] When they considered the issue of mixed-race offspring, most men thought that, judging from what one called the "variation of complexion" to be found, intermarriages were successful. When Byron McKinstry noticed that "the little ones at the trading posts are much whiter than their mothers," he dismissed it: "the cause of this extraordinary phenomenon I shall have to leave to be solved by the learned in such matters."[71]

Only a few men agreed with women on intermarriage. One argued that interbreeding "produced a villainous horde who disgraced the beautiful plains."[72] But numerous men sided with women on Indian men's treatment of women. They were under the impression that Indian men purchased wives for, as one said, "the price of a good horse."[73] An explorer of the 1830s claimed that Indian men compelled their women to do the work, whereas men had "only" to hunt and fight.[74]

Regarding the use of alcohol, white men were less condemnatory than women of Indian drinking habits. Men mentioned that Indians requested whiskey or that visiting Indians did not ask for whiskey.[75] Men who gave accounts of incidents involving drunken Indians did not include censure, as white women did.[76] Given women's fear of drunk men, women had far less tolerance than men for Indians who drank. Instead of passing judgment on Indian drinkers, men condemned the "unprincipled men" who "for the sake of gain, will supply them with the means of drunkenness and destruction."[77]

Men's attitudes were not so flexible when they saw natives eating vermin. Typically, men found this a "disgusting practice." They were further repulsed by Indians' "apparent relish" and "evident gusto."[78] One forty-niner who "saw a woman catching vermin from the head of a little boy, with which she pieced out her supper" never again ate Indian cooking. He said the woman had "fully satisfied his curiosity as to their epicurianism."[79]

Concerning Indians' requests for gifts or appropriating goods for their own use, men were almost as vitriolic as women. Epithets such as "indolent," "thieving," and "begging" punctuated men's accounts.[80] Coming from a Christian society that emphasized hard work, white men could not countenance begging. In addition, they seemed unaware that white migration had caused Indians' poverty. They made frequent derogatory references to panhandling and pilfering Indians. Only occasionally would a man observe industry or ingenuity in American Indians. But, unlike women, men refrained from praising the inventiveness of Native Americans. Although white men may have been slower than women to condemn cultural practices and rituals, they were also slower to recognize a spark of imagination, originality, or enterprise.[81] Evidently, male evenhandedness worked both ways.

Men did, however, join women in learning to discriminate among tribal groups of American Indians.[82] Men's opinions demonstrated great consensus. The Pawnees were "hostile." The Snake Indians were "the greatest beggers in the world." California's "mission" Indians were friendly to settlers.[83] Like white women, white men described the Sioux as powerful, wealthy, and beautiful in form, figure, and dress. The "Diggers," however, were the target of universal opprobrium. Seen as a "thievish and rascally race," they were considered to exist in "the lowest state of human existence."[84]

White men who dealt with Indians or disguised themselves as Indians further upset migrants and settlers. Apparently, some white men, like white women, could see that it was not always Indians who caused turmoil. They admitted that "bad" white men existed as well. One white man described white traders as being "as roguish and treacherous as the Indians themselves." Others thought "white Indians" more dangerous than warlike Pawnees.[85]

These realizations helped white men recognize that, at times, Indians were unfairly condemned. Some whites tried to reach out to Indians to alleviate the rancor that too often resulted from white-Indian contacts. Such white men visited Indian camps and met with leaders to prevent loss of goods or lives. Unfortunately, these meetings were usually formal affairs that did little to foster sympathy or understanding. Following accepted practices, white and Indian men exchanged gifts, smoked the pipe together, and discussed questions of trade, passage, landownership, and other issues. Around the core group of talkers were a large number of onlookers, whose presence added to the tension and impersonality of the situation.[86]

Even though these conferences ended with a feast, stiffness remained.[87] One army officer who smoked the pipe with an Oglala Sioux leader, parleyed, and feasted in the Indian's lodge felt that the "good will" was superficial and very little had been accomplished. His fears were borne out; within a few days the belongings of his men vanished despite the Indian leader's promises to the contrary.[88] The white forty-niner Reuben Shaw also came away from a similar ceremony with a bad impression. When Shaw called on a village of Blackfeet, he was appalled by the "filthy, repulsive interiors" of the dwellings, the "filthy cooking methods" of the women, and the preponderance of dogs. "What struck us as being most abundant about the Indian camp was, first, dirt," he asserted, "second, dogs; third, more dirt." His disgust grew when he had to give gifts of jewelry and buttons to the women and a variety of articles to the leader to obtain hunting rights in the area. Shaw went away convinced that the "crafty" chief—whom he dubbed "Saint Brag" because of the chief's boasting of his exploits—got the best of the bargain. He also reported that, notwithstanding promises, goods disappeared from his party's camp. "We were," he said, "glad to be done with the Blackfeet, though we looked upon them as a very interesting people and as noble types of the American Indians."[89]

These two men's adventures were not unusual. Male contact with Indians failed to foster communication between Indians and whites and to bring native and white men closer in understanding. Consequently, white men seldom experienced changes in their attitudes toward American Indians. Usually committed from the inception of their migration to an adversarial position toward Indians, most men had neither motivation nor opportunity to get to know Indians or develop sympathy for them.[90] Instead, they hung on to their beliefs that their colonialist quest was noble and providential, even if it resulted in the death of Native Americans.[91] Had men changed their attitudes, it might have undermined their effectiveness as invaders and takers of Indian homelands, and perhaps recast history.

Exceptions to pugnacious men did exist. One was Alonzo Delano, who came to believe that white men caused nine-tenths of white-Indian trouble. Yet he concluded that peaceful coexistence was impossible and American Indians would "have to yield because of their obvious inferiority."[92] Another exception was Howard Egan, who found a "good" Indian whom he took back to Salt Lake City as a friend and servant.[93] Such men as missionaries, teachers, fundraisers for missions, explorers, and religiously oriented individuals also expressed compassionate feelings, but they did not adopt these after contact with Indians. Rather, they brought pro-Indian attitudes with them and continued to maintain them.[94]

Yet other men went west claiming to have open minds toward American Indians. One of these, Dr. Thomas White of Indiana, was soon disenchanted. After a few days' exposure to what he called "hateful wretches," he said he had lost any pity that he had for Indians. "I used to think the Emigrants at fault, but I know it is not the case," he insisted.[95] Another medical doctor, traveling on the plains in the 1860s, indicated that the more he saw Indians the more he disliked them. Having observed Omahas, Pawnees, and Sioux, he concluded that all Indians were "filthy," "sneaking," and "treacherous." Having read an acquaintance's description of an Indian council, he was convinced that Indians thought themselves to be superior to whites. Although his evidence was scanty and his "personal observation of their customs" was biased, he advocated that the "tribes of the plains must be given a tremendous thrashing . . . and forced into subjection."[96] A Mormon settler in Salt Lake City urged a similar approach to Utah Indians. He explained that he had "lost all of the good feeling I ever had for them and that was not much." His bellicosity was absolute: "last winter we killed one tribe off and will have to kill a few more before we can make them behave. That is the way to convert them to the Mormon faith."[97]

Clearly, white men's primary tone in this sample was acrimonious and hostile. Although men who migrated with a commitment to aiding American Indians maintained it, those who started out with vague thinking or deep-seated prejudices usually found their pessimistic expectations confirmed. Only a few men converted their cynicism into empathetic views of American Indians. This pattern deviates sharply from the white women considered here, the majority of whom demonstrated positive changes in their reactions toward Indians.

Unarguably, men and women differed in roles and functions in relation to Indians, which provided opportunity to change or not change their attitudes toward Indians. While men usually remained rigid and inflexible in their views, women often altered their ideas regarding American Indians. Neither side, however, was very knowledgeable about Indians or took into account how white migration affected Indian standards of living, morality, and aggressiveness. They simply assumed that whatever Indians were resulted from their character rather than white deeds.

—— White Women's and Men's Interactions with American Indians ——

Given these differences between white men and women, it is understandable that they also differed in their relationships with Native Americans. By necessity, white women concentrated upon family and domestic concerns, values, and other related matters, whereas men focused on fighting, hunting, and conflict. As a consequence, men thought of Indians as foes, whereas women far more often referred to them as guides, assistants, purveyors of provisions, and even friends.

This is not meant to imply that women allowed themselves to be pushed around or intimidated by intrusive Indians. On the contrary, newly confident women resisted Indian demands that they deemed unreasonable. Women short-circuited native commands by actions that ranged from slapping Indians' faces to waving empty pistols under Indians' noses.[98]

White women also resorted to a variety of threats. On one occasion, Susanna Ede evicted an Indian interloper from her kitchen by threatening to pour hot grease on him. In another incident, she raised a pot of boiling water to be thrown on the trespasser.[99] Still other women used direct action. One tore her belongings out of the hands of trespassing American Indians. Some assertive women depended on raw bravado to repel unwelcome requests. Lavinia Porter, for example, refused a demand for bread only to have bleeding scalps thrust at her to count and admire. When she refused to give ground, her would-be oppressor muttered "white squaw no fear" and departed.[100]

Some frontierswomen were even willing to engage in unfeminine, violent action when necessary. To protect stock from nearby Indians, Mary Burrell and Barsina French's mother took turns standing guard with the men.[101] An Arizona woman defended her family's horses and mules by spending a long night shooting at a band of Pima Indians from one end of the stable roof and then the other.[102] An Iowa woman attempted to fend off an abusive Indian with a fireplace poker.[103] And when Susie Van De Wiele's officer husband asked her if she was afraid of Indians near Fort Leavenworth, she replied, "No, give me a pistol."[104]

Apparently, women were learning that their physical weakness was not as severe nor as debilitating as they had been led to believe. They also seemed quite willing to act in a martial fashion when necessary.[105] Still, they more often spoke of occasions of cooperating, trading, or some type of positive encounter with American Indians.[106] The initial pattern of white women's interaction with Indians was exchanges of goods and services. Women who overcame their anxieties traded such items as trinkets, clothing, and foodstuffs. This trade occurred even during the intensified conflict of the 1860s and 1870s.[107] On the trail and in their new homes, women bartered needles and thread, processed foods such as flour, articles of apparel, and trifles with natives, who usually offered fresh foods in return. White women were delighted when Indian men and women brought eggs, potatoes, corn, pumpkins, melons, strawberries, blackberries, venison and other fresh meats, fish, and dried salmon.[108] Women savored these foods, which provided relief from a diet of bread, bacon or salt pork, and beans. "We have so little change in our diet," Miriam Colt, a Kansas settler of the 1850s, wrote, "that almost anything is relished."[109] Similarly, California-bound Martha Moore considered some mountain trout that she purchased from an Indian to be "quite a treat." Another time, she was pleased to have "procured a fine mess of fish."[110]

Many women also desired Indian craft items and grew skillful at bargaining for buffalo hides and robes, antelope and elk clothing, moccasins, baskets, and beadwork.[111] Army wife Cynthia Capron was enthralled by a watertight basket that she purchased for one dollar near Camp Wright during the 1860s.[112] Moccasins were the most popular trade item; some women even ordered them from native women.[113] Buffalo robes were also coveted; at least one woman surrendered her shawl to obtain one.[114] Sadly, some women used as rugs beautifully tanned skins, including beaver and otter, a practice that they came to regret when these items were no longer available.[115]

Some of the women who headed west harboring the worst apprehensions toward American Indians developed into enthusiastic traders. Lucy Cooke, initially in awe of Indians, became an expert bargainer. By the end of her trail experience, Cooke collected a fine cache of furs.[116] Army wife Eveline Alexander overcame her misgivings to barter not only for foodstuffs, but also to purchase shields, bows, and arrows. She considered a war shield that she bought to be "a valuable trophy."[117] And Ada Vogdes, who had spent so much time fearing Indians, acquired enough proficiency in local native dialects to bargain with Native Americans. "I rushed around all day to get a blanket worked with beads which I suceeded in doing," she wrote in triumph.[118]

Women usually carried on such negotiations personally. As women's preconceptions concerning themselves and American Indians dissipated, they were able to enter business dealings with once-dreaded enemies. In so doing, they fulfilled their function as providers of domestic goods. They also demonstrated a relatively gentle style in their contact with

American Indians. And they learned, in Catherine Haun's words, that "the Indian is a financier of no mean ability." Bargains and good deals were not easy to come by, according to Haun: "natives had as strong a streak of Yankee cunning as the Yankees themselves." She added that "though you may, for the time congratulate yourself upon your own sagacity, you'll be apt to realize a little later that you were not quite equal to the shrewd redman."[119] Katherine Dunlap, on her way to Montana in 1864, said that Indian traders not only differentiated between "coin" and "greenbacks," but took "the latter at 50¢ on the dollar,"[120] this in an era where white farm laborers in the East made $0.88 a day and firemen $1.33 a day and probably lacked the same sagacity the Indians demonstrated.[121]

Men also personally traded with Indians. Although some coveted moccasins, buckskins, and buffalo hides, they spent more time dealing in arms, ammunition, tobacco, horses, and other animals.[122] The more accommodating men paid Indians cash or such items as shirts, caps, and ammunition.[123] To white men's credit, the men were judicious in distributing liquor or refused to do so at all.[124] Men also employed, or even kidnapped, Indians to serve as guides because they knew the best trails, grass, and water.[125] Occasionally, men even entrusted their stock to an individual Indian hired to act as a herder.[126] It was not uncommon for men to pay natives "rewards" for locating "lost" stock, but it is impossible to determine whether this was simply a variation of the age-old protection racket.[127]

White men frequently thought amounts of money or goods charged by American Indians were excessive, whereas others viewed the employment of Indian guides, pilots, and herders as extortion.[128] Because of these men's commitment to colonialism, they saw no need to compensate natives for the assistance, land, or other resources they wrested from them. Assuming that whites were superior and Indians were inferior—and perhaps not even human—men regarded all aspects of the West as belonging to them. Due to their belligerent attitudes, such men left resentment in their wake. Moreover, because they refused to pay for Indian assistance, they frequently met with disaster.[129]

White women also hired natives to perform chores for them. Californian Mary Ackley employed some Paiute men to shovel, cut firewood, draw water, and even wash clothes.[130] Other women, evidently free of former anxieties, invited Indians into their homes as domestic helpers. Native men, women, and children performed household chores, including washing dishes and clothes. White female employers, who frequently commented that Indians were "a great help," paid Indian workers with such commodities as sugar, salt, and bread.[131]

The most significant capacity in which women employed both Indian men and women was as nursemaids to their children.[132] In light of white women's fear that American Indians lay in wait to pounce upon white children and carry them away as adoptees or as captives, their employment of Indian nursemaids seems unbelievable. Mothers grew to trust individual Indians enough to bring them into their nurseries. When, in 1868, army wife Eveline Alexander arranged for an Apache girl to care for her newborn baby she wrote to her father in New York: "I wish the grandmothers of the young one, who are so afraid of her 'falling' into the hands of the Apachees could have looked in upon us a while ago." Alexander explained that "they would have seen the infant prodigy awake in her cradle, cooing to herself, and being rocked to sleep by a bona fide wild Apachee, who a week ago was roaming the mountains, guiltless of any other covering but her maiden modesty." Later, Alexander told her father that the Apache nurse seemed "to love to be with the baby" and "is quite useful already in drawing it around in its wagon and rocking the cradle."[133]

Unlike white women in Asian and African empires, those in the West who hired American Indian nurses did not object to them teaching the children native customs, dialects, food preferences, and games.[134] Nannie Alderson was pleased that her baby's "good and faithful" nurse carried the child on her back like a "papoose," as well as crooning native songs to the baby, teaching her a "squaw" dance, making her beaded moccasins, and observing the Indian custom of never spanking the child.[135] Because white people had established their dominance, such women as Alderson could afford to be flexible. Moreover, as whites increasingly moved Indians to reservations, their role in white households became a nonissue. Still, some cross-cultural understanding occurred between white women and Native Americans. During the 1830s, when her male Indian nurse died, Caroline Phelps said that her entire family felt his loss very much: her children cried for him "as much as though he had been a relative." She went on to explain that "he was their friend truly they missed his singing, he used to fix a drum & then sing and drum & have them and the little papooses dance, any one could not tell which was which only by the color, many a time I have went in where they were dancing, all having blankets on, and I could hardly tell my own children . . . they would all sing, but just alike."[136] Later, during the 1850s, a young Puget Sound woman, raised by an Indian nurse, acquired a fondness for native food and gained proficiency in her nurse's language. She also expressed a love for the woman that she said was second only to her feelings for her mother.[137]

White women who treated with fairness their Indian employees fared the best. Rachel Wright, a settler in the Upper Napa Valley, claimed that the key to favorable working relations with American Indians lay with migrants and settlers. Indians could be "an advantage rather than otherwise," she argued, "as they were not only willing but glad to work if they were left free, well treated and properly paid for their labor."[138]

It was in this spirit that many frontierswomen visited American Indians. While such occasions nourished cordiality, it was personal interchanges between white women and Indian men and women that fostered warm feelings. White women who found Indians fearsome in a large group could handle a few at a time. One trail woman of the 1850s who visited Sioux women was impressed by their hospitality and their "skill with a needle."[139] A female migrant of the 1860s recorded frequent and very genial social times between her white friends and "the Cherokee Ladies."[140] A Mormon woman added that Indian women whom she visited were "really friendly." She remarked that they had enjoyed "quite a dish of conversation together."[141]

Others recalled getting to know Indians as children. An Iowa settler of the 1870s explained that she grew up with friendly feelings toward the Indians who roamed the woods and camped in the fields around her home. She attributed this to the fact that her Aunt Liza had regularly taken her and her sister to a nearby native village, where the women had given them beads that they "treasured greatly."[142] An Oklahoma woman recalled a similar experience from her childhood of the 1890s. She often visited a Choctaw woman, whom she called Aunt Sophia.

She loved Aunt Sophia's "wonderfully clean house," extensive collection of handiwork, and the many little kindnesses she extended to her young caller.[143]

Positive contacts between white and native women often blossomed into deeper associations, at least according to white women. Unfortunately, because Indian history is based on oral tradition, the subaltern voice is largely unavailable. In addition, because of different word usage and subtle meanings in Indian languages and in English, even translated accounts are unclear or misleading.[144] Thus, Indian women's views are typically obscure, which leaves white women's writings as the only, and often romanticized, accounts.[145] One tale comes from army wife Alice Baldwin, who after crimping and waving native women's hair, discovered that "thereafter the Indian women were my firm friends, and rendered me various favors and kindnesses." With great insight, Baldwin commented that they were brought together by "feminine vanity and tastes," which she felt were "much the same the world over, no matter what the race or color." On one occasion, Baldwin consented to undress partially so Indian women could see the paraphernalia that she wore. "Crinoline and corsets they marveled at, but did not admire," she remarked. As they examined her various articles of clothing and fussed over her beautifully dressed hair, she was struck by their voices, which seemed "naturally soft and melodious." As she sat among them, "listening to their chatter and laughter, and no doubt passing uncomplimentary comments" about her, she "felt that it all meant sincerity, which does not always prevail in a cultured and fashionable society."[146]

Other white and native women exchanged bits of female knowledge, lore, and folk medicine. For instance, Mormon migrant Eliza Roxey Snow learned about sego roots from native women. Snow claimed that sego "proved to be a nutritious, substantial article of food, and not unpalatable."[147] Similarly, an Oklahoma woman recalled that she learned about "palatable and very healthful" greens and roots by accompanying Indian women on their gathering and digging expeditions into nearby woods.[148] Others learned how to use herb remedies or how to treat a rattlesnake bite with raw turkey meat.[149] At time of childbirth, white women sought Indian midwives and received gifts from Indian women. One California woman raved about "beautiful baskets and elaborate moccasins worked with beads and feathers" that Indian women brought to her mother when her baby, the first white child in that part of the country, was born. Another remembered the Indian woman who brought her persimmon bread and a papoose board intricately worked with beading and fringe.[150]

A representative case of exchanges between white and native women was Leola Lehman, an Oklahoma settler who befriended Indian women. In turn, they visited her, bringing small presents and admiring her new baby. As Baldwin had mentioned, elements of female culture drew Lehman and Indian women into an easy bond. Lehman especially liked one native woman who had come to see her because she thought that Lehman "might be lonesome." Lehman came to regard this native woman, in her words, "as one of the best women she had ever known."[151]

Lehman made an important point when she suggested that positive interchanges between whites and natives were possible if whites would only realize that Indians had heard as many horror stories about whites as whites had heard about Indians. Their inability to understand white language, religion, and culture made them as vulnerable to rumors and alarmism as were whites toward Indians. Having no other information, Indians believed much of what they heard, including legends of Spanish atrocities. Indians were also afraid of whites taking them captive and raping them, killing their babies, and perhaps selling them and their children as slaves and prostitutes.[152] Many despised Catholic priests for establishing sexual liaisons with native women. Adults detested white greed and corruption, and children, who heard that whites would eat them, screamed at the sight of a white face. If Indians acted strange, Lehman said, their behavior stemmed from their "fear of white people."[153]

When other Oklahoma settlers had an opportunity to interact on an amicable basis with their Indian neighbors, they too found that they liked Indians.[154] These settlers occasionally entertained Native Americans in their homes. Occasionally, even a white man and Indian man became close. In one case, an Indian man openly cried when his white friend died. "Not much stoicism there," the deceased man's sister commented.[155] Women's friendships were more common, however, due to the role that female values played in drawing together white and native women. White and Indian women shared interests in home, family, children, and domestic matters, and espoused beliefs that crossed cultures, including being nurturing and supportive, which created a connection largely unavailable to white and Indian men.

Consequently, white women seemed earnest when they spoke of Indian women as friends. When a white woman said "She-wicket was my best friend," the statement carried a ring of veracity.[156] As far as it is possible to judge from mute documents, which are incapable of revealing tone, inflection, or facial expressions, these women seemed to be sincere. Granted, women like Ward or Vogdes may have been aware of the shock value as they wrote their friends about their willingness to share space with an authentic "savage" companion, but most of these women appeared truthful. One even said she was glad to see Indians arrive and sorry to see them leave. "We have parted with white folks that we did not regret so much," she insisted.[157]

White men lacked opportunities available to women. Although men visited native camps and villages, they joined the "braves" and "chiefs" at the fire to smoke the pipe, to talk about land and politics, and to negotiate trades. They were often treated to meals prepared by the women, and sometimes were expected to admire the children, but men were not welcomed into Indians' homes and families as women were. Other situations that existed for women were unthinkable for men. It is unlikely, for example, that a native man would call on a settler, telling him that he thought the white man "might be lonely." And it is ridiculous to picture a male settler partially disrobing so that his new Indian friends could see his intimate apparel. Instead, males helped each other with weapons, stock, hunting, fighting, and similar activities that only infrequently resulted in the mutuality and confidentiality that women so easily shared.

Women not only visited Indians, but regularly attended Indian dances and ceremonies, including cries (mourning ceremonies), weddings, funerals, beef issues (distribution of government rations), stomp dances, war dances, and mock battles. The more generous and sympathetic among them regarded weddings, cries, and funerals as times for respect and empathy.[158] But white women were more reserved about other ceremonies, which often allowed Indians to behave in ways that whites found unacceptable. Indians, who were usually deferential and even ingratiating to whites, were willing to "perform" for white women because it gave them a rare opportunity to act out their dissatisfaction in aggressive ways that would be unacceptable to whites in other situations.[159] As a result, white women generally viewed beef issues as a colorful gathering of native peoples, but were often repulsed by Indians' ferocity as they slaughtered and disemboweled animals.[160] Women usually found ball games and stomp dances entertaining, but sometimes suspected that certain performers ingested drugs and hallucinogens.[161]

Indian war dances and mock battles were even more problematic for white women. Some regarded them as interesting social affairs.[162] Although one woman was pleased when Nez Percé Indians prepared a mock battle for her mother's first visit to Oregon,[163] other women admitted that such performances raised their inner anxieties. Whether they realized it or not, these women reacted to an expression of Indian identity, and perhaps to a subliminal challenging of white hegemony, that permeated these "harmless" exhibitions.[164] In 1875, Wyoming visitor Laura Johnson watched nervously as Sioux filed toward Fort Fetterman to stage a dance. Although impressed with their attire, she felt that the dancers represented "a piece of real savage life." To her, these Sioux were "of the wildest kind, about as savage as any there are." Insightfully, she viewed the male dancers as close to the "real thing" rather than imitation.[165] Similarly, during the 1890s Ellen Biddle observed Indian dancers moving toward Fort Robinson in full regalia. "Few people," she wrote, "can see a tribe of Indians marching toward them, even without their war paint, without feeling a thumping of the heart and a trembling of the limbs; at least that was my experience." She added that the dance, attended by people from miles around the fort, was a "tremendous success," presumably as an exotic form of entertainment.[166]

Other women responded fearfully to the dances that they witnessed. Whatever accommodations they had made with Indians were too recent and wounds too deep for these performances to be innocuous. One women enjoyed a Paiute dance, but, due to recent "unpleasant experience with their neighbors, the Shoshones," she "felt more comfortable when they were gone."[167] Another, stunned by the ferocity of the dancers, worried that the Indians had lured them within range of an ambush.[168] Not only women cringed; men also felt the impalpable aggression in Indian dances and feared possible outcomes. They were correct; Native Americans who were "civilized" and ghettoized, many on reservations, knew better than to express their antagonisms in front of whites. Dances and ceremonies allowed them to do so in an "acceptable" way. Still, whites were concerned that bad feelings might run amok. During the 1860s, the Coloradoan Emma Hill described Indian dances held around fires and lasting late into the night as "dignified and impressive." Yet when American Indians requested permission from town officials to present an exhibition war dance, these whites refused on the grounds that the Indians would get "too excited" during the dance and would harm the settlers.[169]

Even though some women were intimidated by Native Americans attired in battle dress and acting in an aggressive and warlike manner, they usually maintained their equilibrium. After all, such performances emphasized that Indians were still the "other," whereas whites were clearly dominant. The very fact of whites being "guests" at "interesting" Indian ceremonials clearly spelled out who held the power and who did not. Here, too, white women found it easier to adjust to individual Indians than a large number of them. When Laura Johnson attended a Sun Dance involving thousands of Sioux, she focused on the dancing of one handsome and graceful native man.[170]

Gradually, through social relations with Indian women, white women learned to know and like Indian men, who were not as frightening as they thought. Harriet Ward, for example, contradicted earlier attitudes when she declared that her friends back home would "be surprised to see me writing so quietly in the wagon alone . . . with a great, wild looking Indian leaning his elbow on the wagon beside me, but I have not a single fear except that he may frighten the horses."[171] Relieved somewhat of their fears, women asked help of Indian men.[172] For instance, women turned to Indian medical practitioners to treat themselves and children. When her daughter's face got badly burned, Caroline Phelps called in a native doctor who treated the child effectively. In another case, a woman remarked that Indians cared for her people "like a brother should treat a brother." On occasion, white women also aided Native American men. Nannie Alderson restored two "almost frozen" Indian men with a fire and a meal.[173]

Some women not only coped with individual Indian men, but discovered in the process that they liked, admired, and even loved them. Under these circumstances, many white women found it impossible to overcome their sense of superiority to Indians; they could not consider intermarriage. This was the case for Catherine Weldon, a widow from New York who in 1889 traveled to the Standing Rock reservation in Dakota Territory as a representative of the National Indian Defense Association. Weldon especially hoped to help Sitting Bull in his efforts to resist the United States government from appropriating Sioux land. Although Weldon grew close to Sitting Bull, she was shocked and insulted when he proposed marriage. Weldon was put off because Sitting Bull already had several wives and because she thought of herself as a superior white savior to inferior people, hardly a figure to stimulate an Indian man's proposal.[174] For other white women, however, their anathema to intermarriage dissolved.[175] When romantic love blossomed between a white woman and a native man, it often resulted in marriage. In 1886, for example, a young New England woman of genteel family and demonstrated literary ability became a teacher at the Great Sioux Reservation in Dakota Territory. Here, Elaine Goodale came to see Indians as human beings with a complex culture and who were likable as individuals. During her first five years among them, she wrote articles and tracts about them and their problems. In 1891, she married a Sioux physician named Charles A. Eastman, with whom she shared a commitment to helping Sioux people adjust to a changing world. Together, the Eastmans wrote nine books. That Elaine Goodale Eastman's decision to marry an American Indian was not unique among missionary women is supported by references to other instances in frontier accounts.[176]

Another situation that fostered marriages between white females and native males existed in Oklahoma during the 1880s, the 1890s, and the early 1900s. As large numbers of settlers took up land leases on Indian agencies, pushing into the region in land rushes, associations developed between whites and American Indians. These contacts led to a number of intermarriages. A former Texas woman recalled, "I have two nieces who married Commanche Indians, one Clinton Red Elk, and one Buster

Work-a-wam."[177] Other women mentioned that relatives, acquaintances, or they themselves had married full-blood or mixed-blood men.[178]

Such terms as *full-blood* and *half-blood* originated with whites, who established racial and ethnic categories partly to help them administer Indian policies, notably land allotments.[179] In a racist society such racial definitions were necessary to keep those of color in their proper places and behaving in ways that whites found appropriate.[180] Full-blood Indians at least had an unstained background, but mixed-bloods were anathema to many whites and to some Indians. Thus, although some mixed-heritage people admitted their status, others became wary, and even ashamed, of categorizing themselves. One woman remembered that negative feelings caused her father, a "one-half Cherokee," to refuse to prove a land claim because he would not expose his shame at being "part Indian," even to obtain a homestead.[181]

Despite the stigma regarding men with partial Indian "blood," Oklahoma women chose a variety of Indian men as mates. One woman explained that her husband was "a quarter-blood Choctaw Indian" who farmed near the Little Washita River.[182] Another woman said that she married a Cherokee who was a teacher trained at Tahlequah's male seminary. Another, however, chose as her husband "a full blood Chickasaw," an interpreter for the governor of the Chickasaw nation. She married him initially under state law in 1892, and again under Indian law in 1897.[183]

The government recognized these marriages by allowing wives of native men to draw allotments and payments made to "full-blood" Indians. Yet what Americans came to call miscegenation, or mixing of races, was not widely accepted in the West. In Oklahoma, there was opposition from individuals, especially men. One woman spoke of her father's objections to his daughters marrying Native Americans. In a curious twist of fate, after his sudden death, neighboring Indians were so kind to these women that one recalled, "my sister married a full blood and we have always been glad that she did."[184]

Even though it is unclear whether men or women were more, less, or equally accepting of marriages between white women and American Indian men, it is likely that the female value system permitted women to adjust to the idea of intermarriage. Female beliefs allowed women to enter comfortable situations with Indians that led to intimate relationships. In addition, women were not usually as dedicated as men to the eradication of Native Americans and the seizure of their property. Thus, white women were probably more accepting than men of cultural mixing.

Of course, white men—often to the disdain of white women—also married Indians. Although some white male–Indian female relationships were affectional, others contained an element of mutual exploitation. For instance, an Indian wife might be of great use to a white man who traded with Indians, whereas the wife gained status among her people. Because most men considered Indian women inferior, such marriages were almost never legalized or solemnized according to white terms, as were marriages between white females and native males. When a white man did marry a native woman according to white law, it was a matter for comment by whites. In one such case, Alice Baldwin wrote that the man was "the soul of honor," who "had the decent courage to marry her legally."[185] In a very different instance, a woman claimed that Indian tumult was caused in Washington state by white men who not only refused to legalize their unions with native women, but who already had wives back east.[186]

Even though white male–native female alliances have received much coverage in myth and media, little attention had been paid to white female–native male relationships. Beginning with Pocahontas, white men believed they had a mission to rescue native women from primitivism, degraded status, and Indian men's supposedly low sexuality. By allying with an Indian woman, a white man often stood to gain land, stock, and the friendship of the woman's people, as well as the help and affection of the woman herself. Because white men knew that their status would determine that of their wives and children, they were not afraid that they would suffer by marrying a woman from an "inferior" race.[187]

White man–native woman relationships were publicized in popular literature, the press, and more recently, movies and television. From dime novels to the Hollywood movie *Jeremiah Johnson,* illegal and unsolemnized alliances (at least according to white prescriptions) could be presented to general audiences and could even be glorified. Objections to such alliances, which resulted in the use of the epithet "squaw man," receive trifling or sympathetic handling in the media.

White woman–native man relationships, however, must have raised the anxieties of white men. If a white woman chose to marry a native man, what was the attraction that influenced her decision? White women would not gain status, wealth, power, or the approval of society. Could it be that white women found attractive and just the supposedly inferior native male?[188] Worse yet, was it possible that white women chose Indian mates or pined for their native husbands because these men were sexually competent and virile? Media raised this question by occasionally eroticizing Indian men. By the late nineteenth- and early twentieth centuries, white women of Victorian purity read captivity narratives, in which the Indian male's prowess was unspoken yet powerful.[189] If white men acknowledged this possibility, their views of their own superiority would slide. Loss of white men's superior sexuality would be equivalent to loss of control. White men might have to admit that Indian men were not so inferior after all, thus destroying the primary rationale for their anti-Indian policies. If, indeed, women were drawn to elements of native life and to individual Indians, white men would have to add to their list another fear related to Indian men.[190] Typically, white men dealt with this issue by denying the existence or the validity of white female–native male liaisons. Just because white men ignored the situation, it did not go away.

What of the missionary woman married, in legal and religious terms, to an Indian man? Where are the media treatments of such women as Elaine Goodale Eastman? Where is the saga of a female settler who becomes the wife of an Indian and the mother of "half-breed" children? When nineteenth-century media dared to broach this theme, it described female captives who wished to return to Indian husbands and children. The explanation for such behavior was that these women had been dehumanized by contact with American Indians or that they were ashamed to face white society because of their debasement. When late twentieth-century media considered the topic in such movies as *Soldier Blue* and *Tell Them Willie Boy Is Here,* however, it was with a tinge of shame and censure for those involved. For instance, in 1909 in California, Willie Boy had to flee the reservation because the agent interfered in a relationship between Willie Boy and the agent's daughter. Willie Boy's impertinence in connection with a white woman eventually ended with his death.[191]

—— White Women as Captives ——

What of the women facing violation and violence? Did white women taken captive by Native Americans change their attitudes in positive ways? Despite bestselling captivity narratives, white women captives were not always negative toward their captors or to Indians in general. Women's unpublished writings indicate that white women captives understood and sometimes had affection for their captors. Rather than being bitter and malevolent, a significant number were accepting and forgiving.

Of course, attacks, massacres, and captivity were not all they were reputed to be. For one thing, both sides committed "outrages" and took captives. For another, captives of Indians were often accorded fair treatment as prisoners of war, as adoptees, or as potential cultural converts. Nor was captivity by Indians aimed primarily at women and children. A study of captives in New England between 1675 and 1763 showed that 349 were male, 186 female, 22 infants between birth and two years of age, 128 children between two and six, 117 youths between seven and fifteen, 288 over sixteen, and 15 of unknown ages.[192] If such data were collected for the trans-Mississippi West, a similar pattern would most likely emerge. Certainly, anecdotal evidence regarding gender and age of captives in the trans-Mississippi region fails to uphold the belief that natives were intent upon seizing women and children as prisoners.

In addition, little evidence exists that American Indians sexually abused their female captives. Published captivity narratives involving women who were "ravished" appealed to a wide audience, whereas high sales gave visibility and a dominant position to the captivity genre. The popularity of published captivity narratives would gain by suggesting that women accounted for a large number of Indian captives and that they were always raped, forced into unwanted marriages, or otherwise assaulted. Yet numerous unpublished women's accounts do not mention or even hint at sexual threats, nor do they record women's fear of rape by Indian males.[193]

It might be argued that nineteenth-century women, schooled in modesty and an aversion to speaking of sexual matters, refused to comment upon sexual matters. But, using veiled terms, women discussed such issues in published captivity narratives. Women also brought up issues of sexual abuse in petitions, called memorials, that they introduced to the U.S. Congress, asking for compensation for their suffering.[194] Furthermore, captivity accounts include tremendous detail about every type of "atrocity" imaginable. It is difficult to believe that writers of unpublished accounts restrained themselves from including sexual misuse if it was widespread.[195]

Another important question regarding captives was their desire to remain with their American Indian captors. The New England study discussed above revealed that a greater number of females than males chose to remain among Indians. Evidence for the trans-Mississippi West suggests a similar situation. There was, for example, the widely told story of Cynthia Ann Parker, who was a Comanche captive between 1836 and 1860. She married a man who became a noted leader, bore three children, and took the Comanche way of life as her own. When Texas Rangers "liberated" Cynthia Ann and her two-year-old child, Topsannah, she had no desire to go with them. She lost her husband, children, extended family, and friends in one day, and never recovered from her loss. Although the Texas legislature gave Cynthia Ann money and land as compensation for her trials, she made repeated attempts to run away with Topsannah. During the fall of 1863, Topsannah died of a fever. The depressed Cynthia Ann, who eventually refused to eat, followed in 1870.[196]

Another example was Olive Oatman. After being ransomed away from her Indian captors, Oatman spent most of her time longing for and attempting to return to her native husband and children. "For four years she lived with us," a friend explained, "but she was a grieving, unsatisfied woman, who shook one's belief in civilization." Although the Indian tattoo marks were removed from her face, Oatman's white family and friends could not erase what they called "the wild life from her heart."[197]

These cases and similar stories of female captivity were explained away by assertions that these women had been too brutalized by the Indians to function in white society or that they were too ashamed to face their families and friends. These arguments are not upheld by the unpublished writings of female captives.[198] Some female captives expressed favorable feelings toward their captors. Sometimes these cases were recorded secondhand. Texan Harriet Bunyard, leaving her home in 1868 for California, encountered a young woman captive who had been recently ransomed from the Indians and who claimed that they "were very kind to her."[199] Another Texas woman of the 1860s recounted the story of an eleven-year-old female captive who insisted that she had been well cared for by an Indian woman: "as long as I stayed with the Indians she was my adopted mother, and always treated me as her own child."[200] A similar tale revolved around the Fletcher sisters, captured in 1865 in Wyoming by Arapaho Indians. After Amanda Mary was ransomed, she located her baby sister Lizzie. When she wrote to General George Custer about obtaining Lizzie's release, she was told that her sister was "in good health and was kindly cared for by the Indians being considered a great favorite by them." When Amanda Mary pursued the matter, she learned through an interpreter that Lizzie, now fifteen years old, denied being white. Instead, Lizzie claimed she was an Arapaho and refused to be ransomed away from "her" people.[201]

In addition to these tales of female captives who were treated well by American Indians, a number of firsthand captivity accounts reiterate this theme in more detail. In one of the earliest conflicts, that between Indians and Dr. Marcus Whitman's mission in Oregon during the late 1840s, the women involved told of "outrages and "depredations." They also emphasized the aid and support given to them by "friendly" natives. They commended the Nez Percés for saving settlers' lives, for treating them with "decency and respect," and for bringing the responsible Indians in for trial and execution.[202]

During the years following the Oregon turmoil, women felt moved, as one said, "to weep & pray for those dark dying nations."[203] Rather than becoming disillusioned, they took a generous view of the unfortunate events that transpired around the Whitman mission. On the fiftieth anniversary of these events, some women commemorated them.

A ceremony took place at the site, to which the local railroad company gave all survivors free transportation. Also, a monument built to Dr. Whitman dislodged bones and skulls that offered mute testimony to the disastrous nature of the "massacre."[204]

Other captivity stories are from the 1860s and 1870s, the era during which Native American resistance to white invasion of their lands and hunting grounds peaked. Because conflict increased during these decades the number of captivities also proliferated. Women's reactions to Indians did not become more negative as violence intensified. If anything, the troubles of these years convinced many women to intensify their efforts to understand and aid captives. Many women also grew increasingly sympathetic with natives on the issue of taking prisoners of war.[205]

One chronicle of the 1862 New Ulm tragedy in Minnesota, which gained wide circulation in published form, was Mary Renville's *Thrilling Narrative of Indian Captivity.* Renville's account was designed to titillate and shock. The incidents it recounted included the rape of white women captives by several drunken Indian men. Yet a close reading reveals that Renville justified Indian actions by blaming whites, who had a corrupting influence. Who supplied the liquor for the Indians in the first place? Renville asked. And how many crimes committed by Indians have been caused by thoughtless whites? Renville blamed greedy traders and government agents for introducing some of the white's "most flagrant vices" to Native Americans. She concluded her narrative by advising Minnesota settlers not to punish all Indians, which would drive peaceful Indians into the ranks of the warlike. Furthermore, Renville suggested, those settlers who went among American Indians in the future needed to support "Justice, Morality, and Truth" rather than encouraging dishonesty and dissipation.[206]

Another account of the New Ulm affair illustrates that some women liked their captors. Taken prisoner in the 1862 New Ulm conflict, Minnie Carrigan later spoke with fondness of the two Indian women who cared for her during her captivity. "It seems wrong for me to call those two Indian women squaws," she stated. "They were as ladylike as any white women, and I shall never forget them." When the prisoners were dispersed to other camps, Carrigan was protected by a young native woman and was then taken in by an Indian family, who made quite a "pet" of her. "Their conduct toward me was so considerate," she later declared, "that I really liked them."[207]

Perhaps Carrigan's attitude can be understood through a survey of events leading to hostilities. The conflict began with an altercation between begging Indians and resistant whites that led to the death of several settlers. The contretemps escalated into the settlers' severe and dehumanizing retaliation against the natives. Carrigan recalled that white people were given the right to shoot any Indian found off the reservation. When soldiers shot one errant Indian the people brought his body into town and "celebrated" with it in the streets. "The boys put firecrackers in his nose and lit them," Carrigan remembered. "After they were through celebrating, they scalped him and threw him into a ditch." Later, someone removed his head and decided "to have it fixed up in a showcase." This "celebration" was followed by a bad winter, during which the government neglected to pay the Indians their allotments. All of this, Carrigan said, resulted in the Indians becoming "disagreeable and ill-natured." Carrigan did not seem surprised when violence flared, nor did she condemn the Native Americans for their behavior.[208]

Other unpublished narratives involved very young women. Some years before the New Ulm episode, a teenage brother and sister lost their family in a cholera epidemic on the plains. When they continued their trek toward California, they were seized by some Indians along the north fork of the Platte River. During their captivity, the young woman, Ruth, "cured" the chief's daughter of cholera. In the meantime, Ruth's brother Curtis joined the native men in buffalo hunts and other activities. The Indians finally put the two young emigrants back on the road near Fort Laramie, supplying them with blankets and other items. The narrator of the story claimed that a bond of affection existed between the young people and their captors, especially between Ruth and the girl she had aided.[209]

Bianca Babb Bell of Texas related a similar incident, which involved her experience as a young woman when Comanche Indians took her prisoner during the late 1860s. The Comanches killed Bianca's mother, carried her and her brother off in a grueling three-day trek, and neglected to feed her. Later, however, she grew fond of her adoptive mother who, in her words, "was always good to me." Her Indian mother held a "great feast" in Bianca's honor on the night of her arrival, and she showed the girl little kindnesses. "On cold winter nights my Squaw Mother would have me stand before the fire, turning round occasionally, so I could get good and warm," Bell recalled. "Then she would wrap me up in a buffalo robe and tuck me in good and warm." She maintained that her native mother was "always very thoughtful" of her and seemed to care for her as much as if she were "her very own child."[210]

Bell was not only fond of her Indian mother, but respected the other Indians in the group as well. Later, she declared: "The majority of the Indians that I knew were of a jovial, happy disposition, always friendly and playing some kind of joke on the other fellow." She thought they must have had exceptionally well-behaved children, for she never saw them punish one. She added that even though whites thought Indians ignorant, they were well educated in legends and folklore: "All their history was handed down from one generation to the next." When Bianca's father ransomed her from the Indians—to the despair of her native mother—she was glad to return to her own people, but she always retained happy memories of her time among the Comanches.[211]

This is not intended to imply that clashes between whites and natives were less than calamitous or that prisoners of war spent enjoyable interludes away from their families and friends. It is meant to suggest that the captivity scenario presented by myth and by the media was inaccurate. Mired in anti-Indian prejudice and seeking rationalizations for their treatment of natives, many white folks willingly had their biases confirmed by horror stories of attacks and captivity. Yet unpublished women's sources indicate that a discrepancy existed between the scenario and reality.

Even during the height of violence, women were not universally terror stricken by American Indians. Neither were they routinely physically or sexually abused by natives. Nor did women always blame Indians for the ills and strife that plagued so many areas of the frontier. Instead, they put themselves in the place of Indians and became bigger people for doing so.

Clearly, white women and white men developed dissimilar relationships with American Indians. These differences in white female–American

Indian and white male–American Indian relationships derived in large part from gender roles and responsibilities. Because white women had to procure food, clothing, and other domestic goods, they developed a collegial relationship with American Indians. Because white men were cast as aggressors and land grabbers, they became adversaries of Native Americans.

Why did this occur? Although women's roles allowed them to enter warm relationships with individual Indians, sociologists maintain that stereotypes and prejudices do not change solely through positive contact with group members. Rather, education must supplement such contacts. White women did undergo a learning experience. Increased demands on their physical capabilities helped them realize they were not as weak as they had thought. At the same time, the realities of the moral climate showed them that their supposed talent for reform was not as significant as they had believed. As women accepted these alterations in their self-images, they could adjust their attitudes toward others. Thus, white women became susceptible to influences provided by their amicable contact with Indians.

White men did not participate in a similar educational exercise. Convinced of their strength, their right to wrest a livelihood from other peoples' land, and the inferiority of indigenes, men had no reason to modify their convictions. Rather, the stresses and strains of the frontier caused white men to reaffirm such convictions to justify their actions. Men, therefore, treated American Indians in a way that produced the very results that they expected. Because men believed Indians would be contentious, they made displays of their power. Men boasted, brandished weapons, and acted arrogantly. Unsurprisingly, American Indians responded in a militant fashion. When conflict erupted, white men's suspicions were confirmed and their anti-Indian prejudices reinforced. They seldom had pleasant personal contacts with American Indians to alleviate their feelings. Unlike their female counterparts, men had little motivation or opportunity to revise their ideas about American Indians. At the same time, a significant number of women developed a sympathetic stance toward their enemies, which allowed neighborly feeling, friendship, and even affectional relationships to occur, which confirmed women's belief that Indians could be "nice."

As cataclysmic as this finding is, it was not universal, meaning it did not apply to other situations. Only in the West did white women find the right blend of circumstance allowing them to adjust their attitudes. This would not prove to be the case with all groups of "others" that westering women encountered on the American frontier.

——— Chapter Six ———

FRONTIER PLACE: COLONIALISM TRIUMPHANT

White women did not apply their ability to change their views to all racial, ethnic, and religious "others" they encountered on the frontier. Although some women displayed empathy toward American Indians under the most trying circumstances, they did not show the same humaneness to such groups as Mexicans, Asians, African Americans, white members of the Church of Latter-day Saints of Jesus Christ, known as Mormons, or natives along the Panama Route to California. Although many peoples of color lived along westward routes and in western settlements, white women lacked or avoided the opportunity for contact with representatives of these groups.[1] Also, women's self-images did not undergo any changes that affected their feelings about these peoples. Moreover, unlike American Indians, these parties were not as numerous, visible, or pressing in their demands on emigrants and settlers.

White women, therefore, were able to extend their sympathies in a selective manner. Even though they were compassionate toward American Indians, they continued to deprecate most "others." Women had not undergone a sea change. Although their colonialism had moderated somewhat, it still had a firm hold on their minds.

—— Colonialism Critiqued ——

Before considering women's relations with two of the above groups, it is important to understand the extent of white women's dissatisfaction with the results of white colonialism. They were not unique; women of other eras have also opposed white imperialism.[2] Because white women have long believed they are conservators of home, family, and ethnic culture, they are perhaps less likely than white men to destroy the homes, families, and cultures of native peoples. By the mid-nineteenth century, such women as Susan Fenimore Cooper, daughter of James Fenimore Cooper and author of the first American nature book, *Rural Hours* (1850), even argued that women were also conservators of their family's larger homes, the outdoors. This sentiment put white women at the core of the environmental conservation movement emerging after the Civil War.[3] In other words, white women were taught to save rather than tear down and build anew.

Destruction of Native American and western landscapes dismayed a growing number of white women. They were especially upset by the carnage they saw among Indians. White women placed blame on whites in general, on white men, and on the federal government. Moreover, women had ideas concerning solutions, but lacked unanimity.

Women who developed amicable feelings for Indians were especially vehement in their sentiments. While at Fort Laramie during the 1860s, Frances Carrington charged whites with being shortsighted and unfair. She observed that "at the time of my arrival it had become apparent to any sensible observer that the Indians of that country would fight to the death for home and native land, with spirit akin to that of the American soldier of our early history, and who could say that their spirit was not commendable and to be respected?"[4]

Like Carrington, other women who blamed Indian problems on whites called for an understanding of the human condition to be applied to American Indians. One settler of the 1880s agreed that Indians had many faults, but pointed out that whites had character flaws as well. The Indian "has also his trials," she added, so whites should "judge him not harshly." A Kansas settler of the same decade also felt it was unfair of whites to denounce Indians' "state of degradation." She asked, "Are our souls refined and free from all impurity?"[5]

Even women who believed that American Indians were inferior developed a shred of pity for them. An Iowa settler of the 1880s who remembered that Indians had once roamed the prairies around her homestead with "native dignity," were destroyed by white men who "soon became the aggressor." Although not highly supportive of Indians, she empathized with their plight. Gradually, she said, Indians were "compelled to give place to a higher order of civilization." Another woman of the era maintained her conviction that Indians were "murderous savages" capable of "diabolical deeds," yet relented enough to express sadness that the American Indian would "soon be numbered among the extinct races."[6]

Apparently, women who disliked American Indians still commiserated with them. This was true of army wife Frances Roe, who called Indians "dirty, and nauseous-smelling savages," but came to believe that whites' killing of buffalo was unjust in that it deprived the Plains Indians of food, clothing, and tent covering. Of course, whites planned to starve out Indians by killing the buffalo. Although Roe apparently did not understand this, she could see what the policy did to Indians. She wrote bitingly: "If the Indians should attempt to protect their rights it would be called an uprising at once, so they have to lie around on sand hills and watch their beloved buffalo gradually disappear, and all the time they know only too well that with them will go the skins that give them tepees and clothing, and the meat that furnishes almost all of their sustenance."[7]

Other white women also decried the Indians' lack of food and clothing. They pitied the needy Indians, gave what they could, and vented their frustrations in their diaries and journals.[8] "Oh, dear, but they do look so uncomfortable," sighed one emigrant woman of the 1860s, after passing a native village.[9] Army wife Ada Vogdes also mentioned the Indians' destitute condition. When some twenty Indians came into Fort Laramie for food, she logged her compassionate response in her journal. "I did pity these poor things paddling around in the cold & snow," she noted.[10] Other women regretted their inability to help the unfortunate natives. Rather than disparaging Indians as beggars or resenting their demands on their families' resources, these women felt helpless and inadequate. For instance, when Lois Murray turned away a hungry Indian for lack of food he coughed so hard that she later said, "If I could have called him back, I would have given him bread." Murray claimed that she never again refused to aid a needy Indian.[11]

Many other women took the position that it was unjust and immoral for whites to seize Indian lands, a loss that condemned native inhabitants to a life of poverty and homelessness. Much as Indians who had no existence beyond the landscape, white women, especially of the late nineteenth and early twentieth centuries, increasingly felt a bond with land that was, in their view, spiritual and female. As Indians saw land as the center of their universe, women identified with Mother Earth and Mother Nature. As a result, white women often fell somewhere between Indians, who had tremendous empathy for land, and most white men, who viewed land to be "developed," or in today's terms, exploited.[12]

Beside blaming white people in general, other women specifically censured white men. Women complained that male swaggering and braggadocio, petty meanness, and heartlessness in dealings with American Indians caused upheaval. One Iowa settler of the 1840s maintained that she pitied the Indians and expected whites to be as "mean" as the Indians if they were driven out of their lands.[13] Two decades later, another Iowa woman criticized white men's ruthlessness, arguing that "heaped up graves, filled with the victims of starvation, disease, or cruelty" proved that "the supposedly vindictive Indian had his counterpart in white men."[14]

Other white women had additional complaints. Kate Furness, for example, singled out for blame the trail men who created catastrophes along their way. After a young man carelessly shot at some Native American women to startle them, accidentally killing one woman, the Indians seized him and skinned him. "From a peaceful tribe," Furness commented, "these Indians had been turned into demons, a wild, revengeful nation" simply because one young man had indulged in "a foolish, thoughtless act." Another occurrence in the Sierra Nevada area made it even more clear to Furness that the usual male approach to Indians was harmful. When a group of American Indians drew near on horseback, the men of the party surrounded their stock and raised their weapons toward the Indians, who insisted they were peaceful and did not intend to fight. When Furness's mother offered the leader bread and sugar, the gesture convinced the Indians to allow the train to pass. When dealing with Indians, Furness added, it was her mother's custom "to initiate friendly acts, in contrast to the men's belligerent reactions."[15]

What these white women failed to take into account was that masculinity entered most male white-native interactions. Although this would not have been as true for male teachers and missionaries who hoped to help Indians, it would have played a part for white male emigrants and settlers. White men may have thought Indians inferior, but they were still dangerous enemies. In fact, the more dangerous and shifty Indians could be portrayed, the more their defeat assured white males of their own prowess. Any tricks the white man could get away with or damage he could inflict on Indians upped his image in other men's eyes, including fathers, sons, and brothers.[16] Women might have argued that if Indians were inferior they should be treated with kindness by their superiors. These women did not understand the pressures that standards of white masculinity put on men. Nor did Indians understand white masculinity. They could not know that if white men acted more savage than Indians as they imagined Indians to act, they garnered points toward masculinity.

Still other women chided white males for taking advantage of Indians at every turn. An Oregon settler felt that "lecherous white men" who preyed on young Indian women caused the upheaval on the local reservation. A Kansas settler believed that men who cheated Indians in trades also created many difficulties. "Is it right," she queried, that white men paid Indians "three dollar for a buffalo robe, worth twelve at home?"[17]

According to Margaret Carrington of Fort Kearney, military men were especially unethical. She was enthusiastic about an 1866 fort policy barring soldiers from trading with Indians. This policy, she argued, deterred "the possibility of collisions growing out of trades in furs, beads, and other articles, in which the Indian is generally the unlucky one, and often exhibits his disappointment by becoming revengeful and wicked."[18] Other women admonished military men for unnecessary attacks on natives. Rachel Wright mentioned a detachment of soldiers sent to "exterminate" some peaceful Indians in the Upper Napa Valley. According to her, these "harmless natives" stood and stared unsuspectingly at the "strangely clothed men." The soldiers shot into their midst, wounding and killing many of them. Frightened and grief stricken, the Indians fled into nearby canyons. Although a number of white settlers protested to the government, relations between whites and Indians were never restored to their formerly calm state.[19]

Women also accused Civil War troops of making trouble across the frontier. In Oklahoma, soldiers terrorized Choctaw women by tearing earrings from their ears and locking the women in unventilated rooms for days.[20] And in California, Eleanor Taylor condemned Civil War soldiers who perpetuated "horrible butchery" in their battles with natives, displaying "quite as much of the savage nature as did the redskins." When two young soldiers deserted their troop, Taylor applauded their action.[21] The cause of suffering during the Indian wars of the 1870s was also laid at the feet of former Civil War leaders. Caroline Winne, for example, rebuked Sheridan for supposedly being "drunk all the time in Chicago in his fine house," and she blamed Sherman who lived "on his general's pay in Washington, never having fought an Indian & knowing nothing at all about them" for making uninformed and ruinous decisions.[22]

Officials of the United States government came in for their share of the blame as well. Far away from the metropole in Washington, D.C., western settlers carried on a slightly different discourse that put their own needs as first priority.[23] Greedy federal land policies, an inadequate reservation system, and mismanagement of allotments and supplies were all cited by women as sources of American Indian troubles in the West.[24] After an Indian war of the mid-1830s, Oregonian Elizabeth Lord maintained that "there was never any doubt that the Indians were treated unjustly" by authorities who "allowed and supported wholesale seizures of native lands."[25] Mary Ann Tatum, writing in 1870 at Fort Sill, the Kiowa-Comanche Agency, also grumbled about white leaders: "The heart grows sick with the repeated tale of wrongs and broken promises by the whites & government why must it be so, why must the poor untutored redman suffer so from the whites who feel that they are so much further along."[26]

Women reprimanded other specific types of white men for their brutishness. Government agents, renegade Frenchmen, Catholic priests, and representatives of religious groups were accused of corrupting or agitating Native Americans.[27] White thieves were excoriated for stealing from settlers and Indians.[28] One Texas woman of the 1870s thought that white fugitives from other states were the real problem on the Texas frontier. According to her, fear of these "desperadoes" played on her mother's mind "far more than fear of Indians."[29] Renegade and other "unprincipled" white men were also condemned for "inciting" Indians and leading them "on to desperate deeds."[30] Still other women believed that Indian problems in their areas were created by Mormons, who reportedly perpetrated heinous deeds themselves or encouraged Indians to do so.[31] This charge evoked countercharges, with Mormons claiming that it was the "foul tricks" of the emigrants that caused the difficulties for which they had been accused.[32]

Many women realized the need to consider solutions to the events that plagued settlers and American Indians in many areas of the frontier. They thought it apparent that if people expected to attain stability and productivity, violence and acrimony could not be allowed to continue. Conflict eroded the peace of mind and the physical energy of whites and Indians, and led to wanton destruction of resources. Many women thus came to grips with the question of what could be done about the flare-ups that characterized white-Indian relations.

Women did not usually agree with the plan to restore patches of land to Indians through the reservation system. Although some women thought the idea provided partial atonement for past injury, others believed that the reservation concept was white patronization and arrogance, especially by the federal government in Washington, D.C. Although women did not employ the term *internal colonization,* they objected to reservations as internal colonies where Indians had no political rights. "Now the government allows them a portion to themselves as a great favour and taken as such," Oregon-bound emigrant Agnes Stewart Warner contended in 1853, "but this does not make it right." Women like Warner did not realize that government policy intended to keep groups separate and unequal in internal colonies, nor did they credit the argument that keeping Indians on reservations protected white women from them.[33]

Women had other complaints about reservations. When the army wife Eveline Alexander saw eight thousand Navajos confined to a New Mexico reservation in the 1860s, she noted that rations were inadequate. "Not much to support life on, one would think," she concluded. Two decades later, Carrie Strahorn observed Navajo reservations in Arizona and Utah. One of their worst features, she was convinced, was that "the Government divided families by taking them to different localities making them justly angry and revengeful."[34] When, such women wondered, would Manifest Destiny reach the trusteeship phase of imperialism that made natives trustees of themselves?

When they considered solutions, many women talked in vague terms about "civilizing" American Indians."[35] More specifically, whites thought that Indian men should farm and Indian women should take care of the children and house, much like white men and women did. Of course, whites wanted Indians to be farmers, not only to imitate them, but because agriculture provided the means by which whites colonized the West—farmstead by farmstead. With plows and other implements, whites cleared the West of trees, grass, and weeds, planting instead the crops that fed white folks.[36] In such a system, Indians who hunted would have no land on which to hunt, nor would they be controllable by whites. Along with wild landscapes and wild animals, wild Indians had to be subjugated for the good of white hegemony.

As a result, white women complimented Indians who took up farming. In 1885, Alice Fletcher cited the example of Omaha Indian farmers in Nebraska as proof that Indians could indeed be "civilized." Fletcher went on that Omahas demonstrated that "civilization is no fanciful theory" but "within the grasp of all the Indians." Even as many white people questioned whether Indians would work, could be educated, and could become self-sustaining, Omahas were demonstrating that these things were possible.[37] To Fletcher, civilizing American Indians meant turning Indians into productive beings engaged in white-style livelihoods, notably farming, and educating them to become like whites.

Similarly, the reformer Annie K. Bidwell of California took the position that reservations had to be replaced by individual farms. Her rancher husband partially underwrote her scheme by donating land to Indian families. Bidwell added a mission school and a temperance brigade. In a

1904 fundraising letter, Bidwell declared that "these Indians have proven themselves worthy of the position of any white citizen."[38]

For other women, the idea of civilizing American Indians had larger dimensions, such as "elevating" Indians by introducing "white standards" into their lives. This was generally thought to be a job for women, who were regarded as the moral and civilizing forces of American society.[39] In 1840, Abigail Smith wrote to her family from Kansas lamenting the lack of white teachers among natives: "Oh that there might be teachers sent to show them the way to be saved and the arts of civilization."[40] During subsequent decades, more than one white woman arrived on the frontier charged with the duty to supervise Indians' metamorphosis.

Female teachers among Indians easily grew discouraged, however. A white New Mexico field matron admitted that Indians "are learning fast," but recommended the additional harsh policy of relocating young Indian children from their families to schools, for the young "do not have so much to unlearn." Sarah E. Abbott, who lived with native people at First Mesa, Arizona, during the early 1900s was less optimistic. In spite of her efforts, she was at a loss that the "people of Hotevilia still maintain the same obstinate determination to go their own way."[41] Moreover, women who shouldered the task of teaching Indians how to survive in the increasingly white world of the West soon learned that their duties included more than teaching.[42] One teacher in Oklahoma recalled that "I was matron and teacher to say nothing of being nurse and seamstress and besides I usually helped at the Saturday morning bath."[43]

Another potential solution was that religion provide the springboard that would catapult American Indians from primitivism to civilization. Believing that Indians were "buried in ignorance" because they knew "nothing of Christ or the way of salvation," numerous white women tackled the Christianizing of American Indians.[44] One of the earliest was Narcissa Whitman, a young woman so intent on carrying religious teachings to Indians in Oregon that during the 1840s she hastily wed a missionary to meet the church board's requirement that all female missionaries be married. In later decades, missionaries of many faiths competed for Indians' attention.[45] For instance, the Congregationalist missionary Mary C. Collins worked with the Sioux in South Dakota between 1895 and 1910. Also, groups like the Women's Baptist Home

Mission Society and the Women's National Indian Association had a strong missionary bent.[46]

Moreover, as white women realized that American Indians were not stock characters—bestial, wanton, and licentious—they hoped for the salvation of at least some Indians. Because these women's objectives were misguided and based on cultural arrogance, they wanted to replace Indian culture, language, art, and crafts with white ways. After decades of absorbing colonialist tenets stating that white culture provided the center for all Americans, these women failed to realize that such colonized peoples as American Indians did not believe in white superiority and did not want to take on white beliefs and behavior.[47] Yet white women had faith in Indians' ability to adapt, change, and learn. They did not argue, as did many male reformers, that natives were hopeless because they were dying out, obviously incapable of learning, growing, and contributing to white society.[48]

These women extended to Indians their compassion, respect, or even affection. Because whites had prevailed, they were able to be altruistic and solicitous. White women no longer faced a threat of disfigurement, dismemberment, or death at the hands of rancorous Indians. Consequently, they could be gracious, kindhearted, and benevolent. Indians had no such leeway. They were allowed to love nothing, neither their language nor their art nor their culture. As vanquished peoples, they had to remain largely silent, wearing the masks of compliance that whites prescribed for them. Because colonial racism was indirect, meaning that whites disavowed negative feelings and said the problem was "over," the system leached away Indians' self-respect by denying them political rights and economic independence. Those on reservations endured institutionalized racism, whereas those who went to cities found themselves shunned, impoverished, and marginalized. Both had to quash their emotions, at least when whites were around. They lived with two frames of reference, one Indian, one white. Whites only heard Indians when they acted as "wild" and as "savage" as whites thought them to be. Or, like the Indian reformer Sarah Winnemucca, Indians devoted to their cause could be heard by making public spectacles of themselves on the stages of white theaters.[49]

Consequently, only a few white women could imagine Indians

being at their best if left to their own ways, language, and culture. Instead, they judged Indians negatively. For example, when ingenious Indians resisted white efforts by taking from them only what they found useful or meaningful, white women judged them as stubborn or arrogant. When Indians had trouble learning English, white women blamed Indians rather than the differences between Indian languages and English.[50] And when Indians purposely disrupted such displays of white dominance as military parades, inaugurations, and other public ceremonies, whites called them irresponsible and childish. When Indians poached or borrowed, which allowed them to recoup some of the profit of their labor, whites termed them thieves and scalawags. Moreover, because whites had so long vacillated between exterminating Indians physically by killing buffalo, other game, and Indians themselves, or destroying Indians psychologically by eradicating their language and culture, most white women thought in hegemonic terms of assimilation rather than Indian cultural identity. After all, colonization embedded itself in the West by replacing things Indian with things white. The one exception was the Indian as a tourist attraction.[51] The white culture that won dominance and power controlled the symbols, representations, and expressive arts that comprised western culture.[52] Those who objected to assimilation, including white teachers in Indian schools, were discouraged or silenced.[53] Even if white women had accepted Indians' cultural autonomy, it is doubtful that they, being so thoroughly steeped in colonialism, could have countenanced a separate society existing alongside their own. Believing that Indians were inferior, white women had one answer—to destroy all that Indians held dear.

Clearly, a significant number of white women discussed, advocated, or implemented solutions to difficulties that erupted as emigrants and settlers displaced native populations throughout the West. Because they were sympathetic with Indians, they believed that they could have a positive effect on them. They devoted their time and energy to a consideration of the issues, and sometimes invested lifetimes in trying to improve the situation. Concepts of female morality drove these women onward.

In spite of their empathy, few white women asked Indians what they thought about the matter. They continued to send such children as Gertrude Bonnin, a Yankton Sioux woman who called herself Zitkala sa, to places like the White's Manual Labor Institute at Wabash, Indiana, where they experienced programs designed to "civilize" and assimilate what school officials referred to as "savages." Around the turn of the twentieth century, Zitkala sa began to give speeches and to write articles and books asking for racial harmony and American citizenship for Indians; some white women supported her, whereas others did not.[54] Because Indians, especially Indian women, were still thought inferior, their writings were not widely read by whites. Moreover, around the turn of the twentieth century, theories of racial determinism, stating that Indians were incapable of "progress," made assimilation seem hopeless.[55]

One woman of the early twentieth century who thought peaceful coexistence possible was the transplanted New Mexican, Mary Austin, who loved southwestern landscapes and believed they could be redemptive for women. Austin also showed concern for Indians, at times even claiming she was one. She argued that a combination of public health programs, education, and dedicated officials would be a "starter" for a new policy.[56] Austin also thought that whites could learn much from Indians. In articles and books, especially *The Land of Little Rain* (1903), Austin pointed out that Native Americans treated the Southwest with gentleness, which she regarded a far better perspective than Anglo men's concept of land as an exploitable resource.[57]

—— Colonialism in Force ——

White women found it virtually impossible to show the kindheartedness that they extended to Indians to additional groups of "others" along westward trails and in settlements. This occurred, in part, because women continued to operate on a race-based consciousness. They defined themselves and Indians on the basis of race, giving high value to themselves and little to Indians. Racial prejudice short-circuited the process of growth on both sides.

Moreover, women changed only attitudes and not institutions. At the same time that white women became "nicer" to Indians, they continued to inflict on Indians white forms and beliefs. In a sense, women completed in the personal realm the work of colonization that men had begun in the military and political spheres. At the same time that men colonized the body, women colonized the mind. As men took land and forced on Indians structures of white governance, women taught Indians how to talk, dress, and eat like whites. As friends, teachers, missionaries, and employers, women modeled white manners, appearance, customs, beliefs, and aspirations. Clearly, white women needed what today would be called reprogramming, which was unavailable then.[58]

In addition, women failed to generalize the little they had learned about Native Americans. Their "education" was case specific, largely because women did not conceive of themselves as resisting a system—the white colonialist scheme called Manifest Destiny. Although they railed about mistreatment of Indians, found a number of people to blame, and suggested various answers, they failed to realize that they, white men, and American Indians were caught in the larger net of Manifest Destiny. As long as whites thought they were superior and their culture constituted "civilization," the drama in the West had to play out as it did.

Therefore, white women reshaped some beliefs regarding Indians, but they discriminated against virtually everyone else who was not one of them. Because Mexicans, African Americans, and Asians were visibly different from emigrants and settlers in appearance, language, and cultural characteristics, they were easily identified as targets of prejudice. White women took these characteristics as reasons to act stiffly and, although they lacked information, to criticize these peoples.

White women also disliked Mormons, a group of people very much like themselves in appearance, culture, and ethnic origin. Because of these obvious similarities, it might be assumed that Gentile (as Mormons called non-Mormons) women would have had more incentive to associate with members of the Church of Jesus Christ of Latter-day Saints than with Native Americans, but this was not true.

Anti-Mormon prejudice was rampant among white women. Before leaving their eastern homes, they had been indoctrinated with anti-Mormon prejudice by critical sermons, speeches, tracts, novels, newspaper articles, satirical cartoons, and caricatures.[59] Consequently, many women expected Mormons to be more difficult to deal with than

American Indians. One explained that she dreaded Mormons because "the tales told of the Mormons in those days were worse than those of the Indians." Even after learning that the Mormons at Council Bluffs charged reasonable prices and dealt fairly with emigrants, she was delighted when her party bypassed Salt Lake City; she said she had "no desire to see the Mormon settlement."[60] One California-bound emigrant who wintered in Council Bluffs in 1853 came away with a similar impressions of Mormons. "We found before spring," she wrote later, "that with all their zeal and devotion they were a treacherous set and sect." She claimed that these Mormons "made it a business" to steal from the Gentiles. Her party also decided to skip Salt Lake City, a decision that pleased her since she too was averse to Mormons.[61]

Because the Latter-day Saints traveled and lived in tightly knit religious communities, there was seldom little more than superficial contact between Mormon and Gentile women. Consequently, female emigrants and settlers had few experiences with Mormons to offset the incendiary tales they had heard. A common rumor, for instance, was that Brigham Young conserved resources for the Mormons by ordering that no grass or other provisions be given to Gentiles.[62] Because grass and water were spare around Salt Lake, Young may very well have taken his people as his first priority and issued such an edict. Another widely circulated story concerned the Mormons' supposed stealing of stock from emigrants and settlers, which they then blamed on Indians. Accounts flourished of Mormons swooping down on Gentiles to kill them and carry off their possessions, especially animals.[63] After hearing such reports, one female migrant insisted that Mormons believed that "any means to rob the Gentile was commendable."[64] Latter-day Saints were also thought to join American Indians in attacks on emigrants and settlers. In addition, they were blamed for "inciting" Indians to attack whites in hopes of reducing the number of Gentiles settling in the far West.[65]

Feared and hated, Mormons were the target of judgmental comments by female migrants. In light of women's prejudice toward these people, it is unsurprising that they made vitriolic remarks about Mormons. To one woman, Mormon men were "a very hard looking set," whereas to another, the women were "very plain looking, many of them absolutely ugly."[66] Others said that Mormons were "not always inclined to be friendly," that they were "poor, ignorant and dirty," and that their ranks often included "the dregs of some foreign country."[67] One of the most rancorous observations came from Mary Fish. When crossing the plains in 1860, Fish's reaction to seeing Mormon women dragging handcarts behind them was: "They must be sadly in want of husbands to level themselves to brutes & after all their trouble to obtain one 4th or perhaps one 20th part of a man."[68]

Only a few frontierswomen extended understanding to Latter-day Saints they met along the way. One young female migrant who disliked Mormons admitted that some were "good people, but very common."[69] Margaret Hecox, on her way to California in 1846, expressed pity for them. She explained that her party traveled slowly to avoid overtaking a train of Mormons, but were distressed by the badly rutted roads that Mormons left in their wake. They were also upset with bad treatment they received at the hands of people who took them to be Mormons. In Hecox's view, however, the Latter-day Saints could not be "as black as they were painted." When her group caught up with the Mormons, she found their "abject poverty" to be "an extremely pitiful sight." Yet after her train passed the Mormons, she felt "greatly relieved to be clear of them," and anxious that her train move faster "lest they overtake us."[70]

From Mormon women's perspective, Gentile prejudice hurt and isolated them. Increasingly, Mormon and Gentile trains simply passed each other or Mormon trains stuck to the so-called Mormon Trail. Women who had been propelled onto the trail by mob violence, burnings of homes and barns, and killings of family members were already vulnerable. One young woman had left Nauvoo, Illinois, with her mother and siblings after a mob killed her father. Also, these women gave up farms and family businesses, prosperous communities, and hard-built temples. In the face of Gentile prejudice, they turned for succor to their religious beliefs, hope of a promised land ahead, and faith in the second coming of Christ.[71]

At the same time, Gentile women's sentiments hardened as they observed Mormons heading back from Salt Lake to the "States." Women seemed to revel in what they took to be Mormon failure, assuming that these people had their fill of Mormonism and were fleeing Zion.[72] In reality, returning Mormons were not numerous. In addition, the reverse trail included other disillusioned people, including Gentile farmers, miners, and wives with children. Yet Gentile women cast the story of returning Mormons in the worst light. A few claimed that Mormons had confided in them their secret escape from Salt Lake City.[73] Others thought the Mormons pitiful. In 1857, Helen Carpenter described a contingent of returning Mormons as "in rags and tatters and, must I say it, scabs," the "very worst lot" she had seen yet. Carpenter believed that the travelers were only a few of the many who "would be glad to leave Salt Lake if they could only get away."[74]

Predictably, the vitriolic Mary Fish despised returning Mormons. In 1860, she talked with two Mormon women headed for the "States." According to Fish, the women had fled Salt Lake because they could not tolerate being plural wives. One woman was returning to her parents with "four little responsibilities." The other "consoled herself for the loss of a small portion of a man by taking a whole one as she has married a trader."[75]

Throughout the nineteenth century, Gentile women continued to view homebound Mormons as a scourge. In 1884, for example, Mallie Stafford recoiled against her party's occasional encampments with returning Mormons. "They had escaped the terrors of the law and the 'Avenging Angels,'" Stafford proclaimed, "and after a residence of years in Zion, at last were going home." Remarking that "they conversed but little on the subject of Mormonism," she assumed that the slightest reference made to the subject "stirred up a flood of painful and unpleasant recollections."[76]

By the time Gentile women neared the Mormon capital, Salt Lake City, their prejudices had solidified. Although many had little desire to stop, others were intently curious or had to go into the city to replenish their supplies. Some would be glad, as Rachel Rose put it, "to see where folks lived once more."[77] Women who watched Latter-day Saints swarm into their camps to bargain for old clothes, dishes, and other items in exchange for stock, found their interest further aroused.[78] Rumors lured them on, especially those concerning Brigham Young, his elaborate home, and his many wives, sometimes said to be only seventeen in number and other times as many as sixty-one.[79]

They were amazed when they first glimpsed the spiraled city.[80] The emigrants who entered the fabled city of Salt Lake pushed into shops as anxious customers for goods the Mormons were only too willing to sell. To survive in the Utah desert, Latter-day Saints had become a supply station for those on their way to California, who were happy to restock and rest their animals before undertaking the last lap of their trek. The emigrants also explored the city's streets, awestruck by the Mormon Temple, the Mormon Tabernacle, Young's house, the houses of his many wives, and the homes of elders. As Gentile women described it, the city was beautiful, full of adobe homes with well-tended gardens, and crowned by the impressive temple and tabernacle buildings."[81] To one, it looked like "a herd of white castles," whereas another thought it would be "truly beautiful" if not inhabited by Mormons.[82]

When these women entered the Mormon Tabernacle to witness the religious services of the Latter-day Saints, their tone changed. In 1851, one woman claimed that "it was not anything dignified on the Sabbath, but they were very rough and coarse with their remarks." She was upset that the congregation cheered when slurs were hurled against the United States and Mormon leaders threatened to roll rocks down upon the heads of U.S. soldiers should they try to enter the city. She concluded that "their remarks were all coarse; there was nothing refined or elevating in it."[83] A year later, Mary Bailey reported that the Mormon service consisted of people relating "dreamy visions." She was surprised to find that many of the Latter-day Saints were Europeans; she found it strange "that such delusion should spread so far."[84] Another female observer described a service as one that included "a ranting Mormon oration," superb music, and an "overly long" benediction.[85]

In spite of some positive impressions of Salt Lake City and its inhabitants, most white emigrant women did not alter their anti-Mormon views. The ideas they carried into the city were usually the same ideas with which they left. One young woman of the 1870s, who was impressed with the beauty of the city, declared, "Still I should not want to live there, even in the Gentile part and among Gentiles."[86] There were, however, some exceptions. After a winter among the Mormons in the 1850s, Sarah Cooke became a member of the church, yet withstood suggestions that she and her husband engage in plural marriage.[87]

More typical, however, was the fierce statement of a woman who was also in Salt Lake City during the mid-1850s: "To-morrow we turn our back upon the Mormon capital, with its wretchedness, abominations, and crimes," she wrote, "how we rejoice to escape from a region of human depravity, the terrible features of which have opened more and more distinctly to view the longer our sojourn has continued."[88]

Bitter and pitiless, these women could not see the positive side of Mormons. Virtually no one characterized the Saints as industrious folks who had turned persecution to their advantage and wrested a living from an area marred by salt flats and a desert climate. Through grueling effort, Mormons had crowned Salt Lake City with an intricately engineered tabernacle, whose acoustics are still considered remarkable in our technological age. Yet Gentile women usually held the conviction that the Mormon oasis was not Zion, but the center of degeneracy and depravity. Although many entered American Indian villages with disapproval and left with good words on their lips, they could not transform their views of Mormons.

It is not difficult to discern the main reason for Gentile women's hostility. The reason was plural marriage, even though only a portion—about 25 percent—of Mormons practiced it. Gentile women saw plural marriage as a threat to their monogamous marriages.[89] They feared that Mormon men would give their own men ideas. In 1856, Mary Powers said that Mormon women warned her to be vigilant lest her husband be "sucked into the system" before she could prevent it.[90] Moreover, as the carriers of white civilization, Gentile women were committed to a social construction of marriage as one woman and one man. As a result, Gentile women termed plural marriage as "wicked" and "demoralizing." Although they excused "primitive" and "ignorant" American Indians for engaging in plural marriage, they could not accept it among Mormons, who were white, somewhat educated, and Christian. Women thus denounced Latter-day Saints in blistering terms for their "depravity."

Lucene Parsons was one of these. She spent the winter of 1851 in Salt Lake City before continuing on to California. For her, getting to know Mormons did not mean coming to like them. Parsons thought that "a meaner set lives not on this earth." She was dismayed to experience discrimination at the hands of Mormons, who would not hire a Gentile for a job that a Mormon wanted. She did not hesitate, however, to direct prejudice at Mormons. She leveled her worst barrage against plural marriage, which she felt made the Latter-day Saints an "unprincipled sect" who "live like brute creations more than like white folks."[91]

Tales of easy divorce among the Saints also infuriated Gentile women. Although the divorce rate in the United States was at an all-time high in 1850, more women feared divorce than saw it as a liberating force from an unfortunate marriage. In 1847, church officials began parting men from one or more of their plural wives. Because church leaders had no authority over civil marriage, they dealt only with religious couplings. By 1858, Brigham Young was granting a record number of divorces. Although he opposed divorce, he wanted to free what he called "discontented wives." In that year, he relieved George D. Grant of three wives, and a fourth wife several weeks later. Although Young hoped to keep Mormon marriages peaceful by dispatching troubled ones, his church divorces further inflamed Gentiles.[92]

Gentile women, who perceived plural marriage and easy divorce as institutions that white civilized people should shun, blamed Mormon men for their existence. Unsurprisingly, they saw these men—whom they believed to be amoral and in need of female morality—as the cause of the evil.[93] In 1853, Harriet Ward, who radically modified her view of Native Americans, indicted male Mormon leaders. According to her, Mormon men "boasted" that they "owned a plurality of wives for the purpose of raising up a perfect race to inhabit this new Jerusalem forever."[94] Ward dismissed Mormon doctrine, saying that "not any of them believes a word they preach, and they are a miserable lot of extortioners upon whom the wrath of God will yet be poured out." As Ward left the Salt Lake area, she expressed her disgust: "The country through which we have passed today is beautiful and should be inhabited by a different set of beings than the Mormons."[95] In 1865, Sarah Herndon reinforced this view: "This is a beautiful valley. Too good to be possessed by a community of bigamists."[96] Other disgruntled women supported these contentions. One said that men married and unmarried "at pleasure several times a year if they choose." She added that Brigham Young housed his "harem" in a "poor, miserable log and adobe affair, directly in front of his elegant, Gothic-windowed barn!"[97] Parsons claimed that Mormon men treated their wives badly, so that quarreling, desertion, and divorce were common.[98]

Gentile women also worried about Mormon women. As white, Christian, and female, they could not help imagining how they would feel as plural wives.[99] To Herndon, plural marriage was disastrous for Mormon women, who according to her, constituted "a poor heart broken & deluded lot."[100] Another thought Mormon women were "good-natured, stupid fools" for consenting to the idea.[101] Some speculated that Mormon women accepted plural marriage because they were intimidated and fearful of male Mormon leaders. And Gentile women claimed that Mormon women confided to them horrible tales regarding plural marriage. One young woman said that she had not met a Mormon woman "satisfied with her lot," but had received "applications from women that wanted to get away."[102] The newly converted Sarah Cooke even admitted that her friends who were plural wives felt "they would die from the distress of it."[103]

Because Gentile frontierswomen hated plural marriage, they obviously projected their own feelings onto Mormon women. Mormon women's documents tell a different story, however. Mormon women often defended plural marriage.[104] During the 1840s, a plural wife accepted the presence of a second wife because it was a "sacred revelation." She maintained that her family lived happily with no jealousy. She hated those who held Mormon women "up to scorn," and opposed the passage of laws making plural marriage illegal because it would deprive women of lawful husbands and would brand their children as illegitimate.[105] About the same time, Eliza Roxey Snow, a wife of Joseph Smith who migrated to Salt Lake City in 1844, claimed that she had learned to "love" the "principle and design of Plural Marriage." She, too, disliked Gentile critics. During her migration, she wrote, the inhabitants of Des Moines, Iowa Territory, "manifested as much curiosity as though viewing a menagerie of wild beasts."[106]

Other Mormon wives who made the trek to Salt Lake City described their introduction to plural marriage as a "bitter pill," a concept "repugnant to their feelings, and as a crushing trial," but, like Snow, they eventually accepted plural marriage as a religious duty.[107] In 1857, a woman who agreed to her husband taking additional wives after twenty-eight years of monogamous marriage, explained that she was "freer" and able to do "herself individually things she never could have attempted before; and work out her individual character as separate from her husband."[108]

Other Mormon female migrants to Salt Lake also railed against Gentile prejudice. They were against laws that would, in their view, force Mormons to flee the United States so they could follow the sacred precepts of their religion.[109] Others could not understand why Latter-day Saints were so widely maligned.[110] They explained that a man took an additional wife only with the full approval of his other wives; there was nothing secretive, corrupt, or underhanded about it.[111] Moreover, some Mormon women contended that the children of plural marriages were happier, healthier, and "brighter intellectually and physically than those born under the restricted law of Monogamy."[112]

Mormon wife Margaret S. Smoot could not fathom why plural marriage, if all its advantages were conceded, was so "unjustly condemned by the world." In 1847, Smoot came to Salt Lake City as one of two wives. In Salt Lake, she lived what she called a "poor but happy" life among virtuous people. "Vice and prostitution were things unknown to our society," she recalled. The only "houses of ill fame" in the area were those established by "Monagamists, Interlopers and defamers of women." According to another Mormon woman, abortion and infanticide were also unknown among them because extended Mormon families were not like Gentiles, who sought "to destroy the life of an infant before it is born and after because their deeds have been evil."[113]

Was it only from the outside that plural marriages of the Latter-day Saints seemed so reprehensible? Did Gentile women misconstrue plural marriage? Did Gentile women invent unhappy confessions of Mormon wives? Did they perhaps dismiss the feelings of women who favored plural marriage?[114] Recently, one scholar, who was raised as a Mormon, argued that Mormon women were so indoctrinated by the church that they publicly supported controversial issues. According to her, when Latter-day Saints were attacked for plural marriage as they sought statehood during the 1870s, male church leaders encouraged women to defend the practice and assert their right to chose their own style of marriage. She claimed that, under the "guise of women's rights," women were coerced to "participate in their own oppression."[115]

After Utah attained statehood and plural marriage was outlawed, some women remained in or entered plural marriages.[116] Although they had to deny being married, skip around the country to elude authorities, or exile themselves in such countries as England, unsanctioned plural marriage existed.[117] Were these Mormon women accustomed to plural marriage from childhoods spent with several mothers? Did they believe that plural marriage prepared them for the afterlife?

Gentile women ignored such issues. They disdained Mormons for engaging in plural marriage and refused to modify their stance. They did not pity Mormon women, castigating them instead for weak-mindedness. While these same frontierswomen extended understanding, kindness, and even affection to American Indians, they refused to see any good in Latter-day Saints. Women's sympathies were selective, directed toward American Indians and away from Mormons.

White women did not come to like all native peoples, however. Collegial relationships that developed between white women and Native Americans in the trans-Mississippi West involved a complex process, one that did not occur elsewhere. In Panama, for example, white women who encountered natives similar in appearance and culture to American Indians heaped venom and disgust on them. Women who chose the Panama Trail as a fast route to the California gold fields wanted little to do with Panamanians. As they did with Mormons, migrant women judged Panamanians as despicable when they reached the end of the trail as when they began it. Women who carried anti-native prejudices into the eastern part of Panama also carried them, often in an intensified form, out of the western side of the country.

Even though there are no Panamanian voices to tell the story, white women's writings reveal the underside of white-native contact in Panama.[118] Because of the arduous nature of the crossing, female emigrants along the isthmus route were not numerous. The trip, which took anywhere from twenty-one days to a month and a half, involved boarding a steamer in New York; crossing the isthmus on the back of a mule led by a Panama native or, after 1855, crossing by railroad; and boarding another steamer to reach San Francisco. The isthmus portion included seasickness, overcrowding, bad food, boredom, a hot and steamy jungle climate, and resentful natives. Although providing a quick passage, the Panama route presented some of the worst hardships to argonauts and others who chose it.[119]

Even though historians of the isthmus crossing usually insist that numbers of white women were insignificant, they underestimate women's hardiness.[120] A few may have been prostitutes anxious to reap lucrative rewards from their timely appearance among male travelers and gold-seekers, but the cost of the trip would have discouraged these women.[121] In fact, single and married women were passengers on virtually every Panama-bound steamship. On the initial voyage of the California from Panama to San Francisco, 14 of the 364 passengers were women.[122] After a portion of the railroad opened in 1851 and accommodations improved, the number of women making the crossing increased. By 1867, women accounted for a significant proportion of the 400,000 passengers transported across Panama by the railroad in thirteen years.[123]

Like the women who made the overland crossing along the various land routes, these female migrants were fully, if not accurately, informed regarding the treatment they might expect from the natives. Guidebooks published for Panama travelers emphasized the necessity to be "liberal to the men who work the canoe," meaning cash gratuities were expected. White migrants were advised to negotiate written contracts with porters and other native workers.[124] These less than encouraging bits of advice were supplemented by newspaper stories that warned of the rampant vice and corruption, especially an addiction to gambling, among Panamanians.[125] Newspapers also carried lurid accounts of riots and other violent confrontations between natives and emigrants, introduced by dramatic headlines: "Fearful Riot at Panama! Twenty-Five Americans Massacred by the Natives."[126] These stories referred to "excited savages," "a general melee," or "a general massacre." Their authors reported that when Panamanian troops arrived to quell the rioters they joined their "fellows" in attacking white travelers.[127]

After hearing a number of such tales, many women developed intense fear of the land portion of the trip. Sarah Brooks, who migrated with her three-and-a-half-year-old child in 1852, stated that women focused on "that much-dreaded part of the journey," the crossing of the isthmus. "The papers had given accounts of the dangers to be met with there," she explained, including "robbers, loss of baggage, of people being left behind and having to wait for another steamer; and, worst of all, getting the much dreaded Panama fever."[128] Because the women believed in Manifest Destiny they viewed their "little brown brothers" as an inferior race awaiting enlightenment at the hands of white women. White women expected Panamanians to be, as one woman said, "intellectually little above the animals."[129]

After women departed from New York City, some hardly noticed native peoples. Other features of the journey caught their attention, including rough seas and seasickness, magnificent scenery, inadequate meals, friendly companions, and the mule ride across the isthmus.[130] Other women, however, were taken with the native population of Panama. Like women on overland trails, Panama migrants were initially interested in physical appearance and style of dress. They described the nearly naked state of men and children, observing that the men seldom wore anything more than a breechcloth, or as one woman said, a "bit of cloth about their loins."[131] One woman, making the passage in reverse from California to New York in 1854, portrayed the men as "swarthy-visaged, half-naked Carthaginians . . . a mongrel race of natives, whose appearance and features were equally as repulsive."[132] Another woman added unkindly that most of them were "intolerably ugly."[133]

The women of Panama received some compliments from female travelers about their attire. Some white women thought that they dressed "fantastically," although many ruffles and beads made them appear comical.[134] One woman declared that "the females were dressed quite fancifully" in frocks of white gauze, whereas another felt that women's outfits bordered on gaudy.[135] Some female observers were so delighted with these picturesque women that they spent hours watching as they set out wares in the meat market, walked through the streets with baskets on their heads, or spread wash on the grass to dry.[136] One woman asserted that she was so "perfectly fascinated with them and their wares" that she purchased "bananas, oranges and limes and a basket."[137]

When it came to native homes, hotels, and other buildings, women were much less likely to express admiration. They described native huts as filthy thatched dwellings. According to them, they stayed in accommodations so miserable and full of stench that they were, according to one, "obliged to hold our noses and have cologne to go to sleep by."[138] In 1861, Julia Twist denigrated shacks and larger buildings, saying they were "occupied by a race of beings hardly fit to be classed as human."[139]

Apparently, women travelers across Panama expressed great interest in native peoples, which Panama's natives, like American Indians, returned. Women were disconcerted by natives who invaded hotels and other buildings to stand and stare at them "in perfect astonishment."[140] One woman was annoyed at Panamanians who yelled at her as she passed by; she thought them "frightful in the extreme."[141]

White women's judgments were typically unfavorable. Women were harsh, cruel, and spiteful as they described the people who made their trip possible by toting their luggage, leading their mules, piloting their canoes, carrying them on their backs from steamers to shore, and performing other services. Sarah Brooks demonstrated a common attitude toward Panamanians when she stated that they were "desperately ugly in looks" and "proved equally so in character."[142]

Other women were more specific, especially in accusing natives of being greedy and dishonest.[143] One woman believed that they hid mules and bribed boatmen "in order to secure as many pieces of money as possible" from emigrants. To her, Panamanians were crafty yet ignorant.[144] It did not occur to her that natives seeing their homeland invaded by whites might resist, as well as wondering how they could profit from the situation. An 1849 traveler revealed that Panamanians understood the idea of profiting from travelers and tourists. Natives were, she said, "simple, inoffensive people" who "understand perfectly the getting of dimes from the Americans."[145] Another traveler of the same year insisted that the natives "extort all they can from the travelers."[146]

Still other women were upset by what they considered the temperamental nature of Panamanians. The white traveler Jessie Benton Fremont portrayed them as "naked, screaming, barbarous" people. May Ann Harris Meredith thought the "natives were so impetuous and excitable that it was almost impossible to do anything with them." At another point, Meredith declared that "they almost make me crazy."[147]

Other female travelers reported that native tempestuousness was aggravated by their tendency to drink, gamble, and fight.

This unfavorable picture of Panamanians was unrelieved by approving remarks. Unlike their sister migrants on overland routes, white women who crossed the isthmus were oblivious to any expression of personality, creativity, or energy by the natives they encountered. During the relatively short time that it took to traverse Panama, women had neither opportunity nor motivation to revise images of themselves or their conceptions of Panamanians.

Additionally, many women found their prejudices aggravated by outbreaks of violence between migrants and natives. Since most entered Panama expecting brutish treatment, they probably acted in belligerent or arrogant ways that produced the results they anticipated. Considering the boredom, heat, and tension of the situation, travelers' attitudes and actions could have created tragedy between themselves and Panamanians, which would have confirmed their view that such conflict was inevitable.[148]

Like women on other trails, these women commented on native uprisings, massacres, and attacks. In 1852, for example, Sarah Brooks was involved in an altercation with "an ugly set" of boatmen. Due to the heat, one of the men shed his breechcloth and ignored orders to put it back on. The women sheltered themselves with umbrellas, whereas the other boatmen retired to nearby trees for a nap. Rather than letting the situation calm down, white male migrants drew knives and pistols on the natives, who sullenly returned to work.[149]

As a result of such petty squabbles, the Panamanians gained a reputation as bold, insolent, and dangerous people. Crossing Panama in 1854, Mallie Stafford was surprised that in spite of "hordes of merciless savages," huge numbers of gold-seekers chose the route. Along the way, rumors and alarmism beset her at every step. She recalled that the "bare recital" of atrocities and massacres was enough to make "the stoutest female heart quail with apprehension." Stafford did not have an easy crossing. She witnessed a male migrant draw a pistol on a native mule driver who had told him to "go to hell." And she was terrified when a native man pulled her mule off the main trail. She flailed at him with her riding whip, but was rescued by a runner sent out from the destination hotel as a greeter. Stafford talked of thieves, murderers, and brash robbers who held up trains. and women who had been stolen away and murdered.[150]

Other white women had similar troubles. A few years later, in 1856, several women were caught in a riot that occurred in Panama City as a result of rumor, prejudice, and conflict.[151] One of these recollected that during the eighteen-hour siege she saw white families separated and men "knocked down, beaten, left for dead in the streets." Pondering the native rebellion, she suggested that "the natives seemed angry at the constant streams of 'Yankees' who were using their town as convenient stepping stone to the treasure land of California."[152] How right she was.

The flood of migrants moving thoughtlessly and aggressively through Panama had created an incendiary situation. When added to the rigors of the trip, this tension and discord often disrupted the passage. A year after the Panama City riot, Lucy Sexton discovered that a contingent of U.S. Marines would ensure the safety of her party.[153] Like U.S. Cavalry stationed in the American West, marines guarded immigrants from native resistance. As a result, white women had little inclination to adjust their interpretations of Panama's natives. Their memories of the trek were summarized by Mallie Stafford as "a ride over a wild, inhuman country on the back of a wild, irresponsible mule driven by a wild, demoralized, irrepressible son of the tropics."[154]

Numerous white women harbored similar sentiments about their overland passage to the Far West. They thought Mormons and Native Americans barbaric and wily, feared being robbed or murdered, and heard more than they wanted about riots and massacres. Their negative comments were, however, balanced by other women who found much to enjoy in the trip and in Native Americans. The understanding, affection, and empathy that the latter women developed toward American Indians was not extended to all peoples. Rather, the relationship that developed between these frontierswomen and American Indians was unique, not replicated in women's contacts with any other group. Friendly and collegial interchanges between white women and

American Indians demonstrates that the usual interpretation of women and Indians as adversaries is neither accurate nor useful.

Still, white women believed in the tenets of Manifest Destiny, especially white superiority. In white women's interactions with "others," women thought of themselves as occupying the top of a hierarchy. Although they were willing to teach, nurse, and otherwise succor Native Americans, they did so because superior people had a duty to help those beneath them. Even though the American West attracted disparate kinds of people during its frontier era, it did not become a melting pot. Instead, federal policymakers, who often promised eventual incorporation of groups into overall white culture, also institutionalized differences based on race, ethnicity, gender, and social class.[155] Thus, the West's milieu—based on colonialist principles—fostered a legacy that remains problematic today.

—— **Chapter Seven** ——

Frontier Product: A Difficult Legacy

All frontiers have products, some emerging during their existence and some appearing later. Positive product is easily identified. For example, the West has been a model of economic development, with prosperous cities and growing populations. Negative product is more subtle. One of these was an inaccurate image of vulnerable white woman versus rapacious Native Americans.

Legends and myths concerning the nature of white women, Native Americans, and the interaction of the two have exerted tremendous influence from the settlement of Britain's American colonies to the present. Advocating that women were weak and vulnerable, whereas Indians were savage and predatory, myth and media promoted the idea that contact between the two was almost always calamitous. According to typical scenarios—whether they be in prose, poetry, film, or television—women are usually broken in spirit and body from their encounters with American Indians. This belief provided one more rationalization that "unmanageable" Indians must be exterminated or at least physically constrained under the watchful eye of a reservation agent.

In truth, neither white women nor Native Americans were as extreme as thought. Although white women had been taught about their exceptional morality, paired with physical frailty, they discovered through the demands of westward migration that these characteristics had been exaggerated. Meanwhile, rather than being "good" or "bad," American Indians frequently turned out to be curious, helpful, and friendly. Consequently, white women got along far better with Indians than they expected. Unfortunately, white women could not divest themselves of colonialist ideas, especially white superiority, inferiority of peoples of color, and whites' right to take the land of "inferior" natives.

Even though white women gradually warmed to Indians, they continued to view them as lesser than themselves. The deep-seated nature of white colonialism was demonstrated by women's shabby treatment of such other groups as Mormons, or members of the Church of Jesus Christ of Latter-day Saints, and the native people of Panama. This occurred, at least in part, because women criticized the outcomes of colonialism, or Manifest Destiny, in the American West, but did not dispute its underlying assumptions. Thus, even as white women opposed men's violent ways of colonizing the bodies of indigenes, they colonized their minds.[1]

Other negative product can also be teased out of largely white sources. Taking the perspective of Victorio, the Apache chief mentioned earlier who resisted the white invasion of the Southwest between the early 1850s and his death in 1880, shows how negative product is clouded and even ignored. Around 1825, Victorio was born a Warm Springs, or Mimbres, Apache. As a boy, Victorio learned to hunt, fight, and hate Mexicans, often for good reason. In 1835, for example, when Victorio was about ten years of age, Mexican officials in Sonora and Chihuahua reinstated a practice of their Spanish predecessors; they offered cash payments for Apache scalps.[2]

Soon, Victorio also learned to distrust and fear Anglos who came to the Southwest with reductionist notions of Apache society and culture. Anglos seized land and slaughtered buffalo and other game for amusement and to destroy the Apaches' livelihood. Mimbres Apaches resisted, using the very firearms they obtained from unscrupulous white traders. Victorio, who was capable and shrewd, rode with the Mimbres Apaches' fabled leader, Mangas Coloradas. In 1851, Mangas expressed his disappointment with whites who proposed a treaty by saying that he had once believed they "were friends . . . brothers,"[3] but no more. Two years later, in 1853, Mangas and Victorio tried again to establish peace with whites. In that year, the men signed the Fort Webster treaty. A year later, they agreed to try farming, but the U.S. government failed to supply reliable teachers, adequate food, tillable land, and farm implements as they had promised. Eventually, the U.S. Congress refused to ratify its agreements with the Apaches. In other words, Victorio and Mangas were willing to give up their traditional way of life and become pseudo-whites, only to discover that white vows were false.

During these years, the numbers of miners, setters, and travelers increased so rapidly that Victorio's people, who were hunters, faced malnutrition and even starvation. In 1854, Victorio's hopes rose when Dr. Michael Steck came to New Mexico to establish an Indian agency at Fort Thorn. Although Steck became a strong advocate for Apaches, he could not wrest adequate supplies from Washington officials nor could he stop hungry Apaches from raiding settlers' stock. In 1855, Apache leaders were presented with another treaty, this one requiring the Mimbres and Mescalero Apaches to surrender twelve to fifteen thousand square miles of their land to the U.S. government in exchange for food and protection. Because Mangas Coloradas and Victorio mistrusted whites, they refused to sign. Eventually, the U.S. Senate rejected the treaty because deposits of iron, lead, copper, and silver were found on Mimbres land, but not in the areas for which the U.S. government had asked.

During the remainder of the 1850s, and during the 1860s and 1870s, Victorio vacillated between hanging back and actively resisting. Among other white atrocities, Victorio witnessed in 1861 the capture of Cochise and some of his kin during "peace" talks in a white military camp. Another atrocity, also in 1861, concerned Victorio's beloved Mangas Coloradas. White miners in Pinos Altos tied Mangas to a tree, whipping him with ox goads until his back was broken and bloody. Although Victorio knew about Mangas Coloradas's torture, he preserved Mangas's dignity by remaining silent. Two years later, in 1863, a group of Civil War soldiers seized Mangas, shot him, and buried him, only to dig him up, whack his head off, and boil his skull. Victorio was humiliated, for Apaches believed that in the afterworld a person's body had the same condition as at the time of death.[4]

Soon, Victorio took Mangas Coloradas's place as leader of the Mimbres Apaches. He led his followers to reservations like New Mexico's Bosque Redondo, only to see them starve and die there. He then urged his followers to escape from such reservations as Arizona's San Carlos. In between, Mimbres Apaches, along with Mescaleros and Chiricahuas, lived by raiding stock and trading in Mexico. Although white citizens were outraged at the loss of animals and of white lives,[5] U.S. troops—white and black—could not outwit the master strategist that Victorio had become.

During these decades, Apaches scattered. Some of Victorio's people sought refuge at the Indian agency near Fort Stanton, where they lived with Mescaleros. Other Apaches, including Mescaleros, fought with Victorio in onslaughts that took many lives, white and Indian.[6] In 1879, Victorio proclaimed that he would never sign another treaty nor go to another white reservation. Because he knew that a number of white men, some in official positions, advocated reservations or genocide, he decided to fight, launching the Victorio War of 1879–1880.[7] Victorio's resistance to things white terrorized white settlers and decreased the number of Apaches. During these years, Apaches could not protect their loved ones, who might disappear at any time from death or capture. Apaches also lost ownership of their bodies, which became fighting machines, and even their minds, which had to focus on white opponents and on danger rather than on Indian concerns. By the fall of 1880, Victorio's force was diminished, demoralized, and nearly out of supplies. Victorio and his people fled to Mexico, where fighting ended with Victorio's death at Tres Castillos in Mexico. Although a Mexican soldier claimed that he shot Victorio, the Mescaleros who retrieved the bodies said that Victorio had taken his own life rather than be killed by despised Mexicans.

Even though the Victorio War was over, Indian "wars" in the Southwest continued to rage, taking a heavy toll not only on Indian men, but on thousands of women and children who starved, fell ill, or died. Yet hundreds of Apaches preferred, as had Victorio, to die fighting rather than from malnutrition or disease. After an aged Mimbres chief, Nana, took Victorio's place as chief, he organized an attack on white settlers in New Mexico Territory to avenge the deaths of Victorio and others. White military records indicate that in July 1880, Nana "whirled through the territory, plundering and killing a number of people." On August 27, Nana and his soldiers set a successful ambush in Gavilan Canyon in Ruidoso, which disrupted an entire company of the black Ninth Cavalry, who lost three men, about thirty horses, and one hundred rounds of ammunition.

Victorio's warrior sister, Lozen, also tried to avenge him. She fought with Nana and later with Geronimo. In 1886, she was captured with another woman fighter, Tah-des-te. Both were sent on a prisoner-of-war train to an internment camp in Florida. In 1887, Lozen was moved to Mount Vernon Barracks in Alabama, where she died of tuberculosis on an unknown date. According to custom, Apaches buried her secretly in an unmarked grave. The Apaches she left behind were dispossessed, disenfranchised, and prisoners of war.

In the meantime, whites living in New Mexico's Mimbres Valley committed psychological violence against Apaches by appropriating Victorio as a white cultural symbol and commodifying his image.[8] Rather than taking Victorio and Apache culture as a medium to understand Indians, and on a larger level, the human condition, whites used Indians to sell things. During the mid-1880s, a new hotel in Hillsboro, the Victorio Hotel, opened its doors. In Silver City, the Victorio Mining Company operated. During the mid-1890s, the owners of the Mountain Pride Stage Line based in Kingston had a portrait of Victorio painted on the doors of the company's premier coach. Why did whites do these things? A line from a mid-1880s military report suggests that whites were proud of vanquishing Victorio and his people: "the vast section over which the wild and irresponsible tribes once wandered, has been redeemed from idle waste to become a home for millions of progressive people."

The few Mimbres Apaches who currently reside at the Fort Sill agency in Oklahoma, as well as Mescaleros at Fort Sill and at Mescalero, New Mexico, see things differently. After all, creating historical accounts is just another form of discourse, in which the narrators choose dominant tropes. As the Nez Percé Yellow Wolf said sometime around 1877, "The whites told only one side. Told it to please themselves. Told much that is not true. Only his own best deeds, only the worst deeds of the

Indians, has the white man told."[9] Modern Mimbres Apaches and Mescaleros choose to celebrate Victorio, Lozen, and the other Apaches who fought for their people and their culture. But these people live largely divided from the world around them, in a kind of Indian apartheid. The loss of lives, the destruction of much Apache culture, and present-day divisiveness are examples of negative product.

Had white women of the time foreseen the outcome of colonialism, they might have mourned and protested, yet it is unlikely that they could have freed themselves from the shackles of colonialism. And if they had accomplished that Herculean feat, who would have listened? Whites had far more interest in men's adventures on the frontier, and newspaper editors ran male accounts in their newspapers, whereas publishing houses sought out male authors. Nor were women's diaries, letters, and reminiscences collected by libraries and archives. Additionally, few white people paid attention to what American Indians had to say. Most whites viewed Indians as one-dimensional, cardboard-cut-out characters who toured with Buffalo Bill Cody, other Wild West shows, circuses, and expositions. When serious, Indians garnered little attention, but when engaged in antics, whites did notice these eccentric representatives of what most saw as a vanishing breed.

It was not until the 1960s that white Americans questioned their customary assumptions regarding women and Indians. War resisters, second-wave feminists, and African American, Latina, and Latino activists posed questions that made possible in the United States the emergence of a "multi-cultural" awareness. Moreover, environmentalists pointed out that white disdain of Indian ways had encouraged serious environmental damage. Although those protests occurred almost a half-century ago, few whites have come to understand the psychic pain of American Indians. As a result, twenty-first-century Indians continue to suffer acute historical anguish. Victorio's goal, for example, was a simple one. He wanted to take his people to their homeland at Ojo Caliente in New Mexico Territory. Whites, however, imposed their dominance by denying his requests. Yet Ojo Caliente, deep in the Mimbres Mountains, was not a prize for whites. Today, it is sparsely populated. A tumbling-down adobe that stood briefly at the center of a short-lived Apache agency is unmarked. Although archeologists and historians find the site, tourists do not. Consequently, nothing at Ojo Caliente has been trashed or vandalized. The site stands as a reminder of white intransigence and Indian tragedy.

The lesson of Victorio, Lozen, and Ojo Caliente—indeed, of all negative product—is that the time has come to bring the experiences and lessons of contact between white women and American Indians to some kind of fruition. Neutralizing negative product more than has occurred to date is the only way to prevent the dark side of the frontier from living on in the twenty-first century.

NOTES

Introduction

1. See, for example, Robert F. Berkhofer, Jr., *The White Man's Indian: Images of the American Indian from Columbus to the Present* (New York: Alfred A. Knopf, 1978; Vintage Books, 1979).

2. Michael P. Malone, "Beyond the Last Frontier: Toward a New Approach to Western American History," *Western Historical Quarterly* 20 (November 1989): 409–27.

3. Jane Haggis, "White Women and Colonialism: Towards a Non-Recuperative History," 45–75, in *Gender and Imperialism,* ed. Clare Midgley (Manchester, England: Manchester University Press, 1998).

4. For the significance of such sources, see Judy Nolte Lensink, "Expanding the Boundaries of Criticism: The Diary as Female Autobiography," *Women's Studies* 14 (1987): 39–54; Edwin R. Bingham, "American Wests through Autobiography and Memoir," *Pacific Historical Review* 56 (February 1987): 1–24; Andrew P. Norman, "Telling It Like It Was: Historical Narratives on Their Own Terms," *History and Theory* 30 (1991): 119–35; and Brigitte Geogi-Findlay, *The Frontiers of Women's Writing: Women's Narratives and the Rhetoric of Westward Expansion* (Tucson: University of Arizona Press, 1996).

5. Annette Bennington McElhiney, "The Image of the Pioneer Woman in the American Novel" (Ph.D. diss., University of Denver, 1978); Glenwood Irons, ed., *Gender, Language, and Myth: Essays on Popular Narrative* (Toronto: University of Toronto Press); and Barbara Cloud, "Images of Women in the Mining-camp Press," *Nevada State Historical Society* 36 (fall 1993): 194–207.

6. For the usefulness of missionary records, see Vicki Ruiz, "Dead Ends or Gold Mines?: Using Missionary Records in Mexican-American Women's History," *Frontiers* 12 (1991): 35–56.

7. Angela Cavender Wilson, "American Indian History or Non-Indian Perceptions of American Indian History?" 23–26, in *Natives and Academics: Researching and Writing about American Indians,* ed. Devon A. Mihesuah (Lincoln: University of Nebraska Press, 1998).

8. John Frost, *Pioneer Mothers of the West; or, Daring and Heroic Deeds of American Women* (Boston: Lee and Shepard, 1875), 22.

9. Michael G. Kenny, "A Place for Memory: The Interface between Individual and Collective History," *Comparative Studies in Science and History* 41 (July 1999): 420–21; and James C. Scott, *Domination and the Arts of Resistance: Hidden Transcripts* (New Haven, Conn.: Yale University Press, 1990).

10. For the importance of considering many groups, see Susan Armitage and Elizabeth Jameson, eds., *Writing the Range: Race, Class, and Culture in the Women's West* (Norman: University of Oklahoma Press, 1997).

11. Robert J. Hind, "The Internal Colonial Concept," *Comparative Studies of Society* 26 (July 1984): 543–68.

12. That the highpoint of the American West was 1848 to 1889 is argued in Walter Nugent, *Into the West: The Story of Its People* (New York: Alfred A. Knopf, 1999).

13. For what constitutes a western frontier and the West, see Aaron Walker, "Wild Frontiers: Imagined Geographies and the American West" (Ph.D. diss., University of Massachusetts Amherst, 2001); and W. Douglas Seefeldt, "Constructing Western Pasts: Place and Public Memory in the Twentieth-Century American West" (Ph.D. diss., Arizona State University, 2001).

14. Walter Nugent, "Frontiers and Empires in the Late Nineteenth Century," 161–66, in *Trails: Toward a New Western History,* ed. Patricia Nelson Limerick, Clyde A. Milner II, and Charles E. Rankin (Lawrence: University Press of Kansas, 1991); and Robert A. Jackson, "American Regional Theory: Toward a Theory of the Region in the United States and Its Roles in the Production of American Literature and Culture" (Ph.D. diss., New York University, 2001).

15. Christopher Chase-Dunn and Thomas D. Hall, *Rise and Demise: Comparing World-Systems* (Boulder, Colo.: Westview, 1997), 27–58, 200–231; and Hall, "World-Systems Analysis: A Small Sample from a Large Universe," in *A World Systems Reader: New Perspectives on Gender, Urbanism, Cultures, Indigenous Peoples, and Ecology,* ed. Thomas D. Hall (Lanham, Md.: Rowman and Littlefield, 2000), 3–28.

Chapter 1

1. Julie Roy Jeffrey, *Frontier Women: The Trans-Mississippi West, 1840–1880* (New York: Hill and Wang, 1979), 10–13, 22–24; and John Mack Faragher, *Women and Men on the Overland Trail* (New Haven, Conn.:Yale University Press, 1979), 179–87.

2. Cotton Mather, *Ornaments for the Daughters of Zion* (Cambridge, Mass.: Printed by Samuel and Bartholomew Green for Samuel Phillips at Boston, 1692); and Abigail Adams, *Letters* (Boston: Wilkins, Carter and Co., 1848), 416.

3. June O. Underwood, "Western Women and True Womanhood: Culture and Symbol in History and Literature," *Great Plains Quarterly* 5 (spring 1985): 93–106.

4. Helen Papshively, *All the Happy Endings* (New York: Harper Brothers, 1956), xiv–xv; and James D. Hart, *The Popular Book: A History of America's Literary Taste* (New York: Oxford University Press, 1950), 51, 67–68, 85–93.

5. *Ladies Repository* 3 (February 1843), 54.

6. *Ladies Companion* 20 (May 1844), 24–25; and *Ladies Repository* 4 (October 1844), 312.

7. T. S. Arthur, *Advice to Young Ladies on Their Duties and Conduct in Life* (Boston: Phillips and Sampson, 1848), 124–31.

8. Margaret Fuller Ossoli, *Memoirs of Margaret Fuller Ossoli* (Boston: Phillips, Sampson, and Co., 1852), 195.

9. Barbara Welter, *Dimity Convictions: The American Woman in the Nineteenth Century* (Athens: Ohio University Press, 1976), 21.

10. Hester Chapone, *Letters on the Improvement of the Mind* (New York: Evert Dyuckinck, 1826), 151, 160.

11. Harriet Beecher Stowe, *The Minister's Wooing* (New York: Derby and Jackson, 1859), 37.

12. Maria Cummins, *The Lamplighter* (Boston: J. P. Jewett, 1854).

13. Marion Harland, *Alone* (Richmond,Va.: A. Morris, 1855), 282.

14. Caroline Lee Hentz, *Ernest Linwood* (Boston: J. P. Jewett and Co., 1856), 459.

15. *American Monthly Magazine* 9 (March 1837), 290–92.

16. Elizabeth Sandford, *Woman in Her Social and Domestic Character* (London: Longman, Brown, Green, and Longman, 1842), 5.

17. Mrs. A. J. Graves, *Women in America* (New York: Harper, 1844), 67; and Lydia H. Sigourney, *Letters to Young Ladies* (New York: Harpers, 1841), 13.

18. *Ladies Repository* 8 (September 1848), 277–78.

19. Catharine Beecher, *Essay on Slavery* (1837; repr., Freeport, N.Y.: Books for Libraries Press, 1970), 99–100.

20. Catherine Beecher, *The American Woman's Home; or Principles of Domestic Science* (New York: J. B. Ford, 1870), 13, 466.

21. Kathryn Kish Sklar, *Catharine Beecher: A Study in American Domesticity* (New York: W. W. Norton, 1973), 156–58.

22. Ibid., 113–15, 168–83.

23. Catherine Beecher, *Suggestions Respecting Improvements in Education* (Hartford, Conn.: Packard and Butler, 1829), 12; and Beecher, *The Evils Suffered by American Women and Children* (New York: Harper and Brothers, 1846), 12.

24. *Ladies Repository* 4 (October 1844), 313.

25. Lydia Maria Child, *Brief History of the Condition of Women, in Various Ages and Nations,* vol. 1 (New York: C. S. Francis, 1854), 9.

26. Bill Gilbert, "Westward Ho! And Never Mind the Indians," *Smithsonian* 25 (May 1994): 40–53.

27. Elizabeth Furniss, *The Burden of History: Colonialism and the Frontier Myth in a Rural Canadian Community* (Vancouver: University of British Columbia Press, 1999), 63.

28. Susan P. Conrad, *Perish the Thought: Intellectual Women in Romantic America, 1830–1860* (New York: Oxford University Press, 1976), 95–98; and Nancy Cott, *The Bonds of Womanhood: "Woman's Sphere" in New England, 1780–1835* (New Haven, Conn.: Yale University Press, 1977), 200–201.

29. Sarah Josepha Hale, *Northwood,* vol. 2 (New York: H. Long, 1852), 407.

30. Glenda Riley, "Origins of the Argument for Improved Female Education," *History of Education Quarterly* 9 (winter 1969): 455–70; and Sarah Josepha Hale, Letters, Vassar College, Poughkeepsie, N.Y.

31. Glenda Riley, "The Subtle Subversion: Changes in the Traditionalist Image of the American Woman," *The Historian* 32 (February 1970): 210–27.

32. *Godey's Lady's Book* 41 (July 1850), 355.

33. Quote from Burlington (Iowa) *Hawk-Eye,* 9 January 1851.

34. T. S. Arthur, *Ten Nights in a Barroom* (Boston: L. P. Crown, 1854).

35. Ida Husted Harper, *The Life and Work of Susan B. Anthony* (Indianapolis: Bobbs Merrill, 1898), 66–68.

36. *Ladies Repository* 3 (May 1843), 139.

37. Elizabeth Sandford, *Female Improvement* (London: Longmans, 1836); Margaret Coxe, *Claims of the Country on American Females,* vol. 1 (Columbus, Ohio: Isaac N. Whiting, 1842); and *Godey's Lady's Book* 18 (June 1839), 283; 25 (December 1847), 330–32; 43 (August 1851), 122; and 45 (August 1852), 193.

38. *Godey's Lady's Book* 61 (December 1860), 556.

39. Lydia H. Sigourney, *Poems* (Philadelphia: Key and Biddle, 1834), 29; and Sigourney, *Saying of Little Ones* (Buffalo: Phinney and Co., 1855), 244–45.

For Whitman, see Julie Roy Jeffrey, *Converting the West: A Biography of Narcissa Whitman* (Norman: University of Oklahoma Press, 1991); and for Walker, see Violet Tew Kimball, "Mary Richardson Walker: Sidesaddle and Pregnant to Oregon in 1838," *Overland Journal* 13 (winter 1995–96): 4–10. Also helpful is Laurie Winn Carlson, *On Sidesaddles to Heaven: The Women of the Rocky Mountain Mission* (Caldwell, Idaho: Caxton Press, 1998).

40. *Ladies Repository* 8 (January 1848), 17; 1 (April 1841), 113; 8 (January 1848), 17; and 1 (April 1843), 113; and *Godey's Lady's Book* 37 (August 1848), 61–68.

41. *Godey's Lady's Book* 32 (January 1846), 1.

42. Harland, *Alone,* 282.

43. Angelina Grimké, *Appeal to Christian Women* (New York: American Anti-Slavery Society, 1836), 16–18; Elizabeth Chandler, *Political Works and Essays* (Philadelphia: L. Howell, 1836), 17–20, 175, 47–48; and Lydia Maria Child, *The Right Way, the Safe Way* (New York: Published at 5 Beekman Street, 1860), 96.

44. Calvin Stowe, *Harriet Beecher Stowe* (Boston: Houghton Mifflin, 1889), 259–60.

45. Elizabeth Cady Stanton, Susan B. Anthony, and Matilda Joslyn Gage, eds., *The History of Woman Suffrage,* vol. 1 (Rochester, N.Y.: Charles Mann, 1889), 67, 71, 73.

46. *New York Times,* 13 May 1859.

47. *The Knickerbocker* 23 (January 1844), 79–80.

48. *Godey's Lady's Book* 22 (April 1841), 155.

49. Burlington (Iowa) *Hawk-Eye,* 25 December 1850.

50. Maria J. McIntosh, *Woman in America: Her Work and Her Reward* (New York: D. Appleton, 1850), 102.

51. Lydia H. Sigourney, *The Western Home and Other Poems* (Philadelphia: Parry and McMillan, 1854), 27.

52. Charles F. Hoffman, *A Winter in the West by a New Yorker,* vol. 2 (New York: Harper, 1835), 235; and Hector E. Lee, "Tales and Legends in American Western Literature," *Western American Literature* 9 (winter 1975): 239.

53. *Iowa News,* 24 June 1837 and 26 August 1837.

54. Waterloo (Iowa) *Courier,* 10 July 1860.

55. Glenda Riley, *Divorce: An American Tradition* (New York: Oxford University Press, 1991), 73–76, 116, 118.

56. Katherine Sadler, "Petticoats and Votes: The Struggle for Woman Suffrage in Oregon and the West," *Oregon History* 38 (winter 1994–95): 6–7, 22; and Beverly Beeton, *Women Vote in the West: The Woman Suffrage Movement, 1869–1896* (New York: Garland, 1986).

57. Glenda Riley, *Inventing the American Woman: An Inclusive History,* vol. 1 (Wheeling, Ill.: Harlan Davidson, 2001), 258–62.

58. Ibid., 244–45.
59. William W. Fowler, *Woman on the American Frontier; A Valuable and Authentic History of the Heroism, Adventures, Privations, Captivities, Trials, and Noble Lives and Deaths of the "Pioneer Mothers of the Republic"* (Hartford, Conn.: S. S. Scranton, 1880), 3, 33, 359, 365, 502, 505.
60. Riley, *Inventing the American Woman*, vol. 2, 185; and Glenda Riley, *The Female Frontier: A Comparative View of Women on the Prairie and the Plains* (Lawrence: University Press of Kansas), 186.
61. U.S. Department of Commerce and Labor, *Marriage and Divorce, 1867–1906* (Westport, Conn.: 1978 repr. ed.), 1:11–13, 22–24.
62. Riley, *Inventing the American Woman*, vol. 2, 307–8.
63. Glenn Charles Leader, III, "Annie Oakley in Performance: The Evolution of an Image" (Ph.D. diss., Florida State University, 1997); and Roger A. Hall, *Performing the American Frontier, 1870–1906* (Cambridge: Cambridge University Press, 2001), 141–48.
64. Riley, *Female Frontier*, 19–20; Paula M. Bauman, "Single Women Homesteaders in Wyoming, 1880–1930," *Annals of Wyoming* 58 (spring 1986): 39–53; and H. Elaine Lindgren, *Land in Her Own Name: Women as Homesteaders in North Dakota* (Fargo: North Dakota Institute for Regional Studies, 1991).
65. Glenda Riley, *The Life and Legacy of Annie Oakley* (Norman: University of Oklahoma Press, 1994), 112–44.
66. Ibid.
67. Ibid.
68. Ibid., 27–62.
69. Frieda Knobloch, *The Culture of Wilderness: Agriculture as Colonization in the American West* (Chapel Hill: University of North Carolina Press, 1996).
70. Susan-Mary Grant, "Making History: Myth and the Construction of American Nationhood," 88–106, in *Myths and Nationhood*, ed. Geoffrey Hosking and George Schöpflin (New York: Routledge, 1997).
71. Mary Eastman, *Dacotahs* (New York: J. Wiley, 1849); and Arthur J. Larsen, ed., *Crusader and Feminist: Letters of Jane Grey Swisshelm, 1858–1854* (St. Paul: Minnesota Historical Society, 1934), 191.
72. Quoted in Herbert R. Brown, *The Sentimental Novel in America, 1789–1860* (Durham, N.C.: Duke University Press, 1940), 349.
73. See, for example, Ruth Ann Alexander, "Finding Oneself through a Cause: Elaine Goodale Eastman and Indian Reform in the 1880s," *South Dakota History* 22 (spring 1992): 1–37.
74. Carol Carney, "Constructive Narratives of American Culture and Identity: Beadle's Dime Novels By and About Women, 1860–1870" (Ph.D. diss., Claremont Graduate School, 1995).

75. F. A. Briggs, *Buffalo Bill's Witchcraft; or, Pawnee Bill and the Snake Aztecs* (New York: Street and Smith, 1911), 24, 28.

76. Leslie Fiedler, *The Return of the Vanishing American* (New York: Stein and Day, 1968), 77. For examples of white women anxious to be missionaries, see Sara Smith, "Diary," in *First White Women Over the Rockies; Diaries, Letters, and Biographical Sketches of the Six Women of the Oregon Mission Who Made the Overland Journey in 1836 and 1838,* vol. 3, ed. Clifford Merrill Drury (Glendale, Calif.: Arthur H. Clark, 1966), 61–125; and Patricia V. Horner, "Mary Richardson Walker: The Shattered Dreams of a Missionary Woman," *Montana, The Magazine of Western History* 32 (summer 1982): 22.

77. Barbara Welter, "The Cult of True Womanhood: 1820–1860," *American Quarterly* 18 (summer 1966), 158–59.

78. Almira H. Phelps, *The Female Students, or Letters to Young Ladies on Female Education* (New York: Leavitt, Lord, and Co., 1836), 16; Sandford, *Female Improvement,* 14–15; and George W. Burnap, *The Sphere and Duties of Woman* (Baltimore: J. Murphy, 1848), 45, 158.

79. *Godey's Lady's Book* 42 (January 1851), 65.

80. E. D. E. N. Southworth, *Retribution: A Tale of Passion* (Philadelphia: T. B. Peterson, 1856), 173, 188; and James Fenimore Cooper, *Jack Tier; or, The Florida Reef* (1848; repr., G. P. Putnam's Sons, n.d.); and Cooper, *The Sea Lions, or, The Lost Sealers* (1849; repr., New York: D. Appleton, 1901), 223.

81. Catharine Maria Sedgwick, *A Poor Rich Man and a Rich Poor Man* (New York: Harper's, 1836); and Hannah F. S. Lee, *Elinor Fulton* (Boston: Whipple and Damrell, 1837).

82. Hannah F. S. Lee, *Three Experiments of Living* (Boston: W. S. Damrell, 1837); Papshively, *All the Happy Endings,* 45; and E. D. E. N. Southworth, *Capitola* (Stockholm: P. A. Huldberg, 1865), 394.

83. *Godey's Lady's Book* 30 (March 1845), 99–100; 31 (July 1845), 267–69; and 31 (February 1845), 83–88.

84. *Godey's Lady's Book* 34 (April 1847), 215–17; 37 (November 1848), 317; 36 (January), 67; 22 (June 1841), 281; and 23 (July 1843), 41–42.

85. Edward I. Wheeler, *Deadwood Dick's Eagles; or, The Pards of Flood Bar* (Cleveland: Arthur Westbrook, 1899), 8, 10; and Captain C. Carleton, *Dave Bunker; or, The Outlaws of the Frontier* (Cleveland: Arthur Westbrook, 1908), 77–78, 82.

86. Wheeler, *Deadwood Dick's Eagles,* 28; An Old Scout, *The White Boy Chief; or, The Terror of North Platte* (New York: Frank Tousey, 1908), 10–13, 19–20; and An Old Scout, *Young Wild West Surrounded by Sioux; or, Arietta and the Aeronaut* (New York: Frank Tousey, 1917), 10–11, 18.

87. Helen Hunt Jackson, *A Century of Dishonor* (1881; Minneapolis: Ross and Haines, 1969); and Valerie Sherer Mathes, *Helen Hunt Jackson and Her Indian Reform Legacy* (Austin: University of Texas Press, 1990).

88. Chickering Carter, *Kid Curry's Last Stand* (New York: Street and Street, 1907), 5, 11.

89. Sander L. Gilman, *Difference and Pathology: Stereotypes of Sexuality, Race, and Madness* (Ithaca, N.Y.: Cornell University Press, 1985), 15–21; and Homi Bhabha, "Of Mimicry and Man: The Ambivalence of Colonial Discourse," *October* 28 (1983): 125–34. For a fuller discussion of bad Indians, see Richard Slotkin, *Regeneration through Violence: The Mythology of the American Frontier, 1600–1860* (Middletown, Conn.: Wesleyan University Press, 1973).

90. Roy Harvey Pearce, *The Savages of America; A Study of the Indian and the Idea of Civilization* (Baltimore: Johns Hopkins Press, 1965), 3–5; Frederick Turner, "The Terror of the Wilderness," *American Heritage* 28 (1977): 59–62; Alden T. Vaughn, "From White Man to Redskin: Changing Anglo-American Perceptions of the American Indian," *American Historical Review* 87 (November 1982): 917–53.

91. Robert F. Berkhofer, Jr., *The White Man's Indian: Images of the American Indian from Columbus to the Present* (New York: Alfred A. Knopf, 1978; Vintage Books, 1979), 2, 23–28; Ronald T. Takaki, *Iron Cages: Race and Culture in Nineteenth-Century America* (New York: Knopf, 1979), 55–65, 92–107. Two older, yet useful, works are Bernard W. Sheehan, *Seeds of Extinction: Jeffersonian Philanthropy and the American Indian* (New York: W. W. Norton, 1973); and Michael Paul Rogin, *Fathers and Children: Andrew Jackson and the Subjugation of the American Indian* (New York: Vintage, 1975).

92. Rowlandson quoted in Nancy B. Black and Bette S. Weidman, *White on Red: Images of the American Indian* (Port Washington, N.Y.: Kennikat Press, 1976), 41–48; James E. Seaver, ed., *The Story of Mary Jemison* (Canandaigua, N.Y.: J. D. Bemis, 1824); and Emeline Fuller, *Left by the Indians. Story of My Life* (Mount Vernon, Iowa: Hawk-Eye Steam Print, 1892), 29. The legacy of these images is discussed in Christopher Castiglia, *Bound and Determined: Captivity, Culture-Crossing, and White Womanhood from Mary Rowlandson to Patty Hearst* (Chicago: University of Chicago Press, 1996).

93. Stanley B. Kimball, "The Captivity Narrative on Mormon Trails, 1846–65," *Dialogue: A Journal of Mormon Thought* 18 (winter 1985): 81–88; and James F. Brooks, "'This Evil Extends Especially . . . to the Feminine Sex': Negotiating Captivity in the New Mexico Borderlands," *Feminist Studies* 22 (summer 1996): 279–310.

94. Abbie Gardner-Sharp, *The Spirit Lake Massacre and the Captivity of Miss Abbie Gardner* (Des Moines: Iowa Printing Co., 1885); Mary Butler Renville, *A Thrilling Narrative of Indian Captivity* (Minneapolis: Atlas Co., 1863); and Fuller, *Left by the Indians,* 29.

95. Quotes are in Lonnie J. White, "White Women Captives of Southern Plains Indians, 1866–1875," *Journal of the West* 8 (July 1969): 332, 336.

96. *New York Times,* 4 January 1868, 22 September 1851, 4 October 1851, 17 January 1853, 24 January 1853, 2 June 1859, 4 October 1870, 9 October 1870, 28 April 1871, 22 May 1878, 4 June 1878, 6 June 1878, and 11 July 1857.

97. Roy Harvey Pearce, "The Significances of the Captivity Narrative," *American Literature* 19 (1947): 2–6; and James A. Levenier, "Indian Captivity Narratives: Their Functions and Forms" (Ph.D. diss., University of Pennsylvania, 1975), 27, 31–36, 323.

98. James A. Sandos and Larry E. Burgess, *The Hunt for Willie Boy: Indian-Hating and Popular Culture* (Norman: University of Oklahoma Press, 1994). See also Richard Aquila, ed., *Wanted Dead or Alive: The American West in Popular Culture* (Chicago: University of Illinois Press, 1996).

99. Gayatri Chakravorty Spivak, *In Other Worlds: Essays in Cultural Politics* (New York: Methuen, 1987), 77–81.

100. Ward Churchill, *Fantasies of the Master Race: Literature, Cinema and the Colonization of American Indians* (San Francisco: City Lights Books, 1998), 1–3, 6–9.

101. Philip J. Deloria, *Playing Indian* (New Haven, Conn.: Yale University Press, 1998), 38–70; Susan Scheckel, *The Insistence of the Indian: Race and Nationalism in Nineteenth-Century American Culture* (Princeton, N.J.: Princeton University Press, 1998), 15–40; and Margaret McGlone McGrea, "Writing America: Race, Gender and Nationalism in American Frontier Fiction" (Ph.D. diss., City University of New York, 2001).

102. For a fuller discussion of historians of the West, see Kerwin Lee Klein, *Frontiers of Historical Imagination: Narrating the European Conquest of Native America, 1890–1990* (Berkeley: University of California Press, 1997).

103. Francis Flavin, "The Adventurer-Artists of the Nineteenth Century and the Image of the American Indian," *Indiana Magazine of History* 98 (March 2002), 1–29.

104. Old Scout, *White Boy Chief,* 3, 7, 20; and Carter, *Kid Curry's Last Stand,* 8.

105. Devon A. Mihesuah, "Commonalty of Difference: American Indian Women and History," 37–54, in Mihesuah, *Natives and Academics: Researching and Writing about American Indians,* ed. Devon A. Mihesuah (Lincoln: University of Nebraska Press, 1998).

106. Wheeler, *Deadwood Dick's Eagles,* 17.

107. W. Gilmore Simms, *Yemassee* (1853; repr., New York: W. J. Widdleton, Pub., 1878), 113–31.

108. Sherry Ann Sullivan, "The Indian in American Fiction, 1820–1850" (Ph.D. diss., University of Toronto, 1979), 195–97: Mary V. Dearborn, *Pocahontas's Daughter: Gender and Ethnicity in American Culture* (New York: Oxford University Press, 1986); and Scheckel, *Insistence of the Indian,* 41–69.

109. For writers, see Elizabeth Abigail Dillard Russell, "The Princess and the Prostitute: A Study of Eighteenth-Century Representations of Native American Women" (Ph.D. diss., Auburn University, 2001).

110. Jay B. Hubbell, "The Smith-Pocahontas Story in Literature," *Virginia Magazine of History and Biography* (July 1957), 275—300; Bernard W. Sheehan, *Savagism and Civility: Indians and Englishmen in Colonial Virginia* (Cambridge: Cambridge University Press, 1980), 127—31; and Helen C. Rountree, "Pocahontas: The Hostage Who Became Famous," 1—28, in *Sifters: Native American Women's Lives,* ed. Theda Perdue (New York: Oxford University Press, 2001).

111. Lydia H. Sigourney, *Pocahontas and Other Poems* (New York: Harpers, 1841), 32.

112. Richard Godbeer, "Eroticizing the Middle Ground: Anglo-Indian Sexual Relations along the Eighteenth-Century Frontier," 91—111, in *Sex, Love, Race: Crossing Boundaries in North American History,* ed. Martha Hodes (New York: New York University Press, 1999).

113. Benedict Anderson, *Imagined Communities: Reflections on the Origin and Spread of Nationalism* (London: Verso, 1983), 148—50; and Laura Stoler, *Race and the Education of Desire: Foucault's History of Sexuality and the Colonial Order of Things* (Durham, N.C.: Duke University Press, 1995), 9—16, 171—83.

114. James Fenimore Cooper, *The Prairie* (1827; repr., New York: Dodd, Mead, and Co., 1954), 256—57, 346.

115. Berkhofer, *White Man's Indian,* 99.

116. Old Scout, *White Boy Chief,* 24—26.

117. Jeffrey Steele, "Reduced to Images: American Indians in Nineteenth-Century Advertising," 45—77, in *Dressing in Feathers: The Construction of the Indian in American Popular Culture,* ed. S. Elizabeth Bird (Boulder, Colo.: Westview Press, 1996).

118. S. Elizabeth Bird, "Savage Desires: The Gendered Construction of the American Indian in Popular Media," 78—81, in *Selling the Indian: Commercializing and Appropriating American Indian Cultures,* ed. Carter Jones Meyer and Diana Royer (Tucson: University of Arizona Press, 2001).

119. James Hall, *Legends of the West* (New York: T. L. Magagnos, 1854), 317—19; and Caroline Kirkland, *A New Home—Who'll Follow?* (New York: Charles S. Francis, 1841), 45.

120. Cooper, *Prairie,* 315; and *New York Times,* 1 August 1868.

121. Karen Ordahl Kupperman, *Settling with the Indians: The Meeting of English and Indian Cultures in America, 1580-1640* (Totowa, N.J.: Rowman and Littlefield, 1980), 58—59; Jack D. Forbes, *The Indian in America's Past* (Englewood Cliffs, N.J.: Prentice-Hall, 1964), 79, 156—59; and William J. Snelling, *Tales of the Northwest* (Minneapolis: University of Minnesota Press, 1936), 11—12.

122. Ron Tyler, "Artist on the Oregon Trail: Alfred Jacob Miller," *American West* 18 (November–December 1981), 52, 55.

123. Cooper, *Prairie,* 367; Snelling, *Tales of the Northwest,* 101; and Simms, *Yemassee,* 299–300.

124. No author, "Glimpses of Indian Life at the Omaha Exposition," *Review of Reviews* 18 (October 1898): 436–43.

125. Louis S. Warren, "Cody's Last Stand: Masculine Anxiety, the Custer Myth, and the Frontier of Domesticity in Buffalo Bill's Wild West," *Western Historical Quarterly* 24 (spring 2003): 49–69.

126. Regarding William F. "Buffalo Bill" Cody, the most recent biographies are Joseph G. Rosa and Robin May, *Buffalo Bill and His Wild West: A Pictorial Biography* (Lawrence: University Press of Kansas, 1978); Eric V. Sorg, *Buffalo Bill: Myth and Reality* (Santa Fe, N.Mex.: Ancient City Press, 1998); and Robert A. Carter, *Buffalo Bill Cody: The Man Behind the Legend* (New York: John Wiley, 2000). For Cody's problem with the "bottom line," see Sarah J. Blackstone, *Buckskins, Bullets, and Business: A History of Buffalo Bill's Wild West* (Westport, Conn.: Greenwood, 1986). Also useful is Jonathan D. Martin, "'The Grandest and Most Cosmopolitan Object Teacher': Buffalo Bill's Wild West and the Politics of American Identity, 1883–1899," *Radical History Review* (fall 1996): 92–123; Thomas Antony Freeland, "The National Entertainment: Buffalo Bill's Wild West and the Pageant of American Empire" (Ph.D. diss., Stanford University, 1999); and Joy S. Kasson, *Buffalo Bill's Wild West: Celebrity, Memory, and Popular History* (New York: Hill and Wang, 2000).

127. For analysis of Wild West show content, see Paul Reddin, *Wild West Shows* (Urbana: University of Illinois Press, 1999); and Kristine Fredricksson, *American Rodeo: From Buffalo Bill to Big Business* (College Station: Texas A & M University Press, 1985). For coverage of Native Americans and Wild West shows, see Robert E. Bieder, "Marketing the American Indian in Europe: Context, Commodification, and Reception," in *Cultural Transmissions and Receptions: American Mass Culture in Europe,* ed. R. Kroes, R. W. Rydell, and D. F. J. Bosscher (Amsterdam: VU University Press, 1993), 15–23; Cindy Fent and Raymond Wilson, "Indians Off Track: Cody's Wild West and the Melrose Park Train Wreck of 1904," *American Indian Culture and Research Journal* 18, 3 (1994): 235–69; and L. G. Moses, "Indians on the Midway: Wild West Shows and the Indian Bureau at World's Fairs, 1893–1904," *South Dakota History* 21 (fall 1991): 205–29; and Moses, *Wild West Shows and the Images of American Indians, 1883–1933* (Albuquerque: University of New Mexico Press, 1996). An Indian's viewpoint is Chauncey Yellow Robe, "The Menace of the Wild West Show," *Quarterly Journal of the Society of American Indians* 2 (July–September 1914): 224–28. That white women saw reform of show Indians as being in their

jurisdiction is shown in Helen M. Wanken, "Woman's Sphere and Indian Reform: The Women's National Indian Association, 1879–1901" (Ph.D. diss., Marquette University, 1981).

128. David Murray, "Representation and Cultural Sovereignty: Some Case Studies," 80–85, in *Native American Representations: First Encounters, Distorted Images, and Literary Appropriations,* ed. Gretchen M. Bataille (Lincoln: University of Nebraska Press, 2001); Erik Trump, "'The Idea of Help': White Women Reformers and the Commercialization of Native American Women's Arts," 159–89, in *Imagining Indians in the Southwest: Persistent Visions of a Primitive Past,* by Leah Dilworth (Washington, D.C.: Smithsonian Institution Press, 1996), 173–81; Fergus M. Bordewich, *Killing the White Man's Indian* (New York: Random House, 1997), 36–39.

129. Quoted in Ronald Wright, *Stolen Continents: The "New World" through Indian Eyes* (Boston: Houghton Mifflin, 1992), ix.

Chapter 2

1. Jerzy Jedlicki, "Images of America," *Polish Perspectives* 18 (November 1975): 26–28.

2. Helen S. Papshively, *All the Happy Endings* (New York: Harper and Brothers, 1956), 2.

3. Ray Billington, *Land of Savagery, Land of Promise: The European Image of the American Frontier in the Nineteenth Century* (New York: W. W. Norton, 1980), 30.

4. Edward I. Wheeler, *Deadwood Dick's Eagles; or, The Pards of Flood Bar* (Cleveland: Arthur Westbrook, 1899), 8, 10, 28; and An Old Scout, *Young Wild West Surrounded by Sioux; or, Arietta and the Aeronaut* (New York: Frank Tousey, 1917), 18.

5. An Old Scout, *The White Boy Chief; or, The Terror of North Platte* (New York: Frank Tousey, 1908), 3–4, 11, 20; and F. A. Briggs, *Buffalo Bill's Witchcraft; or, Pawnee Bill and the Snake Aztecs* (New York: Street and Smith, 1911), 8.

6. Fergus M. Bordewich, *Killing the White Man's Indian* (New York: Random House, 1997), 33–36; and Ward Churchill, *Fantasies of the Master Race: Literature, Cinema and the Colonization of American Indians* (San Francisco: City Lights Books, 1998), 9–16.

7. François René de Chateaubriand, *Travels in America,* trans. Richard Switzer (Lexington: University of Kentucky Press, 1969).

8. William Cobbett, *A Year's Residence in the United States of America* (Carbondale: Southern Illinois University Press, 1964); Alexis de Tocqueville, *Journey to America,* trans. George Lawrence, ed. J. P. Mayer

(New Haven, Conn.: Yale University Press, 1960); Dr. Albert C. Koch, *Journey through a Part of the United States of North America in the Years 1844 to 1846,* trans. and ed. Ernst A. Stadler (Carbondale: Southern Illinois University Press, 1972); and Moritz Busch, *Travels between the Hudson & the Mississippi, 1851-1852,* trans. and ed. Norman H. Binger (Lexington: University Press of Kentucky, 1971).

9. Isabella L. Bird, *The Englishwoman in America* (Madison: University of Wisconsin Press, 1966), 143.

10. Fredrika Bremer, *The Homes of the New World: Impressions of America,* trans. Mary Howitt (New York: Harper and Brothers, 1868), 555.

11. For a fuller discussion, see Glenda Riley, *Taking Land, Breaking Land: Women Colonizing the American and Kenyan Frontiers, 1815–1915* (Albuquerque: University of New Mexico Press, 2003).

12. Richard D. Wolff, *The Economics of Colonialism: Britain and Kenya, 1870–1930* (New Haven, Conn.: Yale University Press, 1974), 1–2; and John R. Godard, *Racial Supremacy; Being Studies in Imperialism* (Edinburgh, UK: Geo. A. Morton, 1905), 11, 216.

13. George M. Fredrickson, *White Supremacy: A Comparative Study in American and South African History* (New York: Oxford University Press, 1981), 7–13; and V. Y. Mudimbe, *The Idea of Africa* (Bloomington: Indiana University Press, 1994), 212–13.

14. Catherine Hall, *White, Male, and Middle-Class Explorations in Feminism and History* (New York: Routledge, 1992), 75–93; and Mary Poovey, *Uneven Development: The Ideological Work of Gender in Mid-Victorian England* (Chicago, Ill.: University of Chicago Press, 1988), 3–4, 164–201.

15. Ronald Robinson and John Gallagher, *Africa and the Victorians: The Official Mind of Imperialism* (London: Macmillan, 1961), 1–3. See also R. Coupland, *The Exploitation of East Africa, 1856–1890* (London: Faber and Faber, 1939).

16. Rev. Oliver Prescott Hiller, *A Chapter on Slavery* (London: Hodson and Son, 1860), 12.

17. Quote is in Wolff, *Economics of Colonialism,* 134–35.

18. Kathleen M. Tillotson, *Novels of the 1840s* (Oxford: Clarendon Press, 1954), 13–14, 24.

19. Richard D. Altick, *The English Common Reader: A Social History of the Mass Reading Public, 1800–1900* (Chicago, Ill.: University of Chicago Press, 1957), 83–86, 97, 100–110, 128–29, 131–35, 141–42, 152, 173, 188, 191–93, 200, 212–17, 239–40, 260–69, 277, 286, 293, 318, 330–39, 364–68.

20. Allan Nevins, ed., *America through British Eyes* (New York: Oxford University Press, 1948), v–vi, 3, 9; Oscar Handlin, ed., *This Was America* (Cambridge: Harvard University Press, 1949), 1–4, 7–8.

21. D. L. Ashliman, "The American West in Twentieth-Century Germany,"

Journal of Popular Culture 2 (summer 1968): 84–90; and Billington, "Cowboys, Indians and the Land of Promise: The World Image of the American Frontier," Opening Address, XIV International Congress of Historical Sciences, San Francisco, August 22, 1975, Bancroft Library, Berkeley, Calif.

22. Francis J. Grund, *The Americans in Their Moral, Social, and Political Relations* (New York: Johnson Reprint Corp., 1968), 255; W. Faux, *Memorable Days in America: Being a Journal of a Tour to the United States* (New York: A. M. S. Press, 1969), 180;, and Charles Dickens, *American Notes for General Circulation* (New York: Charles Scribner's Sons, 1911), 295.

23. J. P. Brissot de Warville, *New Travels in the United States of America, 1788,* trans. Mara Soceanu Vamos and Durand Echeverria, ed. Durand Echeverria (Cambridge: Belknap Press of Harvard University, 1964), 418.

24. Robert G. Athearn, *Westward the Briton* (New York: Charles Scribner's Sons, 1953), 65.

25. Charles Hooton, *St. Louis Isle or Texiana* (London: Simmonds and Nard, 1847), 51, 53, 149–50.

26. Andrew J. Torrielli, *Italian Opinion on America as Revealed by Italian Travelers, 1850–1900* (Cambridge: Harvard University Press, 1941), 186–87; and Arthur Schlesinger, "What Then Is the American, This New Man?" *American Historical Review* 48 (January 1943): 235–36.

27. Athearn, *Westward the Briton,* 67; and *American Settler,* 16 July 1881.

28. *American Settler,* 9 April 1887 and 5 July 1884.

29. Edouard de Montule, *Travels in America, 1816–1817,* trans. Edward D. Seeber (Bloomington: Indiana University Press, 1951), 142, 112, 174.

30. Charles Sealsfield, *The Americans as They Are* (New York: Johnson Reprint Corp. 1970), 9; and Fredrika Bremer, *America of the Fifties: Letters of Fredrika Bremer* (New York: American-Scandinavian Foundation, 1924), 259.

31. Jane L. Mesick, *The English Traveller in America, 1785–1835* (New York: Columbia University Press, 1922), 89–92; and John G. Brooks, *As Others See Us: A Study of Progress in the United States* (New York: Macmillan, 1908), 309.

32. Athearn, *Westward the Briton,* 36.

33. Alexis de Tocqueville, *Democracy in America* (London: Oxford University Press, 1953), 465–66.

34. Tocqueville, *Journey to America,* 129; Busch, *Travels,* 162; and Francis and Theresa Pulszky, *White, Red, Black: Sketches of Society in the United States during the Visit of Their Guest,* vol. 1 (New York: Negro Universities Press, 1968), 80.

35. Friedrich Gerstäcker, *Wild Sports in the Far West: The Narrative of a German Wanderer beyond the Mississippi, 1837–1843* (Durham, N.C.: Duke University Press, 1968), 200, 233.

36. Frances Trollope, *Domestic Manners of the Americans* (New York: Dodd, Mead, 1927); and Montule, *Travels in America,* 142.

37. Charles Sealsfield, *The United States of North America as They Are* (New York: Johnson Reprint Corp., 1970), 109; and Augustus J. Prahl, "America in the Works of Gerstäcker," *Modern Language Quarterly* 4 (June 1943): 220.

38. Mesick, *English Traveller in America,* 95; and William J. Baker, ed., *America Perceived: A View from Abroad in the 19th Century* (West Haven, Conn.: Pendulum Press, 1974), 31.

39. Sealsfield, *United States of North America,* 119; and Gerstäcker, *Wild Sports,* 239–40.

40. Kalikst Wolski, *American Impressions,* trans. Marion Moore Coleman (Cheshire, Conn.: Cherry Hill Books, 1968), 85.

41. Richard L. Rapson, *Britons View America* (Seattle: University of Washington Press, 1971), 107.

42. William A. Baillie-Grohman, *Camps in the Rockies* (New York: Charles Scribner's Sons, 1910), 22–23.

43. Clarence Evans, "Friedrich Gerstäcker, Social Chronicler of the Arkansas Frontier," *Arkansas Historical Quarterly* 6 (1947): 444; Alice H. Finckh, "Gottfried Duden Views Missouri, 1824–1827," pt. 2, *Missouri Historical Review* (October 1949): 22; Charles Dickens, *American Notes,* vol. 2 (London: Chapman and Hall, 1842), 47; and Charles Lyell, *Travels in North America,* vol. 1 (London: J. Murray, 1845), 57.

44. Harriet Martineau, *Society in America,* vol. 1 (London: Saunders and Otley, 1837), 117, 105.

45. Trollope, *Domestic Manners of the Americans,* 67.

46. Lyell, *Travels in North America,* 1:43; John Xantus, *Letters from North America* (Detroit: Wayne State University Press, 1975), 154; Baker, ed., *America Perceived,* 31–32; and Athearn, *Westward the Briton,* 66.

47. Frederick von Raumer, *America and the American People,* 3 vols., trans. William W. Turner (New York: Johnson Reprint Corp., 1970), 1:499; and Prahl, "America in the Works of Gerstäcker," 220.

48. Ole M. Raeder, *America in the Forties: The Letters of Ole Munch Raeder* (Minneapolis: University of Minnesota Press, 1929), 122–23.

49. Ernest Duvergier de Hauranne, *A Frenchman in Lincoln's America,* trans. and ed. Ralph H. Bowen, vol. 1 (Chicago: Lakeside Press, 1974), 230.

50. Mary S. Owen, "The American Frontiersman: A French Portrait" (unpublished manuscript, n.d., privately held, Man Owens, England), pt. 7, 18–19.

51. Xantus, *Letters from North America,* 154–55.

52. Marilyn M. Sibley, *Travelers in Texas, 1761–1860* (Austin: University of Texas Press, 1967), 105–7.

53. Athearn, *Westward the Briton*, 66–67.

54. Pulszky, *White, Red, Black*, 119; Busch, *Travels*, 136; and Trollope, *Domestic Manners of the Americans*, 68.

55. Sealsfield, *Americans as They Are*, 9.

56. Baker, *America Perceived*, 39–40.

57. Ibid., 45–46.

58. William A. Bell, *New Tracks in North America*, vol. 1 (London: Chapman and Hall, 1869), 16.

59. Charles V. Crosnier de Varigny, *The Women of the United States*, trans. Arabella Ward (New York: Dodd, Mead, 1895), 18–19.

60. Frances Wright, *Views of Society and Manners in America* (Cambridge: Harvard University Press, 1963), 23, 221.

61. Martineau, *Society in America*, 1:108.

62. Harriet Martineau, *Retrospect of Western Travel*, vol. 1 (London: Saunders and Otley, 1838), 24.

63. Bremer, *America of the Fifties*, 245.

64. Martineau, *Society in America*, 1:108.

65. O. Drevdahl, *Fra Emigrationens Amerika 1891* (Oslo: N.p., 1891), unpaginated; and Franklin D. Scott, "Soren jaabaek, Americanizer in Norway," *Norwegian American Studies and Records* 17 (1952): 92.

66. Axel Bruun, *Breve fra Amerika* (Christiana: A. Cammermeyer, 1870), 17.

67. Alan Conway, ed., *The Welsh in America: Letters from the Immigrants* (Minneapolis: University of Minnesota Press, 1961), 257; and William and Robert Chambers, *Journey from New Orleans to California, 1849, and Other Interesting Excerpts from Chambers's Journal* (London: W. and R. Chambers, 1856), 13.

68. *American Settler*, 6 September 1884.

69. James Axtell, ed., *America Perceived: A View from Abroad in the 17th Century* (West Haven, Conn.: Pendulum Press, 1974), 122–23,

70. E. Stanley, *Journal of a Tour in America, 1824–1825* (London: Privately printed, 1930), 152; and Perey G. Ebbutt, *Emigrant Life in Kansas* (London: S. Sonnenschien, 1886), 45. See, for example, Blaine T. Williams, "The Frontier Family: Demographic Fact and Historical Myth," in *Essays on the American West*, ed. Harold M. Hollingsworth and Sandra L. Myres (Austin: University of Texas Press, 1969), 40–65.

71. Athearn, *Westward the Briton*, 65.

72. Tocqueville, *Democracy in America*, 468; William P. Dallmann, *The Spirit of America as Interpreted in the Works of Charles Sealsfield* (St. Louis: Washington University Studies, 1935), 44–45; and Merle Curti and Kendall Birr, "The Immigrant and the American Image in Europe, 1860–1914," *Mississippi Valley Historical Review* 37 (September 1950): 221.

73. Owen, "American Frontiersman," pt. 5, 20–22.

74. Pulszky, *White, Red, Black,* 234–35.

75. Handlin, ed., *This Was America,* 252.

76. Clyde Thogmartin, "Prosper Jacotot: A French Worker Looks at Kansas in 1876–1877," *Kansas Historical Quarterly* 41 (September 1975): 19.

77. Schlesinger, "What Then Is the American," 235–36.

78. *American Settler,* 8 October 1892.

79. Dorothy B. Skardal, *The Divided Heart: Scandinavian Immigrant Experiences through Literary Sources* (Lincoln: University of Nebraska Press, 1974), 57.

80. Simon A. O'Ferrall, *A Ramble of Six Thousand Miles through the United States of America* (London: E. Wilson, 1832), 55–56.

81. Tivador Acs, ed., *Hungarian Pioneers in the New World* (Budapest: Láthatàr Kîadása, 1942), 190; and Skardal, *Divided Heart,* 242–43.

82. Axtell, *America Perceived,* 225; and von Raumer, *America and the American People.*

83. Sealsfield, *United States of North America,* 131.

84. William N. Blane, *An Excursion through the United States and Canada, during the Years 1822–23* (London: Baldwin, Cradoek, and Joy, 1824), 258–59.

85. Mesick, *English Traveller in America,* 99.

86. Robert Barclay-Allardice, *Agricultural Tour in the United States and Upper Canada, with Miscellaneous Notices* (Edinburgh: W. Blackwood and Sons, 1842), 155–56.

87. Finckh, "Gottfried Duden Views Missouri," pt. 2, 21–22. See also George M. Stephenson, "Typical America Letters," *Yearbook of the Swedish Historical Society of America,* 7 (1921–1922): 60.

88. Theodore C. Blegen, *The Land of Their Choice: The Immigrants Write Home* (Minneapolis: University of Minnesota Press, 1955), 76; Michael Chevalier, *Society, Manners and Politics in the United States; Being a Series of Letters on North America* (Boston: Weeks, Jordan, and Company, 1839), 430; and Henry B. Fearon, *Sketches of America* (New York: Benjamin Bloom, 1969), 221.

89. Marcus L. Hansen, *The Atlantic Migration, 1607–1860* (Cambridge: Harvard University Press, 1940), 166; and James Flint, *Letters from America* (Edinburgh: W. & C. Tait, 1822), 192.

90. H. Arnold Barton, *Letters from the Promised Land: Swedes in America, 1840–1914* (Minneapolis: University of Minnesota Press, for the Swedish Pioneer Historical Society, 1975), 42.

91. Thogmartin, "Prosper Jacotot," 19.

92. David T. Nelson, ed., *The Diary of Elisabeth Koren, 1853–1855* (Northfield, Minn.: Norwegian-American Historical Association, 1955), 346.

93. Pauline Farseth and Theodore C. Blegen, eds., *Frontier Mother: The Letters*

of Gro Svendsen (Northfield, Minn.: Norwegian-American Historical Association, 1950), 28.

94. Milo M. Quaife, ed., *A True Picture of Emigration* (New York: Citadel Press, 1968), 91.

95. Busch, *Travels,* 174. See also Gustave Aimard, *The Border Rifles, A Tale of the Texan War* (Philadelphia: T. B. Peterson and Brothers, 1840), 67, 106.

96. *American Settler,* 5 July 1884; Torrielli, *Italian Opinion on America,* 186–87; and Henri Herz, *My Travels in America* (Madison, Wisc.: State Historical Society, 1963), 66.

97. Gustaf Unonias, *A Pioneer in Northwest America, 1841–1858: The Memoirs of Gustaf Unonias,* trans. Jonas Oscar Backlund, ed. Nils William Olsson, vol. 1 (Minneapolis: University of Minnesota Press, 1950), 227–29; and Terry Coleman, *Passage to America, A History of Emigrants from Great Britain and Ireland to America in the Mid-Nineteenth Century* (London: Hutchinson and Company, 1972), 53, 257.

98. Athearn, *Westward the Briton,* 66.

99. Bird, *Englishwoman in America,* 151.

100. Athearn, *Westward the Briton,* 66.

101. Felix P. Wierzbicki, *California as It Is and as It May Be* (San Francisco: Bartlett Co., 1849), 50–51; and Charles Sealsfield, *The Courtship of Ralph Doughby, Esquire* (Stuttgart: J. B. Metzler, 1843), 103–4.

102. Henryk Sienkiewicz, *Western Septet: Stories of the American West* (Cheshire, Conn.: Cherry Hill Books, 1973), 108.

103. See, for example, Auguste Carlier, *Marriage in the United States* (Boston: DeVries, Ifarra, 1837); and Chevalier, *Society, Manners, and Politics.*

104. Sibley, *Travelers in Texas,* 105–7; Patrick Shirreff, *A Tour through North America* (Edinburgh: Simpkin, 1835), 76; and Bremer, *The Homes of the New World,* 190–91.

105. J. W. Schulte Nordholt, "This Is the Place: Dutchmen Look at America," *Delta: A Review of Arts, Life and Thought in the Netherlands* 16 (winter 1973–1974): 46.

106. *American Settler,* 12 December 1885.

107. Nordholt, "This Is the Place," 46–47;, and Varigny, *Women of the United States,* 13–14.

108. Nordholt, "This Is the Place," 58–59, and Charles P. Trevelyan, *The Great New People: Letters from North America and the Pacific, 1898* (Garden City, N.J.: Doubleday, 1971), 113.

109. Herz, *My Travels in America,* 65.

110. John F. Moffitt and Santiago Sebastián, *O Brave New People: The European Invention of the American Indian* (Albuquerque: University of New Mexico Press, 1996), 112–22, 262–87.

111. Hugh Honour, *The European Vision of America* (Cleveland: Cleveland

Museum of Art, n.d.), 1, 4; Phillip D. Thomas, "Artists among the Indians, 1493–1850," *Kansas Quarterly* 3 (fall 1971): 3–6.

112. Thomas, "Artists among the Indians," 7.

113. Honour, *European Vision of America,* 12.

114. Thomas, "Artists among the Indians," 10–11, 8.

115. See, for example, François René de Chateaubriand, *Atala and René* (London: Oxford University Press, 1963); and Chateaubriand, *Travels in America.*

116. Billington, "Cowboys, Indians and the Land of Promise."

117. Preston A. Barba, *Balduin Möllhausen the German Cooper,* vol. 17, *Americana Germanica* (Philadelphia: University of Pennsylvania Press, 1914), 19–20.

118. D. L. A. Ashliman, "The American West in Nineteenth Century German Literature" (Ph. D. diss., Rutgers University, 1969), ii–iii, 47, 54.

119. Philip J. Deloria, *Playing Indian* (New Haven, Conn.: Yale University Press, 1998), 71–94; Richard H. Cracroft, "The American West of Karl May" (Master's thesis, University of Utah, 1963), 1, 153.

120. This phenomenon continues to exist in the United States. See Bryant M. Wedge, *Visitors to the United States and How They See Us* (Princeton, N.J.: D. Van Nostrand, 1965), 73.

121. Chateaubriand, *Travels in America,* 81.

122. Alfred J. Morrison, ed., *Travels in the Confederation, 1783–1784 by Johann David Schopf* (New York: Bergman Publishers, 1968), 281, 283–84, 289.

123. Jens Tvedt, *Sihasapa-Indianerne: Norske Udvandreres Hendelser i Amerika* (N.p.: Stavanger, 1887), 104–5.

124. George R. Brooks, "The American Frontier in German Fiction," in *The Frontier Re-examined,* ed. John F. McDermott (Urbana: University of Illinois Press, 1967), 165.

125. Karl May, *Winnetou* (New York: Seabury Press, 1977), xii–xiv.

126. Louis Philippe, King of France, *Diary of My Travels in America* (New York: Delacorte Press, 1977), 67.

127. Isaac J. Weld, *Travels through North America and the Provinces of Canada 1795–1797* (New York: Augustus M. Kelley, 1970), 217; Fearon, *Sketches of America,* 261; and Paul Wilhelm, Duke of Wurttemberg, *Travels in North America, 1822–1824,* trans. W. Robert Nitske, ed. Savoie Lottinville (Norman: University of Oklahoma Press, 1973), 385.

128. Chateaubriand, *Travels in America,* 178, 27.

129. Pulszky, *White, Red, Black,* 2.

130. Warville, *New Travels in the United States of America, 1788;* and Balduin Möllhausen, *Diary of a Journey from the Mississippi to the Coasts of the Pacific* (New York: Johnson Reprint Corp., 1969), 24.

131. Athearn, *Westward the Briton,* 129; and Billington, *Land of Savagery,* 134.

132. Von Raumer, *America and the American People,* 1:138–39.

133. Grund, *Americans,* 225–27.

134. Lyell, *Travels in North America,* 1:149; Bremer, *America of the Fifties,* 233; and Wright, *Views of Society and Manners,* 135.

135. Axtell, *America Perceived,* 69.

136. Herz, *My Travels in America,* 97; Xantus, *Letters from North America,* 85; and von Raumer, *America and the American People,* 1:137.

137. Rupert Brooke, *Letters from America* (London: Sidgwick and Jackson, 1931), 143.

138. Tocqueville, *Journey to America,* 199.

139. Ibid., 133; Wilhelm, *Travels in North America,* 2:196; and Dickens, *American Notes,* 234.

140. John H. Vessey, *Mr. Vessey of England* (New York: G. P. Putnam's Sons, 1956), 140; and David J. Jeremy, ed., *Henry Wansey and His American Journal, 1794* (Philadelphia: American Philosophical Society, 1970), 51.

141. Thomas Campbell, "Gertrude of Wyoming," in *The Complete Poetical Works of Thomas Campbell,* ed. J. Logie Robertson (London: Henry Fronde, 1907), 50; E. L. Jordan, ed., *America, Glorious and Chaotic Land: Charles Sealsfield Discovers the Young United States* (Englewood Cliffs, N.J.: Prentice-Hall, 1969), 192; and Ulrich S. Carrington, *The Making of an American: An Adaptation of the Memorable Tales by Charles Sealsfield* (Dallas: Southern Methodist University Press, 1974), 47.

142. Tocqueville, *Journey to America,* 133–37, 199–200.

143. Xantus, *Letters from North America,* 88; Frederick Marryat, *Diary in America* (Bloomington: Indiana University Press, 1960), 229; Adam Hodgson, *Remarks during a Journey through North America in the Years 1819, 1820, 1821* (Westport, Conn.: Negro Universities Press, 1970), 75; and Vilhelm Dinesen, "Fra et ophold de Forenede Stater," *Tilskueren* (October–December 1887), unpaged.

144. Billington, *Land of Savagery,* 125; and Athearn, *Westward the Briton,* 126.

145. Wilhelm, *Travels in North America,* 184; and Tocqueville, *Journey to America,* 328.

146. The term *squaw* was probably a European corruption of an Indian word. Its connotation of a demeaned slave seems to have existed originally only in the minds of non-Indians. Susan Gouge, "Let's Ban the Word 'Squaw,'" *Ohoyo: Bulletin of American Indian—Alaska Native Women* 9 (July 1981): 10. See also Jean C. Goodwill, "Squaw Is a Dirty Word," in *Issues for the Seventies: Canada's Indians,* ed. Norman Sheffe (Toronto: McGraw-Hill, 1970), 50–52; and Lillian Schlissel, *Women's Diaries of the Westward Journey* (New York: Schocken Books, 1982), 85.

147. Louis Philippe, *Diary of My Travels,* 85; Franz Loher, *Land und Leute in der Alten und Neuen Welt,* vol. 1 (Gottingen: G. H. Wigand, 1855), 173; and

John V. Cheney, ed., *Travels of John Davis in the United States of America, 1798 to 1802,* vol. 1 (Boston: Privately printed, 1810), 62.

148. Jean Bernard Bossu, *Travels in the Interior of North America, 1751–1762,* trans. and ed. Seymour Feiler (Norman: University of Oklahoma Press, 1962), 131; Gerstäcker, *Wild Sports,* 108; and Montule, *Travels in America,* 155–56.

149. Frederick Marryat, *Narrative of the Travels and Adventures of Monsieur Violet, in California, Sonora, and Western Texas,* vol. 1 (London: Longman, Brown, Green, and Longmans, 1843), 111–12, 131–32.

150. Tocqueville, *Journey to America,* 133.

151. Louis L. Simonin, *The Rocky Mountain West in 1867* (Lincoln: University of Nebraska Press, 1966), 92; Marian Schouten, "The Image of the American West Evoked in the Netherlands" (unpublished manuscript prepared for Ray A. Billington), Huntington Library, San Marino, Calif., 36, 37; and J. C. Beltrami, *Pilgrimage in Europe and America,* vol. 2 (London: Hunt and Clarke, 1828), 145–46.

152. Paul Wilhelm, *Herzog von Württenberg, Erste Reise nach dem Nordlichen Amerika in den Jahren 1822 bis 1824* (Stuttgart: J. G. Cotta, 1835), 179; Jacob H. Sehiel, *Journey through the Rocky Mountains and the Humboldt Mountains to the Pacific Ocean* (Norman: University of Oklahoma Press, 1959), 96–97; and John T. Irving, *Indian Sketches Taken during an Expedition to the Pawnee and Other Tribes of American Indians,* vol. 1 (London: J. Murray, 1835), 170.

153. Weld, *Travels through North America,* 228.

154. Reuben Gold Thwaite, ed., *Early Western Travels, 1748–1846* (Cleveland: Arthur H. Clark, 1906), 223, 271, 325; and Byron Y. Fleck, "The West as Viewed by Foreign Travellers, 1783–1840" (Ph.D. diss., University of Iowa, 1950), 233–34.

155. Weld, *Travels through North America,* 235–36.

156. Cheney, *Travels of John Davis,* 1:62; and Alexander Farkas, *Journey in North America* (Philadelphia: American Philosophical Society, 1977), 122, 136.

157. Wilhelm, *Travels in North America,* 318; and Farkas, *Journey in North America,* 122.

158. Xantus, *Letters from North America,* 34.

159. Bremer, *America of the Fifties,* 229.

160. Trevelyan, *Great New People,* 97.

161. Marryat, *Narrative,* 1:131–32.

162. Percy B. St. John, *The Trapper's Bride* (London: J. Mortimer, 1845), 81–82.

163. Mayne Reid, *The Scalp Hunters; or, Romantic Adventures in Northern Mexico,* vol. 1 (London: C. J. Skeet, 1851), 277–79; and Sygurd Wisniowski, *Ameryka, 100 Years Old; A Globetrotter's View,* trans., ed., and arranged by Marion Moore Coleman (Cheshire, Conn.: Cherry Hill Books, 1972), 64.

164. Gustave Aimard, *Stronghand: A Tale of the Disinherited* (London: J. and R. Maxwell, 1878), 98.

165. J. Martin Evans, *America: The View from Europe* (San Francisco: San Francisco Book Company, 1976), 108–10.

166. Marryat, *Diary in America,* 126.

167. Finckh, "Gottfried Duden Views Missouri," pt. 2, 22.

168. Von Raumer, *America and the American People,* 1:144.

169. Scott, "Soren jaabaek," 92; and Wilhelm, *Travels in North America,* 198.

170. St. John, *Trapper's Bride,* 8–9.

171. Hodgson, *Remarks during a Journey,* 271.

172. Tivador Acs, ed., *A Számüzöttek, Fiala janos, 1848* (Budapest, Hungary: Láthatàr Kîadása, 1943), 245–46.

173. Mor jokai, *Vandoroljatok ki!* (Berlin: Von L. Wechsler, 1893), 29, 50.

174. Wisniowski, *Ameryka,* 67–68.

175. Count Francesco Arese, *A Trip to the Prairies and in the Interior of North America, 1837–1838,* trans. Andrew Evans (New York: Cooper Square Publishers, 1975), 66, 72.

176. Loher, *Land und Leute,* 1:174.

177. Magnus Bech-Olsen, *Min Amerikafaerd* (Copenhagen: S. L. Wulff, 1900), unpaginated; and Fleck, "West as Viewed by Foreign Travellers," 242–44.

178. Cracroft, "American West of Karl May," 57.

179. Bossu, *Travels in the Interior,* 131.

180. Wilhelm, *Travels in North America,* 198.

181. Weld, *Travels through North America,* 221.

182. Bremer, *America of the Fifties,* 232.

183. See, for example, Marryat, *Narrative,* 2:12–13; and James A. Jones, *Traditions of the North American Indians,* vol. 2 (London: H. Colburn and R. Bentley, 1830), 131–40.

184. Wisniowski, *Ameryka,* 64–65.

185. Marryat, *Diary in America,* 234; Marryat, *Narrative,* 2:111–12; and Wilhelm, *Travels in North America,* 316.

186. Frances Brooke, *The History of Emily Montague,* vol. 1 (London: Printed for J. Dodsley, 1769), 18–19.

187. Bossu, *Travels in the Interior,* 132, 171; and Louis Philippe, *Diary of My Travels,* 72.

188. John Bradbury, *Travels in the Interior of America* (Ann Arbor, Mich.: University Microfilms, 1966), 168.

189. Bossu, *Travels in the Interior,* 171.

190. Chateaubriand, *Travels in America,* 88, and Bremer, *Homes of the New World* (1868), 593.

191. Axtell, *America Perceived,* 56, 71; Montule, *Travels in America,* 160; and Handlin, *This Was America,* 13–14.

192. Chateaubriand, *Travels in America,* 32.

193. Ibid., 88; Louis Philippe, *Diary of My Travels,* 71; Gustave Aimard, *The Bee-*

Hunter: A Tale of Adventure (London: J. A. Berger, 1868), 79; Gustave Aimard, *The Pirates of the Prairies: Adventures in the American Desert* (London: Ward and Lock, 1861), 62; and Arese, *Trip to the Prairies,* 164–65.

194. Louis Philippe, *Diary of My Travels,* 72, and von Raumer, *America and the American People,* 281–82.

195. Heinrich Luden, ed., *Reise seiner Hoheit des Herzogs Bernhard zu Sachsen-Weimer-Eisenach durch Nord-Amerika,* vol. 1 (Weimar: W. Hoffman, 1828), 33; and Bremer, *Homes of the New World* (1853), 30.

196. Montule, *Travels in America,* 161.

197. Friedrich Gerstäcker, *Narrative of a Journey Round the World,* vol. 1 (London: Hurst and Blackett, 1853), 356–57.

198. Wilhelm, *Travels in North America,* 338; Fleck, "West as Viewed by Foreign Travellers," 236–44; and Baillie-Grohman, *Camps in the Rockies,* 273–75.

199. Acs, *A Számüzöttek,* 245–46.

200. John U. Terrell and Donna M. Terrell, *Indian Women of the Western Morning* (New York: Doubleday, 1976), 38–40; Karen O. Kupperman, *Settling with the Indians* (Totowa, N.J.: Bowman and Littlefield, 1980), 60–63; and Margot Liberty, "Hell Came with Horses: Plains Indian Women in the Equestrian Era," *Montana, The Magazine of Western History* 32 (summer 1982): 10–19. See also Patricia Albers and Beatrice Medicine, *The Hidden Half: Studies of Plains Indian Women* (Washington, D.C.: University Press of America, 1983).

201. Rayna Green, "Native American Women," *Signs* 6 (winter 1980): 248, 250, 255, 260, 262; Valerie S. Mathes, "Native American Women in Medicine and the Military," *Journal of the West* 21 (April 1982): 41, 47; Susan Armitage, "Western Women: Beginning to Come into Focus," *Montana, The Magazine of Western History* 32 (summer 1982): 4–5; and Liberty, "Hell Came with Horses," 18–19.

202. Cheney, *Travels of John Davis,* 68.

203. Pulszky, *White, Red, Black,* 6.

204. Hodgson, *Remarks during a Journey,* 265

205. Bradbury, *Travels in the Interior,* 89; and Von Raumer, *America and the American People,* 138.

206. Napoleon A. Murat, *America and the Americans* (New York: W. H. Graham, 1849), 212.

207. Xantus, *Letters from North America,* 37.

208. Brooke, *History of Emily Montague,* 1:18–19.

209. Charlotte Lenox, *Euphemia,* vol. 3 (London: T. Cadell and J. Evans, 1790), 190–91; and Gustave Aimard, *The Indian Scout: A Story of the Aztec City* (London: Ward and Lock, 1865), 229; Gustave Aimard, *The Trappers of Arkansas, or, The Loyal Heart* (New York: T. R. Dawley, 1858), 186; and Ashliman, "American West," 154.

210. Cracroft, "American West of Karl May," 153–54.

211. Karen Sacks, "State Bias and Women's Status," *American Anthropologist* 78 (September 1976): 565–69; Liberty, "Hell Came with Horses," 12; and Mathes, "Native American Women," 41.

212. Marryat, *Diary in America,* 248.

213. Terrell and Terrell, *Indian Women,* 37; and Mathes, "Native American Women," 41.

214. Gerstäcker, *Wild Sports,* 110; and Bradbury, *Travels in the Interior,* 146.

215. Bossu, *Travels in the Interior,* 132; Weld, *Travels through North America,* 259; Jeremy, *Henry Wansey,* 51; Möllhausen, *Diary,* 98; and Thwaite, *Early Western Travels,* 22:352.

216. Terrell and Terrell, *Indian Women,* 71–90; and Liberty, "Hell Came with Horses," 13–15.

217. Martineau, *Retrospect of Western Travel,* 1:94; Simonin, *Rocky Mountain West,* 134; and *American Settler,* 19 July 1884.

218. Gustave Aimard, *The White Scalper: A Story of the Texan War* (London: Ward and Lock, 1861), 234–35; Aimard, *Pirates of the Prairies,* 107–8; Aimard, *Trappers of Arkansas,* 191–97; Benedict Henry Revoil, *Le Bivouac des Trappeurs* (Paris: Brunet, 1864), 201–2; and Karl May, *Der Schatz im Silbersee* (Bamberg, West Germany: Karl-May-Verlag, 1973), 340.

219. C. Ax Egerstrom, *Borta dr bram, men hemma dr bdst* (Stockholm: Bonier, 1859), 128.

220. Brooke, *History of Emily Montague,* 1:69.

221. Bremer, *Homes of the New World,* 593.

222. Bremer, *America of the Fifties,* 229–31.

Chapter 3

1. For the types of people who went west, see John C. Hudson, "The Study of Western Frontier Populations," 35–60, in *The American West: New Perspectives, New Dimensions,* ed. Jerome O. Steffen (Norman: University of Oklahoma Press, 1979).

2. Roger G. Barker, "The Influence of Frontier Environments on Behavior," 61–93, in *The American West: New Perspectives, New Dimensions,* ed. Jerome O. Steffen (Norman: University of Oklahoma Press, 1979); David W. Hess, "Pioneering as Ecological Process: A Model and Test Case of Frontier Adaptation," 123–52, in *The Frontier: Comparative Studies,* ed. William W. Savage, Jr., and Stephen I. Thompson, vol. 2 (Norman: University of Oklahoma Press, 1979); and Stephen I. Thompson, "Pioneer Colonization: A Cross-Cultural View," *An Addison-Wesley Module in Anthropology* no. 33 (1973): 1–24.

3. Roger A. Hall, *Performing the American Frontier, 1870–1906* (Cambridge: Cambridge University Press, 2001), 64, 146.

4. Devon A. Mihesuah, *American Indians: Stereotypes and Realities* (Atlanta, Ga.: Clarity Press, 1996), 48–53.

5. Harriet A. L. Smith, "My Trip across the Plains in 1849," California State Library, Sacramento; and Virginia Reed Murphy, "Across the Plains in the Donner Party (1846): A Personal Narrative of the Overland Trip to California," *Century Magazine* 42 (July 1891): 409.

6. Lucy Jennings, interview 10025, vol. 48, Indian-Pioneer Papers, University of Oklahoma, Norman.

7. Lucy H. Fosdick, "Across the Plains in '61," Beinecke Collection, Yale University Library, New Haven, Conn.

8. Emily K. Andrews, "Diary of Emily K. Andrews of a Trip from Austin to Fort Davis, 1874," Barker Texas History Center, University of Texas, Austin.

9. Lola Clark, interview 4547, vol. 18; and Mary Ellen Williams, interview 6877, vol. 98; both in Indian-Pioneer Papers, University of Oklahoma, Norman.

10. Martha Lowrence, interview 7881, vol. 56, Indian-Pioneer Papers University of Oklahoma, Norman.

11. Annie Muthart Baker, interview 10601, vol. 4, Indian-Pioneer Papers, University of Oklahoma, Norman.

12. Mabel Sharpe Beavers, interview 6850, vol. 6, Indian-Pioneer Papers, University of Oklahoma, Norman.

13. Elisha Brooks, *A Pioneer Mother of California* (San Francisco: Harr Wagner Publishing, 1922), 13–15.

14. Robert L. Munkres, "The Plains Indian Threat on the Oregon Trail before 1860," *Annals of Wyoming* 40 (1968): 203.

15. Thomas D. Clark, ed., *Off at Sunrise: The Overland Journal of Charles Glass Gray* (San Marino, Calif.: Huntington Library, 1976), 78; and James A. Pritchard, *The Overland Diary of James A. Pritchard* (Denver: Old West Publishing, 1959), 58.

16. Dr. Jonathan Clark, "The Diary of Dr. Jonathan Clark," *The Argonaut,* 1 August 1925, 3.

17. Lucene Pfeiffer Parsons, "The Women in the Sunbonnets" (1850), Stanford University Library, Stanford, Calif. See also Lydia Waters, "Account of a Trip across the Plains in 1855," *Quarterly of the Society of California Pioneers* 6 (March 1929): 65, 72.

18. Helen Carpenter, "Diary" (1856), Huntington Library, San Marino, Calif.

19. Margaret A. Frink, *Journal of the Adventures of a Party of California Gold-Seekers* (Oakland, Calif.: N.p., 1897), 28–29.

20. Isaac Jones Wistar, *Autobiography of Isaac Jones Wistar, 1827–1905: Half a Century in War and Peace* (New York: Harper and Brothers, 1937), 74.

21. Margaret S. Dart, ed., "Letters of a Yankee Forty-Niner," *The Yale Review* 36 (June 1947): 658.

22. Mallie Stafford, *The March of Empire through Three Decades* (San Francisco: George Spaulding, 1884), 126–27.

23. Clark, *Off at Sunrise*, 78; Jane Augusta Gould, "Diary" (1862), Iowa State Historical Society, Iowa City; Pritchard, *Overland Diary*, 58; Harriet Bunyard, "Diary of Miss Harriet Bunyard from Texas to California in 1868," *Annual Publications, Historical Society of Southern California*, no. 13 (1924): 94, 97; and David M. Kiefer, ed., "Over Barren Plains and Rock-Bound Mountains," *Montana, The Magazine of Western History* 22, no. 4 (1972): 22, 26.

24. Helen Marnie Stewart Love, "Diary" (1853), Huntington Library, San Marino, Calif.

25. Louisa Miller Rahm, "Diary" (1862), Bancroft Library, Berkeley, Calif., and Ellen Tompkins Adams, "Diary of Ellen Tompkins Adams, Wife of John Smalley Adams, M.D." (1863), Bancroft Library, Berkeley, Calif.

26. Fosdick, "Across the Plains."

27. Carpenter, "Diary"; Louise Barry, comp., "Charles Robinson—Yankee '49er: His Journey to California," *Kansas Historical Quarterly* 34, no. 2 (1968): 186; and Andrew F. Rolle, ed., *The Road to Virginia City: The Diary of James Knox Polk Miller* (Norman: University of Oklahoma Press, 1960), 8.

28. Gould, "Diary"; Harriet Bunyard, "Diary of a Young Girl," (1868), Huntington Library, San Marino, Calif., 97; and Laura W. Johnson, *Eight Hundred Miles in an Ambulance* (Philadelphia: J. B. Lippincott, 1889), 43.

29. Munkres, "Plains Indian Threat," 212–15.

30. Catherine Amanda Stansbury Washburn, "Journal, 1853, from Iowa to Oregon Territory," Huntington Library, San Marino, Calif.; Ward G. DeWitt and Florence S. DeWitt, *Prairie Schooner Lady: The Journal of Harriet Sherrill Ward, 1853* (Los Angeles: Westernlore Press, 1959), 46; Ada Millington, "Journal Kept while Crossing the Plains" (1862), Bancroft Library, Berkeley, Calif.; Fosdick, "Across the Plains"; and Bunyard, "Diary," 100.

31. Maria Schrode, "Journal" (1870), Huntington Library, San Marino, Calif.; and Mary Rockwood Powers, "A Woman's Overland Journal to California" (1856), California State Library, Sacramento.

32. Susan Thompson Parrish, "Westward in 1850," Huntington Library, San Marino, Calif.

33. Mary Saunders, "The Whitman Massacre; A True Story by a Survivor of This Terrible Tragedy which Took Place in Oregon in 1847," Bancroft Library, Berkeley, Calif.

34. DeWitt and DeWitt, *Prairie Schooner Lady*, 132.

35. Mary Eliza Warner, "Diary" (1864), Bancroft Library, Berkeley, Calif.

36. Lucy Rutledge Cooke, *Covered Wagon Days: Crossing the Plains in 1852* (Modesto, Calif.: Privately published, 1923), 22.

37. Millington, "Journal."

38. Andrews, "Diary."

39. Warner, "Diary."

40. Katherine Dunlap, "Journal" (1864), Bancroft Library, Berkeley, Calif.

41. Lucy Sexton, *The Foster Family, California Pioneers* (Santa Barbara, Calif.: Press of the Schouer Printing Studio, 1925), 123.

42. Emily McCowen Horton, *My Scrap-book* (Seattle, Wash.: N.p., 1927), 17.

43. Mary Burrell, "Diary of a Journey Overland from Council Bluffs to Green Valley, California, April 27 to September 1, 1854," Beinecke Collection, Yale University Library, New Haven, Conn.

44. Pauline Wonderly, *Reminiscences of a Pioneer* (Placerville, Calif.: El Dorado County Historical Society, 1965): 9.

45. John D. Unruh, *Plains Across: The Overland Emigrants and the Trans-Mississippi West, 1840–1860* (Urbana: University of Illinois Press, 1979), 156, 175–76.

46. Munkres, "Plains Indian Threat," 198–200.

47. Lavinia H. Porter, *By Ox Team to California: A Narrative of Crossing the Plains in 1860* (Oakland, Calif.: Oakland Enquirer Publishing, 1910), 79–83, 95–96.

48. Fosdick, "Across the Plains."

49. Unruh, *Plains Across,* 135.

50. May Callan Tansill, "Narrative" (n.d.), Barker Texas History Center, University of Texas, Austin.

51. Abigail Raymond Smith to her brothers and sisters, 5 May 1840, Beinecke Collection, Yale University Library, New Haven, Conn.

52. In a study of 103 women's overland diaries Lillian Schlissel discovered that only 7 percent recorded attacks by American Indians. Lillian Schlissel, *Women's Diaries of the Westward Journey* (New York: Schocken Books, 1982), 154. Other scholars who have also argued that the Indian threat was vastly exaggerated are Munkres, "Plains Indian Threat," 193–221; and Unruh, *Plains Across,* 9, 135–36, 156–200, 386, 395–96, 408–9.

53. Murphy, "Across the Plains," 409.

54. Margaret W. Chambers, *Reminiscences* (N.p., 1903), 13.

55. Charlotte Stearns Pengra, "Diary" (1853), Huntington Library, San Marino, Calif.

56. Porter, *By Ox-Team to California,* 65, 67, 69–70.

57. Jennings, interview 10025.

58. Williams, interview 6877.

59. Ella Bird-Dumont, "True Life Story of Ella Bird-Dumont, Earliest Settler

in the East Part of Panhandle, Texas" (n.d.), Barker Texas History Center, University of Texas, Austin.

60. Ada Adelaide Vogdes, "Journal" (1866–1872), Huntington Library, San Marino, Calif.; Lizzie Bomhoff, interview 10350, vol. 9, Indian Pioneer Papers, University of Oklahoma, Norman; and Frances M. A. Roe, *Army Letters from an Officer's Wife, 1871–1888* (New York: D. Appleton, 1909), 263.

61. Mrs. M. A. Rogers, "An Iowa Woman in Wartime," pt. 1, *Annals of Iowa* 35 (winter 1961): 526; and Bessie L. Lyon, "Prospecting for a New Home," *The Palimpsest* 16 (July 1925): 226.

62. "Frontier Fear of the Indians," *Annals of Iowa* 3 (April 1948): 315–22.

63. Mary Fokes Locklin, "Experience of Abigail McLennan Fokes and Family as Told by Her Daughter" (n.d.), Barker Texas History Center, University of Texas, Austin; and Doris Faulkner, ed., "Letters from Algona, 1856–1865," *The Palimpsest* 61, no. 6 (November–December 1980), 186–88.

64. Faulkner, "Letters from Algona," 187.

65. Polly Jane Purcell, "Autobiography and Reminiscence of a Pioneer," Graff Collection, Newberry Library, Chicago, Ill.

66. Quoted in Sandra L. Myres, "The Westering Woman," *Huntington Spectator* (winter 1980): 1–2.

67. Bird-Dumont, "True Life Story."

68. Susan Cranston to Huldah P. Fairchild, 6 April 1856, in Susan and Warren Cranston, "Letters, 1852–1859, from Oregon Territory," Bancroft Library, Berkeley, Calif.

69. Margaret I. Carrington, *Ab-sa-ra-ka, Home of the Crows: Being the Experience of an Officer's Wife on the Plains* (Philadelphia: J. B. Lippincott, 1868), 219.

70. Johnson, *Eight Hundred Miles,* 116.

71. Thomas R. Buecker, ed., "Letters of Caroline Frey Winne from Sidney Barracks and Fort McPherson, Nebraska, 1874–1878," *Nebraska History* 62 (spring 1981): 20.

72. Ellen McGowan Biddle, *Reminiscences of a Soldier's Wife* (Philadelphia: J. B. Lippincott, 1907), 134.

73. Anne Ellis, *The Life of an Ordinary Woman* (Lincoln: University of Nebraska Press, 1980), 12; Sondra Van Meter, "Pioneer Women," *Wichita State University Magazine* 2 (winter 1976): 18; Sarah Jane Alice Proctor, interview 9050, vol. 73, Indian-Pioneer Papers, University of Oklahoma, Norman; and Harriet M. Hill Townsend, "Reminiscences" (n.d.), privately held by Frank Kerulis, Waverly, Iowa.

74. Rogers, "Iowa Woman in Wartime," pt. 1, 528; and Louise Sophia Gellhorn Boylan, "My Life Story: Reminiscences of German Settlers in Hardin County, 1867–1883," Iowa State Historical Society, Iowa City.

75. Mollie Dorsey Sanford, *Mollie: The Journal of Mollie Dorsey Sanford in*

Nebraska and Colorado Territories, 1857–1866 (Lincoln: University of Nebraska Press, 1976), 188.

76. Mrs. C. W. Callerman, interview 1080, vol. 15, Indian-Pioneer Papers, University of Oklahoma, Norman.

77. Tansill, "Narrative."

78. Maud Parshall Norris, interview 9837, vol. 67, Indian-Pioneer Papers, University of Oklahoma, Norman.

79. Elizabeth Montgomery Neelley, "History of the Montgomery Family, from 1825 to the Present Time, 1937," Barker Texas History Collection, University of Texas, Austin.

80. Parrish, "Westward in 1850."

81. Sanford, *Mollie,* 152.

82. J. H. Lowry, interview 10332, vol. 56, Indian-Pioneer Papers, University of Oklahoma, Norman.

83. Townsend, "Reminiscence."

84. Minnie Lee Parks, interview 8039, vol. 69, Indian-Pioneer Papers, University of Oklahoma, Norman; Abigail Malick to her children, 8 December 1855, in Abigail Malick, "Letter" (1855), Beinecke Collection, Yale University Library, New Haven, Conn.; Lily Klasner, *My Girlhood among Outlaws* (Tucson: University of Arizona Press, 1972), 78; Rogers, "Iowa Woman in Wartime," pt. 3, *Annals of Iowa* 36 (summer 1961): 26–28; Mrs. Warren R. Fowler, "A Woman's Experience in Canon City" (1884), Bancroft Library, Berkeley, Calif.; Chambers, *Reminiscences,* 45–47; Sanford, *Mollie,* 186–89; and Bessie L. Lyon, "Hungry Indians," *The Palimpsest* 9 (October 1928): 369.

85. Wonderly, *Reminiscences,* 9.

86. Agnes Morley Cleaveland, *No Life for a Lady* (Lincoln: University of Nebraska Press, 1977) 40–41; and Nannie T. Alderson, *A Bride Goes West* (Lincoln: University of Nebraska Press, 1969), 216–17.

87. Jonaphrene S. Faulkner, typescript of novel "Prairie Home" (n.d.), Barker Texas History Center, University of Texas, Austin.

88. Neelley, "History of the Montgomery Family."

89. Elizabeth McAnulty Owens, "The Story of Her Life" (1895), Barker Texas History Center, University of Texas, Austin.

90. Locklin, "Experience"; and Faulkner, "Letters from Algona."

91. Ruth Beitz, "They Guarded Iowa's Last Frontier," *The Iowan* 9 (February–March 1961): 11–12, 46.

92. Robert C. Carriker and Eleanor R. Carriker, eds., *An Army Wife on the Frontier: The Memoirs of Alice Blackwood Baldwin, 1867–1877* (Salt Lake City: Tanner Trust Fund, University of Utah Library, 1975), 105.

93. Frances C. Carrington, *My Army Life and the Fort Phil Kearney Massacre* (Freeport, N.Y.: Books for Libraries Press, 1971).

94. Vogdes, "Journal."

95. Caroline Phelps, "Diary" (1830–1860), Iowa State Historical Society, Iowa City.

96. Rogers, "Iowa Woman in Wartime," pt. 1, 526.

97. Mrs. A. L. Patrick, interview 7773, vol. 69; Annie M. Zeigler, interview 10088, vol. 101; Iona Goar Paxton, interview 9108, vol. 70; all in Indian-Pioneer Papers, University of Oklahoma, Norman.

98. Julia C. Bolen, interview 9113, vol. 9, Indian-Pioneer Papers, University of Oklahoma, Norman.

99. Fowler, "Woman's Experience in Canon City."

100. Lois L. Murray, *Incidents of Frontier Life* (Goshen, Ind.: Evangelical United Mennonite Publishing, 1880), 117, 155–56, 181–84; and Bessie L. Lyon, "Grandmother's Story," *The Palimpsest* 5 (January 1924): 8.

101. Florence Call Cowles, *Early Algona: The Story of Our Pioneers, 1854–1874* (Des Moines, Iowa: The Register and Tribune Company, 1929), 111–12, 115.

102. Kiefer, "Over Barren Plains," 23; Waters, "Account of a Trip," 76; and Owen P. White, *A Frontier Mother* (New York: Minton, Balch, 1929), 81.

103. Bird-Dumont, "True Life Story."

104. Meta Cresse Breuer, interview 10090, vol. 12, Indian-Pioneer Papers, University of Oklahoma, Norman.

105. Munkres, "Plains Indian Threat," 198–200.

106. Unruh, *Plains Across,* 175–76.

107. Mabel Sharpe Beavers, interview 6850.

108. Norris, interview 9837.

109. Bolen, interview 9113.

110. Ellis, *Life of an Ordinary Woman,* 11.

111. Sarah J. Cummins, *Autobiography and Reminiscences* (La Grande, Oreg.: La Grande Printing, 1914), 28.

112. Margaret Hall Walker, *The Hall Family Crossing the Plains* (San Francisco: Privately printed by Wallace Kibbee and Son, 1952), 1:3.

113. Olivia Holmes, "Diary" (1873), Bancroft Library, Berkeley, Calif.

114. Washburn, "Journal."

115. Samuel P. Newcomb, "Diary" (1 January 1865 to 21 December 1865), Barker Texas History Center, University of Texas, Austin.

116. Lois Brown, interview 4496, vol. 12, Indian-Pioneer Papers, University of Oklahoma, Norman.

117. DeWitt and DeWitt, *Prairie Schooner Lady,* 46.

118. Margaret T. Gordon and Stephanie Riger, *The Female Fear: The Social Cost of Rape* (Urbana: University of Illinois Press, 1991), 2–7, 14–24.

119. Susan E. Newcomb, "Diary" (1869, 1873), Barker Texas History Center, University of Texas, Austin.

120. Erwin N. Thompson, "The Summer of '77 at Fort Lapwai," *Idaho Yesterdays* 21 (1977): 14.

121. Carriker and Carriker, *Army Wife*, 78; and Alderson, *Bride Goes West*, 48.

122. Baker, interview 10601.

123. White, *Frontier Mother*, 68.

124. See, for example, Cleaveland, *No Life for a Lady*, 41; and Bird-Dumont, "True Life Story."

125. Milo M. Quaife, ed., *Across the Plains in Forty-Nine* (Chicago: Lakeside Press, 1948), 48–49; and James Hewitt, ed., *Eye-Witnesses to Wagon Trains West* (New York: Charles Scribner's Sons, 1973), 12.

126. Byron N. McKinstry, *The California Gold Rush Overland Diary of Byron N. McKinstry* (Glendale, Calif.: Arthur H. Clark, 1975), 94–96, 101.

127. Ibid.

128. Charles W. Martin, ed., "Joseph Warren Arnold's Journal of His Trip from Montana, 1864–1866," *Nebraska History* 55 (1974): 532.

129. John O. Holzhueter, ed., "From Waupun to Sacramento in 1849: The Gold Rush Journal of Edwin Hillyer," *Wisconsin Magazine of History* 49 (1966): 222.

130. Alonzo Delano, *Life on the Plains and among the Diggings* (Ann Arbor, Mich.: University Microfilms, 1966), 218–19.

131. David M. Potter, ed., *Trail to California: The Overland Journal of Vincent Geiger and Wakeman Bryarly* (New Haven, Conn.: Yale University Press, 1945), 93.

132. María de Guzmán, "Consolidating Anglo-American Imperial Identity around the Spanish-American War (1898)," 97–126, in *Race and the Production of Modern American Nationalism*, ed. Reynolds J. Scott-Childress (New York: Garland, 1999).

133. Gilbert Drake Harlan, ed., "The Diary of Wilson Barber Harlan," pt. 1, *Journal of the West* 3, no. 2 (1964): 153.

134. Barry, "Charles Robinson," 179–88; and Harlan, "Diary of Wilson Barber Harlan," 148.

135. Fancher Stimson, "Overland Journey to California by Platte River Route and South Pass in 1850," *Annals of Iowa* 13 (October 1922): 406.

136. Holzhueter, "From Waupun to Sacramento," 221.

137. Susan Newcomb, "Diary."

138. Samuel Newcomb, "Diary."

139. Waters, "Account of a Trip," 61.

140. Cooke, *Covered Wagon Days*, 58.

141. Quoted in Sandra L. Myres, ed., *Ho for California! Women's Overland Diaries from the Huntington Library* (San Marino, Calif.: Huntington Library, 1980), 271.

142. Julia Lee Sinks, "Reminiscences of Early Days in Texas Taken from Articles

Published in the Dallas and Galveston News, February, 1896," Barker Texas History Center, University of Texas, Austin.

143. Ibid.

144. Burton J. Williams, ed., "Overland to the Gold Fields of California in 1850: The Journal of Calvin Taylor," *Nebraska History* 50 (1969): 142.

145. Buecker, "Letters of Caroline Frey Winne," 6; Howard Egan, *Pioneering the West, 1846 to 1878* (Richmond, Utah: Howard R. Egan Estate, 1917): 23.

146. Mary Butler Renville, *A Thrilling Narrative of Indian Captivity* (Minneapolis: Atlas Co., 1863), 43; Mary Jane Caples, "Overland Journey to California" (1911), California State Library, Sacramento; Eleanor Taylor, "Ross Kin: Early Settlers of the West" (1978), Bancroft Library, Berkeley, Calif.; Rogers, "Iowa Woman in Wartime," pt. 1, 525, 534; Eliza Spalding Warren, *Memoirs of the West: The Spaldings* (Portland, Oreg.: March Printing, 1916), 177; E. Allene Dunham, "Across the Plains in a Covered Wagon" (n.d.), Graff Collection, Newberry Library, Chicago, Ill.; Nancy N. Tracy, "Narrative" (1880), Bancroft Library, Berkeley, Calif.; and Ruth Peterson, comp., "Across the Plains in '57" (1931), California State Library, Sacramento.

147. Douglas C. Comer, *Ritual Ground: Bent's Old Fort, World Formation and the Annexation of the Southwest* (Los Angeles: University of California Press, 1996), 120–22, 219–23; Patricia Seed, *American Pentimento: The Invention of Indians and the Pursuit of Riches* (Minneapolis: University of Minnesota Press, 2001), 2–9; and William G. Robbins, *Colony and Empire: The Capitalist Transformation of the American West* (Lawrence; University Press of Kansas, 1994).

148. Cleaveland, *No Life for a Lady,* 38; Roger, "Iowa Woman in Wartime," pt. 1, 526; and Myres, *Ho for California!,* 149.

149. Jacob H. Schiel, *Journey through the Rocky Mountains and the Humboldt Mountains to the Pacific Ocean* (Norman: University of Oklahoma Press, 1959), 97; and Harlan, "Diary of Wilson Barber Harlan," 153.

150. Walker D. Wyman, ed., *California Emigrant Letters* (New York: Bookman Association), 53, 103.

151. Porter, *By Ox-Team to California,* 36–37.

152. Cleaveland, *No Life for a Lady,* 38; Rogers, "Iowa Woman in Wartime," pt. 1, 526; and Myres, *Ho for California!,* 149.

153. Purcell, "Autobiography and Reminiscence."

154. R. Douglas Hurt, *The Indian Frontier, 1763–1846* (Albuquerque: University of New Mexico Press, 2002), 191–223. For examples, see Klasner, *My Girlhood among Outlaws,* 34–35, 73–77; White, *Frontier Mother,* 34–35; Dora Miller, interview 9373, vol. 64, Indian-Pioneer Papers, University of Oklahoma, Norman.

155. Faulkner, "Letters from Algona," 187–89.

156. Dan L. Thrapp, *Victorio and the Mimbres Apaches* (Norman: University of Oklahoma Press, 1974), 47–67; Eve Ball, James Kaywaykla, Narrator, *In The Days of Victorio: Recollections of a Warm Springs Apache* (Tucson: University of Arizona Press, 1970), 45–53; Jennie Parks Ringgold, *Frontier Days in the Southwest: Pioneer Days in Old Arizona* (San Antonio, Tex.: Naylor, 1952), 14–15; and Mima's diary (1860–1861), in George Wright, "An American Pioneer," unnumbered folio, Lincoln County Historical Society, Carrizozo, New Mexico.

157. Francis Paul Prucha, *American Indian Treaties: The History of a Political Anomaly* (Berkeley: University of California Press, 1996), 237–40, 257–60.

158. Kimberly Moore Buchanan, *Apache Women Warriors* (El Paso: Texas Western Press, 1986); and Ruth McDonald Boyer and Narcissus Duffy Gayton, *Apache Mothers and Daughters* (Norman: University of Oklahoma Press, 1991), 49–59; Virginia Bergman Peters, *Women of the Earth Lodges: Tribal Life on the Plains* (Norman: University of Oklahoma Press, 1995), 165–67; Laura Jane Moore, "Lozen: An Apache Woman Warrior," 92–107, in *Sifters: Native American Women's Lives,* ed. Theda Perdue (New York: Oxford University Press, 2001).

159. Carrington, *My Army Life,* 71.

160. Margaret Cring Adams, interview 8499, vol. 1, Indian-Pioneer Papers, University of Oklahoma, Norman.

161. Unruh, *Plains Across,* 177.

162. Carpenter, "Diary."

163. Unruh, *Plains Across,* 157, 169–70, 177.

164. Porter, *By Ox Team to California,* 79.

165. Sarah Welch Nossaman, "Pioneering at Bonaparte and Near Pella," *Annals of Iowa* 13 (October 1922): 444–45.

166. White, *Frontier Mother,* 23.

167. Klasner, *My Girlhood among Outlaws,* 52.

168. Ibid., 86; and Myres, *Ho for California!,* 166–68.

169. Purcell, "Autobiography and Reminiscence," 4–5.

170. Myres, *Ho for California!,* 167; and Alderson, *Bride Goes West,* 101.

171. Elsie Pierson, interview 8538, vol. 71, Indian-Pioneer Papers, University of Oklahoma, Norman; and Harold F. Taggart, ed., "The Journal of David Jackson Staples," *California Historical Society Quarterly* 22 (June 1943): 146.

172. Sanford, *Mollie,* 123.

173. Lorene Millhollen, interview 8957, vol. 63, Indian-Pioneer Papers, University of Oklahoma, Norman.

174. Fosdick, "Across the Plains."

175. Baker, interview 10601.

176. McKinstry, *California Gold Rush Overland Diary,* 92.

177. Mrs. N. J. Brown, interview 4597, vol. 12, Indian-Pioneer Papers, University of Oklahoma, Norman.

178. Sarah Luster, interview 8530, vol. 56, Indian-Pioneer Papers, University of Oklahoma, Norman.

179. Owens, "Story of Her Life."

180. McKinstry, *California Gold Rush Overland Diary,* 90.

181. Miller, interview 9373.

182. Johnson, *Eight Hundred Miles,* 93–94.

183. Murray, *Incidents of Frontier Life,* 127.

184. Alderson, *Bride Goes West,* 215–16.

185. Baker, interview 10601.

186. Bird-Dumont, "True Life Story."

187. Francena Martin Sutton, "Civil War Experiences of Some Arkansas Women"(n.d.), Barker Texas History Center, University of Texas, Austin. See also LeRoy H. Fischer, ed., "A Civil War Experience of Some Arkansas Women in Indian Territory," *Chronicles of Oklahoma* 57 (summer 1979): 137–63.

188. Alderson, *Bride Goes West,* 99–103, 132–33.

189. "Interview with Nellie Quail," 1 August 1967, Fort McDowell Indian Reservation, held by Arizona State Museum, Tucson. Examples of white brutality are in Warren, *Memoirs of the West,* 20–21; and Johnson, *Eight Hundred Miles,* 61–65.

190. Buecker, "Letters of Caroline Frey Winne," 9–10; and Fosdick, "Across the Plains."

191. McKinstry, *California Gold Rush Overland Diary,* 223.

192. Unruh, *Plains Across,* 184–85, 189.

Chapter 4

1. Carl N. Degler, *At Odds: Women and the Family in America from the Revolution to the Present* (New York: Oxford University Press, 1980), 26–27, 30–31, 150–51, 283, 351–53; John Mack Faragher, *Women and Men on the Overland Trail* (New Haven, Conn.: Yale University Press, 1979), 94–97; Glenda Riley, "The Subtle Subversion: Changes in the Traditionalist Image of the American Woman," *The Historian* 32 (February 1970): 210–27; and Dianne Hales, *Just Like a Woman: How Gender Science Is Redefining What Makes Us Female* (New York: Bantam Books, 1999), 7–15.

2. Leslie Fiedler, *The Return of the Vanishing American* (New York: Stein and Day, 1968), 24, 177; Julie Roy Jeffrey, *Frontier Women: The Trans-Mississippi West, 1840–1880* (New York: Hill and Wang, 1979), 33–34; and Ronald J.

Quinn, "The Modest Seduction: The Experience of Pioneer Women on the Trans-Mississippi Frontier" (Ph.D. diss., University of California, Riverside, 1977), I–iii, 8–9, 11, 15, 18, 23, 30, 39, 45–50.

3. Sarah White Smith, "Diary," in *First White Women over the Rockies: Diaries, Letters, and Biographical Sketches of the Six Women of the Oregon Mission Who Made the Overland Journey in 1836 and 1838*, ed. Clifford Drury, vol. 3 (Glendale, Calif.: Arthur H. Clark, 1966), 87.

4. Annie D. Tallent, *The First White Woman in the Black Hills* (Mitchell, S.D.: Educator Supply Co., 1923), 47.

5. Louisa Miller Rahm, "Diary" (1862), Bancroft Library, Berkeley, Calif.

6. Margaret A. Frink, *Journal of the Adventures of a Party of California Gold-Seekers* (Oakland, Calif.: N.p., 1897), 29–30.

7. Agnes Morley Cleaveland, *No Life for a Lady* (Lincoln: University of Nebraska Press, 1977).

8. Ruth B. Moynihan, "Children and Young People on the Overland Trail," *Western Historical Quarterly* 6 (July 1975): 286.

9. Polly Jane Purcell, "Autobiography and Reminiscence of a Pioneer," Graff Collection, Newberry Library, Chicago, Ill.

10. Martha M. Morgan, *A Trip across the Plains in the Year 1849* (San Francisco: Pioneer Press, 1864), 7.

11. Catherine M. Haun, "A Woman's Trip across the Plains" (1849), Huntington Library, San Marino. Calif.; Susan M. Cranston, "Daily Journal" (1851), Bancroft Library, Berkeley, Calif.; and Frances H. Sawyer, "Overland to California" (1852), Bancroft Library, Berkeley, Calif.

12. Pauline Wonderly, *Reminiscences of a Pioneer* (Placerville, Calif.: El Dorado County Historical Society, 1965), 3–4.

13. Elizabeth J. Goltra, "Journal" (1853), Bancroft Library, Berkeley, Calif.

14. Ada Millington, "Journal Kept while Crossing the Plains" (1862), Bancroft Library, Berkeley, Calif.

15. Ada Adelaide Vogdes, "Journal" (1866–1872), Huntington Library, San Marino, Calif. Other women's views are found in Sherry L. Smith, "Officers' Wives, Indians and the Indian Wars," *Order of the Indian Wars Journal* 1 (winter 1980): 35–46.

16. Mary F. H. Sandford, "A Trip across the Plains" (1853), California State Library, Sacramento; and Ward G. DeWitt and Florence S. DeWitt, *Prairie Schooner Lady: The Journal of Harriet Sherrill Ward, 1853* (Los Angeles: Westernlore Press, 1959), 39–46.

17. Mrs. Nicholas H. Karchner, "Diary" (1862), California State Library, Sacramento.

18. Mary Eliza Warner, "Diary" (1864), Bancroft Library, Berkeley, Calif.

19. Mary Jane Caples, "Overland Journey to California" (1911), California State Library, Sacramento.

20. Allie B. Busby, *Two Summers among the Musquakies* (Vinton, Iowa: Herald Book and Job Rooms, 1886), 75.

21. Lavinia H. Porter, *By Ox Team to California: A Narrative of Crossing the Plains in 1860* (Oakland, Calif.: Oakland Enquirer Publishing, 1910), 26.

22. Sarah R. Herndon, *Days on the Road: Crossing the Plains in 1865* (New York: Burr Printing, 1902), 73.

23. Sarah White Smith, "Diary," 78.

24. Sandford, "Trip across the Plains."

25. Mary Pratt Staples, "Reminiscences ca. 1886," Bancroft Library, Berkeley, Calif.; Sallie H. Maddock, "The Diary of a Pioneer Girl" (1849), California State Library, Sacramento; Margaret M. Hecox, *California Caravan: The 1846 Overland Trail Memoir of Margaret M. Hecox* (San Jose, Calif.: Harlan Young, 1966), 40; and Fleming Fraker, Jr., ed., "To Pike's Peak by Ox Wagon: The Harriet A. Smith Day-Book," *Annals of Iowa* 35 (fall 1959): 132.

26. Louisa Cook to her mother and sisters (Kearney, 1862), in Cook, "Letters" (1860–1865), Beinecke Collection, Yale University Library, New Haven, Conn.

27. Mary C. Fish, "Across the Plaines in 1860," Bancroft Library, Berkeley, Calif.

28. Helen Carpenter, "Diary" (1856), Huntington Library, San Marino, Calif.

29. Esther B. Hanna, "Journal" (1852), Bancroft Library, Berkeley, Calif.; and Rex C. Myers, "To the Dear Ones at Home: Elizabeth Fisk's Missouri River Trip, 1867," *Montana, the Magazine of Western History* 32 (summer 1982): 44; and Sarah White Smith, "Diary," 80, 84–85.

30. Jason Hook and Martin Pegler, *To Live and Die in the West: The American Indian Wars* (Northants, UK: Osprey, 1999), 88–99; Cook to her mother and sisters (Kearney, 1862), in Cook, "Letters"; Thomas R. Buecker, ed., "Letters of Caroline Frey Winne from Sidney Barracks and Fort McPherson, Nebraska, 1874–1878," *Nebraska History* 62 (spring 1981): 67; and Frances M. A. Roe, *Army Letters from an Officer's Wife, 1871–1888* (New York: D. Appleton, 1909), 13.

31. Sandra L. Myres, ed., *Cavalry Wife: The Diary of Eveline M. Alexander, 1866–1867* (College Station: Texas A. & M. University Press, 1977), 79, 100.

32. Leo M. Kaiser and Priscilla Knuth, eds., "From Ithaca to Clatsop Plains: Miss Ketcham's Journal of Travel," pt. 2, *Oregon Historical Quarterly* 62 (1961): 368; and Mrs. B. G. Ferris, *The Mormons at Home* (New York: Dix and Edwards, 1856), 13.

33. Celinda E. Hines Shipley, "Diary" (1853), Beinecke Collection, Yale University, New Haven, Conn.

34. Caroline L. Richardson, "Journal" (1856), Bancroft Library, Berkeley, Calif.

35. Myers, "To the Dear Ones," 47.

36. Hanna, "Journal."

37. Hecox, *California Caravan,* 32.

38. Maria J. Norton, "Diary of a Trip across the Plains in '59," Bancroft Library, Berkeley, Calif.

39. A. D. Fisher, "Cultural Conflicts on the Prairies: Indian and White," *Alberta Historical Review* 163 (1968): 22.

40. Ellen Tompkins Adams, "Diary" (1863), Bancroft Library, Berkeley, Calif.; and Buecker, "Letters of Caroline Frey Winne," 11.

41. Annie M. Zeigler, interview 10088, vol. 101, Indian-Pioneer Papers, University of Oklahoma, Norman.

42. Maddock, "Diary of a Pioneer Girl"; Staples, "Reminiscences"; and Mary Jane Guill, "The Overland Diary of a Journey from Livingston County, Missouri, to Butte County, California, May 5 to September 5, 1860," California State Library, Sacramento.

43. Ferris, *Mormons at Home,* 68.

44. Carrie A. Strahorn, *Fifteen Thousand Miles by Stage* (New York: G. P. Putnam's Sons, 1911), 15; and Mollie Dorsey Sanford, *Mollie: The Journal of Mollie Dorsey Sanford in Nebraska and Colorado Territories, 1857–1866* (Lincoln: University of Nebraska Press, 1976), 122.

45. Herndon, *Days on the Road,* 106, 159.

46. Nellie Slater, "Travels on the Plains in Eighteen Sixty-Two" (Journal), Denver Public Library, Denver, Colo.

47. Algeline J. Ashley, "Diary, Crossing the Plains in 1852," Huntington Library, San Marino, Calif.

48. Mrs. D. B. Bates, *Incidents on Land and Water* (Boston: James French, 1857), 151–52.

49. Helen Marnie Stewart Love, "Diary" (1853), Huntington Library, San Marino, Calif. Intermarried Indian women who became well known are in John S. Gray, "The Story of Mrs. Picotte-Galpin, a Sioux Heroine," *Montana, The Magazine of Western History* 36 (summer 1986): 2–21; and Valerie Sherer Mathes, "Susan Lafleshe Picotte, M.D.: Nineteenth-Century Physician and Reformer," *Great Plains Quarterly* 13 (summer 1993). Culture brokers are discussed in Margaret Connell Szasz, ed., *Between Indian and White Worlds: The Cultural Broker* (Norman: University of Oklahoma Press, 1994).

50. Millington, "Journal."

51. Maria Schrode, "Journal" (1870), Huntington Library, San Marino, Calif.

52. Hecox, *California Caravan,* 29.

53. Thompson, "Summer of '77," 11.

54. Lydia Waters, "Account of a Trip across the Plains in 1855," *Quarterly of the Society of California Pioneers* 6 (March 1929): 61–62.

55. Fish, "Across the Plaines"; and Roe, *Army Letters from an Officer's Wife,* 10.
56. Adams, "Diary of Ellen Tompkins Adams."
57. Hanna, "Journal."
58. Quoted in Sandra L. Myres, ed., *Ho for California! Women's Overland Diaries from the Huntington Library* (San Marino, Calif.: Huntington Library, 1980), 117. For further discussion, see Ruth Spack, *America's Second Tongue: American Indian Education and the Ownership of English, 1860–1900* (Lincoln: University of Nebraska Press, 2002), 13–44.
59. Guill, "Overland Diary"; Buecker, "Letters of Caroline Frey Winne," 10; Hanna, "Journal"; Hecox, *California Caravan,* 28; and Lucy Sexton, *The Foster Family, California Pioneers* (Santa Barbara, Calif.: Press of the Schouer Printing Studio, 1925), 134.
60. Kaiser and Knuth, "From Ithaca to Clatsop Plains," pt. 2, 368.
61. Guill, "Overland Diary"; Norton, "Diary"; Katherine Dunlap, "Journal" (1864), Bancroft Library, Berkeley, Calif.; and Marie Nash, "Diary" (1861), California State Library, Sacramento.
62. DeWitt and DeWitt, *Prairie Schooner Lady,* 78; and Mary Burrell, "Diary of a Journey Overland from Council Bluffs to Green Valley, California, April 27 to September 1, 1854," Beinecke Collection, Yale University Library, New Haven, Conn.
63. Nash, "Diary"; Carpenter, "Diary"; and Millington, "Journal."
64. Julia L. Hare, "Reminiscences" (n.d.), California State Library, Sacramento.
65. Jacqueline Peterson and Jennifer S. H. Brown, eds., *The New Peoples: Being and Becoming Me'tis in North America* (Lincoln: University of Nebraska Press, 1985); Michael Lansing, "Plains Indian Women and Interracial Marriage in the Upper Missouri Trade, 1804–1868," *Western Historical Quarterly* 31 (winter 2000): 413–33; quote is in Cranston, "Daily Journal"; Mary Stuart Bailey, "A Journal of the Overland Trip from Ohio to California" (1852), Huntington Library, San Marino, Calif.; Waters, "Account of a Trip," 64; Charlotte Stearns Pengra, "Diary" (1853), Huntington Library, San Marino, Calif.; Jane Augusta Gould, "Diary" (1862), Iowa State Historical Society, Iowa City; and Sexton, *Foster Family,* 124, 131.
66. Fish, "Across the Plaines."
67. Sawyer, "Overland to California"; and Frink, *Journal,* 47.
68. Peggy Pascoe, "Race, Gender, and Intercultural Relations: The Case of Interracial Marriage," *Frontiers* 12 (1991): 15–18; and Sara Hiveley, "Journal" (1863–1864), Denver Public Library, Denver, Colo.
69. Kaiser and Knuth, "From Ithaca to Clatsop Plains," pt. 2, 371; and Dee Garceau, "Mourning Dove: Gender and Cultural Mediation," 108–26,

in *Sifters: Native American Women's Lives,* ed. Theda Perdue (New York: Oxford University Press, 2001).

70. Sanford, *Mollie,* 137; and Norton, "Diary."

71. Kay Parker Schweinfurth, *Prayer on Top of the Earth: The Spiritual Universe of the Plains Apaches* (Boulder: University Press of Colorado, 2002), 116–17; and Bailey, "Journal."

72. Sandford, "Trip across the Plains"; Mary Horne, "Migration and Settlement of the Latter Day Saints, Salt Lake City" (1884), Bancroft Library, Berkeley, Calif.; Nannie T. Alderson, *A Bride Goes West* (Lincoln: University of Nebraska Press, 1969), 48; Harger Family Papers, privately held by Delores Gros-Louis, Bloomington, Ind.; Sanford, *Mollie,* 128; and Helen E. Clark, "Diary" (1860), Denver Public Library, Denver, Colo.

73. Mrs. H. T. Clarke, "A Young Woman's Sights on the Emigrant's Trail" (Salem, Oregon, 1878), Bancroft Library, Berkeley, Calif.

74. Emily McCowen Horton, *My Scrap-book* (Seattle, Wash.: N.p., 1927), 17.

75. Gilbert Quintero, "Making the Indian: Colonial Knowledge, Alcohol, and Native Americans" (2001): 57–71; and Fraker, "To Pike's Peak," 134.

76. Warner, "Diary."

77. Catherine Jane Bell to Julia, 31 October 1859, Oroville, Calif., Bancroft Library, Berkeley, Calif.

78. Daniel Maltz and JoAllyn Archambault, "Gender and Power in Native North America," 231–41, in *Women and Power in Native North America,* ed. Laura F. Klein and Lillian A. Acherman (Norman: University of Oklahoma Press, 1995); Patricia L. Crown, "Women's Role in Changing Cuisine," 221–66, and Barbara J. Mills, "Gender, Craft Production, and Inequality," 267–300, both in *Women and Men in the Prehispanic Southwest: Labor, Power and Prestige,* ed. Patricia L. Crown (Santa Fe, N.Mex.: School of American Research Press, 2000), 221–66; Millington, "Journal"; Harriet Bunyard, "Diary of a Young Girl," (1868), Huntington Library, San Marino, Calif.; Porter, *By Ox Team to California,* 39; and Sanford, *Mollie,* 164. A counterview is in Martha Harroun, "Of Baggage and Bondage: Gender and Status among Hidatsa and Crow Women," *American Indian Culture and Research Journal* 17 (1993): 121–53.

79. Frink, *Journal;* and Ruth Peterson, comp., "Across the Plains in '57" (1931), California State Library, Sacramento.

80. Leo M. Kaiser and Priscilla Knuth, eds., "From Ithaca to Clatsop Plains," pt. 1, *Oregon Historical Quarterly* 62 (1961): 262; and Miriam D. Colt, *Went to Kansas; Being a Thrilling Account of an Ill-Fated Expedition* (Watertown, N.Y.: L. Ingalls, 1862), 136–61.

81. Caples, "Overland Journey to California."

82. Martha Ann Minto, "Female Pioneering in Oregon" (1849), Bancroft Library, Berkeley, Calif.; Emeline Fuller, *Left by the Indians. Story of My*

NOTES TO PAGES 145–46

Life (Mount Vernon, Iowa: Hawk-Eye Steam Print, 1892), 29; Margaret W. Chambers, *Reminiscences* (N.p., 1903); and Mary A. Hodgson, "The Life of a Pioneer Family" (1922), California State Library, Sacramento.

83. Caroline D. Budlong, *Memories: Pioneer Days in Oregon and Washington* (Eugene, Oreg.: Picture Press, 1949), 38; Colt, *Went to Kansas,* 132; David Edward Blaine, "Letters, 1824–1900," from his wife Kate (no salutation given, Seattle, 1854), Beinecke Collection, Yale University Library, New Haven, Conn.; and Annie D. Tallent, *The Black Hills; or, The Last Hunting Ground of the Dakotahs* (Sioux Falls, S.D.: Brevet Press, 1974), 82.

84. Kate McDaniel Furness, "From Prairie to Pacific" (1853), California State Library, Sacramento.

85. Ellen McGowan Biddle, *Reminiscences of a Soldier's Wife* (Philadelphia: J. B. Lippincott, 1907), 183.

86. Devon A. Mihesuah, *American Indians: Stereotypes and Realities* (Atlanta, Ga.: Clarity Press, 1996), 97–98; and Bonnie Duran, "Indigenous Versus Colonial Discourse: Alcohol and American Indian Identity," 111–28 in *Dressing in Feathers: The Construction of the Indian in American Popular Culture,* ed. S. Elizabeth Bird (Boulder, Colo.: Westview Press, 1996). Examples include Mrs. E. Van Court, "Reminiscences of Her Life in California" (26 March 1914), Beinecke Collection, Yale University Library, New Haven, Conn.; Mary Rice to her sister (Fort Gibson, Okla., 1835), Beinecke Collection, Yale University Library, New Haven, Conn.; Lodisa Frizzell, *Across the Plains to California in 1852* (New York: New York Public Library, 1915), 10; and Sarah May Baldwin, no interview number, vol. 4, Indian-Pioneer Papers, University of Oklahoma, Norman.

87. Rice to her sister (1835).

88. Haun, "Woman's Trip."

89. Ferris, *Mormons at Home,* 63.

90. Alan M. Klein, "The Political-Economy of Gender: A Nineteenth Century Plains Indian Case Study," 143–65, and Patricia C. Albers, "Sioux Women in Transition: A Study of Their Changing Status in Domestic and Capitalist Sectors of Production," 175–223, both in *The Hidden Half: Studies of Plains Indian Women,* by Patricia Albers and Beatrice Medicine (Washington, D.C.: University Press of America, 1983).

91. Pengra, "Diary."

92. Susan Armitage, "Women's Literature and the American Frontier: A New Perspective on the Frontier Myth," in *Women, Women Writers, and the West,* ed. L. L. Lee and Merrill Lewis (Troy, N.Y.: Whitson, 1979), 7–9; and Glenda Riley and N. Jill Howard, "Thus You See I Have Not Much Rest: The Importance of Food on the Oregon Trail," *Idaho Yesterdays* 37, no. 3 (fall 1993): 27–35.

93. Lillian Schlissel, *Women's Diaries of the Westward Journey* (New York: Schocken Books, 1982), 118.

94. Sarah Royce, *A Frontier Lady; Recollections of the Gold Rush and Early California,* ed. Ralph Henry Gabriel (New Haven, Conn.: Yale University Press, 1932), 50.

95. Augusta Pierce Tabor, "Cabin Life in Colorado" (1884), Bancroft Library, Berkeley, Calif.; Rebecca Hildreth Nutting Woodson, "A Sketch of the Life of Rebecca Hildreth Nutting Woodson and Her Family" (1909), Bancroft Library, Berkeley, Calif.; Guill, "Overland Diary"; and Kenneth L. Holmes, ed., "Letters from a Quaker Woman," *American West* 20 (1983): 42.

96. Mary Hall Jatta, "Journal" (1869), Bancroft Library, Berkeley, Calif.; Haun, "Woman's Trip"; and Love, "Diary."

97. Herndon, *Days on the Road,* 235.

98. Tallent, *Black Hills,* 106; Hecox, *California Caravan,* 29; and Eliza Ann Egbert, "Diary" (1852), Bancroft Library, Berkeley, Calif.

99. Guill, "Overland Diary."

100. Mallie Stafford, *The March of Empire through Three Decades* (San Francisco: George Spaulding, 1884), 117.

101. E. Allene Dunham, *Across the Plains in a Covered Wagon* (N.p. [possibly Milton, Iowa]: N.p., [ca. 1920s]), 6–7; Martha M. Moore, "Journal of a Trip to California in 1860," Beinecke Collection, Yale University Library, New Haven, Conn.; Burrell, "Diary"; Buecker, "Letters of Caroline Frey Winne," 7; Gould, "Diary"; Haun, "Woman's Trip"; and Porter, *By Ox-Team to California,* 27, 32–33.

102. Hecox, *California Caravan,* 29; Nash, "Diary"; DeWitt and DeWitt, *Prairie Schooner Lady,* 139; and Margaret Hall Walker, *The Hall Family Crossing the Plains* (San Francisco: Privately printed by Wallace Kibbee and Son, 1952), 29.

103. For Colorado, for example, see Elliott West, *Contested Plains: Indians, Goldseekers, and the Rush to Colorado* (Lawrence: University Press of Kansas, 1998); Libbie B. Bradford to John N. Bradford, 1857, Richfield, Minn., in "The Letters of John N. and Libbie B. Bradford, 1862–1864," privately held by John P. Bradford, St. Paul, Minn.; Curt Harnack, "Prelude to Massacre," *The Iowan* 4 (February–March 1956): 36–39; Rodney Fox, "Stark Reminder of an Indian Raid," *The Iowan* 9 (October–November 1960): 20–21; Hubert E. Moeller, "Iowa's Other Indian Massacre," *The Iowan* 2 (April–May 1954): 40; M. A. Roe, "A Pioneer Woman's Letter," in Alice L. Longley Collection, Division of Archives and Historical Museum, Des Moines, Iowa; Elinore Pruitt Stewart, *Letters of a Woman Homesteader* (Lincoln: University of Nebraska Press, 1961), 120–21; Biddle, *Reminiscences;* Lily Klasner, *My Girlhood among Outlaws* (Tucson:

University of Arizona Press, 1972), 32–35, 73–78; Budlong, *Memories,* 8–9; Mary Richardson Walker, "Diary" (1848), Huntington Library, San Marino, Calif.; and Rachel E. Wright, "The Early Upper Napa Valley" (1928), Bancroft Library, Berkeley, Calif.

104. P. A. M. Taylor, "Emigrants' Problems in Crossing the West, 1830–1870," *University of Birmingham History Journal* 5 (1955): 88; and Schlissel, *Women's Diaries,* 53.

105. Mrs. L. D. Pritchard, interview 8737, vol. 73, Indian-Pioneer Papers, University of Oklahoma, Norman; Lillian Allen, interview 9691, vol. 2, Indian-Pioneer Papers, University of Oklahoma, Norman; and Owen P. White, *A Frontier Mother* (New York: Minton, Balch, 1929), 34–35.

106. Mattie Walker, "A Brief History of the William B. Walker Family" (n.d.), California State Library, Sacramento.

107. Mary Jones, "Papers" (1846–1944), Barker Texas History Center, University of Texas, Austin.

108. Bunyard, "Diary"; Catherine Amanda Stansbury Washburn, "Journal, 1853, from Iowa to Oregon Territory," Huntington Library, San Marino, Calif.; Sawyer, "Overland to California"; Walker, "Brief History"; Kaiser and Knuth, "From Ithaca to Clatsop Plains," pt. 1, 257–58, 284; Dunlap, "Journal"; Harriett A. L. Smith, "My Trip across the Plains in 1849," California State Library, Sacramento; Susan Thompson Parrish, "Westward in 1850," Huntington Library, San Marino, Calif.; Gould, "Diary"; Lucene Pfeiffer Parsons, "The Women in the Sunbonnets" (1850), Stanford University Library, Stanford, Calif.; and Slater, "Travels."

109. Parrish, "Westward in 1850"; Emma S. Hill, *A Dangerous Crossing and What Happened on the Other Side: Seven Lean Years* (Denver, Colo.: Bradford Robinson, 1924), 19; Mary Saunders, "The Whitman Massacre; A True Story by a Survivor of This Terrible Tragedy which Took Place in Oregon in 1847," Bancroft Library, Berkeley, Calif.; and Guill, "Overland Diary"; Hanna, "Journal."

110. Mary Rabb, "Reminiscences" (1875), in Rabb Family Papers (1823–1922), Barker Texas History Center, University of Texas; Austin; Lizzie C. Stillwell Saunders, "Life Experiences of Pickey," and "Reminiscences of Mrs. L. C. Saunders" (1930), both in Barker Texas History Center, University of Texas, Austin.

111. Robert L. Munkres, "The Plains Indian Threat on the Oregon Trail before 1860," *Annals of Wyoming* 40 (1968): 221.

112. Sanford, *Mollie,* 129; Moore, "Journal"; Haun, "Woman's Trip"; Minto, "Female Pioneering"; and Hecox, *California Caravan,* 40.

113. Kaiser and Knuth, "From Ithaca to Clatsop Plains," pt. 2, 392.

114. Maggie Hall, "The Story of Maggie Hall," Bancroft Library, Berkeley, Calif.

115. Blaine, "Letters"; Tallent, *First White Woman,* 138; Buecker, "Letters of Caroline Frey Winne," 8–9; Sanford, *Mollie,* 166; Vogdes, "Journal"; Carpenter, "Diary"; and Lydia S. Lane, *I Married a Soldier; or, Old Days in the Old Army* (Philadelphia: J. B. Lippincott, 1893), 65–66.

116. Hecox, *California Caravan,* 28; Haun, "Woman's Trip"; Georgia Willis Read, "Diary" (1850), California State Library, Sacramento; Pengra, "Diary"; and Lucy Rutledge Cooke, *Covered Wagon Days: Crossing the Plains in 1852* (Modesto, Calif.: Privately published, 1923), 30.

117. Eliza Spalding Warren, *Memoirs of the West: The Spaldings* (Portland, Oreg.: March Printing, 1916), 13, Elizabeth L. Lord, *Reminiscences of Eastern Oregon* (Portland, Oreg.: Irwin-Hodson, 1903), 42; and Frizzell, *Across the Plains,* 18.

118. Barsina French, "Journal of a Wagon Trip" (1867), Huntington Library, San Marino, Calif.; Cynthia J. Capron, "Life in the Army," *Journal of the Illinois State Historical Society* 13 (October 1920): 367; Pengra, "Diary"; Dunlap, "Journal"; and Hecox, *California Caravan,* 33.

119. Lula Nixon, interview 8011, vol. 67; Emma Clayton, interview 9672, vol. 18; Mary Clavin, interview 13643, vol. 18; Mrs. Eddie Brown, interview 7680, vol. 12; Sarah Luster, interview 8530, vol. 56; and Mrs. L. Johnson, interview 10227, vol. 48; all in Indian-Pioneer Papers, University of Oklahoma, Norman.

120. Parsons, "Women in Sunbonnets"; and Hill, *Dangerous Crossing,* 82.

121. Mrs. John Barnes, interview 9735, vol. 5, Indian-Pioneer Papers, University of Oklahoma, Norman; and Hanna, "Journal."

122. Frizzell, *Across the Plains,* 25; Katherine Provost, interview 1419, vol. 73, Indian-Pioneer Papers, University of Oklahoma, Norman; Barbara Baker, interview 10089, vol. 4, Indian-Pioneer Papers, University of Oklahoma, Norman; Lois L. Murray, *Incidents of Frontier Life* (Goshen, Ind.: Evangelical United Mennonite Publishing, 1880), 134; Hodgson, "Life of a Pioneer Family"; Lois Smith Brown, interview 4496, vol. 12, Indian-Pioneer Papers, University of Oklahoma, Norman; and Juliette Fish Walker, "Crossing the Plains," *Noticas* 16 (1970), 4.

123. Haun, "Woman's Trip"; Mrs. John Barnes, interview 9735; and Nixon, interview 8011.

124. Susan S. Magoffin, *Down the Santa Fe Trail and into Mexico: The Diary of Susan Shelby Magoffin, 1846–1847* (New Haven, Conn.: Yale University Press, 1926), 68.

125. Rachel C. Rose, "Diary" (1852), California State Library, Sacramento; Nancy A. Hunt, "By Ox Team to California," Bancroft Library, Berkeley, Calif.; Furness, "From Prairie to Pacific"; Sandford, "Trip across the Plains"; Walker, *Hall Family,* 28; and Hanna, "Journal."

126. Porter, *By Ox Team to California,* 67.

127. Mary E. Hopping, "Incidents of Pioneer Life as I Remember and as I Have Been Told" (1962), California State Library, Sacramento.

128. Porter, *By Ox Team to California,* 79.

129. Wonderly, *Reminiscences,* 4; and Hecox, *California Caravan,* 38.

130. Vogdes, "Journal."

131. Ibid.

132. Glenda Riley, "Women in the West," *Journal of American Culture* 3 (summer 1980): 314–18.

133. Porter, *By Ox Team to California,* 26–27.

134. DeWitt and DeWitt, *Prairie Schooner Lady,* 87, 123, 144, 158, 166.

135. Sandra L. Myres, "Romance and Reality of the American Frontier: Views of Army Wives," *Western Historical Quarterly* 13 (October 1982): 414. Also helpful are Clarity Adams Earley, *One Woman's Army: A Black Officer Remembers the WAC* (College Station: Texas A & M University Press, 1995); and Anne Bruner Eales, *Army Wives on the American Frontier: Living by the Bugles* (Boulder, Colo.: Johnson Books, 1996).

136. Sandra L. Myres, "Army Women's Narratives as Documents of Social History: Some Examples from the Western Frontier, 1840–1900," *New Mexico Historical Review* 65 (April 1990): 175–98; and Smith, "Officers' Wives, Indians and the Indian Wars," 42–43. See also Patricia Y. Stallard, *Glittering Misery: Dependents of the Indian Fighting Army* (San Rafael, Calif.: Presidio Press, 1978).

137. Quoted in Christiane Fischer, ed., *Let Them Speak for Themselves: Women in the American West, 1849–1900* (Hamden, Conn.: Archon Press, 1977), 120–21.

138. Saunders, "Whitman Massacre"; Goltra, "Journal"; Kitturah Penton Belknap, "Reminiscences" (1839), Iowa State Historical Society, Iowa City; and Dunlap, "Journal."

139. Hecox, *California Caravan,* 29; Mary A. Jones, "Recollections" (1915), Bancroft Library, Berkeley, Calif.; Porter, *By Ox Team to California,* 34; Carpenter, "Diary"; DeWitt and DeWitt, *Prairie Schooner Lady,* 77; Sexton, *Foster Family,* 127; Virginia Reed Murphy, "Across the Plains in the Donner Party (1846): A Personal Narrative of the Overland Trip to California," *Century Magazine* 42 (July 1891): 414; Cooke, *Covered Wagon Days,* 30; and Frizzell, *Across the Plains,* 18.

140. Cranston, "Daily Journal," and Fish, "Across the Plaines."

141. DeWitt and DeWitt, *Prairie Schooner Lady,* 139.

142. Lord, *Reminiscences,* 63.

143. Waters, "Account of a Trip," 69.

144. DeWitt and DeWitt, *Prairie Schooner Lady,* 127, 158.

145. Hanna, "Journal."

146. Walker, *Hall Family,* 28.

147. Carpenter, "Diary," and Mihesuah, *American Indians,* 76–78.

148. Bunyard, "Diary."

149. Mary Maverick, "Memoirs" (1881), Barker Texas History Center, University of Texas, Austin; and Parsons, "Women in Sunbonnets."

150. Jean Webster, "The Myth of Hardship on the Oregon Trail," *Reed College Bulletin* 24 (January 1946): 34.

151. Sexton, *Foster Family,* 194–95.

152. Walker, *Hall Family,* 29.

153. Hodgson, "Life of a Pioneer Family," and Hare, "Reminiscences."

154. Capron, "Life in the Army," 367.

155. Hanna, "Journal"; Minnie Lee Cardwell Miller, "The Road to Yesterday" (1937), Bancroft Library, Berkeley, Calif.; and Lord, *Reminiscences.*

156. Hopping, "Incidents of Pioneer Life."

157. Miller, "Road to Yesterday"; and Donald A. Grinde and Bruce E. Johansen, *Ecocide of Native America: Environmental Destruction of Indian Lands and Peoples* (Santa Fe, N.Mex.: Clear Light, 1995).

158. Furness, "From Prairie to Pacific."

159. Belknap, "Reminiscences"; Caples, "Overland Journey to California"; and Olive Cordon Miller, "Pioneer Gordon Family" (n.d.), Bancroft Library, Berkeley, Calif.

160. Gretchen M. Bataille and Kathleen Mullen Sands, *American Indian Women: Telling Their Lives* (Lincoln: University of Nebraska Press, 1984), 2–9.

161. Chambers, "Reminiscences," 13, 47; Mrs. Edward Dyer, "Diary" (1860), Barker Texas History Center, University of Texas, Austin; Jones, "Recollections"; Karchner, "Diary"; Kaiser and Knuth, "From Ithaca to Clatsop Plains," pt. 1, 282, 363; Dwight G. McCarty, *Stories of Pioneer Life on the Iowa Prairie* (Emmetsburg, Iowa: Emmetsburg Publishing, 1974), 20; Valentine McGillycuddy, "Notebook" (1876) and notes kept by his wife, Fanny (1877), Beinecke Collection, Yale University Library, New Haven, Conn.; Norton, "Diary"; and Harriet M. Hill Townsend, "Reminiscences" (n.d.), privately held by Frank Kerulis, Waverly, Iowa.

162. Millington, "Journal."

163. Susan Scheckel, *The Insistence of the Indian: Race and Nationalism in Nineteenth-Century American Culture* (Princeton, N.J.: Princeton University Press, 1998), 70–98.

164. Maverick, "Memoirs"; and Rabb, "Reminiscences."

165. Martha V. Webster Simmons, "The Webster Massacre" (1925), Barker Texas History Center, University of Texas, Austin.

166. Elizabeth McAnulty Owens, "The Story of Her Life" (1895), Barker Texas History Center, University of Texas, Austin.; Mary Fokes Locklin, "Experience of Abigail McLennan Fokes and Family as Told by Her Daughter" (n.d.), Barker Texas History Center, University of Texas, Austin.

167. Rosalie B. Hart Priour, "The Adventures of a Family of Emigrants Who Emigrated to Texas, in 1834; An Autobiography by Rosalie B. Hart Priour" (n.d.), Barker Texas History Center, University of Texas, Austin.

168. Julia Lee Sinks, "Reminiscences of Early Days in Texas Taken from Articles Published in the Dallas and Galveston News, February, 1896," Barker Texas History Center, University of Texas, Austin; Martha N. McFarlin Gray, "Adventures of John Green McFarlin and an Autobiography" (1931), Barker Texas History Center, University of Texas, Austin; Eugenie E. Lavender, "Biography" (n.d.), Barker Texas History Center, University of Texas, Austin; and Mary A. Baylor, "Reminiscences" (n. d.), Barker Texas History Center, University of Texas, Austin.

169. Susan E. Newcomb, "Diary" (1865–1869, 1871–1873), Barker Texas History Center, University of Texas, Austin. For additional stories, see Francis Edward Abernethy, *Legendary Ladies of Texas* (Denton: University of North Texas Press, 1994).

170. Jonaphrene S. Faulkner, typescript of novel "Prairie Home" (n.d.), Barker Texas History Center, University of Texas, Austin.

171. Ella Bird-Dumont, "True Life Story of Ella Bird-Dumont, Earliest Settler in the East Part of Panhandle, Texas" (n.d.), Barker Texas History Center, University of Texas, Austin; Saunders, "Life Experiences"; Margaret Armstrong Bowie, "Diary of Margaret Armstrong" (1872–1877), Barker Texas History Center, University of Texas, Austin; and May Callan Tansill, "Narrative" (n.d.), Barker Texas History Center, University of Texas, Austin.

172. Millie M. Butler, interview 10094, vol. 14, Indian-Pioneer Papers, University of Oklahoma, Norman.

173. Mrs. W. C. Jarhoe, "Papers" (1890–1913), Western History Collections, University of Oklahoma, Norman.

174. Amelia F. Harris, no interview number, vol. 47, Indian-Pioneer Papers, University of Oklahoma, Norman.

175. Adams, "Diary of Ellen Tompkins Adams"; and Pauline Farseth and Theodore C. Blegen, eds., *Frontier Mother: The Letters of Gro Svendsen* (Northfield, Minn.: Norwegian-American Historical Association, 1950), 32.

176. Maverick, "Memoirs"; Sinks, "Reminiscences"; and Fergus M. Bordewich, *Killing the White Man's Indian* (New York: Random House, 1997), 45–50.

177. Theda Perdue, "Cherokee Women and the Trail of Tears," *Journal of Women's History* 1 (spring 1989): 14–30; and Perdue, "Women, Men and American Indian Policy: The Cherokee Response to 'Civilization,'" 90–114 in *Negotiators of Change: Historical Perspectives on Native American Women,* ed. Nancy Shoemaker (New York: Routledge, 1995); Ronald

Wright, *Stolen Continents: The "New World" through Indian Eyes* (Boston: Houghton Mifflin, 1992), 218–21; Mary Ellen Williams, interview 6877, vol. 98; and Julia C. Bolen, interview 9113, vol. 9, both in Indian-Pioneer Papers, University of Oklahoma, Norman. Bolen's first husband was what she called a "full blood Comanche"; after his death she said that she married a "full blood Cherokee."

178. James C. Scott, *Domination and the Arts of Resistance: Hidden Transcripts* (New Haven, Conn.: Yale University Press, 1990), 172–76. Women attending these events included Dora B. Parnell, interview 12091, vol. 69; Mary Archibald, interview 12054, vol. 3; and Fannie J. Bell, no interview number, vol. 7; all in Indian-Pioneer Papers, University of Oklahoma, Norman.

179. Mrs. John Wyers, interview 6244, vol. 101; Bertha Brewer Plummer, interview 4833, vol. 72; Ethel Daniel Pfeiffer, interview 1253, vol. 71; Mrs. Arthur Johnson, interview 9025, vol. 48; and Belle M. Yates, interview 12817, vol. 101; all in Indian-Pioneer Papers, University of Oklahoma, Norman.

180. May Johnson, interview 10498, vol. 48, Indian-Pioneer Papers, University of Oklahoma, Norman.

181. Margaret Cring Adams, interview 8499, vol. 1; Lucy J. Auldridge, interview 5776, vol. 3; Mrs. B. M. Austin, interview 9189, vol. 3; Beaulah Smith Young, interview 10436, vol. 101; and Mrs. Andrew J. Wilson, interview 4507, vol. 99; all in Indian-Pioneer Papers, University of Oklahoma, Norman.

182. Samantha Johnson, interview 12027, vol. 48; Mrs. Frances Johnson, interview 8841, vol. 48; and Mary Bell Boothby, interview 4335, vol. 9; all in Indian-Pioneer Papers, University of Oklahoma, Norman.

183. Mrs. Emma Wiltband, interview 4785, vol. 99; Frances Jeannette Wynn, interview 12794, vol. 101; and Bettie Monahan, interview 8566, vol. 64; all in Indian-Pioneer Papers, University of Oklahoma, Norman.

184. Mrs. C. T. Clay, interview 4045, vol. 18, Indian-Pioneer Papers, University of Oklahoma, Norman.

185. Sarah Cothern Molen, interview 9805, vol. 64, Indian-Pioneer Papers, University of Oklahoma, Norman.

186. Fannie Birdwell, interview 8360, vol. 8, Indian-Pioneer Papers, University of Oklahoma, Norman.

187. Webster, "Myth of Hardship," 28; and Parsons, "Women in Sunbonnets."

188. Kaiser and Knuth, "From Ithaca to Clatsop Plains," pt. 1, 261.

189. DeWitt and DeWitt, *Prairie Schooner Lady,* 76.

190. Ibid., 144.

191. Love, "Diary."

192. Catherine Jane Bell to Julia, 31 October 1859, Oroville, Calif., Bancroft Library, Berkeley, Calif.

193. Sawyer, "Overland to California."

194. Hunt, "By Ox Team to California," 11.
195. Rose, "Diary."
196. Dunham, *Across the Plains*, 4, 7.
197. Strahorn, *Fifteen Thousand Miles by Stage*, 1.
198. Caroline Phelps, "Diary" (1830–1860), Iowa State Historical Society, Iowa City.
199. Hilda Faunce, *Desert Wife* (Lincoln: University of Nebraska Press, 1981), 98–99, 118–19, 158–63, 183–85, 195, 279–80.
200. Myres, "Romance and Reality," 411, 413–14.
201. Robert C. Carriker and Eleanor R. Carriker, eds., *An Army Wife on the Frontier: The Memoirs of Alice Blackwood Baldwin, 1867–1877* (Salt Lake City: Tanner Trust Fund, University of Utah Library, 1975), 41, 78–79, 99, 109.
202. Vogdes, "Journal."
203. Catherine Jane Bell to Julia, 31 October 1859, Oroville, Calif., Bancroft Library, Berkeley, CA; and Norton, "Diary."
204. Susannah Willeford, "Henry County: On Immigration of Pioneers, 1820–1870," Iowa State Historical Society, Iowa City; Staples, "Reminiscences"; and Budlong, *Memories*, 8, 37–39.

Chapter 5

1. Haidi I. Hartmann, "The Family as the Locus of Gender, Class, and Political Struggle: The Example of Housework," *Signs: Journal of Women in Culture and Society* 6, no. 3 (1981): 366–94.
2. Dean L. May, *Three Frontiers: Family, Land, and Society in the American West, 1850–1900* (Cambridge, UK: Cambridge University Press, 1994), 33–35, 143–45, 270–80.
3. Thomas P. Kasulis, *Intimacy or Integrity: Philosophy and Cultural Difference* (Honolulu: University of Hawaii Press, 1992); and Dianne Hales, *Just Like a Woman: How Gender Science Is Redefining What Makes Us Female* (New York: Bantam Books, 1999), 239–78.
4. Leo M. Kaiser and Priscilla Knuth, eds., "From Ithaca to Clatsop Plains," *Oregon Historical Quarterly* 62 (1961): pt. 1, 237–87, and pt. 2, 337–402; and Lillian Schlissel, *Women's Diaries of the Westward Journey* (New York: Schocken Books, 1982), 14.
5. James Hewitt, ed., *Eye-Witnesses to Wagon Trains West* (New York: Charles Scribner's Sons, 1973), 10.
6. William Edmundson, "Diary Kept by William Edmundson, of Oskaloosa, while Crossing the Western Plains in 1850," *Annals of Iowa* 8 (October 1908), 516–35; and Mary Alice Shutes, "Diary" (1862), Division of Museum and Archives, Des Moines, Iowa.

7. Kitturah Penton Belknap, "Reminiscences" (1839), Iowa State Historical Society, Iowa City.

8. Schlissel, *Women's Diaries,* 111–14.

9. [A. W. Harlan], "Journal of A. W. Harlan While Crossing the Plains in 1850," *Annals of Iowa* 11 (April 1913): 32–62; H. C. Ambler, "West Virginia Forty-Niners," *West Virginia History* 3 (October–July 1941–42): 59–75; Helen S. Giffen, ed., *The Diaries of Peter Decker: Overland to California in 1849 and Life in the Mines, 1850–1851* (Georgetown, Calif.: Talisman Press, 1966), 129, 134–35, 183, 187–89; and Charles W. Martin, ed., "Joseph Warren Arnold's Journal of His Trip from Montana, 1864–1866," *Nebraska History* 55 (1974): 463–552.

10. Mary Burrell, "Diary of a Journey Overland from Council Bluffs to Green Valley, California, April 27 to September 1, 1854," Beinecke Collection, Yale University Library, New Haven, Conn.

11. Hales, *Just Like a Woman,* 72–73, 97–98; and David Peterson Del Mar, *Beaten Down: A History of Interpersonal Violence in the West* (Seattle: University of Washington Press, 2002), 46–68.

12. Schlissel, *Women's Diaries,* 14.

13. Harlan, "Journal," 32–62; Ambler, "West Virginia Forty-Niners," 59–75; Giffen, *Diaries of Peter Decker,* 129, 134–35, 183, 187–89; and Martin, "Joseph Warren Arnold's Journal," 463–552.

14. Harlan, "Journal," 141–62.

15. Helen Carpenter, "Diary" (1856), Huntington Library, San Marino, Calif.

16. Jerome Dutton, "Across the Plains," *Annals of Iowa* 9 (October 1910): 466.

17. Ibid., 447–83; Louise Barry, comp., "Charles Robinson—Yankee '49er: His Journey to California," *Kansas Historical Quarterly* 34, no. 2 (1968): 179, 186; Alonzo Delano, *Life on the Plains and among the Diggings* (Ann Arbor, Mich.: University Microfilms, 1966); Harlan, "Journal," 32–62; Georgia W. Read and Ruth Gaines, eds., *Gold Rush: The Journals, Drawings, and Other Papers of J. Goldsborough Bruff, April 2, 1849–June 20, 1851* (New York: Columbia University Press, 1949); James E. Potter, ed., "The Missouri River Journal of Leonard W. Gilchrist, 1866," *Nebraska History* 58 (1977): 275; David Morris Potter, *Trail to California: The Overland Journal of Vincent Geiger and Wakeman Bryarly* (New Haven, Conn.: Yale University Press, 1945); Byron N. McKinstry, *The California Gold Rush Overland Diary of Byron N. McKinstry* (Glendale, Calif.: Arthur H. Clark, 1975); James A. Pritchard, *The Overland Diary of James A. Pritchard* (Denver: Old West Publishing, 1959); Charles Glass Gray, "Diary" (1849–1850), Huntington Library, San Marino, Calif.; Howard Stansbury, *An Expedition to the Valley of the Great Salt Lake* (Ann Arbor, Mich.: University Microfilms, 1966); Fancher Stimson, "Overland Journey to California by Platte River Route and South Pass in 1850," *Annals of Iowa* 13 (October 1922): 403–40; Milo

M. Quaife, ed., *Across the Plains in Forty-Nine* (Chicago: Lakeside Press, 1948); Everett Walter and George B. Strother, eds., "The Gold Rush Diary of Henry Tappan," *Annals of Wyoming* 25 (July 1953): 113–39; and Walker D. Wyman, ed., *California Emigrant Letters* (New York: Bookman Association).

18. John O. Holzhueter, ed., "From Waupun to Sacramento in 1849: The Gold Rush Journal of Edwin Hillyer," *Wisconsin Magazine of History* 49 (1966): 222, 228.

19. Andrew F. Rolle, ed., *The Road to Virginia City: The Diary of James Knox Polk Miller* (Norman: University of Oklahoma Press, 1960), 66.

20. Elizabeth Page, ed., *Wagons West: A Story of the Oregon Trail* (New York: Farrar and Rinehart, 1930), 114.

21. Stansbury, *Expedition*, 44.

22. Quaife, *Across the Plains,* 105.

23. Walter and Strother, "Gold Rush Diary of Henry Tappan," 125.

24. Delano, *Life on the Plains,* 64.

25. Thomas D. Clark, *Gold Rush Diary: Being the Journal of Elisha Douglass Perkins on the Overland Trail in the Spring and Summer of 1849* (Lexington: University of Kentucky Press, 1967), 24.

26. Andrew J. Rotter, "'Matilda for Gods Sake Write': Women and Families on the Argonaut Mind," *California History* 58 (summer 1979): 128–41.

27. Alfred M. Doten, "My Adventures in the California Diggings," *Life* 46 (April 1927): 96.

28. Dutton, "Across the Plains," 464.

29. Giffen, *Diaries of Peter Decker,* 73.

30. E. Allene Dunham, *Across the Plains in a Covered Wagon* (N.p. [possibly Milton, Iowa]: N.p., [ca. 1920s]), 2, 5, 14; Eliza Ann Egbert, "Diary" (1852), Bancroft Library, Berkeley, Calif.; Jane Augusta Gould, "Diary" (1862), Iowa State Historical Society, Iowa City; Catherine M. Haun, "A Woman's Trip across the Plains" (1849), Huntington Library, San Marino, Calif.; Virginia W. Ivins, *Pen Pictures of Early Western Days* (Keokuk, Iowa: n.p., 1905); Sarah Welch Nossaman, "Pioneering at Bonaparte and Near Pella," *Annals of Iowa* 13 (October 1922): 441–53; Caroline Phelps, "Diary" (1830–1860), Iowa State Historical Society, Iowa City; Mary St. John, "Diary" (1858), Iowa State Historical Society, Iowa City. See also John Mack Faragher, *Women and Men on the Overland Trail* (New Haven, Conn.: Yale University Press, 1979), 121–33.

31. Haun, "Woman's Trip."

32. Belknap, "Reminiscences."

33. Ellen R. Fenn, "Sweepin' out the Fabled Ghosts," *The Iowan* 14 (fall 1965): 50.

34. Belknap, "Reminiscences."

35. Oscar O. Winther, ed., *To Oregon in 1852* (Indianapolis: Indiana Historical Society, 1964), 14.

36. Charles R. Berry, ed., "A Prospecting Trip to Idaho: The 1862 Diary of John Green Berry, Jr.," *Idaho Yesterdays* 24 (fall 1980): 18.

37. Shutes, "Diary"; and Haun, "Woman's Trip."

38. Mary Ellis to her mother and sister, 22 February 1857, and Sarah Kenyon to her mother-in-law and sister-in-law, 18 March 1860, Kenyon Family Letters, Iowa Historical Society, Iowa City.

39. McKinstry, *California Gold Rush Overland Diary,* 124–25.

40. Read and Gaines, *Gold Rush,* 31.

41. Harlan, "Journal," 45; and Hiram W. Studley, "Letter Describing a March to Utah in 1859," *Annals of Iowa* 13 (April 1923): 615.

42. Isaac Jones Wistar, *Autobiography of Isaac Jones Wistar, 1827–1905: Half a Century in War and Peace* (New York: Harper and Brothers, 1937), 57; and Francis C. Rosenberger, ed., *Journey to the Gold Fields of California, 1848–1850: The Diary of Zirkle D. Robinson* (Iowa City: Prairie Press, 1966), 5.

43. Truman W. Camp, ed., "The Journal of Joseph Camp, 1859," *Nebraska History* 46 (1965), 33.

44. Potter, "Missouri River Journal," 275.

45. Owen C. Coy, *The Great Trek* (Los Angeles: Powell Publishing, 1931), 250.

46. Studley, "Letter Describing a March," 615.

47. Raymond W. Settle, ed., *March of the Mounted Riflemen* (Glendale, Calif.: Arthur H. Clark, 1940), 83.

48. Richard F. Burton, *The City of Saints and across the Rocky Mountains to California* (New York: Alfred A. Knopf, 1963), 95.

49. Settle, *March of the Mounted Riflemen,* 87.

50. Merrill J. Mattes and Esley J. Kirk, eds., "From Ohio to California in 1849: The Gold Rush Journal of Elijah Bryan Faarnham," *Indiana Magazine of History* 46 (September–December 1950): 308.

51. Nancy B. Parker, ed., "Notes and Documents: Mirabeau B. Lamar's Texas Journal," *Southwestern Historical Quarterly* 84 (January 1981): 326.

52. Niles Searls, *The Diary of a Pioneer and Other Papers* (N.p., 1940), 20; Potter, "Missouri River Journal," 287; Holzhueter, "From Waupun to Sacramento," 224; and Edwin Bryant, *What I Saw in California* (Minneapolis: Ross and Haines, 1967), 10, 15.

53. Wistar, *Autobiography,* 80–81.

54. Barry, "Charles Robinson," 179, 186; Margaret S. Dart, ed., "Letters of a Yankee Forty-Niner," *The Yale Review* 36 (June 1947): 657–65; Delano, *Life on the Plains,* 165–70, 203, 211, 218–19, 273; Howard Egan, *Pioneering the West, 1846 to 1878* (Richmond, Utah: Howard R. Egan Estate, 1917): 23–24, 29; "Emigration from Iowa to Oregon in 1848," *Iowa Journal of History*

and Politics 10 (July 1912): 415–30; Gilbert Drake Harlan, ed., "The Diary of Wilson Barber Harlan," *Journal of the West* 3, no. 2 (1964): pt. 1: 148–53, 156–57; Holzhueter, "From Waupun to Sacramento," 219–31; David M. Kiefer, ed., "Over Barren Plains and Rock-Bound Mountains," *Montana, The Magazine of Western History* 22, no. 4 (1972): 16–29; Martin, "Joseph Warren Arnold's Journal," 530–35; Edward O. Parry, ed., "Observations on the Prairies: 1867," *Montana, The Magazine of Western History* 9 (1959): 25–28; Potter, "Missouri River Journal," 282–83, 286–87, 290, 293–94; Pritchard, "Overland Diary," 58, 109; and Gary C. Stein, ed., "Overland to California," *American History Illustrated* 12 (May 1977): 26–36.

55. Caspar Weaver Collins to His Mother, 20 September 1862, Collins Letters, Beinecke Collection, Yale University Library, New Haven, Conn.; Randolph B. Marcy, *Thirty Years of Army Life on the Border* (Philadelphia: J. B. Lippincott, 1963), 3, 13, 18, 25; and Reuben Gold Thwaite, ed., *Early Western Travels, 1748–1846* (Cleveland: Arthur H. Clark, 1906), 76–77.

56. Burton, *City of Saints,* 64–65.

57. Clark, *Gold Rush Diary,* 44; and Page, *Wagons West,* 114.

58. Parker, "Notes and Documents," 325.

59. Randolph B. Marcy, *The Prairie Traveler: A Handbook for Overland Expeditions* (New York: Harper, 1859), 200, 197.

60. Samuel P. Newcomb, "Diary" (1865), Barker Texas History Center, University of Texas, Austin; Egan, *Pioneering the West,* 174; Thomas D. Clark, ed., *Off at Sunrise: The Overland Journal of Charles Glass Gray* (San Marino, Calif.: Huntington Library, 1976), 78; J. F. Triplett, "The Scout's Story: From the Journal of a Cattleman," *Atlantic Monthly* 135 (April 1925): 493–95; Bryant, *What I Saw in California,* 9; Page, *Wagons West,* 131, 181; Eugene Roseboom, ed., "Charles Tinker's Journal: A Trip to California in 1849," *Ohio State Archeological and Historical Quarterly* 61 (January 1952): 80–81.

61. Wistar, *Autobiography,* 103.

62. Mrs. H. T. Clarke, "A Young Woman's Sights on the Emigrant's Trail" (Salem, Oregon, 1878), Bancroft Library, Berkeley, Calif.; Mrs. B. G. Ferris, *The Mormons at Home* (New York: Dix and Edwards, 1856), 22–24; Lodisa Frizzell, *Across the Plains to California in 1852* (New York: New York Public Library, 1915), 25; Emma S. Hill, *A Dangerous Crossing and What Happened on the Other Side: Seven Lean Years* (Denver, Colo.: Bradford Robinson, 1924), 82; Esther B. Hanna, "Journal" (1852), Bancroft Library, Berkeley, Calif.; Susan S. Magoffin, *Down the Santa Fe Trail and into Mexico: The Diary of Susan Shelby Magoffin, 1846–1847* (New Haven, Conn.: Yale University Press, 1926), 68; Malvina V. Manning, "Diary" (1862), Bancroft Library, Berkeley, Calif.; Lucene Pfeiffer Parsons, "The Women in the Sunbonnets" (1850), Stanford University Library, Stanford, Calif.; and Juliette Fish Walker, "Crossing the Plains," *Noticas* 16 (1970), 4.

63. Mary Stuart Bailey, "A Journal of the Overland Trip from Ohio to California" (1852), Huntington Library, San Marino, Calif.; Carpenter, "Diary"; Mary C. Fish, "Across the Plaines in 1860," Bancroft Library, Berkeley, Calif.; Mary Jane Guill, "The Overland Diary of a Journey from Livingston County, Missouri, to Butte County, California, May 5 to September 5, 1860," California State Library, Sacramento; Helen Marnie Stewart Love, "Diary" (1853), Huntington Library, San Marino, Calif.; Ada Millington, "Journal Kept while Crossing the Plains" (1862), Bancroft Library, Berkeley, Calif.; Martha Ann Minto, "Female Pioneering in Oregon" (1849), Bancroft Library, Berkeley, Calif.; Maria J. Norton, "Diary of a Trip across the Plains in '59," Bancroft Library, Berkeley, Calif.; Caroline L. Richardson, "Journal" (1856), Bancroft Library, Berkeley, Calif.; and Mary F. H. Sandford, "A Trip across the Plains" (1853), California State Library, Sacramento.

64. Barry, "Charles Robinson," 179–88; Camp, "Journal," 32–35; Harlan, "Journal," 51; Kiefer, "Over Barren Plains," 18–21; Martin, "Joseph Warren Arnold's Journal," 472–77; Mattes and Kirk, "From Ohio to California," 300–301, 307–8; McKinstry, *California Gold Rush Overland Diary,* 223–24; Potter, "Missouri River Journal," 291; Pritchard, *Overland Diary,* 73, 96–98; Settle, *March of the Mounted Riflemen,* 40–43, 56–57, 60–61, 72–73, 82–89, 114–15, 150–53, 160–61, 188–91, 202–5, 210–11, 221–24, 229–33, 236, 240–43, 247–55, 262–65, 280–81, 300–301, 306–15, 320–21, 338–39; and Burton J. Williams, ed., "Overland to the Gold Fields of California in 1850: The Journal of Calvin Taylor," *Nebraska History* 50 (1969): 142–45.

65. Eleazar S. Ingalls, *Journal of a Trip to California by the Overland Route across the Plains in 1850–51* (Fairfield, Wash.: Ye Galleon Press, 1979), 32; Rolle, *Road to Virginia City,* 21; Shirley Sargent, ed., *Seeking the Elephant: James Mason Hutchings' Journal of His Overland Trek to California* (Glendale, Calif.: Arthur H. Clark, 1980), 119; Searls, *Diary of a Pioneer,* 33; Kiefer, "Over Barren Plains," 18; and Rev. Samuel Parker, *Journal of an Exploring Tour* (Minneapolis, Minn.: Ross and Haines, 1967), 35.

66. Rolle, *Road to Virginia City,* 125.

67. Potter, *Trail to California,* 77.

68. Settle, *March of the Mounted Riflemen,* 88.

69. Delano, *Life on the Plains,* 316.

70. Stafford, *March of Empire,* 88.

71. Potter, "Missouri River Journal," 291; J. William Barrett, *The Overland Journal of Amos Piatt Josselyn: Zanesville, Ohio to the Sacramento Valley April 2, 1849 to September 11, 1849* (Baltimore, Md.: Gateway Press, 1978), 55; Pritchard, *Overland Diary,* 73; and McKinstry, *California Gold Rush Overland Diary,* 73.

72. Burton, *City of Saints,* 90; McKinstry, *California Gold Rush Overland Dairy,*

223–24, and John S. Wright, *Letters from the West; or, a Caution to Emigrants* (Ann Arbor, Mich.: University Microfilms, 1966), 29.

73. Potter, *Trail to California,* 127.

74. Parker, *Journal of an Exploring Tour,* 53.

75. Potter, "Missouri River Journal," 276.

76. Barry, "Charles Robinson," 34.

77. Parker, *Journal of an Exploring Tour,* 35.

78. Bryant, *What I Saw in California,* 154; and Kiefer, "Over Barren Plains."

79. Clark, *Gold Rush Diary,* 184.

80. Caspar Collins to His Mother, 20 September 1862, Collins Letters; Coy, *Great Trek,* 126–27; Bryant, *What I Saw in California,* 52–53; and Harold F. Taggart, ed., "The Journal of David Jackson Staples," *California Historical Society Quarterly* 22 (June 1943): 119–47.

81. Harlan, "Journal," 57.

82. Lafayette Spencer, "Journal of the Oregon Trail," *Annals of Iowa* 8 (January 1908): 304–10; Mattes and Kirk, "From Ohio to California," 437–68; Parker, "Notes and Documents," 309–30; Wistar, *Autobiography,* 50, 67, 80–81, 101, 219, 221; and M. M. Hoffman, "The First Gazetteer on Iowa," *Annals of Iowa* 17 (July 1932): 383–90.

83. Page, *Wagons West,* 128, 165–66, 237.

84. Ingalls, *Journal of a Trip,* 50; Giffen, *Diaries of Peter Decker,* 131; and Quaife, *Across the Plains,* 119–24.

85. Wistar, *Autobiography,* 67; Clark, *Gold Rush Diary,* 22, 25; Jacob H. Schiel, *Journey through the Rocky Mountains and the Humboldt Mountains to the Pacific Ocean* (Norman: University of Oklahoma Press, 1959), 18–19; W. W. Chapman, "W. W. Chapman's Diary," *Wyoming State Historian Quarterly Bulletin* 1 (15 September 1923): 9; Wyman, *California Emigrant Letters,* 103.

86. Thwaite, *Early Western Travels,* 152–53; Sargent, *Seeking the Elephant,* 125; and Holzhueter, "From Waupun to Sacramento," 229.

87. Delano, *Life on the Plains,* 145.

88. Stansbury, *Expedition,* 254–57.

89. Quaife, *Across the Plains,* 88–89.

90. Although most of the male sources examined showed evidence of little or no change in attitudes toward Indians, especially good examples are Elisha Brooks, *A Pioneer Mother of California* (San Francisco: Harr Wagner Publishing, 1922); James Enos, "Recollections" (ca. 1892), Newberry Library, Chicago, Ill.; Gray, "Diary"; Marcy, *Thirty Years;* Stansbury, *Expedition;* and Quaife, *Across the Plains.* See McKinstry, *California Gold Rush Overland Diary,* 92–94, 96–101, for a male emigrant who realized that the men's adversary stance was frequently unnecessary and even humorous. For a discussion of white Americans' views of American Indians during the nineteenth century, see Alden T. Vaughan, "From White Man

to Redskin: Changing Anglo-American Perceptions of the American Indian," *American Historical Review* 87 (October 1982): 917–53.

91. Krista Comer, *Landscapes in the New West: Gender and Geography in Contemporary Women's Writing* (Chapel Hill: University of North Carolina Press, 1999), 2–23; and Frank Van Nuys, *Americanizing the West: Race, Immigrants, and Citizenship, 1890–1930* (Lawrence: University of Kansas Press, 2002), 9–13.

92. Delano, *Life on the Plains,* 309, 319–20.

93. Egan, *Pioneering the West,* 185.

94. Michael J. Brodhead and John D. Unruh, Jr., eds., "Isaiah Harris' Minutes of a Trip to Kansas Territory in 1855," *Kansas Historical Quarterly* 35 (1969): 373–85; Louise Barry, ed., "Scenes In (And En Route To) Kansas Territory, Autumn, 1854: Five Letters by William H. Hutter," *Kansas Historical Quarterly* 35, 3 (1969): 312–36; Parker, *Journal of an Exploring Tour;* LeRoy R. and Ann W. Hafen, eds., *To the Rockies and Oregon, 1839–1842,* vol. 3 (Glendale, Calif.: Arthur H. Clark, 1955); and Burton, *City of Saints.*

95. Winther, *To Oregon,* 12.

96. Parry, "Observations," 27.

97. John T. Dilworth to His Uncles, 30 March 1851, Bringhurst Family Letters, Beinecke Collection, Yale University Library, New Haven, Conn.

98. Laura Ingalls Wilder, *The First Four Years* (New York: Harper & Row, 1971), 33; and Egbert, "Diary."

99. Barbara B. Zimmerman and Vernon Carstensen, eds., "Pioneer Woman in Southwestern Washington Territory. The Recollections of Susanna Maria Slover McFarland Price Ede," *Pacific Northwest Quarterly* 66–67, 4 (1976): 143, 147.

100. Lavinia H. Porter, *By Ox Team to California: A Narrative of Crossing the Plains in 1860* (Oakland, Calif.: Oakland Enquirer Publishing, 1910), 56.

101. Burrell, "Diary"; and Barsina French, "Journal of a Wagon Trip" (1867), Huntington Library, San Marino, Calif.

102. Christiane Fischer, "A Profile of Women in Arizona in Frontier Days," *Journal of the West* 16 (July 1977): 43.

103. Mary Ann Ferrin Davidson, "An Autobiography and a Reminiscence," *Annals of Iowa* 37 (spring 1964): 256.

104. Susie P. Van de Wiele, "Travels and Experiences in America with Army and Indian Reminiscences," Graff Collection, Newberry Library, Chicago, Ill.

105. Porter, *By Ox Team to California,* 67, 79.

106. Burrell, "Diary"; and Porter, *By Ox Team to California,* 34, 67.

107. Schlissel, *Women's Diaries,* 154.

108. Sarah J. Cummins, *Autobiography and Reminiscences* (La Grande, Oreg.: La Grande Printing, 1914), 42; Mary Saunders, "The Whitman Massacre; A True Story by a Survivor of This Terrible Tragedy which Took Place in

Oregon in 1847," Bancroft Library, Berkeley, Calif.; Almira Neff Beam Enos, "Journal" (1858–1866), Bancroft Library, Berkeley, Calif.; Mrs. M. S. Hockensmith, "Diary of a Trip Overland from the Mississippi to California" (1866), Bancroft Library, Berkeley, Calif.; Julia L. Hare, "Reminiscences" (n.d.), California State Library, Sacramento; Mary E. Hopping, "Incidents of Pioneer Life as I Remember and as I Have Been Told" (1962), California State Library, Sacramento; Margaret A. Frink, *Journal of the Adventures of a Party of California Gold-Seekers* (Oakland, Calif.: N.p., 1897), 46; Louisa Miller Rahm, "Diary" (1862), Bancroft Library, Berkeley, Calif.; Frances H. Sawyer, "Overland to California" (1852), Bancroft Library, Berkeley, Calif.; Guill, "Overland Diary"; Catherine Amanda Stansbury Washburn, "Journal, 1853, from Iowa to Oregon Territory," Huntington Library, San Marino, Calif.; Harriet Bunyard, "Diary of a Young Girl," (1868), Huntington Library, San Marino, Calif., 117, 121; Celinda E. Hines Shipley, "Diary" (1853), Beinecke Collection, Yale University, New Haven, Conn.; Elizabeth J. Goltra, "Journal" (1853), Bancroft Library, Berkeley, Calif.; and Miriam D. Colt, *Went to Kansas; Being a Thrilling Account of an Ill-Fated Expedition* (Watertown, N.Y.: L. Ingalls, 1862), 125.

109. Colt, *Went to Kansas*, 125.

110. Martha M. Moore, "Journal of a Trip to California in 1860," Beinecke Collection, Yale University Library, New Haven, Conn.

111. Fleming Fraker, Jr., ed., "To Pike's Peak by Ox Wagon: The Harriet A. Smith Day-Book," *Annals of Iowa* 35 (fall 1959): 138; Martha M. Morgan, *A Trip across the Plains in the Year 1849* (San Francisco: Pioneer Press, 1864), 7, 12, 15–16; Ellen McGowan Biddle, *Reminiscences of a Soldier's Wife* (Philadelphia: J. B. Lippincott, 1907); Mrs. Edward Dyer, "Diary" (1860), Barker Texas History Center, University of Texas, Austin.

112. Cynthia J. Capron, "Life in the Army," *Journal of the Illinois State Historical Society* 13 (October 1920): 369.

113. Egbert, "Diary."

114. Ferris, *Mormons at Home*, 63.

115. Mary A. Hodgson, "The Life of a Pioneer Family" (1922), California State Library, Sacramento; and Biddle, *Reminiscences*, 83.

116. Lucy Rutledge Cooke, *Covered Wagon Days: Crossing the Plains in 1852* (Modesto, Calif.: Privately published, 1923), 66.

117. Sandra L. Myres, ed., *Cavalry Wife: The Diary of Eveline M. Alexander, 1866–1867* (College Station: Texas A. & M. University Press, 1977), 38, 102.

118. Ada Adelaide Vogdes, "Journal" (1866–1872), Huntington Library, San Marino, Calif.

119. Catherine M. Haun, "A Woman's Trip across the Plains" (1849), Huntington Library, San Marino, Calif.

120. Katherine Dunlap, "Journal" (1864), Bancroft Library, Berkeley, Calif.

121. Scott Derks, ed., *The Value of a Dollar: Prices and Incomes in the United States, 1860–1989* (Detroit: Gale Research, 1994), 11.

122. Frink, *Journal,* 68, 77; Guill, "Overland Diary"; Kate Roberts Pelissier, "Reminiscences of a Pioneer Mother," *North Dakota History* 24 (July 1957): 131; Morgan, *Trip across the Plains,* 15–16; Washburn, "Journal"; Hopping, "Incidents of Pioneer Life"; Bryant, *What I Saw in California,* 166; Settle, *March of the Mounted Riflemen,* 223; Pritchard, *Overland Journal,* 104; G. T. Byron, "The Overland Emigrant," *Cornhill* 65 (June 1892): 643–44; Page, *Wagons West,* 115; Dale Morgan, ed., *Overland in 1846: Diaries and Letters of the California-Oregon Trail* (Georgetown, Calif.: Talisman Press, 1963), 96; Clark, *Gold Rush Diary,* 101; Giffen, *Diaries of Peter Decker,* 72; Potter, *Trail to California,* 138, 152; and Ambler, "West Virginia Forty-Niners," 59–75. Differences in men's and women's trade interests can be seen by comparing Dutton, "Across the Plains," 468–69; Egan, *Pioneering the West,* 47; Pritchard, *Overland Journal,* 104; Thwaite, *Early Western Travels,* 145, 149; with Cooke, *Covered Wagon Days,* 66; Guill, "Overland Diary"; Hopping, "Incidents of Pioneer Life"; Rahm, "Diary"; and Vogdes, "Journal."

123. Maggie Hall, "The Story of Maggie Hall," Bancroft Library, Berkeley, Calif.; Elizabeth L. Lord, *Reminiscences of Eastern Oregon* (Portland, Oreg.: Irwin-Hodson, 1903), 68–69; Charlotte Stearns Pengra, "Diary" (1853), Huntington Library, San Marino, Calif.; and John D. Unruh, *Plains Across: The Overland Emigrants and the Trans-Mississippi West, 1840–1860* (Urbana: University of Illinois Press, 1979), 157.

124. Unruh, *Plains Across,* 166.

125. Carpenter, "Diary"; Unruh, *Plains Across,* 157; Frink, *Journal,* 72; Bunyard, "Diary," 121; French, "Journal"; and Mrs. Nicholas H. Karchner, "Diary" (1862), California State Library, Sacramento.

126. Abby E. Fulkerth, "Diary of Overland Journey of William L. Fulkerth and Wife from Iowa to California in 1863," Bancroft Library, Berkeley, Calif.; Unruh, *Plains Across,* 159; and Lord, *Reminiscences,* 86.

127. Kaiser and Knuth, "From Ithaca to Clatsop Plains," pt. 1, 255; Unruh, *Plains Across,* 163; Caroline D. Budlong, *Memories: Pioneer Days in Oregon and Washington* (Eugene, Oreg.: Picture Press, 1949), 4; Sandford, "Trip across the Plains"; and Barrett, *Overland Journal,* 20.

128. Sanford, "Trip across the Plains"; French, "Journal"; and Unruh, *Plains Across,* 158.

129. Unruh, *Plains Across,* 158.

130. Mary E. Ackley, *Crossing the Plains and Early Days in California* (San Francisco: Privately printed, 1928), 66.

131. Budlong, *Memories,* 38; Nannie T. Alderson, *A Bride Goes West* (Lincoln:

University of Nebraska Press, 1969), 186; Fraker, "To Pike's Peak," 137; Hodgson, "Life of a Pioneer Family"; Albert L. Hurtado, "'Hardly a Farmhouse—A Kitchen without Them': Indian and White Households on the California Borderland Frontier in 1860," *Western Historical Quarterly* 14 (July 1982): 245–70.

132. Alderson, *Bride Goes West,* 131; and Phelps, "Diary."

133. Sandra L. Myres, ed., "Evy Alexander: The Colonel's Lady at Ft. McDowell," *Montana, The Magazine of Western History* 24 (1974): 32; and Laura Stoler, *Race and the Education of Desire: Foucault's History of Sexuality and the Colonial Order of Things* (Durham, N.C.: Duke University Press, 1995), 156–58.

134. Anna Davin, "Imperialism and Motherhood," 152–62, in *Tensions of Empire: Colonial Cultures in a Bourgeois World,* ed. Frederick Cooper and Ann Laura Stoler (Berkeley: University of California Press, 1997).

135. Alderson, *Bride Goes West,* 132, 136.

136. Phelps, "Diary."

137. Sarah McAllister Hartman, "Reminiscences of Early Days on Puget Sound, the Friendliness of the Local Indians, and Experiences during the Indian War of 1855" (n.d.), Beinecke Collection, Yale University Library, New Haven Conn.

138. Rachel E. Wright, "The Early Upper Napa Valley" (1928), Bancroft Library, Berkeley, Calif.

139. Frizzell, *Across the Plains,* 25.

140. Manning, "Diary."

141. Ferris, *Mormons at Home,* 24.

142. Louise Sophia Gellhorn Boylan, "My Life Story: Reminiscences of German Settlers in Hardin County, 1867–1883," Iowa State Historical Society, Iowa City.

143. Edna Hunt Osborne, interview 7387, vol. 68, Indian-Pioneer Papers, University of Oklahoma, Norman.

144. Ruth Spack, *America's Second Tongue: American Indian Education and the Ownership of English, 1860–1900* (Lincoln: University of Nebraska Press, 2002), 109–42.

145. Gayatri Chakravorty Spivak, "Subaltern Studies: Deconstructing Historiography," in *Selected Subaltern Studies,* ed. Ranajit Guha and Gayatri Chakravorty Spivak (New York: Oxford University Press, 1988), 5–15; Spivak, *A Critique of Postcolonial Reason: Toward a History of the Vanishing Present* (Cambridge, Mass.: Harvard University Press, 1999), 67–68, 102–4, 269–73; and Edward Schieffelin and Robert Crittenden, "Remembering First Contact: Realities and Romance," 133–51, in *Remembrance of Pacific Pasts: An Invitation to Remake History,* ed. Robert Borofsky (Honolulu: University of Hawaii Press, 2000).

146. Robert C. Carriker and Eleanor R. Carriker, eds., *An Army Wife on the Frontier: The Memoirs of Alice Blackwood Baldwin, 1867–1877* (Salt Lake City: Tanner Trust Fund, University of Utah Library, 1975), 79, 99–100.

147. Eliza R. Snow, "Sketch of My Life" (1885), Bancroft Library, Berkeley, Calif.

148. Belle M. Yates, interview 12817, vol. 101;; Bertha Brewer Plummer, interview 4833, vol. 72; Fannie Birdwell, interview 8360, vol. 8, all in Indian-Pioneer Papers, University of Oklahoma, Norman; Dan McAllister, "Pioneer Woman," *New Mexico Historical Review* 34, no. 3 (July 1959): 162.

149. Clarke, "Young Woman's Sights."

150. Jean Webster, "The Myth of Hardship on the Oregon Trail," *Reed College Bulletin* 24 (January 1946): 37; and Hodgson, "The Life of a Pioneer Family"; Lorene Millhollen, interview 8957, vol. 63, Indian-Pioneer Papers, University of Oklahoma, Norman.

151. Leola Lehman, "Life in the Territories," *Chronicles of Oklahoma* 41 (fall 1963): 373–75.

152. John F. Moffitt and Santiago Sebastián, *O Brave New People: The European Invention of the American Indian* (Albuquerque: University of New Mexico Press, 1996), 302–17; and Fergus M. Bordewich, *Killing the White Man's Indian* (New York: Random House, 1997), 50–55.

153. Lehman, "Life in the Territories," 375; Carol Douglas Sparks, "The Land Incarnate: Navajo Women and the Dialogue of Colonialism, 1821–1870," 138–39, in *Negotiators of Change: Historical Perspectives on Native American Women,* ed. Nancy Shoemaker (New York: Routledge, 1995); and Lavonee Brown Ruoff, "Reversing the Gaze: Early Native American Images of Europeans and Euro-Americans," 198–223, in *Native American Representations: First Encounters, Distorted Images, and Literary Appropriations,* ed. Gretchen M. Bataille (Lincoln: University of Nebraska Press, 2001).

154. Emma Brown, interview 8543, vol. 12; Emma Clayton, interview 9672, vol. 18; Matilda Clure, interview 4673, vol. 18; all in Indian-Pioneer Papers, University of Oklahoma, Norman.

155. Phelps, "Diary."

156. Mrs. John Barnes, interview 9735, vol. 5, Indian-Pioneer Papers, University of Oklahoma, Norman.

157. Hopping, "Incidents of Pioneer Life"; and Egbert, "Diary."

158. Phelps, "Diary"; Edna Hunt Osborne, interview 7387; Katherine Provost, interview 1419, vol. 73, Indian-Pioneer Papers, University of Oklahoma, Norman; Frances Jeannette Wynen, interview 12798, vol. 101, Indian-Pioneer Papers, University of Oklahoma, Norman; Lucy J. Auldridge, interview 5776, Indian-Pioneer Papers, University of Oklahoma, Norman; Fannie J. Bell, no interview number, vol. 7, Indian-Pioneer Papers, University of Oklahoma, Norman; Plummer, interview 4833.

159. James C. Scott, *Domination and the Arts of Resistance: Hidden Transcripts* (New Haven, Conn.: Yale University Press, 1990), 45–50, 103–7, 156–82.

160. Christiane Fischer, ed., *Let Them Speak for Themselves: Women in the American West, 1849–1900* (Hamden, Conn.: Archon Press, 1977), 146.

161. Mrs. C. C. Clements, interview 9044, vol. 18, Indian-Pioneer Papers, University of Oklahoma, Norman; Lois Smith Brown, interview 4496, vol. 12, Indian-Pioneer Papers, University of Oklahoma, Norman; Loretta C. Morgan, interview 6085, vol. 64, Indian-Pioneer Papers, University of Oklahoma, Norman; Alderson, *Bride Goes West,* 135–36; and Phelps, "Diary." See also Scott, *Domination and the Arts of Resistance.*

162. Fulkerth, "Diary"; and Van de Wiele, "Travels and Experiences," 17.

163. Eliza Spalding Warren, *Memoirs of the West: The Spaldings* (Portland, Oreg.: March Printing, 1916), 20–21.

164. Elizabeth Furniss, *The Burden of History: Colonialism and the Frontier Myth in a Rural Canadian Community* (Vancouver: University of British Columbia Press, 1999), 16–22, 171–72.

165. Laura W. Johnson, *Eight Hundred Miles in an Ambulance* (Philadelphia: J. B. Lippincott, 1889), 61–65.

166. Biddle, *Reminiscences,* 227.

167. Carpenter, "Dairy."

168. Fischer, *Let Them Speak for Themselves,* 146.

169. Hill, *Dangerous Crossing,* 84.

170. Johnson, *Eight Hundred Miles,* 72, 79.

171. DeWitt and DeWitt, *Prairie Schooner Lady,* 78.

172. Nancy C. Pruitt, interview 7855, vol. 73, Indian-Pioneer Papers, University of Oklahoma, Norman.

173. Phelps, "Diary"; Hartman, "Reminiscences"; and Alderson, *Bride Goes West,* 91.

174. Eileen Pollack, *Woman Walking Ahead: In Search of Catherine Weldon and Sitting Bull* (Albuquerque: University of New Mexico Press, 2002).

175. Gary B. Nash, "The Hidden History of Mestizo America," 10–31 in *Sex, Love, Race: Crossing Boundaries in North American History,* ed. Martha Hodes (New York: New York University Press, 1999).

176. Kay Graber, ed., *Sister to the Sioux: The Memoirs of Elaine Goodale Eastman* (Lincoln: University of Nebraska Press, 1978), xi–xii, 172–75; and Emily McCowen Horton, *My Scrap-book* (Seattle, Wash.: N.p., 1927), 17.

177. Mrs. John Barnes, interview 9735.

178. Mrs. William N. Moore, interview 7365, vol. 64; Emma Jean Ross Overstreet, interview 7240, vol. 68; Sarah Scott Phillips, interview 6251, vol. 71; Mrs. J. B. Antics, interview 4163, vol. 2; Harriet Gibbons Oakes, interview 12028, vol. 68; all in Indian-Pioneer Papers, University of Oklahoma, Norman.

179. Devon A. Mihesuah, *American Indians: Stereotypes and Realities* (Atlanta, Ga.: Clarity Press, 1996), 103–6; and Bordewich, *Killing the White Man's Indian,* 67–74.

180. K. Anthony Appiah and Amy Gutman, *Color Conscious: The Political Morality of Race* (Princeton, N.J.: Princeton University Press, 1996), 30–40; and Melissa L. Meyer, "American Indian Blood Quantum Requirements: Blood is Thicker than Family," 231–49, in *Over the Edge: Remapping the American West,* ed. Valerie J. Matsumoto and Blake Allmendinger (Berkeley: University of California Press, 1997). For insight into the practices of other white nations, see Ann Laura Stoler, "Sexual Affronts and Racial Frontiers: European Identities and the Cultural Politics of Exclusion in Colonial Southeast Asia," 198–237, in *Tensions of Empire: Colonial Cultures in a Bourgeois World,* ed. Frederick Cooper and Ann Laura Stoler (Berkeley: University of California Press, 1997).

181. Mrs. B. M. Austin, interview 9189, Indian-Pioneer Papers, University of Oklahoma, Norman.

182. Mrs. Bill Moncrief, interview 4189, vol. 64, Indian-Pioneer Papers, University of Oklahoma, Norman.

183. Alice Parker, interview 4021, vol. 69, Indian-Pioneer Papers, University of Oklahoma, Norman. 184; and Peggy Pascoe, "Race, Gender, and the Privileges of Property: On the Significance of Miscegenation Law in the United States," 215–30, in *Over the Edge: Remapping the American West,* ed. Valerie J. Matsumoto and Blake Allmendinger (Berkeley: University of California Press, 1997).

184. Mollie Beaver, interview 9409, vol. 6, Indian-Pioneer Papers, University of Oklahoma, Norman.

185. Carriker and Carriker, *Army Wife,* 108.

186. Hartman, "Reminiscences."

187. John Brenkman, *Culture and Domination* (Ithaca, N.Y.: Cornell University Press, 1987), 184–227.

188. Dawn L. Gherman, "From Parlor to Tepee: The White Squaw on the American Frontier" (Ph.D. diss., University of Massachusetts, 1975), 216–19.

189. S. Elizabeth Bird, "Savage Desires: The Gendered Construction of the American Indian in Popular Media," 69–74, in *Selling the Indian: Commercializing and Appropriating American Indian Cultures,* ed. Carter Jones Meyer and Diana Royer (Tucson: University of Arizona Press, 2001).

190. Sander L. Gilman, *Difference and Pathology: Stereotypes of Sexuality, Race, and Madness* (Ithaca, N.Y.: Cornell University Press, 1985), 24–25.

191. Pauline Kael, "Americana: Tell Them Willie Boy is Here," 163–65, in *The Pretend Indians: Images of Native Americans in the Movies,* by Gretchen M. Bataille and Charles P. Silet (Ames: Iowa State University Press, 1980).

192. Alden T. Vaughan and Daniel K. Richter, "Crossing the Cultural Divide: Indians and New Englanders, 1605–1763," *Proceedings of the American Antiquarian Society* 90, pt. 1 (Worcester, Mass: American Antiquarian Society, 1980): 55–57.

193. Susan Armitage, "Women's Literature and the American Frontier: A New Perspective on the Frontier Myth," in *Women, Women Writers, and the West,* ed. L. L. Lee and Merrill Lewis (Troy, N.Y.: Whitson, 1979), 7.

194. Fanny Wiggins Kelley, "To the Senators and Members of the House of Representatives of Congress" (undated broadside), Graff Collection, Newberry Library, Chicago, Ill.

195. Rosita Rodriges to Her Father, 15 January 1846, Brazos River, Robertson County, Texas, 1846, Barker Texas History Center, University of Texas, Austin; Emma Polk, "Reminiscence" (n.d.), Iowa State Historical Society, Iowa City; and Martha V. Webster Simmons, "The Webster Massacre" (1925), Barker Texas History Center, University of Texas, Austin.

196. Margaret Schmidt Hacker, *Cynthia Ann Parker: The Life and the Legend* (El Paso: Texas Western Press, 1990), 3–11, 31–41.

197. Parrish, "Westward in 1850."

198. Ibid.; and Dorothy M. Johnson, "Lost Sister," in *Mid-Century, An Anthology of Distinguished Contemporary Short Stories,* ed. Orville Prescott (New York: Washington Square Press, 1973), 11–12.

199. Bunyard, "Diary."

200. Aunt Friendly, *The Children on the Plains* (New York: Robert Carter, 1864), 9–10, 101–16.

201. G. M. Brady, "The Story of Little Silver Hair," *Manuscripts* 28, no. 4 (1976): 294, 299.

202. Warren, *Memoirs of the West,* 31; and Saunders, "Whitman Massacre."

203. Polly Jane Purcell, "Autobiography and Reminiscence of a Pioneer," Graff Collection, Newberry Library, Chicago, Ill.; Matilda S. J. Delaney, *A Survivor's Recollections of the Whitman Massacre* (Spokane, Wash.: Esther Reed Chapter, D.A.R., 1920), 45; and Abigail Smith to My Dear Friend & Sister in Christ, 7 January 1856, Oregon Territory, Beinecke Collection, Yale University Library, New Haven, Conn.

204. Delaney, *Survivor's Recollections,* 45.

205. For another view, see June Namias, *White Captives and Ethnicity on the American Frontier* (Chapel Hill: University of North Carolina Press, 1993).

206. Mary Butler Renville, *A Thrilling Narrative of Indian Captivity* (Minneapolis: Atlas Co., 1863), 19, 43–44.

207. Wilhelmina B. Carrigan, *Captured by the Indians: Reminiscences of Pioneer Life in Minnesota* (Forest City, S.D.: Forest City Press, 1907), 11, 15–16.

208. Ibid., 3–7.

209. Ruth S. Thompson, "The Tragedy of Legion Valley" (1928), Bancroft

Library, Berkeley, Calif.

210. Mrs. J. D. Bell, "A True Story of My Capture by, and Life with the Comanche Indians" (1942), Barker Texas History Center, University of Texas, Austin.

211. Ibid.

Chapter 6

1. Sucheng Chan, Douglas Henry Daniels, Mario T. Garcia, and Terry P. Wildon, eds., *Peoples of Color in the American West* (Lexington, Mass.: D. C. Heath, 1994). Also helpful is Frank Van Nuys, *Americanizing the West: Race, Immigrants, and Citizenship, 1890–1930* (Lawrence: University Press of Kansas, 2002).

2. Lynee Chun Ink, "Decolonizing the Tropics: Gender and American Imperialism in the Pacific and Caribbean" (Ph.D. diss, University of Miami [Florida], 2001).

3. Glenda Riley, *Women and Nature: Saving the "Wild" West* (Lincoln: University of Nebraska Press, 1999), 65–66.

4. Frances C. Carrington, *My Army Life and the Fort Phil Kearney Massacre* (Freeport, N.Y.: Books for Libraries Press, 1971), 45.

5. Allie B. Busby, *Two Summers among the Musquakies* (Vinton, Iowa: Herald Book and Job Rooms, 1886), 19; and Lois L. Murray, *Incidents of Frontier Life* (Goshen, Ind.: Evangelical United Mennonite Publishing, 1880), 92.

6. Susannah Willeford, "Henry County: On Immigration of Pioneers, 1820–1870," Iowa State Historical Society, Iowa City; and Mallie Stafford, *The March of Empire through Three Decades* (San Francisco: George Spaulding, 1884), 118, 171.

7 Frances M. A. Roe, *Army Letters from an Officer's Wife, 1871–1888* (New York: D. Appleton, 1909), 10, 96–97.

8. Leo M. Kaiser and Priscilla Knuth, eds., "From Ithaca to Clatsop Plains," *Oregon Historical Quarterly* 62 (1961): pt. 2: 391; Katherine Dunlap, "Journal" (1864), Bancroft Library, Berkeley, Calif.; Margaret E. Archer Murray, "Memoir of the William Archer Family," pt. 1, *Annals of Iowa* 39 (summer 1968): 368.

9. Sarah R. Herndon, *Days of the Road: Crossing the Plains in 1865* (New York: Burr Printing, House, 1902), 132.

10. Ada Adelaide Vogdes, "Journal" (1866–1872), Huntington Library, San Marino, Calif.

11. Murray, *Incidents of Frontier Life,* 92.

12. Riley, *Women and Nature,* 2–5, 188.

13. Virginia W. Ivins, *Pen Pictures of Early Western Days* (Keokuk, Iowa: n.p.,

1905), 43–44;, and Carrie A. Strahorn, *Fifteen Thousand Miles by Stage* (New York: G. P. Putnam's Sons, 1911), 316.

14. Busby, *Two Summers,* 19.

15. Kate McDaniel Furness, "From Prairie to Pacific" (1853), California State Library, Sacramento.

16. Mary Murphy, "Making Men in the West: The Coming of Age of Miles Cavanaugh and Martin Frank Dunham," 133–71, in *Over the Edge: Remapping the American West,* ed. Valerie J. Matsumoto and Blake Allmendinger (Berkeley: University of California Press, 1997). Also helpful is Gail Bederman, *Manliness and Civilization: A Cultural History of Race and Gender in the United States, 1880–1917* (Chicago: University of Chicago Press, 1995).

17. Caroline D. Budlong, *Memories: Pioneer Days in Oregon and Washington* (Eugene, Oreg.: Picture Press, 1949), 39; Miriam D. Colt, *Went to Kansas; Being a Thrilling Account of an Ill-Fated Expedition* (Watertown, N.Y.: L. Ingalls, 1862), 67.

18. Margaret I. Carrington, *Ab-sa-ra-ka, Home of the Crows: Being the Experience of an Officer's Wife on the Plains* (Philadelphia: J. B. Lippincott, 1868), 75.

19. Rachel E. Wright, "The Early Upper Napa Valley" (1928), Bancroft Library, Berkeley, Calif.

20. Christine Bates, interview 5202, vol. 6, Indian-Pioneer Papers, University of Oklahoma, Norman

21. Eleanor Taylor, "Ross Kin: Early Settlers of the West" (1978), Bancroft Library, Berkeley, Calif.

22. Thomas R. Buecker, ed., "Letters of Caroline Frey Winne from Sidney Barracks and Fort McPherson, Nebraska, 1874–1878," *Nebraska History* 62 (spring 1981): 25.

23. Ann Laura Stoler and Frederick Cooper, "Between Metropole and Colony: Rethinking a Research Agenda," 3–56, in *Tension of Empire: Colonial Cultures in a Bourgeois World,* ed. Frederick Cooper and Ann Laura Stoler (Berkeley: University of California Press, 1997).

24. Busby, *Two Summers,* 76–79.

25. Elizabeth L. Lord, *Reminiscences of Eastern Oregon* (Portland, Oreg.: Irwin-Hodson, 1903), 142.

26. Mary Ann Tatum, "Diary," (1870), Iowa State Historical Society, Iowa City.

27. Mary Butler Renville, *A Thrilling Narrative of Indian Captivity* (Minneapolis: Atlas Co., 1863), 43; Taylor, "Ross Kin"; Mary Ann Rogers, "Iowa Woman in Wartime," pt. 1, *Annals of Iowa* 35 (winter 1961): 525; Eliza Spalding Warren, *Memoirs of the West: The Spaldings* (Portland, Oreg.: March Printing, 1916), 117.

28. Edith E. Kohl, *Land of the Burnt Thigh* (New York: Funk and Wagnall's, 1938), 239.

29. May Callan Tansill, "Narrative" (n.d.), Barker Texas History Center, University of Texas, Austin.

30. Mary Jane Caples, "Overland Journey to California" (1911), California State Library, Sacramento, 89.

31. Elisha Brooks, *A Pioneer Mother of California* (San Francisco: Harr Wagner Publishing, 1922), 29; Ruth Peterson, comp., "Across the Plains in '57" (1931), California State Library, Sacramento; and E. Allene Dunham, *Across the Plains in a Covered Wagon* (N.p. [possibly Milton, Iowa]: N.p., [ca. 1920s]), 11.

32. Nancy N. Tracy, "Narrative" (1880), Bancroft Library, Berkeley, Calif.

33. Agnes Stewart Warner, "Diary" (1853), Huntington Library, San Marino, Calif.

34. Strahorn, *Fifteen Thousand Miles by Stage,* 36.

35. Abigail Smith to My Dear Friend & Sister in Christ, 7 January 1856, Oregon Territory, Beinecke Library, Yale University, New Haven, Conn.

36. Frieda Knobloch, *The Culture of Wilderness: Agriculture as Colonization in the American West* (Chapel Hill: University of North Carolina Press, 1996), 2–5, 57–61, 74–78.

37. Alice C. Fletcher, *Historical Sketch of the Omaha Tribe of Indians in Nebraska* (Washington, D.C.: Judd and Detweiler, 1885), 12.

38. Annie K. Bidwell to Colonel Pratt, 26 April 1904, Chico, Calif., California State Library, Sacramento.

39. Mary E. Arnold and Mabel Reed, *In The Land of the Grasshopper Song* (Lincoln: University of Nebraska Press, 1980), 24.

40. Ada Millington, "Journal Kept while Crossing the Plains" (1862), Bancroft Library, Berkeley, Calif.

41. Quoted in "From Our Matrons," *Ramona Days* (Santa Fe: Ramona Industrial School of the University of New Mexico, 1887), 191; and *Reports of Superintendents and Others in Charge of Indians, Arizona* (Washington, D.C.: Government Printing Office, 1909), 12.

42. Ruth Spack, *America's Second Tongue: American Indian Education and the Ownership of English, 1860–1900* (Lincoln: University of Nebraska Press, 2002), 45–78; Kay Graber, ed., *Sister to the Sioux: The Memoirs of Elaine Goodale Eastman* (Lincoln: University of Nebraska Press, 1978), 32–34; Thisba H., Morgan, "Reminiscences of My Days in the Land of the Ogallala Sioux," *South Dakota Department of History Report and Historical Collections* 29 (1968): 21–62; and Harriet Withers, interview 12066, vol. 99, Indian-Pioneer Papers, University of Oklahoma, Norman.

43. Anna Kellough Wyss, interview 5847, vol. 101, Indian-Pioneer Papers University of Oklahoma, Norman.

44. Esther B. Hanna, "Journal" (1852), Bancroft Library, Berkeley, Calif.

45. "Narcissa Whitman," in *Notable American Women,* ed. Edward T. James

(Cambridge, Mass.: Harvard University Press, Belknap Press, 1971), 595–97.

46. Richmond L. Clow, ed., "Autobiography of Mary C. Collins, Missionary to the Western Sioux," *South Dakota Historical Collections* 41 (1982): 3–64; Mary G. Burdette, ed., *Young Woman among Blanket Indians: The Heroine of Saddle Mountain* (Chicago: R. R. Donnelley and Sons, 1897); and The Missionary Committee, Women's National Indian Association, "Report," November 17, 1885, Braun Library, Southwest Museum, Los Angeles. Also helpful is Ruth Ann Alexander, "Women in South Dakota Missions," *Anglican and Episcopal History* 63 (September 1994): 334–62.

47. For the concept of a cultural center, see Ngugi Wa Thiong'o, *Moving the Centre: The Struggle for Cultural Freedoms* (Nairobi: East Africa Educational Publishing, 1993).

48. Robert Chandler, "The Failure of Reform: White Attitudes and Indian Response in California during the Civil War Era," *The Pacific Historian* 24 (fall 1980): 292–93.

49. Frantz Fanon, *Black Skin, White Masks* (London: Pluto Press, 1986), 83–88, 143–45; Louis Owens, "As If an Indian Were Really an Indian: Native American Voices and Postcolonial Theory," 13–18, 23–24, in *Native American Representations: First Encounters, Distorted Images, and Literary Appropriations,* ed. Gretchen M. Bataille (Lincoln: University of Nebraska Press, 2001); and Siobhan Senier, *Voices of American Indian Assimilation and Resistance* (Norman: University of Oklahoma Press, 2001), 73–120.

50. Spack, *America's Second Tongue,* 79–108. For a fuller discussion of Indian resistance, see Carol Devens, *Countering Civilization: Native American Women and Great Lakes Missions, 1630–1900* (Berkeley: University of California Press, 1992).

51. Leah Dilworth, *Imagining Indians in the Southwest: Persistent Visions of a Primitive Past,* by Leah Dilworth (Washington, D.C.: Smithsonian Institution Press, 1996), 103–24.

52. John Brenkman, *Culture and Domination* (Ithaca, N.Y.: Cornell University Press, 1987), 4, 50–51. For the full story, see Frederick E. Hoxie, *A Final Promise: The Campaign to Assimilate the Indians, 1880–1920* (Lincoln: University of Nebraska Press, 1984); and Brian Dippie, *The Vanishing American: White Attitudes and U.S. Indian Policy* (Lawrence: University Press of Kansas, 1982).

53. Patricia A. Cater, "'Completely Discouraged': Women Teachers' Resistance in the Bureau of Indian Affairs Schools, 1900–1910," *Frontiers: A Journal of Women Studies* 15, no. 3 (1995): 53–86.

54. Spack, *America's Second Tongue,* 110–42; and Jane Hafen, "Gertrude Simmons Bonnin: For the Indian Cause," in *Sifters: Native American Women's Lives,* ed. Theda Perdue (New York: Oxford University Press, 2001).

55. Sherry L. Smith, *Reimagining Indians: Native American through Anglo Eyes, 1880–1940* (New York: Oxford University Press, 2000), 5.

56. Mary Austin, "The Folly of the Officials," *The Forum* 71 (March 1924): 288; and Mary Austin, Clipping File, undated, Center for Southwest Research, University of New Mexico Library, Albuquerque.

57. Smith, *Reimagining Indians,* 165–86.

58. Jürgen Osterhammel, *Colonialism: A Theoretical Overview* (Princeton, N.J.: Markus Wiener, 1997), 25–28, 44–47, 84–88; Ngugi Wa Thiong'o, *Decolonising the Mind: The Politics of Language in African Literature* (repr., Nairobi: East African Educational Publishers, 1996), 2–9; and Homi K. Bhabha, "Difference, Discrimination and the Discourse of Colonialism," 194–99, in *The Politics of Theory: Proceedings of the Essex Conference on the Sociology of Literature, July 1982* (Colchester, UK: University of Essex, 1983).

59. Dunham, *Across the Plains,* 11; Karen Lynn, "Sensational Virtue: Nineteenth-Century Mormon Fiction and American Popular Taste," *Dialogue* 14 (fall 1981): 101–11; and Gary L. Bunker and Davis Britton, *The Mormon Graphic Image, 1834–1914: Cartoons, Caricatures, and Illustrations* (Salt Lake City: University of Utah Press, 1983).

60. Pauline Wonderly, *Reminiscences of a Pioneer* (Placerville, Calif.: El Dorado County Historical Society, 1965), 7.

61. Lucy Sexton, *The Foster Family, California Pioneers* (Santa Barbara, Calif.: Press of the Schouer Printing Studio, 1925), 193–95.

62. Mary Rockwood Powers, "The Overland Route, Leaves from the Journal of a California Emigrant" (1856), Beinecke Collection, Yale University Library, New Haven, Conn.

63. Peterson, "Across the Plains"; and Brooks, *Pioneer Mother,* 14, 29.

64. Emily McCowen Horton, *My Scrap-book* (Seattle, Wash.: N.p., 1927), 27.

65. Helen Carpenter, "Diary" (1856), Huntington Library, San Marino, Calif.

66. Ellen Tompkins Adams, "Diary of Ellen Tompkins Adams, Wife of John Smalley Adams, M.D." (1863), Bancroft Library, Berkeley, Calif.; and Mary C. Fish, "Across the Plaines in 1860," Bancroft Library, Berkeley, Calif.

67. Catherine M. Haun, "A Woman's Trip across the Plains" (1849), Huntington Library, San Marino, Calif.; Stafford, *The March of Empire,* 128.

68. Fish, "Across the Plaines." For a similar opinion, see Maria J. Norton, "Diary of a Trip across the Plains in '59," Bancroft Library, Berkeley, Calif.

69. Mrs. H. T. Clarke, "A Young Woman's Sights on the Emigrant's Trail" (Salem, Oregon, 1878), Bancroft Library, Berkeley, Calif.

70. Margaret M. Hecox, *California Caravan: The 1846 Overland Trail Memoir of Margaret M. Hecox* (San Jose, Calif.: Harlan Young, 1966), 21–24.

71. Glenda Riley, "Sesquicentennial Reflections: A Comparative View of Mormon and Gentile Women on the Westward Trail," *Journal of Mormon History* 24 (spring 1998): 38–41, 48–52.

72. Agnes Stewart Warner, "Diary"; Millington, "Journal."

73. Horton, *My Scrap-book,* 27.

74. Carpenter, "Diary."

75. Fish, "Across the Plaines."

76. Stafford, *March of Empire,* 128–29.

77. Rachel C. Rose, "Diary" (1852), California State Library, Sacramento.

78. Millington, "Journal"; and Clarke, "Young Woman's Sights."

79. Millington, "Journal."

80. Stafford, *March of Empire,* 170–72.

81. Mary E. Ackley, *Crossing the Plains and Early Days in California* (San Francisco: Privately printed, 1928), 28; Mary Burrell, "Diary of a Journey Overland from Council Bluffs to Green Valley, California, April 27 to September 1, 1854," Beinecke Collection, Yale University Library, New Haven, Conn.

82. Ward G. DeWitt and Florence S. DeWitt, *Prairie Schooner Lady: The Journal of Harriet Sherrill Ward, 1853* (Los Angeles: Westernlore Press, 1959), 119.

83. Clarke, "Young Woman's Sights."

84. Mary Stuart Bailey, "A Journal of the Overland Trip from Ohio to California" (1852), Huntington Library, San Marino, Calif.

85. Sexton, *Foster Family,* 135.

86. Jennie Kimball, "Narrative of an Overland Journey from Boston to California and Buck Again" (1876), Beinecke Collection, Yale University Library, New Haven, Conn.

87. Sandra L. Myres, *Westering Women and the Frontier Experience, 1800–1915* (Albuquerque: University of New Mexico Press, 1982), 92–93, 96–97; and Sarah A. Cooke, "Theatrical and Social Affairs in Utah" (1884), Bancroft Library, Berkeley, Calif.

88. Mrs. B. G. Ferris, *The Mormons at Home* (New York: Dix and Edwards, 1856), 205.

89. Julie Roy Jeffrey, "Women on the Trans-Mississippi Frontier: A Review Essay," *New Mexico Historical Review* 57 (October 1982): 398.

90. Mary Rockwood Powers, "A Woman's Overland Journal to California" (1856), California State Library, Sacramento.

91. Lucene Pfeiffer Parsons, "The Women in the Sunbonnets" (1850), Stanford University Library, Stanford, Calif.

92. Riley, "Sesquicentennial Reflections," 45–46.

93. B. Carmon Hardy, "Lords of Creation: Polygamy, the Abrahamic Household, and Mormon Patriarchy," *Journal of Mormon History* 20 (spring 1994): 119–52.

94. DeWitt and DeWitt, *Prairie Schooner Lady,* 119.

95. Ibid., 126; and M. Guy Bishop, "Eternal Marriage in Early Mormon Marital Beliefs," *Historian* 53 (autumn 1990): 77–88.

96. Herndon, *Days on the Road,* 238.

97. Powers, "Woman's Overland Journal."

98. Parsons, "Women in Sunbonnets."

99. Jessie L. Embry, "Effects of Polygamy on Mormon Women," *Frontiers, A Journal of Women Studies* 7, no. 3 (1984): 56–61; Jessie L. Embry and Martha S. Bradley, "Mother and Daughters in Polygamy," *Dialogue* 18 (fall 1985): 99–107; and Carol Cornwall Madsen, "Decade of Detente: The Mormon-Gentile Female Relationship in Nineteenth-Century Utah," *Utah Historical Quarterly* 63 (fall 1995): 298–319.

100. Herndon, *Days on the Road,* 238.

101. Ferris, *Mormons at Home,* 116, 119, 131, 157, 187.

102. Clarke, "Young Woman's Sights."

103. Cooke, "Theatrical and Social Affairs."

104. Myres, *Westering Women,* 93–95.

105. Jane Richards, "Reminiscences" (1880), Bancroft Library, Berkeley, Calif.

106. Eliza R. Snow, "Sketch of My Life" (1885), Bancroft Library, Berkeley, Calif.

107. Jane Richards, "The Inner Facts of Social Life in Utah," (1880), Bancroft Library, Berkeley, Calif.; Phebe W. Woodruff, "Autobiographical Sketch" (1880), Bancroft Library, Berkeley, Calif.; and Clara Decker Young, "A Woman's Experience with the Pioneer Band" (1884), Bancroft Library, Berkeley, Calif.

108. Mary Horne, "Migration and Settlement of the Latter Day Saints, Salt Lake City" (1884), Bancroft Library, Berkeley, Calif.

109. Helena Erickson Rosbery, "History of Helena Rosbery" (1883), Huntington Library, San Marino, Calif.

110. Mary J. Tanner to Mrs. H. H. Bancroft, 29 October 1880, Salt Lake City, in Utah Miscellany, Bancroft Library, Berkeley, Calif.

111. Tracy, "Narrative."

112. Tanner to Bancroft, 29 October 1880; Margaret S. Smoot, "Experience of a Mormon Wife" (1880), Bancroft Library, Berkeley, Calif.

113. Smoot, "Experience of a Mormon Wife."

114. For a quantitative analysis of Mormon wives in plural marriages, see D. Gene Pace, "Wives of Nineteenth-Century Mormon Bishops: A Quantitative Analysis," *Journal of the West* 21, no. 2 (April 1982): 49–57.

115. Marilyn Warenski, *Patriarchs and Politics: The Plight of the Mormon Woman* (New York: McGraw-Hill, 1978), 3–5, 155–56.

116. Carol Cornwall Madsen, "At Their Peril: Utah Law and the Case of Plural Wives, 1850–1900," *Western Historical Quarterly* 21 (November 1990): 425–43.

117. Mary E. Cox Lee, "An Inspired Principle and a Remarkable Lady" (1949), Huntington Library, San Marino, Calif.; Constance L. Lieber, "'The

Goose Hangs High': Excerpts from the Letters of Martha Hughes Cannon," *Utah Historical Quarterly* 48 (winter 1980): 37–48; and Elinore Pruitt Stewart, *Letters of a Woman Homesteader* (Lincoln: University of Nebraska Press, 1961), 263–68, 273–74.

118. Peter Hempenstall, "Releasing the Voices: Historicizing Colonial Encounters in the Pacific," 43–61, in *Remembrance of Pacific Pasts: An Invitation to Remake History,* ed. Robert Borofsky (Honolulu: University of Hawaii Press, 2000).

119. Donald D. Jackson, *Gold Dust* (New York: Alfred A. Knopf, 1980), 77–82, 121–22; and Alex Perez-Venero, *Before the Five Frontiers* (New York: A. M. S. Press, 1978), 79–91.

120. John H. Kemble, *The Panama Route, 1848–1869* (Berkeley: University of California Press, 1943), 149; and Oscar Lewis, *Sea Routes to the Gold Fields* (New York: Alfred A. Knopf, 1949), 35, 61.

121. Lewis, *Sea Routes,* 35.

122. Sandra L. Myres, ed., *Ho for California! Women's Overland Diaries from the Huntington Library* (San Marino, Calif.: Huntington Library, 1980), 6.

123. F. N. Otis, *History of the Panama Railroad* (New York: Harper, 1867), 46.

124. Joseph W. Gregory, *Gregory's Guide for California Travellers via the Isthmus of Panama* (repr., San Francisco: Book Club of California, 1949), 9, 11.

125. *New York Times,* 15 August 1887.

126. *Daily Evening Bulletin,* San Francisco, 1 May 1856.

127. Ibid.; and *Daily Alta California,* San Francisco, 1 May 1856.

128. Sarah M. Brooks, *Across the Isthmus to California in '52* (San Francisco: C. A. Murdock, 1894), 31.

129. Ida F. Fitzgerald, "Accounts of Life of Plummer Edward Jefferis including Voyages from New York to California in 1850 and 1854," Huntington Library, San Marino, Calif.

130. Emeline L. S. Benson, "Diary" (1854), California State Library, Sacramento; Margaret DeWitt to Her Parents, no month, no day, 1849; Steamer "Crescent City," Bancroft Library in DeWitt Family Papers, ca. 1848–1867; Mary E. Durant to Her Cousins, 24 December 1853; Steamer "Sierra Nevada," Bancroft Library, Berkeley, Calif.; Angelina Harvey to Her Cousin Mary Ann, 19 November 1863, Jamestown, California, Bancroft Library, Berkeley, Calif.; Taylor, "Ross Kin"; Mrs. E. Van Court, "Reminiscences of Her Life in California" (26 March 1914), Beinecke Collection, Yale University Library, New Haven, Conn.; Nellie Wetherbee, "Diary" (1860), Bancroft Library, Berkeley, Calif.; Jane McDougal, "Diary" (1849), Huntington Library, San Marino, Calif.; and Niles Searles, *The Diary of a Pioneer and Other Papers* (N.p., 1940), 73–77.

131. Brooks, *Across the Isthmus,* 35, 37; Emeline Hubbard Day, "Journal" (1853), Bancroft Library, Berkeley, Calif.; Mary Ann Harris Meredith, "Diary"

(1859), California State Library, Sacramento; Sexton, *Foster Family,* 251; Mary Jane Cole Megquier, "California Letters" (1849–1856), Huntington Library, San Marino, Calif.

132. Mrs. D. B. Bates, *Incidents on Land and Water* (Boston: James French, 1857), 283.

133. Megquier, "California Letters."

134. Meredith, "Diary."

135. Day, "Journal"; and Julia S. Peck Twist, "Diary" (1861), Bancroft Library, Berkeley, Calif.

136. Mary Bean Simonds Ballou, "Journal" (1851–1852), Beinecke Collection, Yale University Library, New Haven, Conn.; Stafford, *March of Empire,* 18; and Mrs. Charles Wood, "Diary" (ca. 1850), Bancroft Library, Berkeley, Calif.

137. Hannah Bourn Ingalls to Her Husband, 5 October 1865, Steamer "New York," Bourn-Ingalls Family Papers, 1865–1958, Bancroft Library Berkeley, Calif.

138. Mary Pratt Staples, "Reminiscences" (ca. 1886), Bancroft Library, Berkeley, Calif.

139. Twist, "Diary."

140. Megquier, "California Letters."

141. Twist, "Diary."

142. Brooks, *Across the Isthmus,* 35.

143. Stafford, *March of Empire,* 43.

144. Bates, *Incidents on Land and Water,* 284, 288, 308.

145. Megquier, "California Letters."

146. Martha M. Morgan, *A Trip across the Plains in the Year 1849* (San Francisco: Pioneer Press, 1864), 24.

147. Jessie Benton Fremont, *A Year of Adventure Travel: Narrative of Personal Experience* (San Francisco: Book Club of California, 1960), 27; and Meredith, "Diary."

148. John Haskell Kemble, "The Gold Rush by Panama, 1848–1851," in *Rushing for Gold,* ed. John W. Caughey (Berkeley: University of California Press, 1949), 55; and Mark Snyder, "Self-Fulfilling Stereotypes," *Psychology Today* 16, no. 7 (July 1982): 60, 65, 67–68.

149. Brooks, *Across the Isthmus,* 37.

150. Stafford, *March of Empire,* 8, 20, 23, 25–26, 33–35, 38.

151. Fannie Wallace Reading to Her Grandmother, 4 May 1856, San Francisco, Pierson-Barton Correspondence and Papers, 1841–1868, Bancroft Library, Berkeley, Calif.

152. Hester Harland, "Reminiscences" (1940), California State Library, Sacramento.

153. Sexton, *Foster Family,* 251.

154. As with the overland experience, men's comments on the Panama crossing differed from women's in certain respects. Unhampered by hoopskirts, children, and nineteenth-century standards of modesty and privacy,
men were more likely to see the Panama passage as a "pleasant excursion." David Edwards Blaine to Dear Bro. Terry, 5 October 1853, Steamer
"Ohio," Letters, 1824–1900, Beinecke Collection, Yale University Library,
New Haven, Conn. Men were also more interested than women in distances, soil and other resources, and business developments. John Xantus,
Letters from North America (Detroit: Wayne State University Press, 1975),
171–73; William S. Ament, *By Sea to California* (Los Angeles: Powell
Publishing, 1929), 331–43. Many male emigrants who crossed Panama
noted the squalor and nakedness of the natives but argued that Yankee
enterprise was rousing them from their "dreamy lethargy." Quoted in
Myres, *Ho for California!*, 5. Others agreed that the rapid progress of commerce was greatly transforming the country and its people. Myres, *Ho for
California!*, 5; Xantus, *Letters from North America*, 171. Thus, unlike women,
men tended to see Panama less in its sordid present than its promising
future.

155. Ralph Grillo, *Pluralism and the Politics of Difference: State, Culture, and
Ethnicity in Comparative Perspective* (Oxford, UK: Clarendon Press, 1998),
97–118.

Chapter 7

1. David Peterson Del Mar, *Beaten Down: A History of Interpersonal Violence
in the West* (Seattle: University of Washington Press, 2002), 13–45.

2. David R. Maciel and Erlinda Gonzales-Berry, "The Nineteenth Century:
Overview," 12–22, in *The Contested Homeland: A Chicano History of New
Mexico,* ed. Erlinda Gonzales-Berry and David R. Maciel (Albuquerque:
University of New Mexico Press, 2000)

3. Virginia Irving Armstrong, comp., *I Have Spoken: American History through
the Voices of the Indians* (Chicago: Sage Books, 1971), 75.

4. Lee Myers, "The Enigma of Mangas Coloradas' Death," *New Mexico
Historical Review* 41 (October 1966): 287–306.

5. No author, *Old Lincoln County Pioneer Stories* (Lincoln, N.Mex.: Lincoln
County Historical Society, 1940), 1–10.

6. No author, *Record of Engagements with Hostile Indians* (Fort Collins, Colo.:
Old Army Press, facsimile 1972, original c. 1883), 84–85 93–97.

7. Ward Churchill, *A Little Matter of Genocide: Holocaust and Denial in the
Americas, 1492 to the Present* (San Francisco: City Lights Books, 1997),
205–21.

8. Robert Young, *White Mythologies: Writing History and the West* (London: Routledge, 1990), 12–17.

9. Kerwin Lee Klein, *Frontiers of Historical Imagination: Narrating the European Conquest of Native America, 1890–1990* (Berkeley: University of California Press, 1999), 1–12; and Ronald Wright, *Stolen Continents: The "New World" through Indian Eyes* (Boston: Houghton Mifflin, 1992), quote on 4.

INDEX